The Chile Pepper Encyclopedia

The Chile Pepper Encyclopedia

Everything You'll Ever Need to Know
About Hot Peppers,
with More Than 100 Recipes

Dave DeWitt

WILLIAM MORROW AND COMPANY, INC.
NEW YORK

It is the policy of William Morrow and Company, Inc., and
its imprints and affiliates, recognizing the importance
of preserving what has been written, to print the
books we publish on acid-free paper, and we exert our best
efforts to that end.

Library of Congress Cataloging-in-Publication Data
DeWitt, Dave.
The chile pepper encyclopedia : everything you'll
ever need to know about hot peppers, with more than 100
recipes / Dave DeWitt.—1st ed.
p. cm.
Includes index.
ISBN 0-688-15611-8
1. Cookery (Hot peppers)—Encyclopedias.   2. Hot
peppers—Encyclopedias.   I. Title.
TX803.P46D47   1999
641.6'384—dc21   98-29314
CIP

Printed in the United States of America
First Edition

BOOK DESIGN BY DEBBIE GLASSERMAN
www.williammorrow.com

To Mary Jane Wilan,
my partner in life and work—and
she's made both of them fun!

Contents

Acknowledgments

Special thanks to my associate editors on this project, Melissa Stock and Kellye Hunter. Also special thanks to my editors at William Morrow, Justin Schwartz and Christy Stabin, and to copy editor Estelle Laurence.

Additional appreciation to all the exhibitors in the National Fiery Foods Show who have supported me over the years.

I've attempted to keep track of all the chileheads and normal people who have assisted me in the quest for chile pepper knowledge over the past couple of decades and here they are. I apologize if I've left anyone out.

Thanks to:

Bren Ankrum, Alton Bailey, Robert and Mary Jane Barnes, Stefan Bederski, Chel Beeson, Terry Berke, Lou Biad, Paul and Judy Bosland, Jane Jordan Browne, Greg Byfield, Jeff Campbell, Cindy Castillo, Emma Jean Cervantes, Pat and Dominique Chapman, Frank Crosby, Jeanette DeAnda, Rick and Kim DeWitt, Martha Doster, Josefina Durán, Ed and Jan Eckhoff, Victor Espinosa, Chuck Evans, Lois Ellen Frank, Lorenzo Fritz, Frank Garcia, Nancy and Jeff Gerlach, Elaine Gill, Jeanne Gleason, Leslie Hall, Francis Hamilton, Dennis Hayes, J. P. Hayes, Antonio Heras-Durán, Patrick Holian, Sharon Hudgins, David Humphrey, Kellye Hunter, David Jackson, Stewart Jeffrey, Bob and Debbie Jones, Cody Jordan, Doug and Peggy Kane, David Karp, Ellie Leavitt, T. J. and Marti Lelko, W. C. Longacre, Lois Lyles, José Marmolejo, Jay McCarthy, Paul McIlhenny, Mark Miller, John Morton, Gary Paul Nabhan, Leo Nuñez, Jason O'Brien, Christy Ortega, Arthur Pais, David Parrish, Thomas Payne, Marie Permenter, Jim Peyton, Craig Pica, Mark Preston, Paul Prudhomme, Tricia Pursely, Patricia Quintana, Rosa Rajkovic, Cyd Riley, Jennifer Basye Sander, Todd and Krystyna Sanson, Wayne Scheiner, Denice Skrepcinski, Robert Spiegel, Martin and Lillian Steinman, Richard Sterling, Melissa and Dan Stock, Foo Swasdee, Susana Trilling, Javier Vargas, Ben Villalon, Robb Walsh, Andrew Weil, Anne-Marie and Charlie Whittaker, Mary Jane Wilan, Deborah Williams, Phil Wood, Susan Zamora, Nick Zehnder, and Harald` and Renate Zoschke.

Matthioli, "Pepe d'India," 1583.

Preface

They call me "The Pope of Peppers." Yes, that's a totally absurd promotional nickname bestowed on me by my friend Dennis Hayes, but it indicates just how far the hot and spicy movement has progressed over the past couple of decades—it now even has a "religious" leader! When I moved to New Mexico from Virginia in 1974, my only previous experience with chile peppers was an extremely hot conch salad in The Bahamas that I had forgotten about until the locals in Albuquerque tried to "burn out the gringo" with a super-hot green chile stew. They burned me out, all right, but they also caused me to fall in love with a fruit—or is that a vegetable? (See Botany.)

I soon became fascinated with the New Mexicans' obsession with chile peppers, began growing my own chiles, and learned how to cook with them. I spent a lot of time researching them as well, and that led to my first book, *The Fiery Cuisines* (St. Martin's Press, 1984), which was written with Nancy Gerlach, who would co-

author numerous books with me over the years. My obsession with chiles led me from being an interested interloper to a passionate advocate.

In 1986, Nancy and I approached Robert Spiegel with an idea for a publication about chiles, and that led to the launch in 1987 of *Chile Pepper* magazine, which we edited for nine years before it was sold. In 1988, my wife, Mary Jane Wilan, and I founded the National Fiery Foods Show, which we still produce. It became the largest show in the world devoted to chiles and hot and spicy foods. In 1997, with Melissa Stock and Kellye Hunter as editors, Mary Jane and I launched *Fiery Foods Magazine*, a publication for the Fiery Foods Industry.

I have been collecting information on chile peppers for a quarter century and the vast amount of information on the subject never ceases to amaze me. This is because the subject of Capsicums and hot and spicy foods is horizontal in nature, covering a large number of disciplines, including agriculture, botany, chemistry, medicine, and history, not to mention processing, manufacturing, importing, exporting, retailing, marketing, and publishing. A totally complete encyclopedia of peppers would probably be about half the size of the current edition of the *Encyclopaedia Britannica*—if my library, files, and bibliographic citations on the subject are any indication. So, of course, this single volume, thick as it is, cannot be complete. What I've tried to do here is cover the breadth of the subject first, then add as much depth as possible on each entry while considering the indulgence of my editor, who at some point, must scream: "Enough!"

One thing we could not include was a glossary of U.S. varietal names. One has been assembled by James Lusk of PetoSeed that has thousands of entries compiled from hundreds of years of pepper growing. It simply was too long to include in this volume.

The recipes selected were the ones that I thought were the most chile-oriented—using them as much as food as a spice. In the case of recipes from chile-loving countries, I picked the most representative of the various cuisines. Cooks should remember that the recipes are a mere sampling of the thousands of chile recipes prepared worldwide.

The Chile Pepper Encyclopedia

South African peri-peri *chile.*
DAVE DEWITT

Zimbabwe "bird pepper."
PAUL BOSLAND

Achocolatado. "Chocolaty"; in Mexico, another name for pasilla, a reference to its dark brown color.

'Acorchado.' "Corky"; in Mexico, a cultivated variety of jalapeño. The name is a reference to the "corking," or brown streaks, on the pod.

AFRICA

The cooking of the African continent reflects the influences of its explorers, its conquerors, and its traders. Such is the history of chiles in Africa, which were unknown before 1500 but conquered a continent in less than half a century. The Africans embraced the imported Capsicums with a fervor unmatched except, perhaps, by the people of India and Mexico. As African food expert Laurens van der Post observed, "The person who has once acquired a taste in the tropics for African chiles becomes an addict."

There are dozens, if not hundreds, of names for the pungent pods of Africa. The Portuguese there call the chile *pimento*, the English refer to it as *chilli*, the Muslim words for it are *shatta* and *felfel*, and the French word for chile is *piment*. The Swahili words for chile are *pili-pili, piri-piri, pele-pele*, and *peri-peri*, which are regional variations referring to both chiles and dishes made with particularly pungent pods. Tribal names vary greatly: chile is *mano* in Liberia, *barkono* in northern Nigeria, *ata* in southern Nigeria, *sakaipilo* in Madagascar, *pujei* in Sierra Leone, *foronto* in Senegal, and the ominous *fataali* in the Central African Republic.

In much of Africa today, chiles are tolerated weeds. Birds deposit the seeds in peanut or cotton fields, and the plants that sprout are cultivated by the farmers, only in the sense that they do not chop them down. The chiles become associated with the cotton or peanut crops and thrive from the maintenance of those fields. The chile plants are perennial and ripen year-round in the tropical regions. They are expensive to hand-pick, yet have become an important wild-harvested crop in some regions. In some countries, as we shall see, chiles are an important cultivated commercial crop.

North Africa

Since the Arabic countries north of the Sahara are linked culturally, economically, and astronomically more closely with the Mediterranean region than with the rest of Africa, there is little doubt that chiles were first introduced into North Africa. In the first place, the Strait of Gibraltar separates the Iberian Peninsula and North Africa by only a few miles, so it is a logical assumption that chiles would filter southward from Cádiz to Tangier by at least the early 1500s. In the second place, the Turks completed their conquest of North Africa in 1556, and since they had already introduced chiles into Hungary, it makes sense that they also carried them to Tunisia, Algeria, and Libya.

The first chiles to appear in North Africa were probably small, extremely hot *annuums*, closely related to cayennes, which were and still are used mostly in the dried red pod form or are ground into powders. Morocco and Tunisia are the largest producers of chiles in North Africa, followed by Sudan, which sells its chiles to Egypt. By examining the chile recipes that exist today, we can taste dishes that are centuries older because the cuisines of North Africa have hardly changed at all.

A complex and powerful spice compound is the chile-based harissa, of Tunisian origin but found all over North Africa. Harissa is a paste featuring red chiles for heat and color, and curry spices such as cinnamon, coriander, and cumin for flavor. It is used in the kitchen and at the table to fire up soups, stews, and less spicy curries, so it is at the same time a condiment, a marinade, a basting sauce, and a salad dressing. Harissa is often served on the side as a dipping sauce for grilled meats such as kebabs and is also served with couscous.

The most famous North African chile dishes, served from Morocco to Egypt, are called *tajines*, and they are named after the earthenware *tajine* pot in which they are cooked. Just about any meat—chicken, pigeon, mutton, beef, goat, and even camel—can be made into a *tajine*. Due to North Africa's large Muslim population, however, *tajines* rarely feature pork. The meat is usually cubed, and, according to Harva Hatchen: "The cooking liquid is the secret of a *tajine*'s tastiness. This is usually a combination of water and butter or oil (characteristically, olive oil) and seasonings to suit what's being cooked."

The long cooking time allows the ingredients to become very tender, and the cooking liquid to reduce to a thick, savory sauce. *Tajines* vary in consistency and can be either stews or casseroles.

In Morocco, couscous is king, a "national dish." As kings were likely to do, it has invaded the rest of North Africa. In most servings, it has not only its own chiles but is "married" to harissa; that is, they are inseparable. The name of the dish is onomatopoeic, meaning that it emulates the sound the steam makes as the grains of semolina cook.

African "Bird Peppers"

Although chiles probably appeared first in North Africa, they did not spread into the rest of Africa from that region but rather were brought by Portuguese explorers and traders. Even before Columbus, Portuguese exploration of Africa had proceeded down the west coast of the continent between 1460 and 1488. When Vasco da Gama rounded the Cape of Good Hope, crossed the Indian Ocean, and landed in India in 1498, he established the trade route for spices and other goods that the Portuguese controlled for over a century.

By 1482, the Portuguese had settled the western "Gold Coast" of Africa, and by 1505 they had colonized Mozambique on the east coast. By 1510 they had seized Goa in India and had established a colony there. During this time, it is suspected chile peppers were introduced by way of trade routes between Lisbon and the New World. By 1508, Portuguese colonization of the Pernambuco region of Brazil meant that both the *annuum* and *chinense* chiles prevalent there were made available for importation to Africa. The introduction of sugarcane into Brazil in the 1530s and the need for cheap labor was a cause of the trade in slaves, and an active passage of trade goods between Brazil and Africa sprang up.

The most likely scenario for the introduction and spread of chile peppers into Africa south of the Sahara is as follows. Varieties of *Capsicum annuum* and *chinense* were introduced into all West and East African Portuguese ports between 1493 and 1533, with the introduction into West Africa logically preceding that of East Africa. The chiles were first grown in small garden plots in coastal towns by the Portuguese settlers and later by the Africans. Although it has been suggested that chiles were spread throughout Africa by Europeans during their search for new slaves, the simplest answer is the best.

The Portuguese may have been responsible for the introduction of chiles into Africa, but spreading them was for the birds. History and evolution repeated themselves. Precisely in the same manner that prehistoric chiles spread north from South to Central America, chiles conquered Africa.

African birds fell in love with chile peppers. Attracted to the brightly colored pods, many species of African birds raided the small garden plots and then flew further inland, spreading the seeds and returning the chiles to the wild. Chiles thus became what botanists call a *subspontaneous* crop—newly established outside of their usual habitat, and only involuntarily spread by man.

From West Africa, birds moved the peppers steadily east, and at some time chiles either reached the coast of East Africa or met the advance of bird-spread chiles from Mozambique and Mombasa. They also spread chiles south to the Cape of Good Hope. We must remember that these chiles were being spread by birds centuries before the interior of Africa was explored by Europeans. So when the early explorers encountered chiles, it was only natural for them to consider the pods to be native to Africa.

West Africa

The German explorer G. Schweinfurth reported that the natives of West Africa concocted a magic potion from wild chiles that ensured eternal youth! Other explorers observed that chiles were used to spice up dried locusts, which were considered a tasty snack in some parts of Africa. In 1871, when the American Henry Stanley finally found the "lost" Dave Livingstone, he discovered that the Scottish explorer was living on meat and gravy seasoned with wild chiles. Livingstone told him that the native women would sometimes bathe in water to which chile powder had been added in order to increase their attractiveness.

Pierre de Schlippe, a senior research officer at the Yambio Experimental Station in the Congo, reported in 1956 that chiles had become the most important cash crop after cotton in the Zande district with, as he put it, "very little encouragement and no supervision whatsoever." When he asked a Zande tribesman whether he preferred chiles to cotton as a cash crop, the farmer replied, "Do the birds sow my cotton?" De Schlippe noted in his book on the Zande system of agriculture that the tribesman was suggesting that one should never do for oneself what others will do. "It is safe to assume that chiles as a cash crop had no influence on agricultural practice whatever," wrote De Schlippe.

During the early days of chile production in Nigeria, chiles were grown in patches near houses and as field crops under the shade of locust bean trees. They were planted in late May, and the chiles were ripe and ready for picking by November. One source reported that soon after Nigerian farmers began planting chiles, they were getting a 4,000- to 8,000-pound yield per acre and, as early as 1938, were exporting 100 tons a year.

Today, Nigeria and Sierra Leone are major producers of many varieties, including the moderately pungent *funtua* chile. In Nigeria, approximately 150,000 acres are under cultivation with chiles of all varieties, making it the largest producer of chiles in Africa, accounting for about 50 percent of all production. Most of the chile is now consumed domestically, although some is exported to the United Kingdom.

As might be expected, the food of Nigeria is distinguished by an extra infusion of hot chiles. As Ellen Wilson, author of *A West African Cookbook*, has observed: "Learning to eat West African food means learning to enjoy [chile] pepper." She added: "West African dishes can be searing or simply warm, but it is noticeable that the [chile] pepper never conceals the other ingredients; in fact, it seems to enhance them."

Curries are particularly popular in Nigeria, and one of their distinguishing characteristics is that they are served with an inordinate number of accompaniments. In addition to the usual chutneys and raisins and shredded coconut, the Nigerians offer as many as twenty-five condiments, including chopped dates, diced cucumbers, diced citrus fruits, ground dried shrimp, diced mangoes and papayas, peanuts, grapes, fried onions, chopped fresh red chiles, and bananas.

"Nigerians and old African hands," noted Harva Hatchen, "spoon out a portion of everything so their plates become a mound of curry and rice completely hidden by a patchwork of color and tastes."

Approximately 91 percent of the agricultural households in Liberia grow hot peppers, as most of the main dishes of the country contain them. Fresh peppers are marketed, but the dried pods are also ground into powders and made into hot pepper sauce. Most of the varieties grown are local cultivars, but the jalapeño and *yatasufusa*, a Japanese variety, are also grown. There is no export of chiles from Liberia as the entire crop is consumed locally.

In addition to their heavy application in foods, chiles have medicinal uses in West Africa. Fresh green and red pods are eaten whole as a cold remedy, undoubtedly to clear out the sinus cavities. In 1956, L. Stevenel, a French Army officer, noted an interesting medicinal usage of chiles in Africa. Writing in *The Bulletin of the Society of Exotic Pathology*, Stevenel attributed the absence of varicose veins and hemorrhoids in the natives to the constant use of red chiles in their diets. "Native workers on the railroad always carry a supply with them and consider them as a panacea necessary for good health," he wrote. Stevenel claimed that he had cured his own hemor-

rhoid problem and that of his fellow officers by adding red chile pulp to their food. The cure worked quickly—in a matter of days—but only with red chiles; green chiles were ineffective. Although Stevenel did not state why red chiles worked and green did not, we suspect the reason could be connected with the high concentration of vitamin A in red chiles.

East Africa

Historically, East Africa gained importance in the spice world as the principal source of extremely pungent peppers known generically as Mombasa chiles, named after the principal port in Kenya from which they were shipped. But the chiles came not only from Kenya but also from Uganda, Tanzania, and Malawi. The chiles were both cultivated and collected in the wild, and they were varieties of the piquin pod type, which ranged from the spherical "bird's eye" chiles to elongated pods an inch or more in length.

Reputedly, the hottest African chiles are those called Mombasa and Uganda, which are *Capsicum chinense*, probably introduced by the Portuguese from Brazil. In some parts of Africa, these habanero-type chiles are called "crazy-mad" peppers and, reputedly, they were reintroduced into the Caribbean islands during the slave trade.

Chiles in many East African countries are cultivated on plantations amid banana trees, and a chile export industry began in Uganda in the early 1930s. Uganda was the biggest producer and exporter during the first half of the twentieth century, but production dwindled to practically nothing by the mid-1970s (most likely due to political conditions), and the slack was taken up by the islands of Zanzibar and Pemba.

During the same period of time in Kenya, Europeans as well as Africans took to the chiles so much that local consumption caused exports to drop dramatically. Thus it is not surprising to learn that East African foods are as heavily spiced with chiles as are the West African dishes. Kenyans serve a stew called *kima*, which combines chopped beef with red chile powder and curry spices. It is obviously derived from the *keema*, or mincemeat curries of India. East African cooking has been greatly influenced by Indian curries, which are usually not prepared powders but rather combinations of chiles and curry spices that are custom-mixed for each particular dish. Tanzanians are fond of combining goat or chicken with curried stews, or simply charcoal-broiling the meats after they have been marinated in a mixture of curry spices and chiles.

One of the most famous East African dishes is *piri-piri*, Mozambique's "national dish." The same word describes small, hot, dried red chiles, a sauce or marinade made with those chiles, and the recipes combining shrimp, chicken, or fish with the *piri-piri* sauces. Such fiery combinations are so popular in Beira and Maputo that *piri-piri* parties are organized. The dish has even been introduced into Lisbon, where it is served with less chile heat.

Another large East African producer of chiles is Ethiopia, but most of the chiles are used domestically in their highly spiced cuisine. The varieties most commonly grown are *bakolocal* and *marekofana*, known generically as *berbere*, which is the same name as the spice paste made from them. The average daily consumption of chiles in Ethiopia is a little more than half an ounce per person, so they are as much a food as a spice.

Ethiopia is the part of East Africa least influenced by British and Indian versions of curry. Instead, it evolved its own unique curry tradition. According to Daniel Jote Mesfin, author of *Exotic Ethiopian Cooking*, "Marco Polo did not visit our country. And Ethiopia was never conquered. It came under brief Italian rule during Mussolini's time, but for the most part, we did not have direct and intimate dealings with foreign powers. And Ethiopian cuisine remained a secret."

Ethiopia was isolated from Europe, but not from the spice trade. "Since Ethiopia was located at the crossroads of the spice trade," observed Michael Winn, owner of New York's Blue Nile restaurant, "its people began to pay keen attention to blending spices. Fenugreek, cumin, red chiles, and varieties of herbs are used lovingly in creating meat, fish, and vegetable dishes."

The most important spice mixture is a condiment called *berbere*, which is made with the hottest chiles available, plus other spices, and is served as a side dish with meat, used as a coating for drying meats, and is a major ingredient of curried meats. Tribal custom dictated that *berbere* be served with *kitfo*, a raw meat dish that is served warm. According to legend, the more delicious a woman's *berbere* was, the better chance she had to win a husband. Recipes for *berbere* were closely guarded, as the marriageability of women was at stake.

Laurens van der Post philosophized on *berbere* in 1970: "Berbere gave me my first inkling of the essential role played by spices in the more complex forms of Ethiopian cooking. . . . It seemed to me related to that of India and of Indonesia, particularly Java; I suspect that there may have been far more contact between Ethiopia and the Far East than the history books indicate." Chile peppers are obviously extremely important in Ethiopian curries, and they have even inspired a derogatory expression, *ye wend alich'a*, meaning a man who has no pepper in him.

In Ethiopian cookery, *berbere* is an indispensable ingredient in the "national dishes" known as *wa't* or *we't* (depending on the transliteration), which are spicy, curry-like stews of lamb, beef, chicken, beans, or vegetables (never pork).

South Africa

"There is reason to assume that the ambrosia of which the ancient poets spoke of so often was a kind of ginger chile called *pinang* curry," wrote C. L. Leiopoldt, the Afrikaans poet. Chile-laced curries are extremely popular in South Africa because of the unique collisions of culinary cultures.

The Dutch colonized South Africa because of its ideal position halfway between the Netherlands and the Spice Islands. It was a perfect outpost for raising the vegetables and livestock necessary to replenish their ships. In 1652, the Dutch East India Company dispatched a party of officials to the Cape to establish a "revictualing station."

"Within fourteen days of their arrival," wrote Renata Coetzee in *The South African Culinary Tradition*, "these early settlers had laid out a vegetable garden." They planted sweet potatoes, pineapples, watermelons, pumpkins, cucumbers, radishes, and citrus trees such as lemons and oranges.

Late in the seventeenth century, with the revictualing station in operation, commerce between the Dutch East India Company and the new Dutch colony of South Africa picked up considerably because of an important commodity: Malay slaves, referred to in South African literature as "the king of slaves." The men were utilized as farmers, carpenters, musicians, tailors, and fishermen, while the women were expert cooks who not only introduced exotic Spice Islands dishes but also imported the spices necessary to prepare them.

Among the Malaysian spices transferred by the slaves to South Africa were aniseed, fennel, turmeric, ginger, cardamom, cumin, coriander, mustard seeds, tamarind, and garlic. Chiles, of course, were introduced by both birds and the Portuguese traders and eventually were disseminated across South Africa. Curiously, coconuts—so important in the Spice

Islands—do not play a role in South African curries.

The Cape Malays, as the slaves' descendants were called, developed a unique cuisine called, by some, "Old Cape Cookery." It evolved into a mixture of Dutch, English, and Malay styles and ingredients—with an emphasis on the Malay. Predominant among the numerous cooking styles were curries and their accompaniments. As early as 1740, *kerrie-kerrie* dishes were mentioned in South African literature. That terminology had changed by 1797, when Johanna Duminy of the Riviersonderend valley wrote in her diary: "When the evening fell I had the candles lit, the children were given their supper and put to bed. At nine o'clock we are going to have a delicious curry."

Johanna's curry probably was milder than that of today's in South Africa, because for a time the quantity of chiles and fresh ginger were greatly reduced for the Dutch palate. But the Cape Malays relished the heat, and Harva Hatchen, author of *Kitchen Safari*, pointed out: "Curries are as much a part of Malay cooking as they are of Indian."

MADAGASCAR HOT MANGO SALAD

This favorite recipe from Madagascar can be prepared with any fresh green chile, but the hotter the better. Serve it as a side dish to grilled or roasted meat or fish.

MAKES 4 TO 6 SERVINGS
HEAT SCALE: Hot

3 jalapeño chiles, stems and seeds removed, minced
2 green mangoes, pits removed, peeled and julienned
1 onion, minced

2 cloves garlic, minced
2 to 3 tablespoons minced fresh parsley
Juice of 2 limes
3 tablespoons olive oil
Salt to taste

Combine all of the ingredients in a glass bowl, cover, and let sit for 30 minutes to let the flavors blend.

SHRIMP PIRI-PIRI

Shellfish is abundant off the east coast of Africa, and the prawns are so large that a couple will make a meal. The Mozambique marinade not only goes well with shrimp or prawns but also with fish and chicken. Note that this recipe requires advance preparation.

MAKES 4 SERVINGS
HEAT SCALE: Medium

¼ cup butter or margarine
¼ cup peanut oil
2 tablespoons crushed dried hot chile, such as
    piquin or cayenne, seeds included

4 cloves garlic, minced
3 tablespoons fresh lime or lemon juice
1 pound shrimp or prawns, shelled and deveined

In a skillet over medium heat, melt the butter and add the oil and the remaining marinade ingredients, except for the shrimp. Simmer for 2 to 3 minutes to blend the flavors. Remove from the heat and let the mixture cool for 10 to 15 minutes.

In a bowl, toss the shrimp in the marinade and marinate for a couple of hours, covered, in the refrigerator. Drain the shrimp and reserve the marinade.

Thread the shrimp on skewers and grill over hot charcoal or broil until done, 2 to 3 minutes.

In a saucepan over medium-high heat, bring the marinade to a boil (to kill any bacteria from marinating) and serve on the side.

MOROCCAN CHICKEN TAJINE WITH CAYENNE

Tajine Tafarout

This *tajine* honors the flowering of the almond trees and comes from Tafarout, Morocco. This dish is often presented at a wedding feast. Serve with a carrot salad, couscous, and pita bread.

MAKES 4 SERVINGS

HEAT SCALE: **Hot**

One 3- to 4-pound chicken, cut into serving pieces
1/4 cup extra-virgin olive oil
1 large onion, thinly sliced
4 teaspoons ground cayenne
1 teaspoon ground ginger
1 teaspoon ground coriander
1/2 teaspoon ground cumin

1/2 teaspoon ground cinnamon
1/4 teaspoon ground turmeric
2 cups water
1 cup dried apricot halves, soaked in water to
    cover until soft
1 cup whole, blanched almonds
2 tablespoons butter or margarine

In a large skillet over medium heat, brown the chicken pieces in the olive oil, about 5 minutes on each side. Remove the chicken to a dish and pour off all but a few tablespoons of the oil.

Add the onion to the skillet over medium-high heat and cook, stirring, until browned, about 5 minutes. Add the spices and cook, stirring, for 2 minutes more. Add the water and bring to a boil.

Reduce the heat to medium-low, add the chicken pieces and drained apricots, and simmer for 30 minutes, turning the chicken frequently, until the chicken is very tender and starts to fall from the bone. Add more water if necessary.

In another skillet, when the chicken is almost done, over medium heat, brown the almonds in the butter, 3 to 4 minutes. Remove the almonds with a slotted spoon.

To serve, arrange the chicken on a platter, top with the sauce, and garnish with the almonds.

SOUTH AFRICAN HOT LAMB CURRY
Pinang-Kerrie

This very popular South African curry is traditionally served dry, which means that the sauce needs to cook until it is very, very thick. Serve it with rice. Note that this recipe requires advance preparation.

MAKES 4 TO 5 SERVINGS
HEAT SCALE: **Mild**

1 tablespoon imported curry powder

1 teaspoon ground turmeric

4 cloves garlic, minced

½ teaspoon salt

2 tablespoons cider vinegar

1 tablespoon grated fresh ginger

1 teaspoon sugar

1 teaspoon fresh lemon juice or tamarind paste

2 bay leaves

1 pound lamb, cut into 1-inch cubes

2 tablespoons vegetable oil

2 onions, thinly sliced

1½ cups chicken stock or water

In a nonreactive bowl, combine the curry powder, turmeric, garlic, salt, vinegar, ginger, sugar, lemon juice, and bay leaves. Add the lamb and toss it gently to cover it with the marinade. Cover the bowl and let the lamb marinate in the refrigerator for 2 hours.

In a large, heavy skillet over low heat, heat the oil, add the onion, and cook, stirring, until softened, about 5 minutes. Add the lamb with the marinade mixture and cook, stirring, for 1 minute. Add the stock or water, raise the heat to medium-high and bring to a boil. Immediately reduce the heat to low and simmer the mixture for 40 to 50 minutes, uncovered, or until the meat is tender. Remember, the sauce should be very thick, but be careful to keep just enough moisture in the skillet so that the mixture doesn't burn. Remove the bay leaves before serving.

MOZAMBICAN RED CHILE–STEWED SEA BASS
Peite Lumbo

This classic Mozambican seafood dish typically has a large number of chiles. Since the *piri-piri* varieties are not available in North America, substitute cayenne or *santaka* chiles for a hot dish or New Mexican chiles for a milder one. This dish is usually served with dumplings or rice.

MAKES 4 TO 6 SERVINGS
HEAT SCALE: **Medium**

4 to 5 dried New Mexican red chile pods, seeds and
    stems removed
One 3-pound whole sea bass, grouper, or baby
    codfish
1 pound large shrimp, shelled and deveined
2 cups fresh lemon juice
2 cups water
Salt and freshly ground black pepper to taste
3 tablespoons palm or peanut oil

2 bell peppers, deribbed and finely chopped
2 tomatoes, skinned and pushed through a sieve
    or food mill
2 red onions, finely chopped
½ teaspoon ground nutmeg
¾ tablespoon ground dried shrimp (optional)
½ cup coconut milk
½ cup grated unsweetened coconut
¼ teaspoon ground coriander

Rehydrate the chile pods by soaking them in a bowl of boiling hot water to cover for 10 to 15 minutes. Drain and puree in a blender or food processor and set aside.

Clean and eviscerate the fish, leaving the head on and the eyes out. (See if your fishmonger can do this for you.) Wash the fish and lay it in a baking dish. Surround the fish with the shrimp. Add the lemon juice and water and allow to acidulate for a few minutes. Season the fish with salt and pepper inside and out, and refrigerate until ready to cook.

Over medium heat, heat the oil in a skillet and cook the bell peppers, tomatoes, onions, nutmeg, ground dried shrimp, and the reserved chile puree for 7 minutes. Add the coconut milk, grated coconut, and coriander, and simmer, covered but stirring periodically, for 15 minutes. The sauce should be quite thick.

Place the marinated fish and shrimp in a skillet or baking dish large enough to hold it intact and pour the sauce over. Cover, with foil if you don't have a lid, and simmer over medium-low heat for 15 minutes. Stir only once, without breaking the fish, then simmer, covered, for another 10 minutes or so, until the fish flakes off easily. If the sauce is too thick, add water only as needed in small amounts. Spoon the sauce over the fish when serving.

AGRICULTURE, U.S.

Peppers of the *annuum* species were transferred into what is now the American Southwest twice—first by birds and then by humankind. Botanists believe that the wild *annuum* variety known as chiltepins spread northward from Mexico through dissemination by birds long before Native Americans domesticated peppers and made them part of their trade goods. These chiltepins still grow wild today in Arizona and in South Texas, where they are known as chilipiquins.

According to most accounts, chile peppers were introduced the second time into what is now the United States from Mexico by Capitán General Juan de Oñate, who founded Santa Fe in 1609. However, they may have been introduced to the Pueblo Indians of New Mexico by the Antonio Espejo expedition of 1582–83. According to one of the members of the expedition, Baltasar Obregón, "They have no chile, but the natives were given some seed to plant." But by 1601, chiles were not on the list of Indian crops, according to colonist Francisco de Valverde, who also complained that mice were a pest that ate chile pods off the plants in the field. But soon chiles were being grown by Spanish and Indians alike.

We do know that soon after the Spanish arrived, the cultivation of peppers in New Mexico spread rapidly and the pods were grown both in Spanish settlements and native pueblos. In fact, the cultivation was so dedicated that the peppers that were replanted in the same fields for centuries developed into land races (locally adapted varieties) that persist to this very day. These land races, such as 'Chimayó,' 'Velarde,' and 'Española,' developed specific, identifiable traits such as pod shape, high pungency, and early maturing.

During the 1700s, peppers were popping up in other parts of the country. In 1768, according to legend, Minorcan settlers in St. Augustine, Florida, introduced the datil pepper, a land race of the *chinense* species. Supposedly, this pepper was transferred from the Caribbean to Africa and then to Minorca in the Mediterranean, from which it was brought to Florida. However, some historians believe that this story is all bunk and that the datil peppers were introduced into Florida via trade with the Caribbean islands, a simpler explanation that makes a lot more sense.

Other introductions were also occurring during the eighteenth century. In 1785, George Washington planted two rows of "bird peppers" and one row of cayenne at

Harvesting jalapeños, New Mexico. DAVE DEWITT

Load of cayennes, St. Martinville, Louisiana. DAVE DEWITT

Mount Vernon, but it is not known how he acquired the seed. Another influential American, Thomas Jefferson, was also growing peppers from seed imported from Mexico.

By the early 1800s, commercial seed varieties became available to the American public. In 1806, a botanist named McMahon listed four varieties for sale, and in 1826, another botanist named Thornburn listed 'Long' (cayenne), 'Tomato-Shaped' (squash), 'Bell' (oxheart), 'Cherry,' and 'Bird' (West Indian) peppers as available for gardeners. Two years later, squash peppers were cultivated in North American gardens and that same year (1828), the 'California Wonder Bell' pepper was first named and grown commercially.

Around this same time, travelers and historians were beginning to notice the influence of chile peppers in the rather primitive American Southwest. "The extravagant use of red pepper among the [New] Mexicans has become truly proverbial. It enters into nearly every dish at every meal, and often so predominates as entirely to conceal the character of the viands," wrote Josiah Gregg in 1844 in his book *The Commerce of the Prairies*.

In 1849, the first mention of Tabasco peppers occurred in the *New Orleans Daily Delta* of December 7. "I must not omit to notice the Colonel's pepper patch, which is two acres in extent, all planted with a new species of red pepper, which Colonel

White has introduced into our country, called Tabasco [sic] red pepper." The colonel referred to is Maunsell White, one of the earliest growers of Tabasco peppers.

These *frutescens* peppers, introduced into Louisiana from Tabasco, Mexico, were soon grown in quantity by Edmund McIlhenny of Avery Island, who transformed them from obscurity into one of the most famous peppers in history. By experimentation with Tabasco peppers, which were mashed, salted, aged, and then strained and mixed with vinegar, McIlhenny soon produced his famous Tabasco sauce. In 1868, the first 350 bottles of sauce were shipped to wholesalers and by 1870 McIlhenny obtained a patent for Tabasco brand hot pepper sauce. The rest is history as Tabasco became the best-known and best-selling hot sauce in the world.

During the same time period that Tabascos were being grown in Louisiana, the introduction of European pepper varieties into the United States began. In 1867, the 'Sweet Spanish' variety arrived from France, and it was initially called 'Crimson Queen.' By 1888, the Burpee Seed Company's *Farm Annual* offered twenty varieties of peppers, including 'Celestial,' 'Red Squash' ("of Massachusetts origin"), the 'Spanish Monstrous' (six to eight inches long), 'Red Chili' ("best for pepper sauce"), the 'Long Yellow,' and the 'Cranberry,' said to look like one. The Burpee *Farm Annual* was the first in a long line of seed catalogs offering many varieties of peppers, most of which were discontinued or transformed.

The number of varieties available—and their nomenclature—is a problem that will continue to vex botanists, horticulturists, farmers, and home gardeners.

Meanwhile, things were heating up in the West. In 1896, Emilio Ortega, former sheriff of Ventura County, California, brought New Mexican pepper seeds back with him during a visit to New Mexico. He planted them near Anaheim, and they adapted well to the soil and climate there. By the time Ortega opened the first pepper canning operation (1898) in Ventura, the pod type that originated in New Mexico was known as Anaheim, a name that would stick long after Anaheim was paved over and turned into Disneyland. (In 1987, the name of the pod type was changed to the more accurate New Mexican, and 'Anaheim' became a variety of the New Mexican pod type.)

Around the turn of the century, botanists were having a field day cataloging a bewildering number of varieties of peppers. In 1898, H. C. Irish named 43 different varieties, and by 1902 a list by W. W. Tracy of the U.S. Department of Agriculture gave 114 pepper varieties in the United States, of which half were bells. Tracy noted about peppers and other vegetables: "There is such an indiscriminate use of epithets as to make the distinctions of varieties very bewildering. . . . One great source of the confusion in variety names . . . is the use of descriptive words and phrases in multiplying names which frequently mark no varietal differences."

An example Tracy used was 'Ruby King,' which had such incarnations as 'Mammoth Ruby King,' 'Maule's Ruby King,' and 'Burpee Ruby King.' Some now-common pod types appeared on his list, such as squash, bell, cayenne, and cherry.

In 1907, Fabian Garcia, a horticulturist at the Agricultural Experiment Station at the College of Agriculture and Mechanical Arts in Las Cruces, New Mexico (now New Mexico State University), began his first experiments in breeding more standardized chile varieties, and, in 1908, published *Chile Culture*, the first chile bulletin from the Agricultural Experiment Station.

By 1910, the Agricultural Census listed 1,641 farms growing peppers in the United States, with a total acreage of 3,483. The top four states in pepper production were New Jersey, California, Florida, and New Mexico (which was still a territory at the time). New Mexico had 266 farms with a total acreage of 260. The average acreage of a pepper farm in the United States was 3.2.

And during this time, more European varieties were introduced. In 1911, the first pimientos from Spain arrived in Georgia. S. D. Riegel, a talented farmer, developed a line of pimientos from Spain in Spalding County that eventually was released as 'Perfection Pimiento' in 1913. During the years of 1915–16, the South also witnessed the first American production of paprika—in South Carolina. Production was ninety-one tons but the crop was soon abandoned in favor of cotton.

Back in New Mexico, Fabian Garcia, who became director of the experiment station in 1913, expanded his breeding program. Finally, in 1917, after ten years of experiments with various strains of pasilla chiles, Garcia released 'New Mexico No. 9,' the first attempt to grow chiles with a dependable pod size and heat level. The 'No. 9' variety became the chile standard in New Mexico until 1950.

By 1919, the total U.S. acreage in peppers was 15,290, valued at $3.1 million. Seven years later, the acreage in seven important states was about the same (15,430), but the value had climbed to $5 million. New Jersey led all states with 7,500 acres. In 1928, 'Calwonder Bell' was released as an official variety after 100 years of cultivation. During the period of 1930 to 1950, chile pepper acreage in New Mexico averaged between 900 and 1,200 acres.

Duplicate varieties of peppers, complained about by W. W. Tracy in 1902, were gradually phased out of seed catalogs, and by 1930 American seedsmen recorded that a mere thirty different varieties were available. That year, botanist H. C. Irish, writing in *The Standard Cyclopedia of Horticulture*, noted: "Peppers are classed as one of the minor vegetables in that they have not been grown in large quantities in any one locality and the aggregate production is smaller than the so-called truck crops, such as tomatoes, cucumbers, and the like. During the last decade there has been a decided increase in acreage."

There was a flurry of pepper activity during the 1930s as acreage increased but value dropped because of the Depression. In 1931, paprika production began in Southern California, and the following year Hungarian wax peppers were introduced into the United States from Hungary. That same year, botanist A. T. Erwin of Iowa State University bucked the trend of declining numbers of varieties and named 153 different varieties of peppers!

In 1935, H. L. Cochran of the Georgia Experiment Station estimated that 17,000 acres of "green peppers" (undoubtedly bells) were under cultivation, worth a paltry $2.2 million. The 1930s also marked the development of the 'Truhart Perfection Pimiento' in Georgia, and by 1935 Georgia had 11,000 acres of pimientos under cultivation, valued at $450,000.

From 1940 to 1957, sweet pepper acreage doubled in the United States to more than 44,000 acres, and in 1941 the first Hungarian paprika seeds were planted in Washington's Yakima Valley. By 1949, paprika production had resumed in South Carolina and Louisiana, by Yugoslav immigrants, but the industry was not successful.

The year 1950 marked the introduction of 'New Mexico No. 6' by Roy Harper of New Mexico State University, and that variety took over the title of standard variety grown in New Mexico. That same year, the Georgia pimiento crop was 32,000 acres valued at $3.15 million. Meanwhile, California produced 3,850 tons of dry red chile valued at $3 million on 3,932 acres— a yield that would eventually increase.

The bell pepper crop exploded after World War II, and by 1951 production rose to 105,000 tons worth $16.8 million on 34,700 acres. Chile pepper acreage had increased to about 8,500 acres by 1954. The 1950s also witnessed the introduction of many new varieties, including: 'Fresno' (1952 by Clarence Brown Seed Co.); 'Carolina Hot' variety of cayenne (1954); 'Sandia' variety of New Mexican (1956 by Roy Harper); 'New Mexico No. 6-4' (1957, which became, and still is, the number one variety of chile pepper grown in the United States); and 'Cubanelle' (1958 from Italy).

During the 1960s, chili con carne cook-offs became popular, which increased the awareness of chile peppers, especially in Texas and California. The Chili Appreciation Society—International (CASI), which had been founded in 1951, had more than two hundred "pods" (chapters) in Texas during the mid-fifties, and a similar organization, the International Chili Society (ICS) was formed in California. Also in 1960, Roy Nakayama took over the chile pepper breeding program at New Mexico State University from Roy Harper, and by 1963 California paprika production reached 2,900 tons.

The 1970s began with Ben Villalon founding the Texas pepper breeding program at the Agricultural Experiment Station in Weslaco (1970). That same year, Dr. Walter Greenleaf of Auburn University bred the tobacco etch virus–resistant variety, 'Greenleaf Tabasco.' In 1973, the first meeting of the National Pepper Conference was held, proof that peppers were finally being regarded as a serious crop plant in this country.

During 1975, chile pepper acreage in New Mexico climbed to 9,200 and Roy Nakayama released 'NuMex Big Jim.' This variety produced the longest pods of any chile pepper—pods up to an astounding seventeen inches have been reported. Also that year was the publication of the first cookbook solely devoted to hot and spicy foods, *The Hellfire Cookbook* by John Cranwell. During the next twenty-seven years, twenty-three similar titles would follow as U.S. cooks discovered chile peppers and hot and spicy foods. But sweet peppers were gaining ground too, and by the end of the decade bell pepper acreage topped 100,000 for the first time.

In 1980, Tom Williams, a vegetable breeder at Rogers NK seed company, introduced the 'Jupiter' variety of bell pepper, and it soon became the leading pepper variety cultivated in the country. The following year, Ben Villalon at Weslaco introduced 'TAM Mild Jalapeño-1,' which had one third the pungency of the standard jalapeño. It became an immediate hit with growers and consumers, who usually ate them with nachos. Also during the early 1980s, chile pepper acreage in New Mexico topped 17,000, with an additional 5,594 in California and 1,980 in Texas. Louisiana hot pepper acreage was about 200 but would eventually decline to about 75.

PEPPER ACREAGE BY VARIETY IN THE UNITED STATES

There are approximately 125,000 acres of commercially grown Capsicums in the United States, of which 40 percent have pungency

Variety	Acreage
Bell types	65,237
Cascabella	350
Cayenne	4,500
Cheese	125
Cherry Sweet	550
'Cubanelle' types	1,500
'Floral Gem'	125
Hungarian, 'Hot Banana'	700
'Italian White Wax'	25
Jalapeño	5,500
Mild Finger types	100
Misc. Hot (habanero, datil, etc.)	1,100
New Mexican/Anaheim (includes paprika)	38,000
Pepperoncini	25
'Pimiento L'	3,500
Poblano/Ancho	150
'Red Cherry Large Hot'	750
'Santa Fe Grande', 'Caloro'	125
Serrano	150
'Sport' (Mississippi and Louisiana)	150
Sweet Banana	2,150
Tabasco	50

Source: *Lusk's Processor Notebook*, PetoSeed, October 1996

In 1983, the 'Española Improved' variety was released after years of testing by Frank B. Matta at the Española Valley Branch Experiment Station in Alcalde, New Mexico. The variety was developed for cool climates to produce substantial quantities of both green and red pods.

Botanists were still debating the number

Chiles in the wholesale market, Bangkok. DAVE DEWITT

of pepper varieties. In 1985, Charles Heiser's answer to the question was: "There can be no definite answer to that question . . . except to say that there are lots of different kinds of peppers." Later, in 1987, horticulturist Paul G. Smith would add: "The tremendous variation in fruit size, shape, and color, as well as an extremely variable plant habit in *C. annuum* alone make it impossible to devise a practical system of classification that would cover the large numbers of forms known to be cultivated."

Not to be daunted, Paul Bosland, who took over the chile pepper breeding program at New Mexico State University in 1986, devised the "species, pod type, variety" system of identification in *Capsicum Pepper Varieties and Classification* (1989), the method most commonly used today. Other significant pepper events of the 1980s were the founding of *Chile Pepper* magazine by Robert Spiegel, Dave DeWitt, and Nancy Gerlach (1987), the first conference on the wild chiltepin (1988), hosted by Gary Nabhan at the Desert Botanical Gardens in Phoenix, and the beginning of habanero production in California and Texas (1989). By the end of the decade, chile pepper acreage in New Mexico had climbed to 23,650 and nationwide it topped 30,000 for the first time.

In 1991, the acreage of Tabascos under cultivation in Louisiana dropped to a low of 75, and the plants were used mostly for seed. Also in 1991, bell pepper distribution in the United States reached 219,300 tons (including imports), up from the year before by 23,550 tons. The top bell-producing states were Florida, California, New Jersey, Texas, North Carolina, and Georgia. The top importing countries were Mexico and the Netherlands. Also in 1991, the Chile Institute was founded at New Mexico State University to assemble a permanent archive of *Capsicum* information and to promote chile peppers world-wide.

AGRICULTURE, WORLD

Until recently, it has been very difficult to find accurate chile pepper production statistics from various countries around the world. The problem has been a combination of lax record keeping and the lack of publication of such data. But in 1988, the Asian Vegetable Research and Development Center in Taipei, Taiwan, held an international conference on tomato and pepper production. The results of that conference, published as *Tomato and Pepper Production in the Tropics*, is now available and contains much valuable data on world production.

Below is a table listing statistics extracted from reports given at the conference. There still are problems with the statistics because of various factors, but these are the most reliable figures to date. Readers should be warned that these statistics reflect only reported commercial operations and do not include small home farm plots. Some countries do not report whether their figures are for fresh or dry weight so assumptions have been made based on the varieties grown. Fresh or green production figures have been converted to dry equivalent tons at the ratio of 8:1.

COUNTRY	YEAR	ACREAGE	YIELD (DRY EQUIV. TONS)
India	1986	2,202,746	707,900
Mexico	1988	156,840	536,000
Indonesia	1986	498,940	387,000
China	1988	148,200	212,500
Korea	1986	326,331	202,841
Thailand	1985	143,652	116,501
Ethiopia	1971	600,704	102,200
U.S.A.	1988	31,201	49,921
Taiwan	1986	7,047	21,218
Malaysia	1985	2,848	13,836
Japan	1984	351	400

The biggest statistical problems are closest to home: Mexico and the United States. As J. A. Laborde and E. Rendon-Poblete point out, "The statistics for (Mexican) peppers are not very reliable, because they are expressed in two different ways: as 'pungent' and 'nonpungent' or as 'dry and green peppers.' Current figures do not specify which peppers are included in which group." Thus, the Mexican figures may include bell peppers but may not include Tamaulipas State, the main producer of serranos. However, chile pepper data from the National Chile Conference held at San Miguel de Allende in 1984 compare favorably to the Laborde and Rendon-Poblete figures and do not include bells.

In the United States, some states collect data on chile pepper production (New Mexico and California), while others do not (Texas, Arizona, Louisiana). The U.S. Agricultural Census keeps only acreage data. Thus the U.S. figures are extrapolated from a number of sources and years from 1978 to 1988.

Yield depends to a certain extent on the varieties grown. Varieties with smaller pods will produce less weight per acre. Figures do not include bell pepper production. The countries are ranked by total yield. Also, some notable chile pepper producing countries, such as Burma, Pakistan, Peru, Bolivia, Bangladesh, Tanzania, and Hungary were not included in the Asian Vegetable Research and Development Center study.

According to a 1993 study by the Texas Agricultural Experiment Station, India again was ranked first in pepper acreage. The United States was eleventh (bell pepper production included) and Mexico was sixth. Remember that yield varies by variety and cultural practices.

COUNTRY	ACREAGE
India	2,230,000
Ethiopia	608,000
Indonesia	541,000
Korea	331,000
China	215,000
Mexico	204,000
Bangladesh	197,000
Nigeria	193,000
Thailand	151,000
Pakistan	144,000
U.S.A.	125,000
Sri Lanka	101,000

◣ *Ahumado.* "Smoked-cured"; in Mexico, referring to chipotle chiles.

◣ *Ají.* The common name for chiles in South America and some parts of the Caribbean; usually *Capsicum baccatum*.

◣ *Ají amarillo.* "Yellow chile"; in Peru, the commonest chile grown and eaten. This *Capsicum baccatum* var. *pendulum* is three to five inches long and matures to a deep orange color. It has a medium-hot pungency and is grown in all regions of the country. Also called *ají escabeche*.

◣ *Ají ayucllo.* In Peru, a semicultivated pungent variety of undetermined species. It matures to a bright orange color, is small, thick-fleshed, and oval-shaped.

➤ *Ají cereza.* "Cherry chile"; cultivated in backyards in Peru, this semidomesticated chile is round and about one and a half inches in diameter. It is extremely pungent and matures to a deep red color. It is either *Capsicum chinense* or *baccatum*.

➤ *Ají charapa.* In Peru, a wild chile that is harvested near the city of Iquitos. It is spherical, about a quarter inch in diameter, and very pungent. Fruits mature to red or yellow color. The species is either *Capsicum chinense* or *baccatum*.

➤ *Ají chombo.* A name for the *chinense* species in Panama.

➤ *Ají escurre-huéspedes.* In Cuba, the term for a chile that "makes the guests sneak away."

➤ *Ají lengua de pájaro.* "Bird's tongue chile"; in Cuba, a variety of piquin.

➤ *Ají limo.* Popular on the northern coast of Peru, this *Capsicum frutescens* is very pungent and matures to a yellow, orange, or red color. They are two to three inches long. The word *limo* has no known meaning; the species is *Capsicum frutescens*.

➤ *Ají mono.* "Monkey chile"; grown in the Peruvian jungles, this chile matures to bright red and measures four to five inches

long. It has high pungency and is thought to be *Capsicum baccatum*.

➤ *Ají norteño.* "Northern chile"; in Peru, this chile is grown in northern coastal valleys. The ripe pods mature to yellow, orange, and red and measure three to four inches long. They have moderate pungency and are commonly eaten fresh with seafood. Thought to be *Capsicum baccatum*.

➤ *Ají panca.* Thought to be *Capsicum frutescens*, this Peruvian chile grows from three to five inches long and has a mild pungency. It is deep red to purple when ripe and dries to a dark purple color.

➤ *Ají pinguita de mono.* "Little monkey penis chile"; found in Peru's central valley of Chanchamayo, these are wild or semicultivated chiles of unknown species that are one half to one inch long, very elongated; they mature to a bright red color. The species is *Capsicum chinense* or *baccatum*.

➤ *Ají yaquitania.* A name for the *chinense* species in Brazil.

➤ *Aleppo.* A Syrian chile powder.

➤ *'Altamira.'* In Mexico, a cultivated variety of serrano.

➤ *Amarillo.* In Mexico, any yellow chile, but specifically *chilcoxtle*.

⌖ *Amash.* A piquin chile that grows wild in the Mexican states of Tabasco, Chiapas, and Yucatán. Very hot and consumed in the green form. Thought to be the progenitor of the pods transferred to Louisiana and called tobasco or Tabasco; if true, then *amash* is *Capsicum frutescens*.

⌖ *Amatista.* A South American purple ornamental, probably *Capsicum annuum*.

AMAZONIA

After the Andes region, chiles in South America are most prevalent in Brazilian cookery and occur in many dishes. In Brazil

Malagueta *chile, Brazil.* DAVE DEWITT

and the Amazon Basin, there are two main species we are concerned with, *Capsicum chinense* and *C. frutescens*, the habanero and Tabasco relatives respectively. The *malagueta* pepper grows wild in the Amazon Basin in Brazil, where the species probably originated. It is cultivated in scattered small plots, according to some sources. No domesticated *frutescens* has ever been found in an archaeological site in Central or South America, but ethnobotanists speculate the domestication site was probably Panama, and, from there, it spread to Mexico and the Caribbean. The pods are borne erect and measure from one half to one and a half inches long and one quarter to three eighths of an inch wide. Immature pods are yellow or green, maturing to bright red.

An interesting botanical mystery crops up with the *malagueta* pepper from Brazil because it has virtually the same name as the *melegueta* pepper from West Africa. The mystery arises from the fact that the two peppers are completely unrelated botanically and in appearance. The African *melegueta* (*Aframomum melegueta*) is a reed-like plant with red berries, while the Brazilian *malagueta* is very similar to the Tabasco chile that is the basis of the famous sauce.

The *melegueta* pepper enjoyed great popularity during the Elizabethan Age in England, primarily through trade with Portugal. Some food historians consider that since the word "*melegueta*" was already a Portuguese term for spicy berry, this name was transferred to a Brazilian red chile pepper of even more pungency, sometime after the Portuguese settlement of Brazil. This scenario follows a pattern that Christopher Columbus began when he misnamed chiles as pepper. The chile peppers, it seems, were given the closest common name when they were "discovered" by Europeans. Interestingly enough, the African *meleguetas* were eventually imported into Surinam and Guyana, where they were grown commercially.

But we are concerned with the *Capsicum* version of the *malagueta* in this book. The most common use for the pods is making hot sauces; the *malaguetas* are crushed, salted, fermented, and combined with vinegar. The *malagueta* pods can also be used fresh in salsas and can be dried for adding to stir-fry dishes.

As far as the habanero relatives are concerned, the Amazon Basin was the center of origin for the *chinense* species, famous for having the hottest chiles of all. The oldest known *chinense* ever found was the 6,500-year-old intact pod found in Guitarrero Cave in Peru.

Bernabe Cobo, a naturalist who traveled throughout South America during the early seventeenth century, was probably the first European to study the *chinense* species. He estimated that there were at least forty different varieties of chiles, "some as large as limes or large plums; others, as small as pine nuts or even grains of wheat, and between the two extremes are many different sizes. No less variety is found in color . . . and the same difference is found in form and shape."

Chinense is the most important cultivated pepper east of the Andes in South America. There is a great diversity of pod shape (from chiltepin-sized berries to elongated pods) and heat levels ranging from zero to the hottest ever measured. They are green at immaturity and mature to red, orange, yellow, purple, or white. The wild *chinense* varieties have numerous local names in Spanish, Portuguese, and Indian dialects that translate as "fish eye," "parakeet's eye," and "blowgun pepper." At some point in time, Native Americans transferred the *chinense* from the Amazon Basin into the Caribbean, where land races (locally adopted varieties) developed on nearly every island.

The popularity of chiles in Brazilian cookery is the result of three factors: the prevalence of chiles in the Amazon Basin, their combination with foods introduced by the Portuguese, and the fact that the first African slaves readily adopted the native chiles. Brazilian cuisine was influenced more by African sources than its own native Indian tribes because, in colonial times, the Portuguese colonials totally depended upon African cooks who utilized both Brazilian and imported West African foodstuffs. There is even a saying in Brazil today, "*A mais preta a cozinheira, o melhor a comida,*" "the blacker the cook, the better the food."

According to Tita Libín, who researched the subject, chiles and religion collide in Bahia. "Bahia is where the African religions blended with Catholicism," she wrote, "creating a very unique synthesis, transforming their magical gods into the form of Catholic saints. It was necessary for the African slaves to make this transformation because their religion was deemed unacceptable to the authorities of the day. The slaves pretended to adopt Catholicism, but instead incorporated the Saints into their own religion, hiding the statues for rituals such as Magic Candomble ceremonies which only the 'initiated' were allowed to witness."

Libín went on to describe the ceremonies. "Nowadays outsiders and tourists are sometimes permitted as spectators at these 'voodoo' ceremonies, but very few understand the sequence of the ritual. The followers who congregate to receive a particular Orixa or Saint are always dressed in white. At certain times in the ceremony, a specific Orixa possesses the body of one of the initiated for a few moments, promising the rest of the followers of the sect better times ahead. After the sacred ordeal is over, the people partake in a feast prepared with the favorite foods of the participating Saint."

In addition to a favorite food, each Orixa has a specific Catholic saint counterpart, greeting, color of dress, day, and element. A recurring ingredient in most of the Orixa recipes is the *malagueta* chile. In the coastal city of Salvador, Bahia, the dish is very spicy, with either dried or fresh chiles added.

BRAZILIAN BLACK BEAN STEW WITH MALAGUETAS
Feijoada Completa

This recipe features smoked meats and the Brazilian favorite, black beans. To serve it without black beans would be sacrilege to a Brazilian! This stew is so popular it is thought of as the national dish of Brazil. The smoked tongue and *carne seca* are available in Latin markets, but feel free to substitute other smoked meats.

MAKES 10 TO 12 SERVINGS
HEAT SCALE: **Medium**

1 smoked beef tongue
2 pounds black beans, soaked overnight and
    drained
2 pounds carne seca (dried beef), soaked
    overnight and drained
2 pounds linguiça (seasoned Brazilian pork
    sausage) (or substitute chorizo)
½ pound bacon, in 1 piece
½ pound smoked loin of pork
½ pound salt pork, cubed

2 tablespoons vegetable oil
2 onions, minced
2 cloves garlic, crushed
2 tomatoes, seeded and chopped
2 bay leaves
3 fresh malagueta chiles, seeds and stems
    removed, minced (or substitute piquins or red
    serranos)
2 tablespoons finely chopped fresh parsley
4 oranges, peeled and sliced

Place the tongue in a large pot and add water to cover. Bring to a boil, lower the heat to medium-low, and simmer, covered, until tender, about 2½ hours. Drain and when the tongue is cool enough to handle, remove the skin and any gristle. Place the beans, *carne seca*, *linguiça*, bacon, pork loin, and salt pork in a very large skillet. Add cold water to cover. Place over high heat on top of the stove and bring to a boil, then lower the heat to medium-low and simmer, covered, 1 hour. Check occasionally to see if the liquid is being absorbed too quickly by the beans. Add boiling water as necessary to keep the ingredients barely covered. Add the tongue and continue cooking 1 hour until the beans are tender.

Heat the oil in another skillet, add the onions and garlic, and cook, stirring, until soft, about 5 minutes. Add the tomatoes, bay leaves, chiles, and parsley and simmer for 5 minutes. Remove about 2 cups of the black beans from the casserole with a slotted spoon and mash them into the onion-tomato mixture. Cook, stirring constantly, about 2 minutes. Remove and slice the meats. Arrange them on a large platter with the tongue in the center. Garnish with orange slices. Add the thick bean sauce to the remaining black beans in the casserole. Cook, stirring, about 2 minutes. Remove and discard the bay leaves. Place the beans in a soup tureen. Serve the *feijoada* with rice, greens, and hot pepper sauce.

 ## GUYANESE GARLIC-CHILE PORK

This is a very traditional variation on a Portuguese-influenced dish that originated in Guyana. The usual preparation method is to slaughter a pig, cut it up, and marinate it in a huge mass of garlic, malt vinegar, and fresh thyme. After a week, the meat is cooked in a large pot, creating its own garlic-oil. Note that this recipe requires advance preparation.

MAKES 6 TO 8 SERVINGS
HEAT SCALE: **Hot**

¼ pound garlic cloves (4 or 5 heads)
2 tablespoons chopped fresh thyme or
    4 tablespoons dried
2 onions, chopped
1 habanero chile, seeds and stem removed,
    chopped

2 teaspoons salt
Juice of 1 lime
2 cups white vinegar
4 pounds boneless pork leg or shoulder, cut into
    1-inch cubes
¼ cup vegetable oil for frying

Combine all the ingredients except the pork and oil and puree in a blender in batches until smooth. Pour the mixture over the pork and marinate, covered, in a nonmetallic bowl in the refrigerator for at least 2 days and preferably 1 week.

Drain the pork, discard the marinade (see Variations), and pat it dry. Heat the oil in a frying pan over medium-high heat and fry the pork cubes, a few at a time, turning often, until they are browned on all sides, about 5 to 7 minutes. Add more oil for each batch if necessary.

Drain the pork on paper towels, keep warm in an oven, and serve with a salad and boiled rice.

VARIATIONS: Some cooks brown the pork slightly and then finish the cooking in a 350°F oven for about 30 minutes in a covered ovenproof casserole, adding some water or marinade. For garlic lovers, simmer the marinade until thick and serve it over the pork cubes.

BRAZILIAN SEAFOOD IN SPICY GINGER-PEANUT SAUCE

Vatapá

This recipe is typical of Bahia, Brazil; it has the African influences of palm oil, red chiles (usually *malaguetas*), bananas, and coconuts. The food of Salvador, the capital, also plays a central role in Jorge Amado's novels, including *Doña Flor and Her Two Husbands*. *Vatapá* is the food of Ogun, the Bahian Orixa of iron and war.

MAKES 4 SERVINGS

HEAT SCALE: **Medium**

1 pound snapper or catfish fillets, cut in 2-inch cubes

½ cup dried shrimp, finely chopped

2 to 3 tablespoons olive oil

¼ cup chopped scallions

1 small onion, minced

1 teaspoon minced fresh ginger

2 cups chopped tomatoes

2 teaspoons crushed malagueta chile (or substitute piquin)

1 cup coconut milk

½ cup cashew nuts, chopped

1 cup chunky peanut butter

2 slices bread, soaked in water

½ teaspoon freshly ground black pepper

½ teaspoon ground cloves

1 tablespoon palm oil (or substitute vegetable oil with 1 teaspoon ground paprika)

2 cups water

¼ cup chopped fresh cilantro

In a large skillet over medium-high heat, cook the fish and shrimp in the oil, stirring, until just done, 5 to 6 minutes. Remove from the skillet and keep warm.

Add the scallions, onion, and ginger to the skillet and cook, stirring, until soft, about 5 minutes. Stir in the tomatoes and simmer for 5 minutes. Add the remaining ingredients, except the cilantro. Bring to a boil, then reduce the heat to medium-low and simmer, uncovered, until the sauce has thickened, about 15 minutes.

Return the fish and shrimp to the skillet. Add the cilantro and heat through. Serve with rice and beans.

◣ *Amomo.* A variety of piquin chile in Mexico.

◣ **Anaheim.** The name that the California produce industry gave the New Mexican pod type. Typically a long, mild chile primarily used in the green form, Anaheim is now considered to be a cultivated variety of the New Mexican pod type.

◣ **Ancho.** "Wide" or "broad"; a dried poblano chile. In Mexico and the United States, it is a large, broad, mild chile with a raisiny aroma and flavor. Confusingly, ancho is called pasilla in Morelia, Michoacán, and chile *joto* in Aguascalientes. It is also called pasilla in some Northern states and in California, U.S.A.

ANCHO/POBLANO

A pod type of the *annuum* species. The name ancho means "wide," an allusion to the broad, flat, heart-shaped pods in the dried form. The fresh pod is called poblano.

The Plant

Anchos are multiple-stemmed and compact to semierect, semiwoody, and about twenty-five inches high. The leaves are dark green and shiny, approximately four inches long and two and a half inches wide. The corollas are off-white and appear at every node. The flowering period begins fifty days after sowing and continues until the first frost. The pods are pendant, vary between three to six inches long, and are two to three inches wide. They are conical or truncated and have indented shoulders. Immature pods are dark

Poblano chiles. PAUL BOSLAND

green, maturing to either red or brown. The dried pods are a very dark reddish-brown, nearly black. They are fairly mild, ranging from 1,000 to 1,500 Scoville Units.

Agriculture

This variety is one of the most popular peppers grown in Mexico, where about 37,000 acres of it are under cultivation. The ancho/poblano varieties grow well in the United States but only about 150 acres are planted. Growers in the Eastern United States reported their plants topped four feet and needed to be staked to keep them from toppling over. They produced well but the pods never matured to the red stage before the end of the growing season. The usual growing period is 100 to 120 days and the yield is about fifteen pods per plant, although there are reports of thirty pods per plant.

Culinary Usage

Fresh poblanos are roasted and peeled, then preserved by canning or freezing. They are often stuffed to make chiles *rellenos*. The dried pods can be stored in airtight containers for months, or they can be ground into a powder. Anchos are commonly used in sauces called *moles*.

ROASTED POBLANO CHILES STUFFED WITH SPICED GOAT CHEESE

Poblano chiles impart a distinctive taste to these *rellenos* and they are usually milder than the New Mexican ones. The filling is a combination of traditional Mexican and New Southwestern ingredients.

MAKES 4 SERVINGS
HEAT SCALE: **Mild**

2 teaspoons ground red New Mexican chile

½ cup goat cheese

½ cup ricotta cheese

1 cup walnuts, finely chopped

½ cup dark raisins

¼ teaspoon ground cinnamon

¼ teaspoon ground cloves

4 large poblano chiles, roasted and peeled (page 146), stems left on

All-purpose flour for dredging

4 large eggs, separated

½ cup flour

2 teaspoons baking powder

1 tablespoon water

¼ teaspoon salt

Vegetable oil for frying

In a bowl, combine the red chile, cheeses, walnuts, raisins, cinnamon, and cloves to make the filling. Make a slit in the side of each chile and stuff with the filling. Roll each stuffed chile in the flour and shake off the excess.

In a clean bowl, beat the egg whites until stiff. In another bowl, combine the egg yolks, ½ cup flour, baking powder, water, and salt and gently fold the mixture into the egg whites to make a batter.

Carefully dip the chiles into the batter and coat well. Heat 2 to 3 inches of oil in a large skillet over high heat to 350°F. Add the chiles and fry until lightly browned (about 2 to 3 minutes per side), turning them once. Remove and drain on paper towels.

Ají amarillo, *a common Andean chile.* DAVE DEWITT

ANDES REGION

The country people of the Andean region of Peru, Chile, Ecuador, and Bolivia still eat basically Incan food that has been only slightly modified by the meats and vegetables introduced by the Spanish. But despite the basic nature of the cuisine of this region, chiles are used extensively, and they are among the hottest in the world.

Although the habanero relatives of the *chinense* species of the *Capsicum* genus do occasionally appear in the Andes, the two major chiles of choice in the region are *ajís* and *rocotos*. The *baccatum* species, familiarly termed "*ají*" throughout South America, originated either in Bolivia or in Peru and, according to archaeological evidence, was probably domesticated in Peru about 2500 B.C.

Extensive *baccatum* material found at the Huaca Prieta archaeological site in Peru shows that the species was gradually improved by the pre-Incan civilizations. From tiny, berry-like pods that were deciduous (dropped off the plant), the fruit size increased, and the fruits gradually became non-deciduous and stayed on the plants through ripening. There are two wild forms (var. *baccatum* and *microcarpum*) and many domesticated forms. The domesticated forms have a great diversity of pod shape and size, ranging from short, pointed pods borne erect to long, pendant pods resembling the New Mexican varieties of the *annuum* species. The *baccatum* species is generally distinguished from the other species by the yellow or tan spots on the corollas of the flowers. One variety of *ají, puca-uchu*, grows on a vine-like plant in home gardens. *Baccatums* are cultivated in Argentina, Colombia, Ecuador, Peru, Brazil, and Bolivia. They are used fresh in salsas, and the small yellow varieties are prized for their lemony aroma. The pods of

Hummingbird feeding on chile flower in pre-Incan pottery design. SUNBELT ARCHIVES

all *ajís* are also dried in the sun and then crushed into powders.

The other chile of choice in the Andes is the red or yellow, apple-shaped *rocoto,* of the *pubescens* species. It is grown today in the Andes from Bolivia to Colombia, mostly in small family plots. It is also cultivated in highland areas of Central America and Mexico. The *rocotos* are renowned for their pungency, and there is a Peruvian expression about them, *"llevanta muertos,"* meaning they are hot enough to raise the dead. According to chile expert Dr. Jean Andrews, in the town of Huanta, Peru, *rocotos* are described as *"gringo huanuchi,"* "will kill a gringo." They are highly aromatic and flavorful in addition to their heat. The ripe pods are used fresh because their thick flesh makes them difficult to dry. They are often stuffed with cheese or sausage and baked.

Rocotos are the only chiles with black seeds, and *pubescens* is the only domesticated species with no wild form; however, two wild species, *C. cardenasii* and *C. eximium,* are closely related. The center of origin for this species was Bolivia, and according to botanist Charles Heiser, it was probably domesticated about 6000 B.C., making it one of the oldest domesticated plants in the Americas. Heiser went on to cite Incan historian Garcilaso de la Vega (1609), that *pubescens* was "the most common pepper among the Incas, just as it is today in Cuzco, the former capital of the Incan empire." It was in the Andes that the great Inca civilization came to depend upon the *ajís* and *rocotos* as their principal spice and a

major crop. Farming determined nearly every aspect of Incan society: the calendar, religion, law, and even war. It has been estimated that more kinds of foods and medicinal plants were systematically cultivated in the Andes than anywhere else in the world at any time. The result of the Incan agricultural expertise included 240 varieties of potatoes, nearly as many kinds of beans, 20 types of maize, plus sweet potatoes, peanuts, pineapples, chocolate, avocados, papayas, tomatoes, and—of course—many varieties of the beloved chile pepper.

Garcilaso de la Vega, known as El Inca, wrote in detail about chile peppers and their place in Incan culture. In his *Royal Commentaries of the Incas* (1609), he noted that chiles were the favorite fruit of the Indians, who ate them with everything they cooked, "whether stewed, boiled, or roasted."

One reason for the popularity of the pods was that the Incas worshiped the chile pepper as one of the four brothers of their creation myth. *"Agar-Uchu,"* or "Brother Chile Pepper," was believed to be the brother of the first Incan king. Garcilaso de la Vega observed that the chile pods were perceived to symbolize the teachings of the early Incan brothers. Chile peppers were thus regarded as holy plants, and the Incas' most rigorous fasts were those prohibiting all chiles. The Aymaras, an Andean tribe conquered by the Incas in the fifteenth century, had a saying that went: "Am I your salt or chile that you always have me in your mouth and speak ill of me?"

According to El Inca, the Incas raised three or four varieties of chiles. The first was called *rócot uchu*, "thick pepper," which described the long, thick pods that matured to yellow, red, and purple. Despite the adjective *"rócot,"* the most likely identification of these chiles would be the *ají* species, *C. baccatum*. De la Vega forgot the name of the next type but wrote that it was used exclusively by the royal household. The third chile he described was *chinchi uchu*, which "resembles exactly a cherry with its stalk." This type, with its name and cherry-like pods both still intact, has survived to this day in Peru and Bolivia; it is the *rocoto*. El Inca noted that the *chinchi uchu* was "incomparably stronger than the rest and only small quantities of it are found, wherefore it is most esteemed."

The varieties of *ajís* were used extensively with Andean foodstuffs such as maize, potatoes, and quinoa, three of the most common vegetable crops grown by the Incas. According to historian Bernabe Cobo, "of whole maize with some greens and chile they make a dish called *motepatasca*, cooking the maize until it burst." Maize was extremely important to the Incas, and it was primarily used to make breads and *chicha*, a beer that was their favorite intoxicant. *Locro*, a thick stew, was made with corn kernels, potatoes, *ajís*, meat, and beans.

Most of the common folk ate the grains and potatoes, while the meats were generally reserved for the Inca nobility. Some of the meat and *ají* dishes were rather unusual, such as raw liver or llama entrails chopped up with fresh *rocoto* pods, as well as the infamous Andean rodent, the guinea pig or *cuy*. According to Bernabe Cobo, "The Indians eat this little animal with the skin on, only removing the hair as if it were a suckling pig. For them it is a great delicacy, and they cook it whole, gutted, with much chile and smooth pebbles from the river." The pebbles were heated in a fire and were used to cook the guinea pig. The *cuy* today provides more than 50 percent of the animal protein eaten in Peru!

Other meats combined with *ajís* included the American camels, the wild guanaco and vicuña, and the domesticated alpaca and llamas. Llamas were reserved exclusively for the Inca royalty, and none of the commoners were allowed to kill or eat them. The hearts of the camels were particularly prized, and the Incas probably invented the dish that lives on today, *anticuchos*, chunks of heart (beef is used now) that have been marinated in a spicy vinegar and are then grilled and basted with *ají*-spiced oil.

Today, the pervasiveness of chiles in the Andes lives on. The hottest city in the region is Arequipa, at the foot of the Misti Volcano in southern Peru. The dishes from that city are so hot that restaurants in Lima list menu items as *"arequipeño,"* meaning that diners should use caution when eating them.

CHILEAN AJÍ SALSA
Pebre

Here is the classic hot sauce of Chile, one that is served with grilled or roasted meats. The types of chiles used vary considerably, depending on availability and the cook's preference. Note that this recipe requires advance preparation.

MAKES 1½ CUPS
HEAT SCALE: **Hot**

2 tablespoons olive oil

1 tablespoon red wine vinegar

⅓ cup water

4 fresh ají chiles, seeds and stems removed, minced
    (or substitute 1 jalapeño or 1 habanero)

2 cloves garlic, minced

½ cup minced onion

½ cup minced fresh cilantro

1 teaspoon minced fresh oregano

Salt to taste

Combine the olive oil, vinegar, and water in a bowl and beat with a whisk. Add the remaining ingredients, mix well, and let stand for 2 hours to blend the flavors. It can be stored in a glass jar in the refrigerator for up to a week.

PERUVIAN GARLIC-ROCOTO CHICKEN
Pollo al Ajo y Rocoto Estilo Peruano

This classic poultry dish of the Andes is made with *rocoto* chiles, which are rare in North America. Serve this garlic chicken garnished with boiled potatoes, topped with a dollop of plain yogurt.

MAKES 6 SERVINGS
HEAT SCALE: **Hot**

½ cup vegetable oil

3 onions, chopped

6 cloves garlic, minced

4 rocoto chiles, seeds and stems removed, minced
   (or substitute jalapeños)

½ teaspoon ground cinnamon

1 tablespoon cumin seeds, crushed

1 teaspoon dried basil

2 cups roasted peanuts, coarsely chopped

½ cup freshly grated Parmesan cheese

One 3½-pound chicken, poached, meat removed
   from the bones, and chopped

¾ cup low-fat plain yogurt, at room temperature

Salt and freshly ground black pepper to taste

Boiled potatoes for garnish

Heat the oil in a large saucepan over medium-high heat and cook the onions and garlic, stirring, until the onion is soft, about 5 minutes. Add the chiles, cinnamon, cumin, basil, peanuts, cheese, and the chicken meat to the saucepan and fold together gently. Cook until heated through.

Two or 3 minutes before serving, stir in the yogurt and add salt and pepper. Serve with the boiled potatoes.

PERUVIAN MIXED SEAFOOD CEVICHE
Ceviche Mixto de Mariscos Peruano

This particular ceviche has a fair amount of crushed *ajís* or whatever dried chiles you have available. The use of corn and sweet potatoes shows that this dish is typically Peruvian. Serve it as an entree for lunch or dinner on those hot and sweltering days of summer. Note that this recipe requires advance preparation.

MAKES 4 SERVINGS
HEAT SCALE: **Medium**

¾ cup fresh lime juice

¾ cup fresh lemon juice

3 dried ají chiles, seeds and stems removed, crushed in a mortar (or substitute 2 New Mexican chiles [mild] or 6 piquins [hot])

1 clove garlic, minced

1 large red onion, sliced paper-thin

1 teaspoon salt

¼ teaspoon freshly ground black pepper

½ pound whitefish fillets, such as catfish, cut into 1-inch pieces

1 pound cleaned shellfish (clams, oysters, mussels, or a mix)

1 teaspoon paprika (optional)

1 tablespoon chopped fresh parsley, Italian preferred

3 sweet potatoes, peeled and cut into 1-inch-thick slices

3 ears of fresh corn, cleaned and cut into 2-inch-thick slices

4 Bibb lettuce leaves

Combine all the ingredients except the potatoes, corn, and lettuce in a large ceramic bowl, mix well, cover tightly, and refrigerate for 3 to 5 hours. If the citrus juice doesn't cover the fish, add more in equal amounts.

Just before serving, bring a large pot of salted water to a boil. Add the sweet potatoes and boil for 10 minutes. Then, add the rounds of corn to the pot and boil for another 10 minutes. Drain the vegetables thoroughly.

Drain the fish in a colander to remove the marinade and arrange the fish on the lettuce on 4 dinner plates. Garnish with the sweet potatoes and the rounds of corn.

ANNUUM SPECIES

Annuum means annual, which is an incorrect designation, as peppers are perennials. This species includes most of the commonest varieties, such as New Mexican, jalapeño, bell, and wax.

The most likely ancestor of the common *annuum* varieties grown in the garden today is the wild chiltepin (*Capsicum annuum* var. *aviculare*). Botanists believe that these wild chiles are the closest surviving species to the earliest forms of chiles that developed in Bolivia and southern Brazil long before mankind arrived in the New World. The wild chiles spread all over South and Central America and up to what is now the United States border millennia before the domesticated varieties arrived. In fact, some botanists believe that chiltepins have the widest distribution of any Western Hemisphere chile variety, ranging from Peru north to the Caribbean, Florida, Texas, and Louisiana and west to Arizona.

By the time the Spanish arrived in

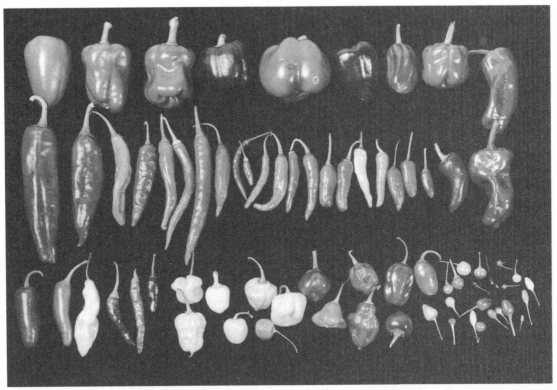

Pod variations in the annuum *species.* NMSU

Mexico, Aztec plant breeders had already developed dozens of *annuum* varieties. According to historian Bernardino de Sahagún, who lived in Mexico in 1529, "hot green peppers, smoked peppers, water peppers, tree peppers, beetle peppers, and sharp-pointed red peppers" existed. Undoubtedly, these peppers were the precursors to the large number of *annuum* varieties found in Mexico today. Christopher Columbus took *annuum* seeds back to the Old World, and they were planted extensively in the Portuguese and Spanish colonies in Africa, India, and Asia, resulting in even more diversification of the species.

C. annuum is the most extensively cultivated species in the world, both commercially and in home gardens. It is the principal species grown in Hungary, India, Mexico, China, Korea, and the East Indies. Because the varieties cross-pollinate so easily, probably thousands of different types exist around the world. Each has a common name, making identification difficult. In Mexico, for example, more than 200 common names for peppers are used—but only about fifteen *annuum* pod types are cultivated commercially.

Annuums used to be divided into two categories, sweet (or mild) peppers and hot (or chile) peppers. However, modern plant breeding removed that distinction because now hot bell varieties and sweet jalapeño and New Mexican varieties have been bred.

➤ *'Apaseo.'* In Mexico, a cultivated variety of pasilla.

➤ *'Ardida do chile.'* A commercial variety of *Capsicum baccatum* grown in Brazil.

ASIAN CHILES

Chiles were not indigenous to Asia but were transferred there through trade. Although hard evidence is lacking, ethnobotanists theorize that either Arab, Hindu, or Portuguese traders—or some combination—carried chiles from India to Malacca, on the Malay Peninsula across from Sumatra, between 1510 and the late 1520s. From there, Portuguese traders introduced the fiery fruits into Thailand,

Cambodian flame tongue chile. DAVE DEWITT

and numerous trading groups took them to Java, Sumatra, New Guinea, Macao, and the Philippines.

From the varieties present today in Asia, it appears that the *Capsicum annuum* and *frutescens* species were the primary chiles transferred to the region. Whatever their species, they quickly became a very important element in the cuisines of all the countries in the region. As Thai food expert Jennifer Brennan described the process, chile peppers were "adopted by the Thai with a fervor normally associated with the return of a long-lost child."

In 1529, a treaty between Spain and Portugal gave the Spanish control of the Philippines and the Portuguese control of Malaysia. Since the Spanish also controlled Mexico, it was easier to administer the Philippines from that colony, so regular shipping routes between Manila and Acapulco were established. Mexican chiles and other foodstuffs were transferred directly from the New World to the Old across the Pacific.

By 1550, chiles had become well established in Southeast Asia, probably spread as much by birds as by human trade and cultivation. It is an ironic culinary fact that the imported chiles became as important as many traditional spices in Southeast Asian cuisines, thus illustrating how the pungency of chiles has been combined with indigenous flavors to fire up most of the cuisines of the region.

Chiles are most predominant in Southeast Asia, particularly Thailand, Korea, western China, Indonesia, and Malaysia.

They play a lesser role in the agriculture and cuisines of two other important Asian countries, Japan and the Philippines.

Capsicums were introduced into Japan in the late 1500s or early 1600s and were used as a vegetable, spice, and ornamental plant. By the late 1800s, cultivation was extensive, and the Japanese varieties known as "santaka" and "hontaka" became famous for their high pungency. Today, a mere 350 acres are planted for chile peppers, less than one thirtieth the total *Capsicum* acreage—the Japanese are far more fond of bell peppers.

In the Philippines, "hot pepper is a minor crop," according to one agricultural expert. Production is limited to very small, scattered areas and the most popular variety is "*matikis.*" The *siling labuyo*, either a *C. frustescens* or *C. chinense*, is an extremely hot "bird pepper" that grows both wild and cultivated. (See China; Korea; Spice Islands—Indonesia, Malaysia, and Singapore; and Thailand and Its Neighbors.)

➤ **ASTA.** American Spice Trade Association. ASTA Units are a measurement of the degree of red coloration in peppers. The higher the ASTA value, the brighter the color and the more valuable the pepper for use in extraction oleoresins. A value of 300 ASTA is considered to be superior.

➤ *Ata.* The generic term for chile pepper among the Yoruba of Nigeria. *Ata funfun* resembles the jalapeño, while *ata wewe* is a Tabasco-like chile. *Ata rodo* is *Capsicum chinense*, the habanero relative.

BACCATUM SPECIES

The word *baccatum* means berry-like. The *baccatum* species of the genus *Capsicum*, familiarly termed *"ají"* throughout South America, originated either in Bolivia or in Peru and, according to archaeological evidence, was probably domesticated in Peru about 2500 B.C. Extensive *baccatum* material found at the Huaca Prieta archaeological site in Peru shows that the species was gradually improved by the pre-Incan civilizations. Fruit size increased and the fruits gradually became nondeciduous and stayed on the plants through ripening. There are at least two wild forms (var. *baccatum* and *microcarpum*) and many domesticated forms. The domesticated *ajís* have a great diversity of pod shape and size, ranging from short, pointed pods borne erect to long, pendant pods resembling the New Mexican varieties. One variety of *ají*, *pucauchu*, grows on a vine-like plant in home gardens. The *baccatum* species is generally distinguished from the other species by the yellow or tan spots on the corollas, and by the yellow anthers.

Baccatums are cultivated in Argentina, Colombia, Ecuador, Peru, Brazil, and Bolivia, and the species has been introduced into Costa Rica, India, and the United States. In the United States, it is grown to a very limited extent in California under the brand-name Mild Italian and in Nevada under the brand-name *Chileno*.

The *baccatums* are tall, sometimes reaching five feet, have multiple stems and an erect habit, occasionally tending toward sprawling. The large leaves are dark green, measuring up to seven inches long and four inches wide.

The flower corollas are white with distinctive yellow or tan spots; anthers are yellow or tan. The pods usually begin erect and become pendant as they mature; they are elongated in shape, measure between three and six inches long and three quarters to one and a half inches wide. They usually mature to an orange-red, but yellow and brown colors also appear in some

Pod variations in the baccatum *species.* DAVE DEWITT

varieties. The pods measure between 30,000 and 50,000 Scoville Units.

The *baccatum* plants tend to stand out in the garden like small trees. Their growing period is up to 120 days or more, and the plants can produce forty or more pods.

The pods have a distinctive, fruity flavor and are used fresh in ceviche (lime-marinated fish) in South America. They are also used fresh in salsas, and the small yellow varieties are prized for their lemony aroma. The pods of all *ajís* are also dried in the sun and then crushed into colorful powders.

PERUVIAN SPICY GRILLED BEEF
Anticuchos Picantes

Peruvian people love really hot food. The marinade and sauce used with this version of *anticuchos* make this dish rather pungent. Substitute steak for the heart if you wish. Note that this recipe requires advance preparation.

MAKES 10 TO 16 SERVINGS
HEAT SCALE: Hot

1 beef heart

Marinade

6 to 8 cloves garlic, pressed

2 fresh ají chiles, seeds and stems removed, minced (or substitute red jalapeños)

2 tablespoons ground cumin

½ tablespoon dried oregano

Salt and freshly ground black pepper to taste

1½ to 2 cups red wine vinegar

Sauce

⅓ cup crushed dried ají chiles (or substitute New Mexican chiles)

⅓ cup warm water

1 tablespoon vegetable oil

Salt to taste

Clean the beef heart thoroughly, removing all nerves and fat. Cut into 1-inch cubes and place the cubes into a nonreactive bowl. Place in the refrigerator.

To make the marinade, combine the garlic, chiles, cumin, oregano, salt and pepper, and 1½ cups of the vinegar. Pour this over the meat. Add more vinegar, if necessary, to cover it completely. Marinate the meat in the refrigerator for 12 to 24 hours. Then, about 1 hour before grilling, remove the meat from the marinade and thread on skewers. Reserve the marinade.

For the sauce, soak the crushed chiles in the warm water for 30 minutes. In a blender or food processor, combine the chiles and their soaking water with the oil and salt. Add enough of the reserved and boiled marinade (about ¾ cup) to make a thick sauce, and puree.

Brush the skewered meat with the sauce and grill it over hot coals or under a broiler, turning and basting to cook quickly on all sides. The *anticuchos* are best cooked medium well, about 4 to 6 minutes per side on the grill, depending on the heat of the fire. Serve with the remaining sauce for dipping.

⩗ *'Bakolocal.'* A cultivated variety of chile in Ethiopia.

⩗ *'Balín.'* "Bullet"; in Mexico, a cultivated variety of serrano chile.

⩗ *Bandeño.* In the state of Guerrero, Mexico, a name for the green *costeño.* The name refers to the bank of a river.

⩗ *Barkono.* Term for chile in northern Nigeria.

BELL PEPPERS

Bell is a pod type of the *annuum* species. It is multistemmed with a growing habit that is subcompact tending toward prostrate, growing between one and two and a half feet tall. The leaves are medium-green, ovate to lanceolate, smooth, and are about three inches long and one and a half inches wide. The flower corollas are white with no spots. The pods are pendant, three- or four-lobed, blocky, and blunt. Their immature color is dark green, usually maturing to red, but sometimes to yellow, orange, or purple. The pungent variety, 'Mexi-Bell,' has only a slight bite, ranging from 100 to 400 Scoville Units.

Agriculture

Bells are the most commonly grown commercial peppers in the United States with approximately 65,000 acres under cultivation. Mexico follows with about 22,000 acres, and most of their bells are exported to the United States. More than

An early engraving of an English bell pepper. SUNBELT ARCHIVES

100 varieties of bell peppers have been bred, and we have chosen our selections on the basis of color, pungency, disease resistance, and availability to the home grower.

Bells grow well in sandy loams with good drainage. The hotter varieties are usually grown in the home garden. The growing period ranges from 80 to 100 days, depending on whether it is picked green or at the mature color. A single plant produces ten to twenty pods. A recommended variety is 'Mexi-Bell.'

Culinary Usage

Most bells are used in the fresh form, cut up in salads or stuffed with meats and baked.

Pungent bells are also used in fresh salsas. Both kinds can be preserved by freezing.

⌁ *Berbere.* The Amharic word for chile; in Ethiopia the term refers generically to both the pod and a paste made from the pods.

BEVERAGES

There's a crisis these days in the world of etiquette: What drinks should be served with hot and spicy foods? The turmoil has been caused by the fact that more and more Americans are consuming hot and spicy dishes from a number of world cuisines, yet most cookbook authors and magazine writers on the subject have avoided matching beverages to the sizzling entrees. Should peppery cocktails, such as those made with chile pepper vodkas, be served with spicy foods, or is such a practice culinary overkill? Which wines should be matched with the enormous variety of exotic, incendiary dishes? What role does beer play in this question? And isn't it only polite to provide cool-down drinks for guests whose palates have not yet adapted to the heat levels of the fiery food being served?

Peppery Cocktails

Since cocktails always precede the meal, it makes perfect sense that a burning beverage is the best way to prepare guests for the fiery feast to follow. The most basic peppery cocktail is one that has the heat already in it—namely, a liquor that has been treated with some variety of chile pepper.

It is ironic that chile pepper–flavored liquors originated in a country virtually devoid of fiery foods: the Soviet Union. The word vodka is the Russian diminutive for "water," which gives a fairly good indication of just how basic and important this liquor is in the Soviet Union. In fact, the people there love it so much they cannot leave it alone. They blend about forty different flavors of various herbs and spices with their vodkas, including combinations of heather, mint, nutmeg, cloves, cinnamon—and, of course, cayenne powder.

A favorite brand of Russian chile pepper

Jalapeño vodka. CHEL BEESON

vodka is Stolichnaya Pertsovka, the famous "Stoly," which has been infused with white and black pepper, combined with cayenne powder, and then filtered to remove all solids. Unfortunately, the reddish tint of the vodka is the result of added caramel coloring rather than the chiles, but it still tastes great and has a nice bite. Other popular brands of hot vodkas are Absolut Peppar from Sweden and America's own Gordon's Pepper Flavored Vodka.

Today, Bloody Marys (see the recipe on page 49) are often made with the chile-infused vodkas, and variations on the Bloody Mary include replacing the vodka with tequila—which creates a Bloody Maria—or with Japanese sake for a Bloody Mary Quite Contrary. The cocktail can be made with one of the chile pepper vodkas to supply the pungency, or it can be spiced up with a favorite brand of bottled hot sauce. Since the various chiles used in these sauces all have their own unique flavor, the taste of the Bloody Marys can vary significantly. Tabasco sauce, the trademarked brand of the McIlhenny Company, is still the most commonly used hot sauce to spice up this drink, but these days people are experimenting with hot sauces based upon the cayenne, habanero, jalapeño, and even chipotle chiles.

It is always embarrassing to discover—after you've served the peppery cocktails—that one of your guests has recently been discharged from an alcohol treatment center. So for guests on the wagon, serve them a volatile Virgin Mary, which retains the hot sauce but eliminates the vodka.

Matching Wines and Beers with Spicy Entrees

The fiery main courses have been selected, whether at home or in a restaurant. But what beverages should accompany such incendiary dishes as the ones contained in this book? Certainly not the same peppery cocktail you've been drinking before the meal because the pungency of the drink will mask the complex flavors and spiciness of the entree. Since wines and beers are traditionally served with meals all over the world, the crucial questions to answer are: Will the fiery foods overwhelm the wine, and do wines and beers extinguish the fire of the chiles?

Wine expert Roy Andries de Groot believes that wines do indeed cut the heat of chile dishes. He suggests serving cold white wines with most spicy foods and claims that a Chablis, Chenin Blanc, or Colombard is "excellent for putting out chile fires." Undoubtedly, he has heard the argument that beer and wine have some efficacy as cool-downs because capsaicin—the chemical that gives chiles their heat—dissolves readily in alcohol but does not mix with water. This theory holds that the alcohol dilutes the capsaicin and thus reduces the heat sensation. However, since both beer and wine are more than 80 percent water, the alcohol content actually has little effect on the heat levels.

So do not expect wines and beers to reduce the pungency of the dishes being served. Although the cool temperature at which many beers and wines are served may give the illusion of reducing heat, in reality they do not temper the sting of capsaicin very much and in some cases may even increase it. Beverage consultant Ronn Wiegand, writing in Marlena Spieler's book *Hot & Spicy*, warns, "the tannin content of most young red wines can actually magnify the heat."

With beer and wine accompaniments, the heat level is not nearly as important as a harmonious blending of flavors and textures. For example, we usually drink beer with the hottest Mexican and Chinese foods because it is a perfect complement, not because of its reputation as a cool-down. With some of the spicy New Southwest meals, slightly fruity white wines such as Chenin Blanc or Riesling seem to be a better pairing.

Roy Andries de Groot has studied the problem of what wines to serve with fiery foods and advises, "My theory of the successful marriage of wine with these cuisines is to know (and separate) the gentle dishes, the spicy dishes, and the fiery dishes. The menu is then planned so that each group of dishes is paired with the wine that adds certain essential contrasts and harmonies."

For example, he recommends a Bordeaux or a Cabernet Sauvignon as the best wine to accompany the chocolate-flavored *mole* poblano and calls the combination "one of the more memorable marriages of exotic gastronomy." For curries, De Groot suggests a Fumé Blanc or a soft Semillon; for the entrees that top the heat scale he has surprising advice—an American light wine. Since he believes that white wine cuts the heat, he advises that the wine should be low in alcohol so it can be consumed in great quantities without discomfort.

Ronn Wiegand recommends serving the wine that your budget can comfortably afford. He suggests that fine and rare wines are not perfect beverages with fiery foods because their flavor nuances "are overwhelmed by the strong spices" but admits that there are times when no other drink will do. "At such times," he writes, "simply upgrade the quality of the wine you would normally serve with a given dish, and enjoy the inevitable fireworks."

When deciding which beers to offer guests who are about to assault their senses with chile heat, one logical solution is to do a regional match: Carta Blanca with Mexican foods, a Tsingtao with Sichuan dishes, Tusker with African entrees, Red Stripe with Jamaican foods, and so on. With American spicy specialties, such as New Mexican or Cajun, we suggest forgetting every American beer that is advertised on TV—they are all mediocre at best. Instead, serve one of the finer regional specialty beers such as Augsburger from Wisconsin or Anchor Steam from San Francisco.

Incidentally, some writers insist that dark beers should never be served with spicy foods because they are traditionally served in cool climates rather than tropical ones. Such a judgment makes little culinary sense because often one needs a heavy, dark beer to match a meal measuring high on the heat scale. Besides, the theory is proven false in Mexico, where such fine beers as Negra Modelo and Dos Equis are commonly served with the hottest meals.

For hosts still in a quandary about which beers and wine to offer, why not present a number of selections to your guests and have them decide—by tasting them all—which wines and beers go best with the fiery foods being served?

After-Dinner Cool-Downs

Believe it or not, some chile addicts believe that every course of the meal should burn. After peppery cocktails, fiery appetizers, spicy soup, and three different incendiary entrees, they have the nerve to serve jalapeño sorbet for dessert. Fortunately, the vast majority of chile cooks believe that enough is enough and prefer a soothing cool-down as a perfect finish for a fiery feast.

As with beers and wines, a debate rages over precisely which drinks actually tame the heat of chiles. Recommendations range from ice water to hot tea to lemon juice to one of our favorites, Scotch on the rocks. Most of these liquids can be dismissed out of hand. Ice water is totally useless because capsaicin and water don't mix. As soon as the water leaves the mouth, the fire rages on. Hot tea is a legendary Vietnamese remedy, but there is no logical reason for it to work because it is 99 percent water. Lemon juice seems to help some people, but somehow we can't picture our guests sitting around the table sucking on lemons after a marvelous fiery feast. And as for Scotch on the rocks, well, if you drink enough of it, you soon won't care about cooling down.

Actually, it was East Indian cooks who perfected the solution to the problem of after-dinner cool-downs. They discovered that the most effective antidote for capsaicin is dairy products, particularly yogurt. The Indian yogurt and fruit drink called *lassi* is commonly served after hot curry meals, and it is sweet, refreshing, and effective. No one seems to know precisely why milk, sour cream, yogurt, and ice cream cut the heat, but they do. Some experts suggest that the protein casein in the milk counteracts the capsaicin, but all we know is that it works.

CHILE-INFUSED VODKA

The raisiny flavor of the pasilla melds with the apricot overtones of the habanero and the earthiness of the New Mexican chile to create a finely tuned, fiery sipping vodka. Of course, use an excellent vodka like Stolichnaya or Absolut. Note that this recipe requires advance preparation.

MAKES ABOUT 1 QUART
HEAT SCALE: **Varies**

1 liter vodka
1 pasilla chile, seeds and stem removed, cut into thin strips
½ dried red New Mexican chile pod, seeds and stem removed, cut into quarters

¼ habanero chile, seeds and stem removed, left whole

Open the bottle of vodka and drink some of it to make room in the bottle. Add the chiles and recap. Let sit for at least 3 days to generate some heat. The vodka will get progressively hotter over the weeks. As you drink the vodka, replace it with more fresh vodka, and the process will go on for some time.

TEX-MEX TEQUILA

Nearly any small, red chile pepper can be used in this recipe, but the chiltepins (called chilipiquins in Texas) work particularly well because they are small enough so the whole pod can fit through the neck of the bottle. Flavored liquors are often prepared in the Southwest with sliced jalapeños too. Obviously, the longer the chiles are left in, the hotter the tequila will be. Serve this tequila extremely cold in shot glasses, over ice, or in tomato juice for an "instant" Bloody Maria. Note that this recipe requires advance preparation.

MAKES 1 LITER
HEAT SCALE: **Varies, but usually hot**

6 dried chiltepin chiles, left whole , stems removed   1 liter white tequila (Herradura preferred)
   (or substitute any small, hot dried chiles)

Place the chiltepins in the tequila, seal the bottle, and let them steep for a week or more. Periodically taste the liquor and remove the chiles when the desired heat has been obtained.

PUNGENT BLOODY MARY

Here is the ultimate Bloody Mary designed for the ultimate peppery cocktail snob. Canned tomato juice is permitted only when fresh, vine-ripened tomatoes are not available.

MAKES 1 SERVING
HEAT SCALE: **Medium**

½ teaspoon of your favorite bottled hot sauce (or   *1 teaspoon freshly squeezed lime juice*
   more to taste)   *⅛ teaspoon soy sauce*
1½ ounces (3 tablespoons) fine vodka such as   *1/16 teaspoon brown sugar*
   Stolichnaya or Absolut (or use the Chile-Infused   *Dash salt*
   Vodka, page 48)   *Freshly ground black pepper to taste*
4 ounces (½ cup) tomato juice, freshly made from   *1 slice fresh serrano or jalapeño chile for garnish*
   vine-ripened tomatoes, or more to taste—get
   out your juicer!

Combine all ingredients except the garnish in a cocktail shaker or jar with a lid and shake with ice cubes. Serve garnished with a slice of fresh serrano or jalapeño chile.

SANGRITA WITH HOT SAUCE

This particular version of sangrita, or "bloody little drink," comes from Chapala, Mexico, where the bartenders have not succumbed to the temptation of adding tomato juice to this concoction, as the gringos do. The bloody color comes from the grenadine, so this is truly a sweet heat drink that is also salty. Some people take a sip of tequila after each swallow of sangrita, while others mix one part tequila to four parts sangrita to make a cocktail.

MAKES ABOUT 3 CUPS
HEAT SCALE: **Medium**

2 cups fresh orange juice
¾ cup grenadine syrup

2 teaspoons Mexican hot sauce of your choice (or
     substitute any habanero hot sauce)
1 tablespoon salt

Combine all ingredients in a jar with a lid, shake well, and chill.

⊯ *Bhere khorsani.* In Nepal, wolf chile.

"BIRD PEPPERS"

A "bird pepper" is defined as any small, erect-podded *Capsicum* consumed and dispersed by birds. According to botanists, the genus *Capsicum*, to which all chiles belong, originated in the remote geologic past in an area bordered by the mountains of southern Brazil to the east, by Bolivia to the west, and by Paraguay and northern Argentina to the south. Not only does this location have the greatest concentration of wild species of chiles in the world but here, and only here, grow representatives of all the major domesticated species within the genus. Some botanists believe that the location for the origin of chile peppers was further east, in central Bolivia.

Scientists are not certain about the exact time frame or the method for the spread of both wild and domesticated species from the southern Brazil–Bolivia area, but they suspect that birds were primarily responsible. The wild chiles (as well as their undomesticated cousin of today, the chiltepin) had erect, red fruits that were quite pungent and very attractive to vari-

Pod variations in "bird peppers." DAVE DEWITT

small seeds. Mammals perceive a burning sensation from capsaicin but birds do not.

There are more than fifty varieties of chiles worldwide that are called "bird peppers," including about twenty undomesticated species such as *C. cardenasii* from Bolivia, *C. chacoense* from Argentina, and *C. galapagoense* from the Galápagos Islands. (See Chiltepin.)

⬊ *'Blanca, La.'* "The white one"; a cultivated variety of *mirasol* in Mexico.

⬊ *Bola.* "Ball" or "marble." (See *Cascabel.*) Also, in Jalisco, Mexico, a word for a spherical piquin.

⬊ *Bolita.* "Little ball." (See *Cascabel.*)

⬊ *Boludo.* "Bumpy." (See *Cascabel.*)

⬊ *Bonda man Jacques.* Name for the *Capsicum chinense* species in Martinique and Guadeloupe.

⬊ **Bonney pepper.** Name for the *chinense* species in Barbados; considered to be the Red Caribbean pod type.

BOTANY

Peppers are perennial subshrubs, native to South America, which are grown as annuals in colder climates. They are a part of the large nightshade family, or *Solanaceae,* and are closely related to tomatoes, potatoes, tobacco, and eggplants. They are not related to black pepper, *Piper nigrum.* In

ous species of birds, who ate the whole pods. The seeds of those pods passed through their digestive tracts intact and were deposited on the ground encased in a perfect fertilizer. In this manner, chiles spread all over South and Central America long before the first Asian tribes crossed the Bering land bridge and settled the New World. The small pods of the undomesticated species are commonly called "bird peppers" in languages all over the world.

Botanists believe that birds are immune to the capsaicin in the pods and that the chemical evolved to protect chile peppers from mammalian predators. Scientists have long speculated that plants produce secondary metabolites, chemicals that are not required for the primary life support of the plant. These metabolites fight off animal predators and perhaps even competing plant species.

Capsaicin in chiles may be such a metabolite. It prevents animals from eating the chiles, so that they can be consumed by fruit-eating birds that specialize in red fruits with

botany, chile pods are berries, while in horticulture, they are fruits. The fresh pods are considered to be vegetables in the produce industry. The dried pods and powder are defined as spices in world trade.

The genus *Capsicum* includes all the peppers, from the mild bell to the hottest habanero. There are twenty-three species of *Capsicum* identified at this time, but experts continually argue about that number. The taxonomy of *Capsicum* is:

Kingdom	*Plantae*
Division	*Magnoliophyta*
Class	*Magnoliopsida*
Order	*Solanales*
Family	*Solanaceae*
Genus	*Capsicum*
Species	*annuum* (or other species)
Pod-type	Bell (for example)
Cultivar	'Oriole' (for example)

The pepper genus is *Capsicum*, from the Greek *kapto*, appropriately enough, meaning "to bite." The domesticated species are:

Purple flower of Capsicum pubescens. PAUL BOSLAND

annuum, meaning annual, which is an incorrect designation, as peppers are perennials. It includes most of the commonest varieties, such as New Mexican, jalapeño, bell, and wax.

baccatum, meaning berry-like. It consists of the South American peppers commonly known as *ajís*.

chinense, meaning from China, is also an incorrect designation since the species originated in the Amazon Basin. It includes the extremely hot habaneros.

frutescens, meaning shrubby or brushy. It includes the familiar Tabascos.

pubescens, meaning hairy. It includes the South American *rocotos* and the Mexican *manzanos*.

A simple key to identifying the five domesticated species of *Capsicum* follows.

Description	Species or Go To
1. Seeds black, corolla purple	*C. pubescens*
1. Seeds tan	Go to 2
2. Corolla with spots	*C. baccatum*
2. Corolla without spots	Go to 3
3. Corolla white	Go to 4
3. Corolla greenish	Go to 5
4. Flowers solitary and filament nonpurple	*C. annuum*
4. Flowers 2 or more per node and filament purple	*C. chinense*
5. Flowers solitary	*C. frutescens*
5. Flowers 2 or more per node	*C. chinense*

⤅ *Bravo.* "Brave, wild, savage"; in Mexico, a local name of chile *de árbol.*

BREEDING

Breeding peppers to create new varieties and improve old varieties is fun and easy. Amateur plant breeders usually work to improve traits that are fairly easy to change, such as fruit shape, fruit color, pungency, or plant size.

Plants reproduce two ways, asexually and sexually. Asexual, or vegetative reproduction, occurs without the fusion of reproductive cells. An example of asexual reproduction is a strawberry that produces runners that take root and form new plants. Plants originating from asexual reproduction are usually identical clones to the parent plant. Asexual reproduction can also be accomplished artificially on pepper plants by means of cuttings.

To reproduce pepper plants from cuttings, with a sterile knife, cut a nonwoody branch section with at least six leaves. Just above the end of the cutting, make a shallow incision in what is now the stem. Dip the end of the cutting in a rooting hormone powder such as Rootone to just above the incision and place it in a rooting medium such as vermiculite in plastic cell packs. The best results occur when the cuttings are gently misted. Some cuttings will likely die, but some will take root. Check them periodically and when a cutting has formed a root ball, it can be transplanted.

Sexual reproduction involves the union of male and female gametes to produce a

Chile plants under netting to prevent breeding cross-pollination, Las Cruces, New Mexico. NMSU

seed. Because of the passage of genes, plants originating from seed can be quite different from the parents and one another. Plant breeders can selectively develop new varieties by manipulating sexual reproduction in peppers.

The flowers of peppers contain both male and female organs. The sexual organs are easy to distinguish, so crossing peppers is relatively easy. Pollination is the transfer of pollen from an anther to a stigma. When the anther is mature, it opens and releases pollen. Two kinds of pollen transfers exist, cross-pollination and self-pollination. With cross-pollination, the pollen is transferred from the anther of a flower on one plant to the stigma of a flower on another plant. With self-pollination, the pollen is transferred from the anther to the stigma of the same flower, or to the stigma of a flower on the same plant.

Cross-pollination is quite common in peppers grown outdoors. Studies indicate that from 30 to 70 percent of pepper flowers can cross-pollinate, depending on location and season. Honey bees are common visitors to gardens, and usually pollinate peppers.

Plants, like animals, inherit traits from their parents. The laws of heredity explain why different traits are inherited by offspring of the same parents. By observing (and recording) the offspring's different traits, growers can discover the genes of the parent plants and how the genes interact. If a self-pollinated plant produces offspring that are identical to itself, it has bred true.

Cross-pollination is used to develop new varieties. Once the plant breeds true for a specific trait, self-pollinating the plant and its offspring will cause that trait to continue to appear. Sometimes traits such as yield, earliness, or level of pungency cannot be fixed. Many plants may have to be grown to produce a few plants showing the desired trait.

Equipment required for plant breeding is relatively inexpensive and easy to use. The basic items include rubbing alcohol, a pair of narrow-pointed forceps, a spear needle, a hand lens, a pencil, string tags, and a notebook. The notebook will be used to record the parents' characteristics, as well as how the resulting seedlings perform.

Self-pollinating a pepper to produce pure seed requires keeping insects away from the flower, and growing the peppers in a greenhouse is the simplest method. Insect-isolation cages can be used to self-pollinate peppers outdoors, and they can be made from any netting material, including drapery backing and nylon window screening. The entire plant can be caged, or just a branch. A simple technique is to enclose the plant branch with the flowers in a small paper bag for a week. After the flowers have self-pollinated, remove the bag and tag the pods as selfed. Another technique is to place a gelatin capsule over the flower bud. This will keep the flower closed until it has self-pollinated. As the fruit grows, it pushes the capsule off. Again, tag the selfed pods to separate them from others that might be insect-pollinated.

Extremely high temperatures or moist conditions are harmful to pollen. For best results, pollinate plants on dry days during the cool morning hours. Crosses can be made at any time during daylight, but the best time is between one hour after sunup and approximately 11 A.M. The main objective in crossing is not to let the flower self-pollinate, which would make the flower useless for experimentation.

Prepollination is the technique used to avoid self-pollination, and it should begin before the flower opens. Peppers bloom over a period of time, and even if some of the flowers on a plant have bloomed before they are prepared for crossing, there will be others that have not opened. Choose flower buds that are one to two days from opening. These buds are plump and white. Using forceps, remove the petals and stamens (this is called emasculation), leaving the calyx and pistil (the female organ). Use a magnifying glass for more accurate emasculation. From the male parent, either pull the anther from an opened flower and gently touch the anther to the stigma to transfer pollen, or take the spear and glean pollen from the anther and place that on the stigma. Label the pollinated flowers with a string tag, and record on the tag the mother plant, the father plant, and the pollination date.

Because peppers are not wind-pollinated, and insects will not visit the flower after the petals are removed, no other flower protection is necessary. After five to seven days, the flower will fall off if the cross did not take. Otherwise, the fruit will grow and mature and can be picked when it has reached the mature fruit color. Several flower buds should be pollinated at one time to increase the chance of the cross taking. The tools must be disinfected with rubbing alcohol between different crosses or selfs, to reduce cross-pollination. The alcohol must dry on the tools before they are used, or the alcohol will kill the pollen or ruin the stigma.

Most pepper types in this book belong to the species *annuum*. Any *annuum* pepper can be crossed with any other *annuum*. Any two varieties of the same pod type or species will cross, such as jalapeños crossing with piquins. Within the *annuums*, all varieties of all pod types will cross. Among the five species, the following scenarios occur.

Annuum: Crosses prolifically with *chinense*, sporadically with *baccatum* and *frutescens*; does not cross with *pubescens*.

Baccatum: Crosses sporadically with *annuum*, *chinense*, and *frutescens*; does not cross with *pubescens*. However, *baccatum* produces only sterile hybrids with other species.

Chinense: Crosses prolifically with *annuum*, sporadically with *frutescens* and *baccatum*; does not cross with *pubescens*.

Frutescens: Crosses sporadically with *annuum*, *baccatum*, and *chinense*; does not cross with *pubescens*.

Pubescens: Does not cross with any of the other species.

Byadgi. A variety of *annuum* in India that resembles a wrinkled, dried cayenne.

Caballo. "Horse"; another name for *rocoto* in Mexico.

Cabe (also *cabai*). General term for chile peppers in Indonesia and Malaysia. *Cabe hijau* means green chiles; *cabe merah*, red chiles; *cabe rawit*, bird chiles (*Capiscum frutescens*).

Cachucha. "Cap" chile; term for *rocotillo* in Cuba.

Cambray. A long, narrow chile grown in San Luis Potosí, Mexico, and marketed in Monterrey.

Canario. "Canary"; in Mexico, a yellow variety of the *rocoto*, or chile *manzano*.

CAPSAICIN

The active principle that causes heat in chile peppers is a crystalline alkaloid generically called capsaicin. It is produced by glands at the junction of the placenta and the pod wall. The capsaicin spreads unevenly throughout the inside of the pod and is concentrated mostly in the placental tissue.

Capsaicin is an incredibly powerful and stable alkaloid, seemingly unaffected by cold or heat, which retains its original potency despite time, cooking, or freezing. Because it has no flavor, color, or odor, the precise amount of capsaicin present in chiles can be measured only by a specialized laboratory procedure known as high performance liquid chromatography (HPLC). Although it has no odor or flavor, it is one of the most pungent compounds known, detectable to the palate in dilutions of 1 to 17 million. It is slightly soluble in water, but very soluble in alcohols, fats, and oils.

P. A. Bucholtz in 1816 first discovered that the pungent principle of peppers could

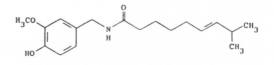

Graphic formula of capsaicin. SUNBELT ARCHIVES

be extracted from the macerated pods with organic solvents. In 1846, L. T. Thresh reported in *Pharmacy Journal* that the pungent principle could be extracted in a crystalline state. It was Thresh who named the substance capsaicin. In 1878, the Hungarian medical scientist Endre Hogyes extracted capsaicin, which he called capsicol, and discovered that it stimulated the mucous membranes of the mouth and stomach and increased the secretion of gastric juices. Capsaicin was first synthesized in 1930 by E. Spath and F. S. Darling.

The word capsaicin actually describes a complex of related components named capsaicinoids by Japanese chemists S. Kosuge and Y. Inagaki in 1964. Capsaicinoids are the chemical compounds that give chile peppers their bite. Scientists have identified and isolated five naturally occurring members of this fiery family and one synthetic cousin, which is used as a reference gauge for determining the relative pungency of the others.

The major capsaicinoids that are contained in the crystalline extract and their percentages are capsaicin (69 percent), dihydrocapsaicin (22 percent), and three minor related components: nordihydrocapsaicin (7 percent), homocapsaicin (1 percent), and homodihydrocapsaicin (1 percent).

The synthetic capsaicinoid vanillylamide of n-nonanoic acid (VNA), was administered to sixteen trained tasters by researchers Anna Krajewska and John Powers at the University of Georgia. The tasters compared the heat of VNA to the four natural capsaicinoids and the results were as follows.

The mildest capsaicinoid was nordihydrocapsaicin (NDHC), which was described as the "least irritating" and "fruity, sweet, and spicy." Next was homodihydrocapsaicin (HDHC), a compound described as "very irritating," and one that produced a "numbing burn" in the throat, which also was the most prolonged and difficult to rinse out.

The two most fiery capsaicinoid compounds were capsaicin (C) and dihydrocapsaicin (DHC), which produced burning everywhere from the mid-tongue and palate down into the throat. Evidently, all of the capsaicinoids work together to produce the pungency of peppers, but capsaicin itself is still rated the strongest.

Capsaicin is so powerful that chemists who handle the crystalline powder must work in a filtered "tox room" in full body protection. The suit has a closed hood to prevent inhaling the powder. Said pharmaceutical chemist Lloyd Matheson of the University of Iowa, who once inhaled some capsaicin accidentally: "It's not toxic, but you wish you were dead if you inhale it." "One milligram of pure capsaicin placed on your hand would feel like a red-hot poker and would surely blister the skin," said capsaicin expert Marlin Bensinger.

It has long been believed that capsaicin was present only in the pods of the *Capsicum* genus and in no other plant or animal material. However, during our research we uncovered a quote from W. Tang and G. Eisenbrand in *Chinese Drugs of Plant Origin*: "Capsaicin, the pungent principle of

Capsicum species, was isolated from ginger rhizome." Chemical engineer and capsaicin expert Marlin Bensinger strongly believes this finding to be in error. He says the proper chemical precursors are simply not found in ginger. (See Oleoresins from Capsicums.)

⩗ *Capsicum.* The genus chiles belong to. In Southeast Asia, this means bell pepper.

⩗ *Capón.* An emasculated chile; one with the seeds removed.

CARIBBEAN ISLANDS

The first peppers to inhabit the islands of the Caribbean Sea were the small, spherical pods the Mexicans call chiltepins and many people around the world call "bird peppers." These are of the species *Capsicum annuum,* but they are the progenitors from which such varieties as jalapeños and anchos evolved, with human assistance. They were spread by birds throughout the tropical and semitropical regions of the Americas. The birds were attracted to the bright red fruits, which provided valuable vitamin A for their brilliant plumage.

These "bird peppers" grow from the Northern Range in Trinidad west to Jamaica. They are sometimes raised in backyards as perennial providers of tiny-podded peppers to add to soups and stews, and they are the pepper of choice for flavored vinegars and sherries.

The other popular peppers of the

Rocotillo chile from the Cayman Islands. DAVE DEWITT

Caribbean Basin belong to the species *Capsicum chinense* (see *Chinense* Species). Introduced from the Amazon Basin, where the species originated, the seeds were carried and cultivated by Native Americans, and the *chinense* species hopped, skipped, and jumped around the West Indies, forming—seemingly on each island—specifically adapted pod types that are called land races of the species. These land races were given local names in the various islands and countries, although the terms Scotch bonnet, goat pepper, and habanero are also used generically throughout the region.

In the eastern Caribbean, habanero relatives are called Congo peppers in Trinidad and bonney peppers in Barbados. In the French Caribbean islands of Martinque and Guadeloupe, *le derrière de Madame Jacques* describes the hot peppers, and in Haiti, *piment bouc,* or goat pepper. In the western Caribbean are the familiar Jamaican Scotch bonnets, Puerto Rican *rocotillos,* and the Cuban *cachucha* ("cap") peppers, which are what the Cubans call *rocotillos.*

The habanero variety, which is thought

to have originated in Cuba, was transferred to the Yucatán Peninsula, where it was given the name that means "from Havana." These land races with the colorful names became the dominant spicy element in the food of the Caribbean.

Another member of the *chinense* species that is commonly used, especially in the eastern Caribbean, is the seasoning pepper. It is a medium-hot, elongated pepper that is an ingredient for seasoning pastes in Trinidad, Barbados, St. Lucia, and other islands.

One of the most common uses for hot peppers in the Caribbean is in hot sauces. The Carib and Arawak Indians used pepper juice for seasoning and, according to researcher Shirley Jordan, "the Caribs were

accomplished pepper sauce makers. Not knowing how to extract salt from the sea, they flavored their food with *coui*, a sauce of hot peppers and cassava juice. The tradition has persisted. Almost all West Indians like hot peppers in their food, and when a dish is not spicy enough they reach for the ever-present bottle of hot sauce. This is made in many homes by steeping diced hot peppers in vinegar, rum or sherry."

After the "discovery" of chile peppers by Europeans, slave ship captains combined pepper juice with palm oil, flour, and water to make a "slabber sauce" that was served over ground beans to the slaves aboard ship. The most basic hot sauces on the islands were made by soaking chopped Scotch

Barbadian chile products. DAVE DEWITT

bonnets in vinegar (making pepper pickles) and then sprinkling the fiery vinegar on foods. Over the centuries, each island developed its own style of hot sauce by combining the crushed chiles with other ingredients such as mustard, fruits, or tomatoes.

Homemade hot sauces are still common on the islands of the Caribbean, and there are numerous commercial sauces available in North America.

Islands in the eastern Caribbean have their own hot and spicy traditions. Barbados is famous for its mustard-based hot sauces, of which there are dozens and dozens of commercial brands in addition to the restaurant-made sauces. They are made with the bonney peppers—the Barbadian equivalent of the Congo peppers of Trinidad—which also appear in the herb seasonings that parallel those of Trinidad.

The French Caribbean has a well-deserved reputation for fiery foods. "Martinique is an island where, in the finest French tradition, people love to talk about food even more than they love to talk about politics," notes food writer Bob Payne. "And if there is one thing they agree on, it's that to eat food the way it was meant to be eaten means that you can't forget the pepper—by which they mean the hot pepper."

"If a native of Guadeloupe warns you that a dish may be hot, take heed," warn Caribbean food experts Jinx and Jefferson Morgan. "Our notes on *le crabe farci de Grand Terre* say: 'Scotch bonnets marinated in gasoline.'" They also mentioned that at La Créole Chez Violetta in the town of Gosier, "a huge mason jar of her homemade

hot sauce stood in the middle of the table. Rumor has it that the recipe is a state secret known only to the French space agency." Curried dishes are also popular in the French islands, where the word for curry is *colombo*, named for the capital of Sri Lanka. A typical *colombo*, such as the Christmas specialty with pork from Martinique, begins with a *colombo* paste that contains, in addition to some standard curry spices, crushed fresh garlic, ginger, and those *le derriére de Madame Jacques* chiles.

In the western Caribbean, some islands are hot and some are not. The Spanish islands such as Puerto Rico, Cuba, and the Dominican Republic are not hotbeds of chile peppers, although Cuba does have some spicy dishes. The spicy haven of the area is Jamaica, and its fiery cuisine is as varied as that of Trinidad—but the pepper nomenclature leaves a lot to be desired.

During several visits to Jamaica, we had futilely endeavored to differentiate between Scotch bonnets and country peppers, two terms that seemed to be interchangeable. According to vendor Bernice Campbell in the Ocho Rios market, country peppers were more elongated than Scotch bonnets, were milder, and had more flavor. With a typical pepper contrariness, cook Betty Wilson of Port Antonio disagreed. She claimed country peppers were hotter than Scotch bonnets but were more "flavored." Our room attendant at Ciboney Resort in Ocho Rios, Carol Burrell, insisted that no, country peppers were milder than Scotch bonnets. To add to the confusion, habanero grower Graham Jacks had written to us that: "One of these country peppers is a deep brownish purple when ripe, and is truly ferociously hot; much hotter than the Scotch bonnet."

Other mysterious Jamaican peppers had cropped up in various books. A variety called 'Jamaican Hot' was described by author and chef Mark Miller, in his guide *The Great Chile Book*, as "smaller than the habanero but similar in shape." It is possible that this variety is the same as the 'West Indian Hot' mentioned by Jean Andrews in *Peppers: The Domesticated Capsicums*, but pepper importer Joe Litwin had told us that the "hots" are generic terms used in the United States but not in Jamaica. A search of the 1994 edition of *Seed Savers Yearbook* revealed common names of cultivated varieties to be 'Jamaica Large Red,' 'Jamaica Orange,' 'Jamaica Small Red,' and the appellation 'Scotch bonnet' with the descriptors "orange," "yellow," and "red" added. The nomenclature had become increasingly murky.

We were on our way to tour the Good Hope Great House when we asked our guide, David Brown, if they had a garden there. David replied yes, and that there would probably be some peppers in the garden.

"We have many peppers that are hot," he observed while driving us through St. Ann's Parish. "Scotch bonnets stand out because of their incomparable flavor. From our East Indian ancestors came the long, thin cayenne that is very hot and coolie peppers, those long green ones like the ones you grow in New Mexico. Old lady peppers are also called grandmother's pepper, and we have kitchen peppers that grow outside of kitchen windows, and 'bird peppers' that grow wild and are extremely hot. The 'bird peppers' were not commonly used until people started jerking pork. They are less expensive than Scotch bonnets and are often used when Scotch bonnets are not abundant. [See Jerk Foods.]

"Scotch bonnets are country peppers but not all country peppers are Scotch bonnets. Country pepper is just a general term for garden peppers. Any cultivated pepper is a country pepper. Say a man goes into a restaurant and sees hot sauce and black pepper on the table. Those are two kinds of pepper but he wants another. He says to the waitress, 'Do you have any pepper?' The waitress would say, 'Country pepper?' The man would say, 'Yes, what kind do you have?' The waitress might say, 'Scotch bonnet and kitchen pepper,' and then the man might order some freshly chopped Scotch bonnets. Country peppers could even be sweet peppers, what you call bell peppers."

In addition to their use in hot pepper sauces, Scotch bonnets are also pickled whole and in crushed form. In Jamaican cooking, yellow Scotch bonnets are used with escovitch fish, which are fillets cooked with the pepper slices in vinegar, lime juice, and pimento (allspice). The whole pods are often floated in stews or stewed dishes such as oxtail soup, curry goat, fricasseed chicken, and stewed peas and rice, and are removed just before serving. Cooks take care not to let the pods burst or the meal may be too hot to eat!

In nearby Cuba, several questions have sprung up regarding chiles and hot and spicy foods. Do habaneros—supposedly from Havana—still grow in Cuba? And is any Cuban food hot and spicy? The answer to the first question was easy, because we have grown Cuban habaneros from seed passed on to us from Cuban immigrants. Some writers insist that only *rocotillos*—the related mild *chinense* variety—grow in Cuba, but we have discovered that there are several varieties of Cuban habaneros.

Is any Cuban food hot and spicy? We asked Rodolfo de Garay and Thomas Brown, who have written extensively on the subject. "Ask any Cuban-American about the spicy heat of Cuban food and you'll get a leery look," was the reply. And truly the Cuban dishes known to North Americans are rarely spicy. *Ropa vieja, picadillo, boliche,* and *escabeche* all depend on peppers for fla-

vor, but nearly always the mild and sweet kinds: 'Cubanelles,' bells, and pimientos.

"But then remind that incredulous Cuban of recipes such as shrimp *enchilado*, baby goat *chilindrón*, chicken with habanero glaze, *rabo encendido*, or tamales *pican* or no *pican*—that bite or don't bite. You could also remind them of the *guaguao* (or piquin) peppers pickled in vinegar, the light heat of the *cachuchas* (or *rocotillo*), which add crunch and perfume to black beans and are sold as a staple produce in Miami supermarkets. Most Cuban homes, whether in Cuba or Miami—where an estimated 600,000 Cuban-Americans reside—have one or two chile plants growing in their yard. They are usually piquin, which is known simply as '*ají picante*,' or hot pepper. The home cook uses the peppers with discretion according to family tastes."

 ASHER SAUCE

Island legend holds that the name of this sauce is a corruption of "Limes Ashore!" the phrase called out by British sailors who found limes growing on the Virgin Islands. The limes, originally planted by the Spanish, would save them from scurvy. It is presumed that the "bird peppers" would save them from bland food. Add this sauce to seafood chowders. Note that this recipe requires advance preparation.

MAKES 2 ½ CUPS
HEAT SCALE: **Hot**

15 limes, Key limes preferred
1 cup salt
3 cups water
10 whole "bird peppers," such as piquins or
    chiltepins, or 2 habaneros, halved
½ cup white vinegar
½ cup sugar

2 cardamom pods or ½ teaspoon ground
    cardamom
1 tablespoon whole cloves
5 allspice berries
¼ teaspoon freshly ground black pepper
4 cloves garlic, sliced
1 bunch scallions, white part only, chopped

Quarter the limes but do not cut all the way through. Spread open each lime and rub with salt. Place the limes on cutting boards, cover with cheesecloth, and set in the sun for about a week. Protect them from rain.

The limes will shrink and their skins will turn brown. Rinse the limes to remove as much salt as possible. Place the limes in a large pan, cover with the water, and add the remaining ingredients. Bring to a boil, reduce the heat to low, and simmer, uncovered, for 1 hour. Cool and strain the sauce. It will keep for several weeks in the refrigerator.

CALLALOO AND CRAB SOUP WITH CONGO PEPPER

This is the famous callaloo of Trinidad. There are numerous variations, including this one made with the large blue land crabs of that island.

MAKES 8 TO 10 SERVINGS
HEAT SCALE: **Medium**

2 tablespoons butter

1 medium onion, diced

½ cup chopped celery

1 clove garlic, minced

1 quart chicken stock

1 cup coconut milk

½ pound smoked ham, diced, or 1 small ham hock

2½ cups washed, coarsely chopped, firmly packed callaloo (dasheen) (or substitute spinach leaves)

1 cup sliced okra

1 teaspoon dried thyme

¼ teaspoon freshly ground black pepper

1 Congo pepper (habanero), seeds and stem removed, minced

1 pound cooked crabmeat, chopped

1 tablespoon melted butter (optional)

Salt

Heat the butter in a large saucepan over medium-high heat and cook the onion, celery, and garlic, stirring, for 2 to 3 minutes. Add the chicken stock, coconut milk, and ham and bring to a boil. Add the callaloo or spinach, okra, thyme, black pepper, and the Congo pepper.

Reduce the heat to low and simmer, covered, stirring occasionally, until the callaloo is thoroughly cooked, about 50 minutes.

Whisk the soup until it is very smooth, or puree it in small batches in a blender. Add the crabmeat and heat thoroughly. Add the melted butter, swizzled over the top, and add salt to taste.

 TRINIDADIAN BULJOL

The name of this eastern Caribbean salad of shredded salt fish comes from the French *brûlé*, meaning burnt, and *geule*, slang for mouth. Since it is served at room temperature, the burning is obviously the result of the Congo pepper. Traditionally, *buljol* is served for breakfast or a Sunday brunch. Note that this recipe requires advance preparation.

MAKES 4 SERVINGS
HEAT SCALE: **Hot**

8 ounces salt codfish (or substitute any cooked, flaky whitefish fillet)
1 large onion, minced
1 large tomato, minced
1 Caribbean seasoning pepper (or substitute 1 'Hungarian Yellow Wax Hot'), seeds and stem removed, minced
1 Congo pepper (habanero), seeds and stem removed, minced
Freshly ground black pepper
3 tablespoons olive oil
Lettuce leaves
Sliced hard-boiled eggs for garnish
Sliced avocado for garnish

If using salt cod, place the fish in a bowl and pour boiling water over it. Allow to sit for an hour, pour off the water, and repeat. Drain the fish, remove any skin or bones, and squeeze out all the water.

In a bowl, combine the fish with the onion, tomato, seasoning pepper, Congo pepper, black pepper, and olive oil and mix well. Serve this mixture on lettuce leaves and garnish with the eggs and avocado.

GRENADIAN-STYLE CURRIED GOAT

Use a good-quality imported curry powder for this dish; the domestic curry powders just don't have the taste or the punch needed here. Serve the goat with rice and peas or fried plantains or cooked yams. Note that this recipe requires advance preparation.

MAKES 8 SERVINGS
HEAT SCALE: Medium

2 pounds fresh goat or lamb, cut into large pieces and washed

2 tablespoons fresh lime juice

¼ cup grated fresh ginger

1 teaspoon salt

¼ cup vegetable oil (use coconut oil if available)

¼ cup sugar

2 hot Scotch bonnet (or habanero) chiles, seeds and stems removed, minced

6 cloves garlic, minced

2 cups chopped onions

1 tomato, seeded, chopped

¾ cup tomato sauce

¼ cup imported curry powder

3 teaspoons dried thyme or 4 sprigs fresh thyme

1 cup water, if necessary

Put the cut-up goat in a large, shallow glass dish. Drizzle the lime juice over the meat, and spread the ginger over the meat. Sprinkle the meat with the salt, then cover the dish and marinate in the refrigerator for 4 to 6 hours.

Heat a very large, heavy skillet to a high heat, add the oil and the sugar, and allow the mixture to caramelize, about 3 minutes. Add the drained meat, remove the skillet from the heat, and let the meat sit, without stirring, to brown for 30 seconds. Return the pan to the heat, stir the meat, and finishing browning it, about 2 minutes.

Turn the heat down to medium and cook, carefully turning and stirring the meat, for 10 to 15 minutes.

Add the chile peppers, garlic, and onions; reduce the heat to low and simmer, covered, for 20 minutes, stirring twice. Then add the remaining ingredients, cover, and simmer for 1½ to 2 hours, or until the meat is tender. Stir the meat occasionally and check to make sure it doesn't burn. Add water, if necessary.

JAMAICAN JERK CHICKEN WINGS

Jerk huts are everywhere in Jamaica, especially in Kingston, where many a steel drum has been converted to a grill. There is also an ongoing controversy as to what part of Jamaica (and what particular place) has the best. So far, the unofficial taste troop has designated Boston Beach. Note that this recipe requires advance preparation.

MAKES 4 TO 6 SERVINGS
HEAT SCALE: **Medium**

1 onion, chopped

2/3 cup minced scallions, both green and white
    parts

2 cloves garlic

1/2 teaspoon dried thyme, crumbled

1 1/2 teaspoons salt

1 1/2 teaspoons ground allspice

1/4 teaspoon freshly grated nutmeg

1/2 teaspoon ground cinnamon

1/2 teaspoon minced habanero chile

1 teaspoon freshly ground black pepper

10 drops commercial habanero hot sauce, or to
    taste

2 tablespoons soy sauce

1/4 cup vegetable oil

18 chicken wings (about 3 1/4 pounds), wing tips
    cut off and reserved

In a food processor or blender, puree all of the ingredients except for the chicken.

In a large, shallow dish, arrange the wings in one layer and spoon the marinade over them, rubbing it in. Let the wings marinate, covered, in the refrigerator, turning once, for at least 1 hour, or preferably overnight.

Preheat the oven to 450°F. Arrange the drained wings in one layer on an oiled rack set over a foil-lined roasting pan, spoon the boiled marinade over them, and bake the wings in the upper third of the oven until cooked through, 30 to 35 minutes.

⌣ ***Caribe.*** A variety of *güero* grown in Aguascalientes; usually found fresh, it has a conical shape, is about one and a half inches long, and is colored yellow.

⌣ ***Carrocillo.*** A name in central Mexico for the *güero*.

⌣ ***Cascabel.*** "Jingle bell" or "rattle"; an allusion to the seeds rattling in the pods of this oval chile about one and a half inches in diameter and dark red in the dried form. In the fresh form it is called *bola, bolita,* and *boludo.* Dried, *cascabels* are also known as *coras* and *guajones.* Grown in the Mexican states of Jalisco and Guerrero.

⌣ ***Casero.*** "Homemade"; in the Mexican state of Guerrero, a name for the green *costeño.*

⌣ ***Catarina.*** A dried chile from the Mexican state of Aguascalientes; it is one to two inches long, a half inch wide, and the seeds rattle in the pods. Possibly a variety of *de árbol.*

CAYENNE

The word "cayenne" seems to come from *kian,* the name of the pepper among the Tupi Indians of northeastern South America. The pod type probably originated in what is now French Guiana and was named after either the Cayenne River or the capital of the country, Cayenne.

It owes its spread around the world to Portugal, whose traders carried it to Europe,

'Carolina Cayenne' variety. DAVE DEWITT

Africa, India, and Asia. Although it probably was introduced into Spain before 1500, its circuitous route caused it to be transferred to Britain from India in 1548.

A plant resembling cayenne was described in 1552 in the Aztec herbal *The Badanius Manuscript,* indicating their medical use for such hot peppers: treating toothache and scabies. In 1597, the botanist John Gerard referred to cayenne as "ginnie or Indian pepper" in his herbal, and in his influential herbal of 1652, Nicholas Culpepper wrote that cayenne was "this violent fruit" that was of considerable service to "help digestion, provoke urine, relieve toothache, preserve the teeth from rottenness, comfort a cold stomach, expel the stone from the kidney, and take away dimness of sight." Cayenne appeared in Miller's *The Gardener's and Botanist's Dictionary* in 1768, proving it was being cultivated in England—at least in home gardens.

The Plant

Cayenne is a pod type of *Capsicum annuum*. The cayenne plant is tree-like, with multiple stems and an erect habit. It grows up to three feet tall and two feet wide. The leaves are ovate, smooth, and medium green, about three and a half inches wide and two inches long. The flower corollas are white with no spots. The pods are pendant, long, and slender, measuring up to ten inches long and one inch wide. They are often wrinkled and irregular in shape. A mature plant can easily produce forty pods. The cayenne is very pungent, measuring between 30,000 and 50,000 Scoville Units.

Agriculture

Grown commercially in New Mexico, Louisiana, Africa, India, Japan, and Mexico, the cayenne has a growing period of about ninety days from transplanting. Surprisingly, perhaps, New Mexico is leading the way in production of cayenne chiles for hot sauces. In 1995, more than 1,000 acres of cayenne were planted in New Mexico.

Cayenne acreage in the United States rose from 2,500 acres in 1994 to 4,500 acres in 1995. About 105 million pounds of cayenne mash (crushed cayennes with about 20 percent salt) was produced in the United States, with Reckitt & Colman, producers of Durkee's Red Hot, accounting for nearly half that amount. In fact, 75 to 85 percent of all cayenne mash in the world is produced in the United States. Retail sales (not including food service) of cayenne pepper sauces topped $82 million in 1995.

Culinary Usage

Cayennes can be used fresh in the immature green form in salsas, but the most common use is to grind the dried red pods into powder. In Louisiana, numerous hot sauces are made with cayennes. Although the term "cayenne" is commonly used in commerce, the cayenne you buy may not be made from the cayenne pod type—in fact, it probably is not. Virtually any small, hot red chile can be ground and placed in a gelatin capsule and called cayenne. But this is not necessarily an indictment because there is no difference in the composition of the different pod types and varieties of the *annuum* species, except in heat level. In summary, a capsule of ground piquin pods will virtually be the same in chemical composition as a capsule of ground cayenne pods. In fact, the American Spice Trade Association considers the term "cayenne" to be a misnomer and prefers the more generic term "red pepper."

FRESH CAYENNE HOT SAUCE

Here is a quick and easy twist on Louisiana hot sauce. The key here is to use fresh rather than dried chiles. Serve this sauce over fried foods such as crawfish or alligator.

MAKES 1 CUP
HEAT SCALE: **Hot**

10 large fresh red cayenne chiles, stems and seeds removed, halved lengthwise
2 cloves garlic, halved

¾ cup white vinegar
Salt

Preheat the broiler. Place the cayennes, cut side down, on a broiler rack. Broil for about 5 minutes or until the skin blisters and blackens. Transfer the peppers to a plastic bag for about 10 minutes. Peel when cool.

Place the chiles and garlic in a blender or food processor. With the machine running, slowly add the vinegar until the mixture is well blended. Add salt to taste. Keep covered and refrigerated until use. It will keep for weeks in the refrigerator.

CENTRAL AMERICA

Central America has pockets of heat. As is true of South America, the cuisines of some countries have embraced chile peppers with more fervor than others. Panama and Costa Rica, for example, have some spicy dishes, but the overall cuisine is not as spicy as those of Belize or Guatemala. Guatemala has a fiery cuisine second only to Mexico in terms of chile usage—perhaps because of its Mayan heritage. (See "The Spicy Legacy of the Maya," page 184.)

Central America is becoming quite a chile pepper growing mecca. The McIlhenny Company of Avery Island, Louisiana, grows the majority of Tabascos for its famous sauce in Mexico, Honduras, and Colombia. Costa Rica is the source of habaneros and other chiles for hot sauces, and there are substantial growing operations in Panama and Guatemala.

NICARAGUAN JALAPEÑO PORK SALAD
Ensalada de Cerdo con Jalapeños

In Latin America, pork is often treated with a generous squeeze of lime. The citrus flavors serve as a wake-up call to the flavors of the meat and works well with the heat of the jalapeño.

MAKES 6 TO 8 SERVINGS
HEAT SCALE: **Medium**

2 pounds boneless pork butt or shoulder, cut into
   1-inch cubes
½ cup water
Salt and freshly ground black pepper
1 large tomato, cored
2 tablespoons vegetable oil

4 tablespoons fresh lime juice
3 cups finely shredded cabbage
½ cup minced onion
3 or 4 fresh jalapeño chiles, seeds and stems
   removed, minced
Lime wedges

Preheat the oven to 400°F. Place the pork in a 10 by 15-inch roasting pan. Add the water. Cover the pan tightly with aluminum foil and bake until the meat is very tender when pierced, about 1 hour. Uncover and continue roasting, stirring occasionally, until all the liquid evaporates and the meat is well browned, about 15 minutes longer. Add salt and pepper to taste.

While the meat cooks, cut 2 wedges from the tomato and dice the remainder. In a large bowl, combine the diced tomato, oil, 3 tablespoons lime juice, cabbage, and salt and pepper to taste; cover and chill. In a small bowl, combine the remaining 1 tablespoon of lime juice, onion, and chiles; cover and chill.

When the meat is well browned, lift with slotted spoon onto a serving platter. Arrange the cabbage over the top and spoon the chile-onion salsa over all. Garnish with the tomato wedges and lime wedges.

CHICKEN IN RED CHILE PIPIAN SAUCE
Pollo en Salsa de Pipian Rojo

The squash seeds make this a very New World dish, as squash has been a staple of the Central American diet since it was domesticated millennia ago. The Mexican green tomatoes, called tomatillos, are available at Latin American markets and even in some chain grocery stores.

MAKES 4 SERVINGS
HEAT SCALE: Medium

One 3½-pound chicken, cut into serving pieces, loose skin and fat discarded
4 cups water
1 teaspoon salt, or to taste
1½ cups chopped ripe tomatoes
½ cup chopped tomatillos
1 pasilla chile, seeds and stem removed
1 guajillo chile, seeds and stem removed (or substitute New Mexican)
¼ cup fresh lime juice

½ cup sesame seeds
1 tablespoon squash seeds (pepitas)
1 cinnamon stick, 1 inch long, broken up
2 teaspoons crushed hot New Mexican red chile
One 3-inch slice of French bread
¼ cup chicken or vegetable broth
¼ teaspoon achiote (annatto seed)
1 tablespoon all-purpose flour
Squash and sesame seeds for garnish

In a skillet, cook the chicken in 3 cups of the water and the salt over medium heat for 30 minutes. Remove the chicken, keep warm, and reserve the broth for the sauce.

In the empty skillet, combine the tomatoes, tomatillos, chiles, remaining 1 cup water, and lime juice and cook over medium heat for 10 minutes.

In a dry skillet over low heat, toast the sesame seeds, squash seeds, cinnamon stick, and crushed chile, stirring occasionally, for about 10 minutes.

Cut the bread into cubes, and moisten with the chicken broth. Set aside.

In a food processor or blender, process the toasted ingredients. Add the cooked tomato mixture and process to make a smooth paste. Add the bread, *achiote,* 2 cups of the reserved chicken cooking liquid, and flour, and process until smooth. Return the sauce to the skillet and heat through.

Place the cooked chicken on a platter and cover with the red sauce. Sprinkle the squash and sesame seeds over the top. Serve with Colombian Coconut-Habanero Rice (page 74).

GUATEMALAN BEEF IN TOMATO AND CHILE SAUCE

Carne en Jocon

This spicy beef dish is found throughout Guatemala; it is a famous and traditional favorite that is usually served with hot rice. The tomatillos add an interesting taste dimension with a hint of lemon and herbs.

MAKES 6 TO 7 SERVINGS
HEAT SCALE: **Medium**

3 to 4 tablespoons vegetable oil
1 cup chopped onion
2 cloves garlic, minced
1 bell pepper, seeded and chopped
2 fresh serrano chiles, seeds and stems removed, chopped (or substitute jalapeños)
3 pounds boneless beef, cut into 1-inch cubes
1/2 teaspoon salt
1/4 teaspoon freshly ground black pepper

10 ounces fresh tomatillos, husks removed, diced (or substitute one 10-ounce can tomatillos)
3 tomatoes, chopped
1 bay leaf
1/4 teaspoon ground cloves
1 teaspoon oregano
3/4 cup beef stock
2 small corn tortillas

Heat the oil in a large, heavy skillet over medium-high heat and add the onion, garlic, and peppers. Cook until the onion is softened, about 5 minutes. Push the mixture to one side of the skillet and add the beef. Cook the meat, stirring, until lightly browned, about 5 minutes. Mix together the meat and the onion mixture.

Add the remaining ingredients, except the tortillas, and bring the mixture to a boil. Reduce the heat to low, cover, and simmer gently for 2 hours.

Soak the tortillas in cold water to cover for a few minutes. Squeeze the water out and finely crumble the tortillas onto the beef. Stir the crumbled tortillas into the beef and simmer until the meat mixture thickens, about 3 minutes. Remove the bay leaf before serving.

COLOMBIAN COCONUT-HABANERO RICE
Arroz con Coco y Ají Habanero

Rice cooked with coconut milk and hot chiles has a unique flavor and is part of the Spanish-Indian cuisine of Colombia. The Colombians on the coasts prefer rice, just as those in the interior depend on corn and potatoes. As a side dish, this flavorful rice can be served with grilled meats or fish. Note that this recipe requires advance preparation.

MAKES 6 SERVINGS
HEAT SCALE: **Medium**

2 cups shredded unsweetened coconut
4 cups water
½ teaspoon salt
3 tablespoons butter
1 teaspoon sugar

½ cup dark raisins
½ habanero chile, seeds and stem removed, minced (or substitute 1½ jalapeños)
¼ cup minced onion
1½ cups white rice

In a bowl, soak the coconut in the water for at least 3 hours. Drain the coconut milk through a colander into another bowl, squeezing out as much juice as possible. Reserve the coconut milk and discard the meat.

Pour 3 cups of the coconut milk, salt, 2 tablespoons of the butter, sugar, raisins, and habanero into a large saucepan over medium-high heat. Bring the mixture to a boil, then reduce the heat to medium-low and simmer gently for 3 minutes.

Meanwhile, melt the remaining 1 tablespoon butter in a small skillet over medium-high heat and add the onion. Cook, stirring, until the onion is softened, 3 to 5 minutes. Add the onion to the simmering mixture and stir in the rice. Cook this mixture, covered, for 20 to 25 minutes and stir once or twice to check for sticking. If the mixture starts to stick, add some of the remaining coconut liquid and stir thoroughly.

Guatemalan woman with her chiles. PAUL BOSLAND

⊾ *Charapilla.* A name for the *chinense* species in Peru.

⊾ *Chawa.* Mexican word for a variety of the wax pod type.

⊾ **Cherry pepper.** Originally thought to be *Capsicum cerasiforme*; now a pod type of the *annuum* species that resembles a large cherry. Introduced into England from the West Indies in 1759. The cherry type is familiar because the pods are commonly pickled and served as an accompaniment to sandwiches. Varieties include 'Cherry Sweet' and 'Red Cherry Hot.'

⊾ *Chiapas.* A name for the chiltepin in Chiapas, Mexico.

⊾ *Chilaca.* Fresh form of the pasilla chile. This term is also used to refer to fresh New Mexican pod types grown in Durango and Chihuahua, Mexico.

⊾ *Chilacate.* A chile eaten both fresh and dry in Jalisco, Mexico, which resembles a small New Mexican type. Also called *de la tierra*.

⊾ *Chilaile.* See *Mora*.

⊾ *Chilango.* Slang term for natives of Mexico City.

⊾ *Chilcoxle.* A dried yellow chile used in the *mole amarillo* of Oaxaca, Mexico. Also spelled *chilcostle* and *chilcoxtle*.

⊾ **Chile *caribe*.** Coarse ground chile powder; a red chile paste made from crushed or ground red chiles of any type, garlic, and water.

⊾ **Chile colorado.** Generally, any red chile; usually *guajillo*.

⊾ *Chile con queso.* A cheese and chile dip.

⊾ *Chile pasado.* Literally, "chile of the past"; in New Mexico it is a roasted, peeled, and sun-dried green chile. The dried chile is later rehydrated for use in cooking.

🖝 **Chile** *seco.* Any dried chile; in various states of Mexico this refers to different chiles. For example, in the state of Colima, the term most often refers to *guajillos*. In other parts of Mexico it refers to chipotles.

🖝 *Chilhuacle.* In Mexico, a Oaxacan chile primarily used in *moles*. Some sources say that it is a regional variety of *guajillo*, but to our eyes it more closely resembles a small poblano. There are three forms, *amarillo*, *rojo*, and *negro*. Also spelled *chilguacle*.

CHILI CON CARNE

Chili con carne is a stew that consists of meat, hot chile peppers, a liquid such as water or broth, and spices. It may or may not contain such ingredients as onions, tomatoes, or beans. Everything about chili con carne generates some sort of controversy—the spelling of the name, the origin and history of the dish, the proper ingredients for a great recipe, the awesome society and cook-off rivalries, and even what the future holds for the bowl o' red. Perhaps the fiery nature of the dish is responsible for such controversy, driving usually rational men and women into frenzies when their conception of the truth is challenged.

As far as the spelling of the dish is concerned, etymologists report that there is enormous confusion about the terms that describe the Capsicums and the recipes prepared with them. Writers who must use these terms quite often have reached an informal agreement: chile, the original Spanish-Mexican spelling, refers to the plant and the pod, while chili is an abbreviated form of chili con carne, which is a curious combination of the Anglicized chili (from chile) and carne, Spanish for "meat." New Mexicans, however, still use Spanish words, so chile there refers to the plant, pod, and the bowl o' red.

Origins

Another endlessly debated controversy is the origin of the bowl o' red itself. Although archaeological evidence indicates that chile peppers evolved in Mexico and South America, most writers on the subject state flatly that chili did not originate in Mexico. Even Mexico disclaims chili; one Mexican dictionary defines it as: "A detestable dish sold from Texas to New York City and erroneously described as Mexican."

Despite such protestations, the combination of meat and chile peppers in stew-like concoctions is not uncommon in Mexican cooking. Elizabeth Lambert Ortiz, in her book *The Complete Book of Mexican Cooking*, has a recipe for chile con carne made with ancho chiles, which she describes as "an authentic northern Mexican style of cooking . . . as distinct from the version that developed in Texas." Mexican *caldillos* (thick soups or stews), *moles* (meaning "mixture"), and *adobos* (thick sauces) often resemble chili con carne in both appearance and taste because they all sometimes use similar ingredients: various types of chiles combined with meat (usually beef), onions, garlic, cumin, and occasionally tomatoes.

But chili con carne fanatics tell strange tales about the possible origin of chili. The story of the "lady in blue" tells of Sister Mary of Agreda, a Spanish nun in the early 1600s who never left her convent in Spain but nonetheless had out-of-body experiences during which her spirit would be transported across the Atlantic to preach Christianity to the Indians. After one of the return trips, her spirit wrote down the first recipe for chili con carne, which the Indians gave her: chile peppers, venison, onions, and tomatoes. An only slightly less fanciful account suggests that Canary Islanders, transplanted to San Antonio as early as 1723, used local peppers and wild onions combined with various meats to create early chili combinations.

E. De Grolyer, a scholar, chili aficionado, and multimillionaire, believed that Texas chili con carne had its origins as the "pemmican of the Southwest" in the late 1840s. According to De Grolyer, Texans pounded together dried beef, beef fat, chiltepins (piquins), and salt to make trail food for the long ride out to San Francisco and the gold fields. The concentrated, dried mixture was then boiled in pots along the trail as sort of an "instant chili."

A variation on this theory holds that cowboys invented chili while driving cattle along the lengthy and lonely trails. Supposedly, range cooks would plant oregano, chiles, and onions among patches of

Armadillo Breath Chili Team. SUNBELT ARCHIVES

mesquite to protect them from cattle. The next time they passed along the same trail, they would collect the spices, combine them with beef (what else?), and make a dish called "trail drive chili." Undoubtedly, the chiles used with the earliest incarnations of chili con carne were the wild chiltepins, called chilipiquins in Texas, which grow wild on bushes—particularly in the southern part of the state.

The most likely explanation for the origin of chili con carne in Texas comes from the heritage of Mexican food combined with the rigors of life on the Texas frontier. Most historians agree that the earliest written description of chili came from J. C. Clopper, who lived near Houston. He wrote of visiting San Antonio in 1828: "When they [poor families of San Antonio] have to pay for their meat in the market, a very little is made to suffice for the family; it is generally cut into a kind of hash with nearly as many peppers as there are pieces of meat—this is all stewed together."

Except for this one quote, which does not mention the dish by name, historians of heat can find no documented evidence of chili in Texas before 1880. Around that time in San Antonio, a municipal market—El Mercado—was operating in Military Plaza. Historian Charles Ramsdell noted that "the first rickety chili stands" were set up in this marketplace, with the bowls o' red sold by women who were called "chili queens."

"The legendary chili queens," wrote Ramsdell, "beautiful, bantering, but virtuous, made their first appearance. All night long they cooked, served, and flirted in the picturesque flare from hand-hammered tin lanterns, in the savory haze rising from clay vessels on charcoal braziers."

A bowl o' red cost visitors like O. Henry and William Jennings Bryan a mere dime and was served with bread and a glass of water. O. Henry later wrote a short story about the chili stands entitled "The Enchanted Kiss." In it, a young San Antonio drugstore clerk eats chili in the *mercado* and hallucinates that he is the former captain of the Spanish army in Mexico who has remained immortal since 1519 by eating chili con carne!

The fame of chili con carne began to spread and the dish soon became a major tourist attraction, making its appearance in Mexican restaurants all over Texas—and elsewhere. At the World's Fair in Chicago in 1893, a bowl o' red was available at the "San Antonio Chili Stand."

Given the popularity of the dish, some commercialization of it was inevitable. In 1898, William Gebhardt of New Braunfels, Texas, produced the first canned chili con carne, which appeared in San Antonio under the Gebhardt brand, a name still in existence today.

The chili queens were banned from San Antonio in 1937 for health reasons—public officials objected to flies and poorly washed dishes. They were restored by Mayor Maury Maverick (a real name, folks) in 1939, but their stands were closed again shortly after the start of World War II. However, Texans have never forgotten their culinary heritage, and in 1977 the

Texas legislature proclaimed chili con carne to be the "Official Texas State Dish."

Recently, San Antonio has been staging what they call "historic reenactments" of the chili queens, complete with some of the original queens like songstress Lydia Mendoza, who would serenade the chili eaters. The "Return of the Chili Queens Festival," held each year in Market Square, re-creates the era of the chili queens and celebrates the dish that, no matter what its origin, will live forever in the hearts, minds, and stomachs of Texans.

Original San Antonio Chili

According to legend, this is one of the original recipes of the San Antonio chili queens. Some minor changes have been made to take advantage of modern ingredients.

MAKES 8 TO 10 SERVINGS
HEAT SCALE: **Medium**

All-purpose flour for dredging
2 pounds beef shoulder, cut into ½-inch cubes
1 pound pork shoulder, cut into ½-inch cubes
¼ cup suet
¼ cup pork fat
3 medium onions, chopped
6 cloves garlic, minced

1 quart water
4 ancho chiles, seeds and stems removed, minced
1 serrano chile, seeds and stems removed, minced
5 dried red New Mexican chiles, seeds and stems removed, minced
1 tablespoon cumin seeds, finely ground
2 tablespoons dried Mexican oregano

Lightly flour the beef and pork cubes. Quickly heat the suet and pork fat, stirring often, in a large pot over medium-high heat. Add the beef and pork cubes and cook until browned, about 5 minutes. Add the onions and garlic and cook until softened, about 5 minutes. Remove all pieces of fat. Add the water to the mixture and bring to a simmer. Reduce the heat to low and simmer for 1 hour.

Grind all the chiles together in a blender with a little water to make a paste. Add to the meat mixture and stir. Add the remaining ingredients and simmer, uncovered, for an additional 2 hours. Skim off all the fat and serve.

BUZZARD'S BREATH CHILI

Tom Griffin, a Houston stockbroker, was the Chili Appreciation Society–International (see page 17) Terlingua champion in 1977 with this interestingly named chili.

MAKES 12 SERVINGS
HEAT SCALE: **Medium**

8 pounds boneless beef chuck, cut into ⅜-inch
　cubes and trimmed of gristle and fat
¼ cup vegetable oil
Two 8-ounce cans tomato sauce
2 cups water
2 large onions, chopped
5 cloves garlic, crushed and chopped
2 jalapeños, wrapped in cheesecloth
¼ cup chili powder

2 teaspoons ground cumin, plus a bit more
　(optional)
¼ to ½ teaspoon dried oregano
Cayenne powder to taste
Salt to taste
1 quart beef stock, homemade preferred
Masa harina (optional)
1 to 2 teaspoons paprika

In a cast-iron skillet over medium-high heat, brown the meat, about 2 pounds at a time, in the oil until gray in color, about 5 minutes per batch. Place the meat in a large, cast-iron chili pot.

Add the tomato sauce and water and mix. Add the onions, garlic, jalapeños, and chili powder.

Bring the mixture to a boil, then reduce the heat to low, and simmer for 20 minutes. Add the cumin, oregano, cayenne, and salt. Raise the heat to medium-high and add the beef stock. Bring to a simmer again, reduce the heat to low, and simmer, covered, until the meat is tender, about 2 hours, stirring occasionally.

Add the *masa harina* to achieve the desired thickness, if needed. Add the paprika for color and cook 10 minutes more. Correct the seasoning to taste, discard the jalapeños, and serve. A small amount of additional cumin enhances the aroma when added during the last 10 minutes.

ICS-STYLE CHILI

This chili utilizes many of the ingredients and techniques common to the International Chili Society (see page 17).

MAKES 6 SERVINGS
HEAT SCALE: **Medium**

3 pounds sirloin steak, cut into ¼-inch cubes
¼ cup vegetable oil
1 cup chorizo sausage (see page 196)
1 large onion, minced
3 cloves garlic, minced
1 stalk celery, minced
2 cups beef broth
2 cups tomato sauce
One 12-ounce bottle Corona beer

¼ cup New Mexican red chile powder (your choice, hot or mild)
3 tablespoons chili powder
½ cup diced New Mexican green chiles
1 tablespoon ground cumin
2 teaspoons dried Mexican oregano
Salt, freshly ground white pepper, cayenne, and brown sugar to taste

In a skillet over medium-high heat, cook the steak in the oil, stirring, until lightly browned, about 5 minutes. With a slotted spoon, remove the steak and reserve. Add the sausage to the same skillet and cook, stirring, for 5 minutes. With a slotted spoon, remove the sausage and reserve. Add the onion, garlic, and celery to the skillet and cook, stirring, until the onions are soft, about 5 minutes. Remove with the slotted spoon and reserve.

Transfer the steak, sausage, and onion-garlic-celery mixture to a chili pot or Dutch oven over medium-high heat. Add the beef broth, tomato sauce, and beer and bring to a boil. Reduce the heat to low and simmer for 30 minutes.

Add the New Mexican chile powder, chili powder, green chiles, cumin, and oregano, and simmer, uncovered, for 1 hour, stirring occasionally.

The next step is the most difficult. Taste the chile and add salt, white pepper, cayenne, cumin, and brown sugar to make the chili perfect. Simmer an additional 15 minutes.

CHILI COOK'S HINTS: Experiment with other spices to make your chili unique. Some suggestions are: ¼ to ½ teaspoon of paprika, coriander, dried cilantro, dried sage, and dried basil. You also might want to draw attention to your chili by floating a habanero chile on top, but omit the cayenne and take care that the habanero does not burst!

⤳ *Chilillo.* "Little chile"; a variety of piquin in Yucatán, Mexico.

⤳ *Chilpaya.* A variety of chiltepin in Veracruz, Mexico.

CHILTEPIN

Botanists believe that these wild chiles (*Capsicum annuum* var. *aviculare*) are the closest surviving species to the earliest forms of chiles that developed in Bolivia and southern Brazil long before mankind arrived in the New World. The small size of their fruits were perfect for dissemination by birds, and the wild chiles spread all over South and Central America and up to what is now the United States border millennia before the domesticated varieties

Chiltepin chile. DAVE DEWITT

arrived. It is possible that chiltepins have the widest distribution of any chile variety; they range from Peru north to the Caribbean, Florida, and Louisiana and west to Arizona.

There is a wide variation in pod shapes, from tiny ones the size and shape of BBs to elongated pods a half inch long. By contrast, domesticated piquins have much longer pods, up to three inches. The chiltepins most prized in Mexico are spherical and measure five to eight millimeters in diameter. They are among the hottest chiles on earth, measuring up to 100,000 Scoville Units.

The word chiltepin is believed to be derived from the Aztec language (Nahuatl) combination of *chilli* plus *tecpintl*, meaning "flea chile," an allusion to its sharp bite. That word was altered to *chiltecpin*, then to the Spanish *chiltepín*, and finally Anglicized to chilipiquin, as the plant is known in Texas. A nonaccented chiltepin is the English term for the plant and fruit.

In Sonora and southern Arizona, chiltepins grow in microhabitats in the transition zone between mountain and desert, which receive as little as ten inches of rain per year. They grow beneath "nurse" trees such as mesquite, oak, and palmetto, which provide shelter from direct sunlight, heat, and frost. In the summer, there is higher humidity beneath the nurse trees, and legumes such as mesquite fix nitrogen in the soil—a perfect fertilizer for the chiltepins. They also protect the plant from grazing by cattle, sheep, goats, and deer. Chiltepins planted in the open, without nurse trees, usually die from the effects of direct solar radiation.

Although the chiltepin plant's average height is about four feet, there are reports of individual bushes growing ten feet tall, living twenty-five to thirty years, and having stems as big around as a man's wrist. Chiltepins are resistant to frost but lose their leaves in cold winter weather. New growth will sprout from the base of the plant if the top part of the plant freezes, but the root system remains intact.

There is quite a bit of legend and lore associated with the fiery little pods. In earlier times, the Papago Indians of Arizona traditionally made annual pilgrimages into the Sierra Madre range of Mexico to gather chiltepins. Dr. Gary Nabhan of Native Seeds/SEARCH in Tucson wrote that the Tarahumara Indians of Sonora value the chiltepins so much that they build stone walls around the bushes to protect them from goats. Besides spicing up food, Indians use chiltepins for antilactation, the technique where nursing mothers put chile powder on their nipples to wean babies. Chiltepins are also an aid in childbirth because when powdered and inhaled they cause sneezing, which reputedly starts the birth contractions. And, of course, the hot chiles induce gustatory sweating, which cools off the body during hot weather.

In 1794, Padre Ignatz Pfefferkorn, a German Jesuit living in Sonora, described the chile: "A kind of wild pepper which the inhabitants call *chiltipin* is found on many hills. It is placed unpulverized on the table in a salt cellar and each fancier takes as much of it as he believes he can eat. He pulverizes it with his fingers and mixes it with his food. The *chiltipin* is the best spice for soup, boiled peas, lentils, beans and the like. The Americans swear that it is exceedingly healthful and very good as an aid to the digestion." In fact, even today, chiltepins are used — amazingly enough — as a treatment for acid indigestion.

Padre Pfefferkorn realized that chiltepins are one of the few crops in the world that are harvested in the wild rather than cultivated. (Others are piñon nuts, Brazil nuts, and some wild rice.) This fact has led to concern for the preservation of the chiltepin bushes because the harvesters often pull up entire plants or break off branches. Dr. Nabhan believes that the chiltepin population is diminishing because of overharvesting and overgrazing. In Arizona, a chiltepin reserve has been established near Tumacacori at Rock Corral Canyon in the Coronado National Forest. Native Seeds/SEARCH has been granted a special use permit from the National Forest Service to initiate permanent marking and mapping of plants, ecological studies, and a management plan proposal. (See "Bird Peppers.")

CHILTEPIN HOUSE SAUCE
Salsa Casera

This diabolically hot sauce is also called chiltepin pasta (paste). It is used in soups and stews and to fire up *machaca,* eggs, tacos, tostadas, and beans. This is the exact recipe prepared in the home of Josefina Duran in Cumpas, Sonora.

MAKES 2 CUPS
HEAT SCALE: **Extremely hot**

2 cups chiltepins
8 to 10 cloves garlic
1 teaspoon salt
1 teaspoon dried Mexican oregano

1 teaspoon coriander seeds
1 cup water
1 cup cider vinegar

Combine all ingredients in a blender and puree on high speed for 3 to 4 minutes. Refrigerate, covered, for 1 day to blend the flavors. It keeps indefinitely in the refrigerator.

Sonoran Enchiladas

These enchiladas are not the same as those served north of the border. The main differences are the use of freshly made, thick corn tortillas and the fact that the enchiladas are not baked.

MAKES 4 TO 6 SERVINGS
HEAT SCALE: **Hot**

For the sauce
15 to 20 chiltepins, crushed
15 dried red New Mexican chiles, seeds and stems
    removed
1 teaspoon salt
3 cloves garlic
1 teaspoon vegetable oil
1 teaspoon all-purpose flour

For the tortillas
2 cups masa harina
1 large egg
1 teaspoon baking powder
1 teaspoon salt
Vegetable oil for deep frying

To assemble and serve
2 cups grated queso blanco or Monterey Jack
    cheese
Shredded lettuce
3 to 4 scallions (white part only), minced

To make the sauce, in a saucepan, combine the chiles, salt, and enough water to cover. Boil until the chiles are quite soft, 10 to 15 minutes.

Allow the chiles to cool and then puree them in a blender along with the garlic. Strain the mixture, mash the pulp through a strainer, and discard the skins.

Heat the oil in a saucepan over medium heat and add the flour. Cook the flour, stirring, until browned, taking care that it does not burn, about 5 minutes. Add the chile puree and boil until the sauce has thickened slightly, 5 to 10 minutes. Set aside and keep warm.

To make the tortillas, in a bowl, mix the first 4 ingredients together thoroughly, adding enough water to make a dough. Using a tortilla press, make the tortillas. Add the oil to a depth of about an inch in a large skillet over high heat. Heat until very hot. Deep fry each tortilla until it puffs up and turns slightly brown, about 2 minutes on each side, flipping once. Remove and drain on paper towels and keep warm.

To assemble and serve, place a tortilla on each plate and spoon a generous amount of sauce over it. Top with the cheese, lettuce, and scallions.

CHINA

Because of dialects and difficulties in transliteration, chile peppers from China have been called *la-chio* and *la-chiao* in various sources, but more recently translated material from China indicates that the generic term *la-jiao* is now preferred. A wild chile known as *xiao mi jiao* grows in the virgin forest area of Xishuangbanna Prefecture of the Yunan Province. Hot chiles are common in the diet in the provinces of Gansu, Shaanxi, Sichuan, Guizhou, Yunan, Hunan, Hubei, and Jiangxi.

In international chile pepper production, China ranks fourth in yield, after India, Mexico, and Indonesia. In 1988, China had 148,200 acres under cultivation with a yield of 212,500 dry equivalent tons. As might be expected, acreage and production were considerably less in Taiwan. In 1986, about 7,000 acres of chiles were under cultivation in Taiwan, yielding about 3,000 dry equivalent tons. Approximately twenty cultivars of both sweet and hot peppers are grown commercially in mainland China and about nine in Taiwan. In China, some of the more popular varieties are 'Shi Feng Jiao' and the hot cultivar grown in Sichuan, 'Chi Ying Jiao.' In Taiwan, the varieties have English names and the pungent ones are 'Goat's Horn,' 'Szuchuan,' 'New Comer,' and 'Hot Beauty.'

Some experts speculate that chiles were imported into China from Singapore, or carried inland from Macao, where hot dishes are more popular today than in neighboring Canton. More likely is the theory that chiles were introduced into Sichuan by sixteenth-

'Hot Beauty' Chinese chile. TERRY BERKE

century Indian Buddhist missionaries traveling the "Silk Route" between India and China. After all, western Sichuan is closer to India than to either Macao or Singapore. No matter how they arrived in western China, chiles soon became enormously important to the food of the people.

E. N. Anderson, who has studied the chile situation in China extensively, described the effect of chiles on the cuisines of the Far East as "epochal." The use of the large varieties of *Capsicum annuum* was important because of the addition of vitamins A and C to low-vitamin grains such as rice. In western China, chiles were easy to grow, simple to preserve, and soon became vital to life there. Anderson observed, "Tomatoes and chiles not only transformed the taste of southern Chinese cooking, they also provided new and very rich sources of vitamins A and C and certain minerals, thus improving the diet of the south Chinese considerably. Easy to grow, highly productive, and bearing virtually year round in the subtropical climate, these plants eliminated the seasonal bottlenecks on vitamin availability."

Cooks in Sichuan and Hunan provinces depend mostly upon chile pastes and oils to provide the heat in their meals. Fresh peppers are more commonly used in Hunan than Sichuan, where small, dried *santaka*-type chiles are commonly added whole, seeds and all, to stir-fry dishes. Other commonly used seasonings in the cooking of Sichuan and Hunan are chile paste with garlic, an aromatic chile vinegar, and chile oils.

Chile in such forms is often combined with ground rice, sesame seeds, and peanuts as a snack or a coating for grilled meats. The combination of chiles with nutty products like sesame seeds and peanuts is called *ma la* and is one of the essential flavors of western Chinese cooking.

Contrary to popular belief, chefs cooking in Sichuan or Hunan style are not trying to incinerate the people who eat their creations. Howard Hillman, an expert on world cuisines, has written of the way heat is applied in western China: "Even on the peasant level, the people prefer the dishes on the table to have degrees of hotness varying from mild to fiery. This is in contrast to the monotonous everything-as-hot-as-possible approach favored by many non-Chinese Sichuan restaurant-goers. Making one Sichuan dish hotter than another is not a measure of a chef's talent; all it takes is the addition of extra chile, a feat that could be performed by a trained monkey. Epicures judge a Sichuan chef by the subtly complex overtones of his sauces and whether they complement the other ingredients in his dishes."

Perhaps the most obscure fiery cuisine of Asia is that of Xinjiang Autonomous Region, China's largest province. Located in the northwest part of the country, surrounded by Tibet, Russia, Kazakhstan, Jammu, Kashmir, Mongolia, Afghanistan, and Pakistan, Xinjiang is the land of the Uighurs, the Mongols, the Tartars, and other peoples related to Turkic Central Asians. The capital of Xinjiang is Urümqi, the most inland city in the world. Here, where most of the population is Muslim, pork is replaced by lamb, which is commonly combined with chile peppers.

A favorite lamb and chile dish from Xinjiang is *Kao Yang Ruo Chuan*, Xinjiang Lamb and Chile Grill (page 91) in which lamb kebabs are marinated in a garlic, lemon, and extremely hot chile oil sauce and then barbecued with jalapeño-type chiles. Other lamb and chile dishes from the region include: a sliced lamb meal with onions and jalapeño-type chiles; *la tiao-ze*, which combines noodles and lamb with a garlic and chile pepper sauce; and lamb-filled potstickers with hot chile-vinegar-soy sauce.

China's hot sauces are quite varied, from simple chile oils and sauces to hot bean sauces to pastes—even commercial hoisin sauce has a little dried red chile in it. Chinese chile oil is made by simply steeping hot chiles in peanut oil; the oil can be used as a replacement for vegetable oils in salads and for frying. Some commercial brands include House of Tsang oils and Lee Kum Kee's Chili Oil and Hot Sesame Oil.

"Bean sauce is vital to authentic Sichuan and Hunan cooking," wrote Asian food expert Bruce Cost. "Usually added with chile peppers in some form, bean sauce—more than soy sauce— flavors the many fiery country-style dishes." Commercial brands include Lan Chi, Sze Chuan, and Lee Kum Kee.

There are quite a few Chinese chile sauces available, including Kimlan in Taiwan and Lee Kum Kee's Guilin Chili Sauce. "There are many proprietary Chinese chilli [English spelling] sauces available on the market," wrote our friend Pat Chapman, England's spicy food expert. "These vary markedly in flavour, consistency and heat strength—ranging from sweet to hot or even extra hot."

SICHUAN CHILE SAUCE

Here is a classic chile sauce from one of the hottest regions—foodwise—in China. It can be used in stir-fry dishes, added to soups, or sprinkled over rice.

MAKES ABOUT 1¼ CUPS
HEAT SCALE: Hot

2 tablespoons vegetable oil
4 cloves garlic, minced
One 1-inch piece fresh ginger, minced
1 small onion, minced
6 fresh red chiles, such as jalapeños, seeds and
    stems removed, minced

¼ cup Chinese rice vinegar, preferably red
1 tablespoon sugar
2 tablespoons tomato ketchup
2 tablespoons Chinese rice wine
2 teaspoons salt

Heat the oil in a wok or frying pan over high heat, add the garlic and ginger and cook, stirring, for 30 seconds. Add the onion and cook, stirring, for another minute.

Add the chiles and vinegar and simmer for 10 minutes, adding water if it gets too dry.

Add the remaining ingredients and simmer for 5 minutes more.

Remove from the heat and allow to cool. Transfer the mixture to a food processor or blender and process to a fine puree, adding water as necessary to achieve the desired consistency.

Place the sauce in bottles, cover, and refrigerate.

SICHUAN BEEF WITH HOT SAUCE

The most important thing to remember in preparing this classic Sichuanese recipe is that the beef should be stir-fried until it is dry and crispy, but not burned. Use the shredding blade of a food processor to cut the celery and carrot. Serve over steamed rice.

MAKES 2 SERVINGS
HEAT SCALE: **Medium**

For the marinade
½ teaspoon cornstarch
2 tablespoons soy sauce
1 tablespoon rice wine (or substitute dry vermouth
   or white wine)

8 ounces flank steak, cut into 2-inch-long julienne
   strips with the grain

For the sauce
2 tablespoons soy sauce
2 tablespoons rice wine (or substitute dry
   vermouth or white wine)
½ tablespoon sugar
3 tablespoons hot bean sauce

½ tablespoon sweet bean sauce
½ teaspoon sesame oil
1 tablespoon Sichuan Chile Sauce
   (page 89)

To stir-fry
¼ cup peanut oil
1 tablespoon minced garlic
1 tablespoon minced fresh ginger
1 scallion (white part only), minced
1 large stalk celery, shredded
1 carrot, shredded
2 green New Mexican or poblano chiles, roasted
   and peeled (page 146), seeds and stems
   removed, cut into julienne strips

Combine the ingredients for the marinade in a large bowl, stir well, and add the beef. Toss the beef in the marinade and let sit, covered, for 30 minutes.

In a bowl, combine all the sauce ingredients and mix well.

To stir-fry, heat a wok over high heat and add 3 tablespoons of the peanut oil. Just when it begins to smoke, add the drained marinated beef and cook, stirring, until the beef is browned to the point of being crispy, about 8 minutes. Remove the beef with a slotted spoon and set on paper towels to drain.

Add the remaining 1 tablespoon peanut oil to the wok, heat, and add the garlic, ginger, and scallion, and cook, stirring, for 15 seconds. Then add the celery, carrot, and chiles. Cook, stirring, for 30 seconds, then add the beef. Stir briefly to mix the beef with the vegetables, add the reserved sauce, and cook, stirring, for 30 seconds to 1 minute. Adjust the heat with more Sichuan Chile Sauce.

XINJIANG LAMB AND CHILE GRILL
Kao Yang Ruo Chuan

Xinjiang, which borders Mongolia, is noted for its barbecued lamb even though lamb is rarely eaten in other parts of China. In fact, the Mongolian tribes introduced lamb to the rest of China. This simple barbecue could easily be prepared by the nomads on the plains of Xinjiang. Note that this recipe requires advance preparation.

MAKES 6 SERVINGS
HEAT SCALE: **Medium**

1/4 cup chile oil
1/2 cup fresh lemon juice
2 tablespoons rice wine (or substitute dry vermouth or white wine)
4 cloves garlic, minced
2 teaspoons crushed Sichuan peppercorns
1/4 teaspoon salt

1/4 teaspoon sugar
2 pounds lamb, cut into 2-inch cubes
8 whole jalapeño chiles
6 sesame seed buns
Chopped scallions, including the greens
Chopped fresh cilantro

In a large bowl, combine the chile oil, lemon juice, rice wine, garlic, peppercorns, salt, and sugar. Add the lamb and jalapeños and marinate in the refrigerator preferably overnight or for at least 2 to 3 hours.

Thread the drained lamb on skewers, alternating with the jalapeños. In a saucepan, boil the marinade for 2 minutes, then reserve.

Grill or broil the skewers, basting frequently with the reserved marinade until done.

Serve the drained lamb and chiles in the buns with the chopped scallions and cilantro.

ORANGE CHICKEN WITH RED CHILES

This chicken and chile dish is a standard in western China, were the flavors of poultry and citrus are often combined. Dried orange peel is available in Asian markets. Any small, dried red chiles may be used in this recipe. Serve it over steamed rice or rice pilaf.

MAKES 2 SERVINGS
HEAT SCALE: **Medium**

For the marinade

½ tablespoon cornstarch

1 tablespoon rice wine (or substitute dry vermouth or white wine)

½ pound boneless chicken breast, cut into ½-inch pieces

For the sauce

½ tablespoon minced fresh ginger

½ tablespoon minced garlic

1 whole scallion, minced

½ teaspoon ground Sichuan peppercorns

1 tablespoon rice wine (or substitute dry vermouth or white wine)

2 tablespoons soy sauce

1 tablespoon hot bean sauce

2 tablespoons dried orange peel, soaked in hot water for ½ hour and shredded

2 teaspoons sugar or honey

½ teaspoon sesame oil

To stir-fry

2 tablespoons peanut oil

6 small dried hot red chiles, such as Japónes or de árbol

In a bowl, combine the ingredients for the marinade, stir well, and add the chicken. Let sit for 30 minutes.

In another bowl, combine all the sauce ingredients, stir well, and set aside.

To stir-fry, heat a wok over high heat. Add the peanut oil and when it just begins to smoke, add the chiles and drained marinated chicken. Cook, stirring, for about 1 minute. Add the sauce and cook, stirring for an additional 30 seconds. Remove the chiles before serving.

⊾ *Chinchi-uchu.* Indigenous name for the *chinense* species in Peru.

CHINENSE SPECIES

This entire species is often referred to as "habanero," but that appellation is a misnomer because there are hundreds of varieties, and the name habanero refers to a specific pod type from the Yucatán Peninsula of Mexico. (See Habanero.)

The Amazon Basin was the center of origin for the *chinense* species, famous for having the hottest peppers of them all. The oldest known *chinense* ever found was the 6,500-year-old intact pod found in Guitarrero Cave in Peru.

Bernabe Cobo, a naturalist who traveled throughout South America during the early seventeenth century, probably was the first European to study the *chinense* species. He estimated that there were at least forty different varieties of chiles, "some as large as limes or large plums; others, as small as pine nuts or even grains of wheat, and between the two extremes are many different sizes. No less variety is found in color . . . and the same difference is found in form and shape."

The species was first noted in 1768 in *The Gardener's and Botanist's Dictionary* by Phillip Miller, who identified it as *Capsicum angulofum,* a West Indian pepper with wrinkled leaves and a bonnet shape. The species was then misnamed *Capsicum chinense* in 1776 by Nikolaus von Jacquin, a Dutch physician who collected plants in the Caribbean for Emperor Francis I from 1754 to 1759. Jacquin, who first described the species as

Pod variations in the chinense *species.* NMSU

"chinense" in his work *Hortus botanicus vin-dobonensis*, wrote, mysteriously, "I have taken the plant's name from its homeland."

Why would Jacquin write that a plant native to the Western Hemisphere was from China? Jacquin had never collected plants in China, and considering the fact that the first Chinese laborers to the West Indies would not arrive in Cuba until the early 1800s, it is unlikely that Jacquin crossed paths with any suspected Chinese "importers" of the species. It is likely that this pepper mystery will never be solved, so we are stuck with a totally inaccurate species name of a supposedly Chinese pepper that's not from China. And so far, no taxonomist has gone out on a limb to correct this obvious error.

Chinense is the most important cultivated pepper east of the Andes in South America. There is a great diversity of pod shape and heat levels ranging from zero to a reported 577,000 Scoville Units. At some point in time, Native Americans transferred the *chinense* from the Amazon Basin into the Caribbean.

The seeds were carried and cultivated by Native Americans, and the *chinense* species hopped, skipped, and jumped around the West Indies, forming—seemingly on each island—specifically adapted pod types that are called land races of the species. These land races were given local names in the various islands and countries, although the terms Scotch bonnet, goat pepper, and habanero are also used generically throughout the region.

In the eastern Caribbean, habanero relatives are called Congo peppers in Trinidad and bonney peppers in Barbados. In the French Caribbean islands of Martinique and Guadeloupe, *le derrière de Madame Jacques* describes the hot peppers, and in Haiti, *piment bouc,* or goat pepper. In the western Caribbean are the familiar Jamaican Scotch bonnets, Puerto Rican *rocotillos,* and the Cuban *cachucha* ("cap") peppers. These land races with the colorful names became the dominant spicy element in the food of the Caribbean.

The pods of the *chinense* species vary enormously in size and shape, ranging from chiltepin-sized berries one-quarter inch in diameter to wrinkled and elongated pods up to five inches long. The familiar habaneros are pendant and lantern-shaped, and some are pointed at the end. Caribbean *chinenses* are flattened at the end and resemble a tam, or bonnet. Often the blossom ends of these pods are inverted. The pods are green at immaturity and usually mature to red, orange, yellow, or white. Purple and brown mature pods have also been described. *Chinense* pods are characterized by a distinctive, fruity aroma that is often described as "apricot-like." Interestingly enough, that aroma is present regardless of the variety, heat level, or the size of the pod.

The heat level of the *chinense* species has been the subject of much discussion. Phrases like "hottest pepper in the world" and "a thousand times hotter than a jalapeño" have been bandied about for years, but they don't really tell the story. In actuality, the species does have nonpungent varieties, just like the bell peppers of the *annuum* species. Thus the heat scale ranges from zero to 577,000 Scoville Units, the hottest *chinense* ever measured. In terms of the average number of Scoville Units, a habanero, for example, is about fifty times hotter than a jalapeño—as measured by machines, not the human mouth. Because humans have varying numbers of taste buds, reaction can vary enormously from person to person.

Another member of the *chinense* species that is commonly used, especially in the eastern Caribbean, is the seasoning pepper. It is a medium-hot, elongated pepper that is used in quantity for seasoning pastes in Trinidad, Barbados, St. Lucia, and other islands.

In the Yucatán Peninsula, the *chinense* is called habanero, which means "from Havana," hinting of a transference to Mexico from the Caribbean. It long has been rumored that habaneros no longer grow in Cuba, but pepper aficionado Richard Rice sent us seeds in 1990 given to him by Cuban refugees. The seeds did indeed produce habaneros, proving they are still grown in Cuba today. The species was transferred to Africa during the colonization of Brazil or during the later traffic in slaves, and today there are many *chinense* varieties in Africa.

The different varieties of the *chinense* species vary greatly. They range between one and four and a half feet tall, depending on environmental factors. Some perennial varieties have grown as tall as eight feet in tropical climates, but the average height in the U.S. garden is about two feet. It has multiple stems and an erect habit. The leaves are pale to medium green, large and wrinkled, reaching six inches long and four inches wide, the flowers have white corollas and purple anthers, and the plant sets two to six fruits per node. The pods are pendant, campanulate (a flattened bell shape), and some are elongated and pointed at the end. Others are flattened at the end and resemble a tam, or bonnet. They are usually about two and a half inches long and one to two inches wide, green at immaturity, and mature to red, orange, yellow, or white. Although the *chinense* range in heat from zero to the hottest ever measured, they average between 80,000 and 150,000 Scoville Units.

The seeds tend to take a long time to germinate. The *chinense*, being tropical plants, do best in areas with high humidity and warm nights. They are slow growers, especially in the Southwest, and the growing period is 80 to 120 days or more. The yield varies enormously according to how well the particular plants adapt to the local environment; some plants have as few as ten pods while others may have fifty or more.

Habaneros are grown commercially in the Yucatán Peninsula of Mexico, where about 1,500 tons a year are harvested. They are cultivated to a lesser extent in Belize and there are small commercial fields of other *chinense* varieties in Jamaica, Trinidad, and to a limited extent on other islands, such as The Bahamas. In Costa Rica, a variety of *chinense* called 'Rica Red,' developed by Stuart Jeffrey and Cody Jordan of Quetzál Foods, is grown commercially, with about 200 acres under cultivation in 1992. In the United States, there are two significant commercial growing operations: one in California and the other in the Texas Hill Country with about 500 acres under cultivation. The datil pepper, a *chinense* variety grown for about 300 years in St. Augustine, Florida, is processed into sauces and jellies, but growers there jealously protect their seeds and none are available commercially. Although Mexican varieties have been developed and named, none are commercially available to home gardeners. In the United States, most commercial habanero seeds are generic.

Interestingly enough, in the Amazon region of Brazil, mildly pungent *chinense* varieties have been crossed with bell peppers to produce sweet hybrids that are more disease-resistant than *annuums* under hot and humid conditions. S. S. Cheng, the researcher responsible for the experiment, notes: "The advantages of *C. chinense* cultivation are the longer harvest periods, no pesticide application requirement, and low production cost. A breeding program is under way to transfer fruit quality from *C. annuum* to *C. chinense*."

The *chinense* pods are used fresh in salsas, and are commonly used to make very hot, liquid sauces when combined with carrots and onions. They can be dried and ground into powder, but be sure to wear a protective mask. (See Habanero.)

◢ *Chino.* Another term for a dried poblano chile, especially in central Mexico and San Luis Potosí.

CHIPOTLE

Generally speaking, chipotle in English refers to any smoked chile pepper. The Spanish word *chipotle* is a contraction of *chilpotle* in the Nahuatl language of the Aztecs, where *chil* referred to the hot pepper and *potle* was derived from *poctli*, meaning smoked. The word was apparently reversed from Nahuatl, where it originally was spelled *pochilli*. Other early spellings in Mexico are *tzilpoctil*, *tzonchilli*, and *texochilli*.

The most commonly smoked chiles are jalapeños, named for the city of Jalapa in the state of Veracruz. They are also known in Mexico as *cuaresmeños*, or Lenten chiles. In Puebla, central Mexico, and Oaxaca, jalapeños are known as *huachinangos*, while in coastal Mexico and Veracruz they are called chiles *gordos*.

Smoked chiles had their origin in the ancient civilization of Teotihuacán, north of present-day Mexico City. It was the largest city-state in Mesoamerica and flourished centuries before the rise of the Aztecs. Chipotles also made an appearance in the marketplaces of Tenochtitlán, the capital city of the Aztecs that is now called Mexico City. Certain varieties of fleshy chiles, called jalapeños, would not dry properly in the sun—their thick flesh would rot first. However, like meats, they could be preserved by the process known as smoke-drying.

Bernardino de Sahagún, a Spanish friar who lived in Mexico in the early 1500s, described a dish called *teatzin* that was served in Cholula in the state of Puebla. It contained a combination of chipotle and pasilla sauces for stewing fresh jalapeños and lenten palm flowers.

In 1575, a Spanish visitor to Mexico, Juan de la Cueva, described a dish that combined the seedless chipotles (*capónes*), onions, piñon nuts, and a broth with meat juice and *pulque* (agave beer). The sauce was simmered with chunks of meat to create *pipián de piñon*.

For hundreds of years after the Aztecs, smoked chiles were found predominantly in the markets of central and south Mexico, in areas such as Puebla, Oaxaca, Veracruz, and Chiapas. In the state of Veracruz, a salsa made with tomatoes, peanuts, and chipotles has been made for centuries. It is called *tlatonile*.

The true chipotle is grayish-tan, quite stiff, and is often described as looking like a cigar butt. It is deeply imbued with smoke and is both hot and flavorful. This main variety is also called chile *ahumado* (smoked chile); chile *meco* (blackish-red chile—*meco* is close to *seco*, meaning dry); the double terms chipotle *meco* and chipotle *típico*; and just *típico*. Further confusing the issue is a cultivated variety of jalapeño that is also named 'Típico.' The 'Típico' variety is often smoked to become a *típico* chipotle.

Other varieties of smoked jalapeños are mistaken for the *típico* chipotle. The most common one is called *morita*, which means "little blackberry" in Spanish. The color of this smoked chile is dark red, sometimes approaching purple in color. Often the *morita* is referred to as a smoked serrano

Chipotle chiles. PAUL BOSLAND

chile, but this is inaccurate. Both the *típico* and the *morita* are smoked jalapeños; the difference is that the *morita* is not smoked nearly as long, and thus it remains very leathery and pliable. Not only is the smoky flavor much more intense in the *típico*, its flavor is much richer.

But the *morita* is commonly marketed as the *típico* chipotle because it can bring two to four dollars more per pound with that name. Unfortunately, most of the "*chipotles*" being sold in markets in the United States are in actuality the inferior *moritas*. This is because most of *chipotles* produced in Mexico are eaten there, leaving little for export.

To make up for lack of the *típico* variety to export, producers in the northern states of Mexico, particularly Chihuahua, have turned to the *moritas*, which are much less expensive to produce. Unfortunately, they call the *moritas* "chipotles" and sometimes claim that they have never heard of the *típico* variety. To further confuse the issue, in the interior, the *típico* is known by brokers as "*Veracruz.*"

Other varieties of smoked chiles include:

De cobán —A piquin chile that is smoked in southern Mexico and Guatemala.

Pasilla de Oaxaca—A variety of chile that is smoked in Oaxaca and is used in the famous *mole negro*.

Jalapeño *chico*—Jalapeños that are smoked while still green. Usually, they are culls from the fresh market that need to be preserved, and the smoke-drying process obscures any blemishes.

Capónes—This rare smoked chile is a red jalapeño without seeds; the term means "castrated ones." They are quite expensive and are rarely exported.

Habanero—Recently, a smoked habanero product has been introduced into the United States. It is used as a very hot substitute for chipotles.

The heat scales of smoked chiles vary considerably. The *de cobán* and habaneros are the hottest of the smoked chiles and the *morita* and *típico* are the mildest. Since jalapeños themselves have medium heat, when smoked they retain the same heat level, which ranges from about 5,000 to 10,000 Scoville Units, measured in the dried form. By comparison, New Mexican chiles are typically 500 to 1,000 Scoville Units, and habaneros range from 80,000 to more than 500,000 Scoville Units. When many chipotles are added to a dish, the result can be quite pungent. (See Smoking Chiles.)

CHIPOTLE CHILE SAUCE
Salsa de Chipotle

From Tlaxcala, Mexico, comes a wonderful sauce that utilizes any type of smoked chile. Most commonly, chipotles are smoked red jalapeños. This is a table sauce served at room temperature to spice up any main dish, including meats and poultry. Note that this recipe requires advance preparation.

MAKES ABOUT 2½ CUPS
HEAT SCALE: **Hot**

10 dried chipotle chiles
4 mulato chiles (or substitute anchos)
½ onion, chopped
10 cloves garlic
¼ cup olive oil
1 tablespoon sesame seeds
10 black peppercorns

10 cumin seeds
½ cinnamon stick
1 teaspoon dried Mexican oregano
½ teaspoon salt
¼ cup vegetable oil
¼ cup white vinegar
1 cup water

In a bowl, soak the chiles in hot water to cover until soft, about 1 hour. Drain the chiles and remove the seeds and stems.

In a food processor or blender, combine the chiles, onion, garlic, 2 tablespoons olive oil, sesame seeds, peppercorns, cumin seeds, cinnamon stick, Mexican oregano, and salt and process to a paste.

Heat the remaining olive oil and vegetable oil together in a saucepan over medium heat. Add the paste and heat until it is aromatic, stirring constantly, for about 5 minutes. Add the vinegar and water, remove from the heat, and stir well.

CHIPOTLE DIP

Chipotles a la Cordobesa

This dip is a classical Mexican way to use chipotles. It can be served with tortilla chips or the fresh vegetables suggested here.

MAKES 10 TO 12 SERVINGS
HEAT SCALE: **Medium**

2 cups water

2 cups red wine vinegar

6 dried chipotle chiles, stems and seeds removed

1 cup packed dark or light brown sugar

Salt to taste

1/3 cup olive oil

2 medium onions, chopped

4 cloves garlic, minced

1/2 teaspoon salt

1/4 teaspoon dried thyme

1/4 teaspoon dried Mexican oregano

1 bay leaf

2 cups sour cream

1 cup mayonnaise

1 tablespoon fresh lemon juice

One 1-pound bag of carrots, quartered lengthwise, cut into sticks 3 inches long

Place the water, vinegar, chiles, brown sugar, and salt in a saucepan. Bring to a boil, then reduce the heat to low, and cook until the chiles rehydrate and the peel is easily loosened, about 20 minutes. Remove the chiles and peel off the skin. Puree in a blender with 2 tablespoons of the rehydrating solution, then reserve.

In another saucepan, combine the olive oil, onions, garlic, salt, thyme, oregano, and bay leaf and cook over medium heat, stirring well, for 5 minutes. Drain off the excess oil and remove the bay leaf.

In a bowl, mix together the pureed chiles, onion mixture, sour cream, mayonnaise, and lemon juice. Serve with the carrots, or fresh vegetables of your choice.

ﻻ *Chombo.* Local name for *Capsicum chinense* in Panama.

ﻻ **Chorizo.** In Latin America, a spicy sausage made with pork, garlic, and red chile powder.

ﻻ *Cili.* Alternate Malaysian term for chiles. *Cili padi* are apparently the same as *cabe rawit*, the small bird chiles, while dried red chiles are *cili kering*. Chile powder is *serbuk cili*. In the Czech Republic, *cili* is chile powder, usually pungent paprika, used in many dishes.

ﻻ *Cobán.* A smoked Guatemalan piquin chile. Also *de cobán*.

ﻻ **Coffee pepper.** Local Trindadian name for a wild *Capsicum annuum* variety that resembles a coffee bean.

ﻻ *Cola de rata.* "Rat's tail"; a term for a long, thin variety of chile *de árbol* in Nayarit, Mexico.

ﻻ *Colombo.* A type of hot curry introduced into the French Caribbean in the 1800s by migrant Indian workers mostly from Bengal.

ﻻ **Colorado.** Another term for a dried red New Mexican chile.

ﻻ *Comapeño.* A small, orange chile consumed both fresh and dry in Veracruz, Mexico. Also called *ozulyamero*.

ﻻ **Congo.** Local name for the Trinidad pod type of *Capsicum chinense*; the term is said to mean large or powerful.

ﻻ *'Cora.'* A cutivated variety of *cascabel* grown in Nayarit, Mexico, where it is also called *acaponeta* and *cuerudo*. It is eaten both fresh and dry. The name is the same as an Indian tribe.

ﻻ *Corazón.* A spicy, heart-shaped poblano grown in Durango, Mexico.

ﻻ *Corriente.* In the state of Guerrero, Mexico, a name for the green *costeño*.

ﻻ *Costeño.* A small dried red chile about an inch long that is a variety of chile *de árbol*. Commonly found in the states of Veracruz, Oaxaca, and Guerrero, Mexico. Also spelled *costeña*. Other regional terms for this chile are *bandeño*, *casero*, *criollo*, and *corriente*.

ﻻ *'Cotaxtla.'* A cultivated variety of serrano in Mexico.

ﻻ *Coui.* In the Caribbean, an ancient Carib Indian sauce of hot peppers and cassava juice.

ﻻ *Covincho.* Local name for the wild *Capsicum chacoense* in northern Argentina.

ﻻ *Cuaresmeño.* See Jalapeños. The name refers to Lent, probably an allusion to the planting of the chile at that time of year.

❧ **Cuauhchilli.** In Jalisco, Nayarit, and Aguascalientes, Mexico, a variety of *de árbol*.

❧ **Cuban.** A pod type of the *annuum* species. These mild pods are much loved when fried. There are two basic types: the long-fruited ones like 'Key Largo' and 'Biscayne' and the short-fruited types like 'Cubanelle.' Recommended varieties include 'Aconagua,' 'Biscayne,' and 'Cubanelle.'

❧ **Cuerno de oro.** "Horn of gold"; Costa Rican name for *Capsicum baccatum*.

❧ **Cuicatleco.** A variety of chile consumed by the indigenous people of the district of Cuicatlán, Oaxaca, Mexico.

CURRY

The word curry refers to both a spice mixture and a style of cooking. The spice mixture usually contains chile peppers in the form of a hot powder along with up to thirty other spices and herbs. The cooking style is essentially stewing meats, seafood, poultry, and/or vegetables in the spice mixture plus a liquid.

Commercial curry products. CHEL BEESON

Curry's oldest tradition, of course, is in India. Some of the spices used in curries — namely cumin, saffron, and fennel — were being ground on stones as early as 4000 B.C. in the Indus Valley. Eventually this Harappa culture of the Indus Valley declined, and since their clay seals have never been translated, we have no idea if the spices they ground were actually used in curry-like dishes. We also do not know if the spices were cultivated, collected in the wild, or acquired through trade with other peoples.

Although there is no definitive proof, it is believed that curries originated in southern India because the Malabar Coast of Kerala became the first spice-growing region of India. Black pepper, cinnamon, turmeric, and cardamom first grew wild there, and then were cultivated for centuries before they were spread into the other regions.

The Portuguese forever changed curries by introducing chile peppers, which became the principal hot spice in curries from then on. Christopher Columbus brought chile peppers and their seeds back from the New World in 1493, and they were grown mostly by monks in monasteries. Portuguese explorers carried the chiles to their ports in Africa and Goa, India, shortly thereafter. Although the exact date of their introduction into India is not known, most experts believe that it was in the early 1500s.

Most curry cooks recommend using only freshly ground spices; however, there are many convenient commercial curry preparations. *Masalas* are spice blends that usually lack turmeric. Curry powders contain turmeric (the yellower the powder, the more turmeric it contains) and a large percentage of coriander. Imported powders are generally superior to domestic ones. Curry pastes are sealed, moist blends of herbs, spices, and other ingredients such as coconut, onions, fresh chiles, and ginger. They are imported from India, Thailand, Indonesia, and Sri Lanka.

QUICK CURRY POWDER
Bafat

Contrary to the popular belief that Indians make curry powder from scratch, in India, commercial curry powders have become an integral part of middle-class family life. This quick curry powder, called *bafat*, is from the southwestern region of India. It can be used for meat, fish, or vegetable dishes. Traditionally, the spices are sun-dried for 3 days and then roasted.

MAKES ABOUT 2 CUPS
HEAT SCALE: Medium

1/3 cup coriander seeds
1/4 cup cumin seeds
2 tablespoons yellow mustard seeds
2 tablespoons black peppercorns
2 tablespoons whole cloves
1 tablespoon fenugreek seeds

2 tablespoons ground cardamom
2 tablespoons ground cinnamon
2 tablespoons powdered turmeric
1/4 cup freshly ground, hot chile powder, such as New Mexican

Preheat the oven to 200°F. On a large sheet pan, dry the whole spices in the oven for 15 minutes, taking care they do not burn. Remove them from the oven, cool, and grind them together with the ground spices in a spice mill. Place in a jar and seal. It will keep indefinitely in a cool, dark cupboard.

INDIAN MINCED MEAT CURRY
Keema Bafat

This is a popular dish from the coastal region of Karnataka, India, using Quick Curry Powder (see previous recipe). It is traditionally prepared with lamb, but chicken may be substituted and the cooking time reduced by 7 minutes. *Ghee* is clarified butter, available in Asian markets.

MAKES 4 SERVINGS
HEAT SCALE: Mild

2 tablespoons vegetable oil
1 tablespoon ghee (optional)
1 large onion, chopped
6 cloves garlic, minced
1 tablespoon minced ginger

1 tablespoon Quick Curry Powder (page 104)
   (or substitute imported Indian curry powder)
1 pound minced lamb meat (or substitute chicken)
Salt to taste
¼ cup chopped fresh cilantro or mint leaves

In a skillet over medium heat, heat the oil for 1 minute. Add the *ghee* and onion and cook, stirring, until the onion wilts, about 1 minute. Add the garlic and ginger and cook, stirring, for 1 minute. Add the Quick Curry Powder, reduce the heat to low, and simmer for 1 minute.

Add the minced meat, mix well, and cook for 20 minutes over low heat. Add the salt. Garnish with cilantro or mint leaves and serve.

PORK CURRY GURKHA-STYLE

Gurkhas, the sturdy soldiers from Nepal, took this curry formula wherever they went, be it Malaya or the Falkland Islands. The use of yogurt in this curry tempers the chiles. Note that this recipe requires advance preparation.

MAKES 6 SERVINGS
HEAT SCALE: **Medium**

1 teaspoon white vinegar
1 tablespoon cayenne powder
2 pounds lean boneless pork, cut into 1-inch cubes
2 cups plain yogurt
2 tablespoons minced ginger
1 teaspoon vegetable oil
¼ cup ghee (or substitute vegetable oil)
1 teaspoon freshly ground black pepper

1 teaspoon powdered turmeric
1 cup water
Salt to taste
½ cup chopped fresh cilantro leaves
1 teaspoon ground cumin
1 teaspoon ground nutmeg
½ teaspoon ground cloves
½ teaspoon ground cardamom

In a large bowl, combine the vinegar and cayenne powder and toss the meat in it. Add the yogurt and ginger and marinate the meat for about 3 hours in the refrigerator.

Heat the oil in a skillet over low heat for 1 minute. Add the *ghee*, the pork with its marinade, black pepper, turmeric, water, and salt, raise the heat to medium-high, and bring to a rapid boil. Reduce the heat to low, cover the skillet, and simmer for 40 minutes.

Add the cilantro, cumin, nutmeg, cloves, and cardamom, stir in well, and serve hot.

MOGHLAI CHICKEN CURRY
Nimbu Masala Murgh

The Moghlai dishes, popular across India, but particularly in Delhi and the neighboring Uttar Pradesh, owe their ancestry to the sixteenth- and seventeenth-century Moghul rulers, Akbar and Shehjehan, who were connoisseurs of music, literature, architecture, and food. Unlike their immediate ancestors, who invaded India and were too busy consolidating their empire to pay much attention to cuisine, Akbar and Shehjehan recruited the best chefs in northern India, and encouraged them to create dishes that carried the influence of the ingredients of central Asia and India. Note that this recipe requires advance preparation.

MAKES 4 SERVINGS
HEAT SCALE: **Medium**

2 large onions, chopped, plus 1 large onion, cut into rings, for garnish

One 2-inch piece of ginger, peeled

10 cloves garlic

2 cups plain yogurt

Salt to taste

1 teaspoon cayenne powder

1 tablespoon cumin powder

1 tablespoon coriander powder

1 tablespoon commercial garam masala

1 chicken, cut up into serving pieces

¼ cup ghee *(or substitute vegetable oil)*

1 teaspoon yellow mustard seeds

4 green chiles, such as serranos, stems removed, minced

¼ cup fresh lime juice

1 lime, cut into small pieces with peel on, for garnish

½ cup cashew nuts for garnish

1 large tomato, diced, for garnish

¼ cup chopped fresh cilantro or mint leaves for garnish

In a food processor or blender, grind the chopped onions, ginger, and garlic into a smooth paste. Combine the paste with the yogurt, salt, cayenne powder, and half of the cumin, coriander, and *garam masala*. Add the chicken pieces, mix well, and marinate in the refrigerator for 6 hours.

Place the drained chicken in a large skillet and cook, covered, for about 12 minutes over low heat.

In another skillet, heat the *ghee* or oil over medium heat for 2 minutes. Add the mustard seeds, and when they begin to pop, add the chiles. Pour the *ghee* or oil (along with the mustard and chiles) over the chicken, and continue cooking for 8 to 10 minutes, or until the moisture evaporates.

Place the chicken in a serving dish. Squeeze the lime juice over the meat, and sprinkle the remaining cumin, coriander, and *garam masala* over the mixture. Garnish with the lime pieces, cashew nuts, diced tomato, onion rings, and cilantro.

'Dandicut cherry.' Cultivated chile in Pakistan.

Dar feller. Yemeni for chile pepper.

Datil. Local name for *Capsicum chinense* in St. Augustine, Florida.

De agua. "Water chile"; in Mexico, a fairly long (to four inches) conical chile that grows erect on plants in Oaxaca. It is used both in its green and dried red forms in sauces and stews. Some sources say it is a variety of poblano, but that is doubtful. When red and smoke-dried, it is called pasilla *oaxaqueño*.

De árbol. "Tree chile"; in Mexico, the bush resembles a small tree. In the United States, a pod type of the *annuum* species. The hot pods are red and about one-quarter inch wide by one and a half to three inches long. Also called *puya, cuauhchilli, alfilerillo, pico de pájaro,* and *cola de rata.* Grown primarily in Jalisco and Nayarit, Mexico. Varieties

include 'NuMex Sunburst,' with bright orange, three-inch, medium-hot pods; 'NuMex Sunflare,' bright red, three-inch, medium-hot pods; and 'NuMex Sunglo,' bright yellow, three-inch, medium-hot pods.

De chorro. "Irrigated chile"; in Mexico, a variety of poblano that is so named because each plant is irrigated separately. Grown only in Guanajuato and Durango. The pods are used only in the green form.

De color. "Of color." There are two types in Mexico: chile *pasera*, a dried poblano that is left on the plant until the pods turn red and then are removed and dried in the sun, and *chilessecadora*, which is a green poblano that is removed from the bush and dried in a dehydrator.

De la tierra. In Mexico, another term for a dried red New Mexican chile.

De monte. "Hilly chile"; in Mexico, a general term for wild chiles, the chiltepins.

A hot and spicy cheesecake. CHEL BEESON

⊌ *De onza.* "By the ounce"; in Mexico, a small dried, brick-red Oaxacan chile about three inches long and a half inch wide. It is used in *moles*.

⊌ *Derrière de Madame Jacques, Le.* A name for the *chinense* species in Guadeloupe.

⊌ *De siete caldos.* A chile from Chiapas, Mexico, that is supposedly so hot that one is enough to spice up seven pots of soup.

DESSERTS AND SWEETS

The idea of combining sweet and heat has been around for more than 1,000 years. The Maya were the first to mix the luscious tastes of chocolate with chile powder and honey to create a fiery chocolate drink. They believed this treat was inspired by the gods. Today, hot and sweet foods have become an increasingly popular part of the growing two-billion-dollar fiery foods industry. Products include everything from jams and jellies to chocolates, cheesecakes, dessert sauces, cookies, cakes, pies and breads, suckers, nuts, gummy chiles, and even chocolate and chile-covered fruit. Not surprisingly, there is an entire cookbook devoted to the subject of hot desserts, called *Sweet Heat*, by Melissa T. Stock and Dave DeWitt (Ten Speed Press, 1996). This book has more than 150 chile-inspired desserts, from red chile carrot cake to well-spiced custards, sorbets, cookies, and breads. The following is a sampling of some sweet hot desserts that are sure to please.

PIÑON PEPPER BRITTLE

With the native chile and pine (piñon) nuts, it's not surprising that this is one of New Mexico's favorite candies.

MAKES 4 CUPS
HEAT SCALE: Mild

½ teaspoon green chile powder (or substitute red chile powder)
1 tablespoon New Mexican red chile powder
½ teaspoon salt

3 tablespoons vegetable oil
½ cup sugar
2 cups pine nuts

In a bowl, combine the ground chiles and salt.

Pour the oil into a 12-inch frying pan over medium-high heat. When the oil is hot, add the sugar and cook, stirring, until the sugar is melted and begins to turn a golden color, about 4 minutes. Add the pine nuts to the pan and cook, stirring, until the melted sugar is a rich caramel color, about 4 minutes more. Add the ground chiles and salt mixture and cook, stirring, about 1 minute more; remove from the heat immediately if the mixture begins to scorch.

Immediately pour the candy mixture onto a large sheet of aluminum foil, spreading it with a spoon to make the nuts 1 layer thick. Let the candy cool and harden, about 20 minutes. Next, break the candy into small pieces and serve.

CHOCOLATE CHESS AND CHILE PIE

Chess pie is a very traditional Southern dessert. Adding red chile gives this dessert a subtle heat. It can be made ahead of time. Use your favorite pie crust recipe.

MAKES 6 TO 8 SERVINGS
HEAT SCALE: **Mild to medium**

4 large eggs
1 cup sugar
1 teaspoon red chile powder, plus ⅛ to ¼
    teaspoon (optional)
6 ounces (1 cup) semisweet chocolate chips,
    melted

1 cup heavy cream
6 tablespoons melted, unsalted butter
One 9-inch prebaked pie crust
¼ cup confectioners' sugar
½ teaspoon vanilla extract

Preheat the oven to 325°F.

In a medium mixing bowl, beat the eggs and sugar together until light and fluffy. Add the red chile powder and beat until well blended. Add the melted chocolate chips, ½ cup of the heavy cream, and the melted butter. Mix until well blended. Pour this mixture into the prebaked pie crust. Bake until the mixture is set, 30 to 35 minutes. Remove the pie from the oven and let cool on a wire rack, then chill. Just before serving, whip the remaining ½ cup cream until soft peaks form, add the confectioners' sugar and vanilla, and continue beating until firm peaks form. Serve the pie with a dollop of whipped cream. For chile lovers you can add ⅛ to ¼ teaspoon of red chile powder to the whipped cream for a double dose of chile.

SANTA FE–STYLE HOT CHOCOLATE

This is a Santa Fe–style adaptation of an ancient Mayan drink. The hot chocolate is accented with red chile. On cold Santa Fe nights, the Kahlúa warms the body and soul. Try substituting brandy for the Kahlúa for a different flavor. If you prefer, you can eliminate the liquor and still have a rich-tasting drink.

MAKES 4 SERVINGS
HEAT SCALE: **Mild**

¼ cup sugar
¼ cup cocoa
½ teaspoon New Mexican red chile powder
½ tablespoon flour
1 cup water

2 cups half and half
1 cup milk
1 teaspoon vanilla extract
¼ cup Kahlúa or coffee-flavored liquor (optional)

In a large saucepan, combine the sugar, cocoa, red chile, and flour with the water. Stir and whisk until blended very well. Heat the mixture on low until bubbling and just beginning to simmer. Gradually add the half and half, then the milk, stirring constantly. Beat with a whisk. Add the vanilla and mix. Pour the hot chocolate into mugs or heat-proof cups. If desired, carefully spoon 1 tablespoon of Kahlúa on top of each cup.

WHITE CHOCOLATE MOUSSE WITH GREEN CHILE PISTACHIOS

This is a decadent, rich dessert. The green chile pistachios give the wonderful mousse a definite kick. It's an unusual combination of flavors that truly complement each other. If green chile pistachios are not available in your area, substitute the same amount of plain pistachios and 1 to 2 tablespoons of finely minced canned green chiles. Be sure the green chile is drained well and any excess moisture removed as this will affect the consistency of the mousse.

MAKES 4 TO 6 SERVINGS
HEAT SCALE: **Mild**

8 ounces white chocolate, cut into small chunks
2 cups heavy cream
½ cup sifted confectioners' sugar
½ teaspoon vanilla extract

⅓ cup chopped green chile pistachios
   (see above)
Sweetened whipped cream and chopped green
   chile pistachios for garnish (optional)

Slowly melt the white chocolate in a heavy saucepan, stirring constantly. Remove from the heat and cool until lukewarm.

While the chocolate is cooling, in a mixing bowl, beat the heavy cream until soft peaks form. Mix in the confectioners' sugar and vanilla. Gently fold about one quarter of the whipped cream into the chocolate, then fold in the remaining whipped cream. Stir in the green chile pistachios. Spoon the mousse into individual serving dishes, and chill until ready to serve. If desired, garnish with a dollop of sweetened whipped cream and a few chopped green chile pistachios.

⌐ *Diente de tlacuache.* "Oppossum tooth"; in Mexico, the name for chiltepins in Tamaulipas.

⌐ **Dominica pepper.** Name for the *chinense* species in the U.S. Virgin Islands.

⌐ *Dulce.* "Sweet"; in Mexico, a term for bell peppers and pimiento.

⌐ *'Dutch.'* A hot variety of *Capsicum annuum* from the Netherlands that was developed from Indonesian varieties.

Color variations in New Mexican chiles.
PAUL BOSLAND

Canario chiles in Mexico City market. DAVE DEWITT

Ají *harvest.* DAVE DEWITT

'Jigsaw,' variegated chiles. DAVE DEWITT

Bonney peppers, Barbados.
DAVE DEWITT

Serrano chiles in Mexico City market.
DAVE DEWITT

Growing datil *peppers, St. Augustine, Florida.*
DAVE DEWITT

Chiles in Bangkok wholesale market.
DAVE DEWITT

Seasoning pepper, Trinidad.
DAVE DEWITT

Habanero harvest, U.S.A.
DAVE DEWITT

Habanero harvest, Belize.
DAVE DEWITT

Fataali pepper, Africa.
DAVE DEWITT

Capsicum pubescens, *Costa Rica.*
PAUL BOSLAND

"Fiesta" chiles, New Mexico State University demo garden.
DAVE DEWITT

Red habanero, Costa Rica.
DAVE DEWITT

"Red Caribbean" habaneros. DAVE DEWITT

Caribbean seasoning peppers.
DAVE DEWITT

Chiltepin harvest.
DAVE DEWITT

Cayenne harvest. DAVE DEWITT

"Round Pepper," *Trinidad.* DAVE DEWITT

Hot sauces at National Fiery Foods Show. CHEL BEESON

Ají limo, *South America.* DAVE DEWITT

Tabasco plants, Avery Island, Louisiana. DAVE DEWITT

Tabasco harvest, Avery Island, Louisiana. DAVE DEWITT

Chiltepin, Sonora, Mexico. DAVE DEWITT

Aerial view, National Fiery Foods Show. DAVE DEWITT

Ristras, *Las Cruces, New Mexico.* DAVE DEWITT

Habanero harvest. DAVE DEWITT

Congo pepper seedlings, Botanic Station, Tobago. DAVE DEWITT

Chilhuacle rojo in market, Oaxaca, Mexico. DAVE DEWITT

Ají harvest. DAVE DEWITT

Rocoto *chile, Peru.*   DAVE DEWITT

Congo pepper, Trinidad.   DAVE DEWITT

'Ancho 101,' New Mexico State University demo garden.
PAUL BOSLAND

HOTTER   MEDIUM   HOT

Hot sauce tasting, National Fiery Foods Show.   CHEL BEESON

Ripening poblano chile.   DAVE DEWITT

Canario chile showing black seeds.   CHEL BEESON

MULATO $18.00
ANCHO $14.00
ANCHO
GUAJILLO $8.00
ARBOL $12.00
AJONJOLI $8.00

Chiles in Mexico City market.   DAVE DEWITT

Scotch bonnets in Jamaican market. DAVE DEWITT

Chimayó chile, New Mexico.
DAVE DEWITT

Chile jewelry by
Leslie Hall.
DAVE DEWITT

'NuMex Centennial,' New Mexico State University
demo garden. DAVE DEWITT

Paprika. DAVE DEWITT

Serrano harvest. DAVE DEWITT

Chile de agua, *Oaxaca, Mexico.* DAVE DEWITT

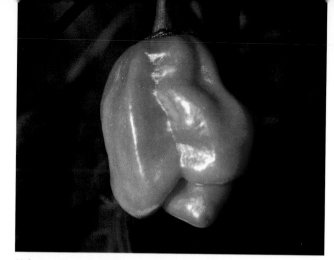

Habanero, Yucatán, Mexico. DAVE DEWITT

Chile from Turkey. DAVE DEWITT

Chiltepin harvest, La Aurora, Mexico. DAVE DEWITT

Lal mirch *chile, India.* DAVE DEWITT

'Thai Hot' chiles. PAUL BOSLAND

⤏ **'Esmeralda.'** "Emerald"; in Mexico, a cultivated variety of poblano.

⤏ **'Espinateco.'** "Spiny"; in Mexico, a cultivated variety of jalapeño.

Harvesting jalapeños, New Mexico. DAVE DEWITT

⚑ *Fataali.* *Chinense* variety grown in the Central African Republic.

⚑ *Felfel al har.* Arabic term for chile pepper in North Africa.

⚑ *Filfil.* General Arabic term for chile pepper.

⚑ *'Flor de Pabellón.'* "Flower of the Pavillion"; in Mexico, a cultivated variety of poblano.

FOLKLORE AND MYTHOLOGY

The ritual uses of the genus *Capsicum* range from the innocuous to the murderous, but the fiery pods are always powerful. In astrology, Capsicums fall under the dominion of Mars, ancient god of war, so that should be some indication of respect. Fuentes y Guzmán wrote in 1690 that those who frequently ate red pepper were protected against poison, while the Incas prohibited the use of chiles at initiation and funeral rites. It is not known why the pods were precluded by the Incas but Capsicums were associated with lightning bolts in Incan mythology, another allusion to their power.

One of the commonest household uses of chile peppers in cultures all over the world is burning them as a fumigant for vermin ranging from bedbugs to rats. Since fumigation in ancient times was also believed to be protection against vampires and werewolves, we have a good introduction to the concept of the mystical powers of peppers.

"Chile is used as an amulet, probably because of its well-known protective pharmacological properties, and in religious ceremonies, witchcraft, and conjuring; its fiery potency is considered a powerful means to any end," observed Beatrice Roeder, author of *Chicano Folk Medicine from Los Angeles, California.*

Chiles are considered to be a cleanser for evil eye (*mal de ojo*), bad luck, and bewitchment among Hispanics in the

United States, a practice imported from Mexico. This parallels usage among the Indians in Guatemala. When a child is thought to have the evil eye, the parents spray the child's face with a mixture of rue, then a little *aguardiente* mixed with a crushed hot pepper is rubbed on the child's feet. Another cure for the evil eye calls for mixing a little *annatto* with chile peppers in a cloth bag and passing it over the child's body while making the sign of the cross. Then the bag is thrown into a fire.

In a remarkable parallel usage between totally different cultures, the East Indian population of Trinidad wraps seven red pepper pods with salt, onion, and garlic skins in a paper and passes it seven times around a baby to remove *najar*, the evil eye, which is believed to cause unnecessary crying. Also, green peppers are dropped around the doorway to keep away evil spirits. However, black Hispanics from islands like Cuba and Hispañola believe that red pepper pods on a doorstep are the sign of a malignant influence, and may give a man the "hot foot."

Likewise, chiles are associated with the *luban oko*, or "red demon" of the Tsachila or Colorados Indians of the Amazon. This demon sucks the blood out of its victims, leaving them "as white as a boiled yuca." The chiles are served in food and also burned and the demon is foiled in two ways: He is asphyxiated by the fumes, and cannot eat any of the food because it is too hot. This legend seems to be related to the rubefacient effects of chiles, and their consistent linking to the circulatory system.

There is also a chile-witchcraft remedy. In the American Southwest, two nails are tied together in the shape of a cross with a piece of wire and put in the fire; when it is red hot, it is removed from the fire. A *ristra* (string) of small chiles is placed on it, and then some rock salt. The resulting vapors are said to banish any witchcraft in the area.

But in the Ozarks and Deep South of America, an African-American legend holds that in order for peppers to grow out and be hot, you have to be very angry when you plant them. The best peppers are planted by a lunatic!

There are additional references to the darker side of chiles. "A case of death has been reported due to eating of excessive quantity of chillies," warned R. N. Chopra in his classic book, *Poisonous Plants of India*. Chiles are one of the ingredients in the arrow poison of indigenous Bajak tribesmen of Borneo. And R. N. Chopra adds: "In the past, chillies were frequently used in the Orient for the purpose of torture, some of the common methods being by introducing them into the nostrils, eyes, vagina or urethra, burning under the nose . . ."

In northern Mexico, chiles are still used as a part of spells to make people ill, or even to kill them. One "potion" consisted of a rag that contained chile seeds, scorpions, sow bugs, mustard, and a strand of red silk. In one case recorded by Isabel Kelly in her 1965 book *Folk Practices in North Mexico:* "Another time they threw chiles through the door of the butcher shop. They were two large chiles anchotes [probably anchos], wrapped in a newspaper. The chiles were 'prepared.' They stuck the package in, through a hole in the door. May God receive him, because he fell ill and died."

Lorenzo Fritz, a pepper enthusiast and South American traveler, reported to us in 1994 that the negative side of chiles was countered by a positive spin. The Aymara Indians of Bolivia conduct a spiritual cleansing ritual in which a mixture of various herbs, flowers, and *locoto* chile (*Capsicum pubescens*) are placed in a pail of boiling water. The subject sits on a stool nearby, and a blanket is placed over him and the pail to form a mini-sauna. Fritz, who observed the ceremony, noted: "This exercise is said to be an exorcism for *malas energías*, or bad energies."

Ethnobotanist Dr. Gary Nabhan revealed that the Tarahumara Indians of Sonora, Mexico, use the tiny chiltepins in curing ceremonies—not to rid someone of a current affliction, but to prevent maladies as a result of future witchcraft. According to Gary, "Such witchcraft is caused by a *sukurame* sorcerer who uses a special bird called a *disagiki* as a pathogenic agent to transmit illness. He is the only one who can see the bird, which is no bigger than a finger tip but lives on meat and tortillas. It flies into houses crying 'Sht! Sht!' and then eats your food or defecates on you. The only way to prevent its coming is to throw some *chiltepins* into the air and eat some yourself. The bird is like no other birds. More like evil people than its feathered kind, it cannot stand chiles."

Neither can sharks, if the Indians of the Cuna Islands off Panama can be believed; they tow chiles behind their boats to ward them off.

But apparently the ancient mystical remedies are not enough for devoted chile aficionados. In 1997, a newly formed "cult" posted its own Web site on the Internet: the Transcendental Capsaicinophilic Society. According to the tongue-in-cheek site, the cult is devoted to the worship of chiles, the lifelong dedication to chile consumption, and making fun of people who "just can't take that spicy food." In the "Chants and Rituals" portion of the site, there is the "Litany Against Pain," "to be repeated silently when tempted to complain of burning":

Teach me, Chile, and I shall Learn.
Take me, Chile, and I shall Escape.
Focus my eyes, Chile, and I shall See.
Consume more Chiles.
I feel no pain, for the Chile is my teacher.
I feel no pain, for the Chile takes me beyond
*   myself.*
I feel no pain, for the Chile gives me sight.

FOLK MEDICINE

Chile peppers have been used for centuries all over the world in a remarkable number of cures. Without exhaustive testing, of course, there is no way to judge their efficacy. Modern scientists and doctors are just beginning to examine the healing powers of peppers that began with folk cures such as the ones that follow.

Beauty and Punishment

The role of chiles in appearance and behavior modification has been strong in many cultures. David Livingstone, the famed African explorer, reported that West African women bathed in water to which ground red pepper—he called it paprika—had been added because they believed it would make them more beautiful. The Maya also used chile as a beauty aid, specifically for skin care. However, their technique left a lot to be desired. The women washed their skin with hot urine, applied chile powder, and then repeated the procedure.

Various parts of the chile plant are ingredients in hair dyes in numerous cultures—in Taiwan, for example, a decoction of the stem and leaf is said to be an effective hair dye for jet-black hair. And chiles are reputedly a cure for baldness in the West Indies. Fiery hot chile oil is rubbed into the scalp and the resultant tingling is said to be the start of the hair-growing process. This makes some sense when we consider that capsaicin is an ingredient in a dandruff remedy called Denorex. Apparently the advertising agency for this product realized that the shampoo had to give the illusion of doing something when it was applied to the scalp. So, they added an irritant—in this case a minute amount of oleoresin capsicum—and it produced the tingling sensation of the shampoo "doing something." But what is it doing? Are the capsaicin molecules gobbling up the dandruff flakes? We think not. And we don't think that the capsaicin is growing hair, either.

As usual, there's a darker side of chiles—their use as behavior modifiers and as punishment. Sometimes the usage is rather benign, as in Mexico and other Latin American countries, where chile powder is rubbed on children's thumbs to prevent sucking. But in the *Codex Mendocino*, one of the few remaining books that survive from the Aztecs, there is a rather graphic illustration of a boy being held by an adult in the smoke of burning chiles. Chile expert Jean Andrews noted: "Today, a Popolocan Indian group near Oaxaca still punishes disobedient children in this manner."

Lazy and delinquent children of the Kallawaya Indians of the Andes are corrected by burning chiles and their seeds. "This makes them sneeze, forget their mischievousness, and become docile and obedient children," said one herbalist. Many parents fervently wish that this were so, but are reluctant to attempt the burning chile technique because it would violate cruelty to children statutes.

The Maya, of course, were not bound by such rules; they threw chile powder into the eyes of young girls who stared at boys or men, and they squirted chile juice on the private parts of unchaste women. It gets worse. The Carib Indians of the Caribbean rubbed chile juice into the wounds of youths during their ritual of passage to become a warrior. Worse yet, the Caribs, legend holds, marinated the flesh of captured Arawak Indians in chile before they barbecued and ate them.

On the lighter side of behavior modification by chiles, they are occasionally cited as being an aphrodisiac. In North African legend, they are an occasional ingredient in spice mixtures such as *ras al hanout*, which also includes numerous other spices and cantharis beetles, the notorious Spanish fly. The beetles are also an ingredient in Samoan *kava*, the potion of love and virility—except that if you drink too much, you'll pass out before, well, the act. But in case the chile works too well as an aphrodisiac, the root of the chile plant is used in Indonesia as a treatment for gonorrhea.

A tincture of chile pods is used to treat poor memory in Venezuela, but how does the patient remember to take the remedy? A fascinating cure for "mental sluggishness" comes from the American Amish community, who eat bell pepper seeds for nine days, starting with one and doubling the dosage each day until 256 are consumed on the final day. The point is, if you can remember how many to take, you're cured.

More seriously, chile is often listed as a treatment for alcohol-related disorders. Cayenne in large doses is recommended in herbal lore for control of delirium tremens and, in India, chile powder with cinnamon and sugar in a water-based drink is prescribed for alcoholism and delirium tremens, as it is said to lessen the craving for alcohol. Interestingly enough, an identical chile-cinnamon-sugar cure is used in the Philippines. This treatment corresponds to a homeopathic remedy to suppress the desire for alcohol: ten to fifteen drops of tincture of capsicum in the diet per day, usually in hot tea or beef broth.

Chile seeds also play a role in such treatments. In his book *Indian Medicinal Plants*, published in 1918, K. R. Kirtikar quotes a Surgeon-Major Gray of Lahore: "A dose of ten grains of finely powdered Capsicum seed, given with an ounce of hot water, two or three times a day, sometimes shows wonderful effects on delirium tremems."

On the lighter side of the alcohol issue, a broth laden with chiles is a classic hangover cure in Mexico, as is *menudo*, a tripe soup with chiles served in northern Mexico and the American Southwest. *Menudo* is called "the breakfast of champions" because of its reputed ability to banish the demons of drink.

Chiles are also associated with other drugs. For example, chile powder is mixed with tobacco snuff to make it "more effective" for some tribes in the northwest Amazon. Some of the tribes in the region actually smoke a tobacco and chile powder mixture, not to get high but to come down. The Waorani Indians smoke the mixture to counteract hallucinogenic *yage* (or *ayahuasca*) intoxication—one of the most powerful hallucinogens known. Apparently, the Waorani believe that chiles have the power to counter the vivid hallucinations. The Kulinas of the same region eat chile as they ingest the drug to temper its power. But the most daring drug story of all comes from Bolivia, where powdered chiles are mixed with powdered cocaine and snorted for what is supposedly the ultimate rush.

And then there are the mysteries. Thomas Rutherford, who lived for many years in West Africa, wrote to us about chiles and babies. "In Liberia, chile peppers are boiled, and the water is used to give the babies enemas and to rinse their faces. I have not actually seen the enemas, but I have watched the face-rinsing in the village. The mother lays the baby on her lap. Scoops up the pepper water with her hand and allows it to drip into the baby's eyes as well as over the face. As the baby cries, the mother laughs happily. The reason for this, whether medicinal or as a tonic, was never explained to me."

The Chilehead's Head

Both externally and internally, chiles play a significant role in folk medicine for treating ailments related to the head. Headaches, one of the most common afflictions of mankind, are thought to respond to a variety of chile treatments. A poultice of pepper leaves is applied as a treatment in the Philippines, while biting into a serrano chile in Mexico is a cure because it is thought to be a distracting influence on the headache. In Bolivia, ground chile powder in a poultice is applied to the forehead to relieve headaches.

Just how far-fetched are such cures? Well, capsaicin compounds—mostly powerful creams—are used to treat the victims of cluster headaches, a type of migraine that is probably the most painful of all headaches. But headaches are not the only head ailment treated by chiles as a folk medicine: the Maya applied chile powder to the head to cure vertigo, and chiles are consumed to relieve the effects of stroke in the Peruvian Amazon.

Anyone who has accidentally spread the juice of fresh chiles into his eyes while cleaning or chopping them knows the incredibly sharp pain and tearing blindness that results. So why would anyone in his right mind apply chile juice directly onto his eyeballs? Malingerers, for one. We have read reports of workers in Africa who imitate the condition of conjunctivitis as an excuse not to work by using the juice from fresh pods as an eyewash. Interestingly enough, nineteenth-century Peruvians believed that a capsaicin infusion from the juice of crushed chiles was a cure for conjuntivitis. Some African tribes use chile pepper eyedrops as a way to relieve headaches—apparently the pain of the eyes overwhelms that of the head. Perhaps more soothing is a cure for opthalmia in the West Indies: juice from the leaves is used rather than the hot pods.

The Incas believed that eyesight was improved by eating chiles, and one Mexican source states that "two roasted chiles should be eaten with all meals" for better eyesight. The vitamin A in red chiles is known to fortify vision, and in Hungary, night blindness was treated with a paprika tea.

The ears are not immune from chile treatment either—the mashed chile pods are used for earache treatment in Jamaica. Among the ancient Maya, the blossom of the *pepino* (cucumber), the blossoms of the chile plant, and the flower of an herb we only know as *algodon atabacado* are all mashed together, combined with cotton-wool, and squeezed into the afflicted ear. The Maya also cured ear infections and earache by mixing the resin of the herb *coyoxochtil* with chile powder and applying it three times per day, expelling pus and mucus. Later, during the colonial era in Mexico, a cure for earache was to mix wine and chile powder for use as eardrops. In the Philippines, in combination with *chinchona*, chiles are used to treat tympanitis.

Since the most common usage of chiles is consuming them orally, it is no wonder that they are readily linked to the mouth. Chiles are an ingredient to mask the unpleasant taste of other medicinal drinks among the Kamsá medicine men of the northwest Amazon. Bernardino de Sahagún, a Franciscan friar living in Mexico in the sixteenth century, noted the use of chiles for: "An injury to the tongue, biting of the tongue, laceration of the tongue. Its treatment is to cook chile with salt, which is to be spread on. Then bee honey or thickened maguey syrup is to be spread on." In another tongue-related chile cure, in northern Nigerian bush veterinary medicine, there is a disease of cattle and horses called *chizol*. The patient's hard, black tongue is scarified and treated with a mixture of chile powder, *natron*, and soot.

Swollen gums are treated with masticated chiles by the Kallawaya herbalists of the Andes in Peru. Similarly, gum infections are treated with crushed chile pods in the state of Veracruz, Mexico. The Kallawayas also treat toothache by placing a chile seed on the sore tooth, while the Mayna Jivaros of Peru apply the broken or crushed pods directly to sore teeth. Also in the Peruvian Amazon, chiles are a gen-

eral dental analgesic for any kind of mouth or tooth pain, while the leaves are used to treat toothache in China and Southeast Asia. Interestingly enough, commercial dental poultices contain capsicum (probably small amounts of oleoresin capsicum), sassafras root, hops, and benzocaine. A drop or two of tincture of capsicum applied on a cotton swab was recommended as a remedy for toothache by the Dublin Medical Press in 1850.

Moving slightly downward, we find that one of the most common bush medicine chile treatments involves the throat—both externally and internally. External applications include a rub of macerated pods in Cuba for sore throat and laryngitis, and the super-hot *malagueta* chiles are crushed and used as a throat rub in Brazil for similar ailments. A poultice of crushed pods is applied to the throat to treat tonsilitis in Peru.

For general throat soreness, there are a large number of chile cures: leaf tea is gargled in Trinidad, while pod tea is used in Argentina, Jamaica, and Honduras. Pepper tea is also very popular with the Tarahumara Indians of northern Mexico. In India, a chile pepper tea is strongly recommended for what is descriptively called "putrid sore throat." The classic Mayan cure for sore throat was to combine honey, crushed chiles, and tobacco leaf and swallow it. Inflamed tonsils and swollen throat are treated by drinking the extremely pungent juice of *locoto* or *rocoto* chiles in Bolivia. This is reportedly a horribly painful cure, but one that always works. There are a number of sore throat cures combining cayenne and other herbs. The effectiveness of chiles on sore throat probably involves the depletion of substance P (a neurotransmitter that sends pain signals to the brain). (See Medicinal Uses; Taste and Flavor.)

Other ailments are treated by applying chiles to the throat. In northern New Mexico, swollen glands in the throat are treated by boiling a dry red chile until soft, then applying it as a poultice. In Jamaica, whooping cough is treated with "bird" or Scotch bonnet chiles that are crushed with salt and the root of mimosa trees and used as a throat swab. In some parts of Africa, garlic with a chile-water mixture is said to be a cure for laryngitis, while in India, hoarseness is treated with a lozenge made from chile powder, sugar, and an herb called *tragacanth* (*astralagus* species). One of the more perplexing cures comes from Peru and illustrates our early comment about chiles sometimes being a cause and cure of the same malady. There, chile pod tea is said to cure hiccups—which is a direct contradiction, because hot chiles are known to cause hiccups.

Topical and Sometimes Tropical Cures

As we combed dozens and dozens of books on medicinal plants and folk medicine searching for chile pepper citations, one of the most frequent references we found were those linking chile peppers to the treatment of skin problems of all kinds. Generally speaking, chiles are commonly thought to be rubefacients, treatments that bring blood to the skin when applied externally. (Some experts say they are not true rubefacients because the skin is not reddened enough after their application.) Thus they are used as a treatment for frostbite in China, and their blood-drawing capabilities probably play a role in many of the herbal skin cures below. Also, in general, eating chiles causes gustatory perspiration, which in turn causes the body to cool off. In many tropical countries, large amounts of chiles are eaten during extremely hot weather to induce sweating; such a "cure" is common, for example, among the East Indian population in Trinidad.

Chile in various forms is believed to be efficacious in treating minor skin problems. For example, chile powder is a cure for itching in Peru and for pimples and scabies, a disease of the skin caused by mites, in Indonesia. In Venezuela, a poultice of leaves is placed on boils and pimples. Similarly, in the Philippines, chile leaves are pounded with lime juice and used as a poultice to reduce swelling and to cure skin ulcers. A combination of the pods and leaves is used to treat boils in Fiji, the Cook Islands, and Tonga in the Pacific Ocean. In Tonga, for example, the pods and leaves are crushed together with the hands and spread over a skin inflammation called *kolokula*. A similar treatment in The Bahamas is placed on a boil to draw it to a head, while in Venezuela, powdered chiles are mixed with animal fat and spread over boils. Paprika plasters are used to banish boils in Hungary while in parts of Africa ringworm (a fungal disease) is thought to be cured by the juice of hot chiles. Also in Africa, an ointment made with concentrated chile juice extracted from the hottest pods is used to treat skin infections of all kinds.

When an insect bites or stings you in the garden, what do you do? Pick some chile pods and apply them to the wound immediately, of course. Freshly crushed chile pods are applied to insect bites in Peru, and poultices of dried, toasted chile powder are also used to treat beestings, spider bites, and scorpion stings in that country. The poultices are sometimes coated with honey before being applied. In a similar fashion, chiles are used to reduce the swelling and "draw out the poison" of beestings among the Pueblo Indians in New Mexico, a practice identical to methods applied in Southeast Asia to treat insect stings and bites of all kinds.

There are reports out of Colombia and India that chiles are used to draw out the venom of poisonous snake bites; however, we'd place bets on the cobras' and bushmasters' venom being triumphant in these circumstances. Also, we read a report of chile powder being applied to crocodile bites in India, but we feel that such a bite is more akin to a severe wound than a sting, which brings up chile usage in wounds of all kinds.

We ran across many instances of open wounds treated by chile powder to stop bleeding, and chile leaves are generally regarded in folk medicine to be antibiotic. In fact, the leaves, pounded with shark oil, castor oil, or lard, are a poultice for wounds and sores in Trinidad and other parts of the West Indies, including Curaçao and Jamaica.

Paprika powder has been sprinkled on wounds in Hungary for centuries to stop bleeding and as a disinfectant, and cayenne has long been used as a styptic for minor cuts in England. Many varieties of hot chiles are used in the same manner along the U.S.–Mexico border for razor cuts in particular, which brings up images of switchblade fights in bordertown bars that end with the combatants dousing themselves with salsa to stop the bleeding. In Peru, dried crushed chiles are mixed with white corn flour and vegetable oil to treat wounds; this same remedy is used in Bolivia to cure boils. Hispanics in California split a long chile pod, boil it, and use it as a poultice for swollen glands or to draw out pus from an infected sore.

But as usual in the world of chiles as a medical treatment, stranger skin ailments are treated with Capsicums. Chile powder poultices were a powerful treatment used against gangrene by the Cherokee Indians of the United States The Kallawaya herbalists of the Andes treat facial paralysis by rubbing the inside skin of a chile on the inflicted area. Aches and pains from colds and arthritis are also treated this way.

In northern New Mexico, infected sores on the fingers and toes are treated with a sequence of rehydrated red chile pods until the pus is drawn out; tumors and cancers are treated with crushed chiles mixed with tallow in Venezuela. Also in Venezuela, in a bizarre cure, lumbago is treated by the people of Elmina by making cuts in the shoulders of the patient and rubbing chile powder and lime juice into the wounds!

Indian Ayurvedic medicine calls for the entire chile plant—leaves, pods, stems, branches, and roots—to be boiled in milk and applied to swellings and tumors on the skin. And where else but India would the fumes from chiles roasting on smoldering cow dung cakes be used in the treatment of scabies? Such usage recalls the use of chile smoke as a fumigant for vermin.

Fevers, Diseases, and the Lungs

In many cultures throughout the world, such as Russia, where the pods are a diaphoretic, chiles in various forms are used to treat colds and fevers. For treatment of the common cold and fevers in general among the Mano people of Liberia, the root of *suo longo* (*Ethulia conysoides*) is chopped into small pieces, three hot chile peppers are added, and the mixture is boiled in a few cups of water. The concoction is removed from the heat and is allowed to steep all night. In the morning, a half teaspoon of salt is added, and one cup is consumed. This cure is also considered to be a cathartic and diuretic. Salt also appears with crushed chiles among the Indians of the Vichada area of Colombia as a general tonic known as *yuquitania*.

Chile powder is commonly used to relieve general fever in Paraguay and malarial fevers in Jamaica and Costa Rica. Incidentally, the people of the Tapanti region of Costa Rica supposedly cured *conquistadores* of their fevers, and that was how the Spanish learned of the healing powers of peppers.

In Jamaica and other parts of the Caribbean, a concoction called *mandram* is believed to prevent attacks of malaria. It is made with cucumbers, onions, lime juice, and chile powder.

We would be remiss if we didn't mention the external use of Capsicums to relieve some of the same maladies. In Mexico, to relieve fevers, the head is washed with a pepper leaf tea, while the Cherokee Indians utilized chile powder poultices placed on the feet to relieve fevers.

More serious diseases than colds have also been treated with chile pepper concoctions in folk medicine. A treatment for flu in Peru is to eat large quantities of chiles with *chicha*, corn beer, primarily to induce sweating and "break" a fever. Chile powder was an early treatment for typhus and dropsy in India, when mixed with "Peruvian bark," presumably quinine. Also in India, a decoction of chile pods with opium and asafetida was used as a cure for cholera, and tincture of Capsicum was used against malarial fevers, although we found no connection with quinine with that usage. Other diseases treated with chiles include plague, where the Luo tribe of Africa applies the pepper leaf to the bubo; cholera, malaria, and scarlet fever are treated by the simple consumption of chile pods in the Malay Peninsula.

Although chile powder is notorious for causing sneezing and coughing among those who inhale it, there is anecdotal evidence of the use of Capsicums in breathing and lung problems. For example, chile powder is used as a snuff when breathing is difficult among the Amazonian Indians around the Rio Apaporis.

The Aztec remedy for cough was to eat large amounts of chiles to eliminate mucus and a similar usage occurs in modern-day Veracruz, Mexico, with chiles as a decongestant. A chile soup was often the food used. It is well known that eating chiles causes gustatory rhinitis, which is a technical term for a runny nose. The ancient Maya treated asthma and "white phlegm" by combining five chile pods and a little salt in a pan and boiling it well. It was put out "in the dew until dawn." Then it was reheated and drunk as a tea before breakfast.

Pepper leaf tea is used in Trinidad and Honduras to treat asthma, coughs, and chest colds, while Hispanics in California eat chile to prevent tuberculosis. The Tarahumara Indians of northern Mexico use chiltepin tea to fight bronchitis, and an infusion of crushed chiles is a cure for cough in Venezuela.

Red Hot Muscles and Joints

One of the banes of mankind is back pain, but of course, there are herbal chile cures for this condition. Hispanics in California split a long green chile pod in half lengthwise, boil it, and place it on the back as a counterirritant to "neutralize" back pain. In Indian Ayurvedic medicine, a plaster of chile powder with garlic, black pepper, and an herb called *silaras* (*Storax officinalis*) is applied to the back for relief of crippling pain.

A decoction of leaves and roots is placed in a hot bath to relieve general body aches and pains in Paraguay, and according to Whitelaw Ainslie, M.D., in his 1826 book, *Materia Indica,* "With hog lard, Capsicum forms a good liniment for paralytic limbs."

There are many chile folk cures associated with relieving the conditions of rheumatism. Peruvians massage areas sore from rheumatism with chile powder, as do Hawaiians. Tinctures and liniments made with chiles are used in Peru, while the pods are macerated in alcohol and used as a rub for rheumatism, lumbago, and sciatica in Paraguay. A poultice of pods is applied to sore areas in Honduras, while a lotion made from the pods is used for rheumatism relief in Southeast Asia. In American Indian lore, chiles are soaked in vinegar, and a cloth steeped in the liquid is applied to the aching area.

In Bolivia, freshly ground *locoto* or *rocoto* chiles are mixed with the bark of *uña de gato,* or cat claw, and used as a poultice on the afflicted area. A black cloth is wrapped around the poultice and is left on for three days. Similarly, poultices of leaves and crushed pods are a common treatment for rheumatism, lumbago, and "unbroken chilblains" in Africa and in Jamaica and Trinidad, where the leaves are used more than the pods for rheumatism relief.

A fascinating rheumatism treatment by the Mano people of Liberia calls for making a rubbing chalk from common white clay or preferably the clay from the mushroom-shaped anthills that are the nests of the termites *Termes mordax.* The clay is mixed with water, lime leaves, and the seed of *suo,* or chile peppers, as well as the seed of *xylopia* species, called "spice" by the Liberians. The chalk is made into cones and is dried in the shade. The afflicted area is wetted and the chalk is rubbed onto it.

Jules Rengade, in his book *Las Plantas que Curan* (1887), wrote that a paper made from chile pepper extract in Spain was called Lardy paper. Crushed hot chiles were spread over absorbent paper and allowed to dry. It was then applied to the skin and the effect was similar to that of a mustard plaster. The skin would begin to heat up and the pain would diminish. Lardy paper was also used to treat sciatica, lumbago, bronchitis, and neuralgia.

Surprisingly, although arthritis pain is commonly treated with capsaicin cream today, we did not come across very many folk remedies for the condition involving chiles. However, from our friend Lorenzo Fritz, we learned of an unusual treament in Bolivia. Arthritis pain is treated there with automobile grease mixed with finely ground hot *ají* chiles. The salve is placed on the sore spot, is wrapped in black cloth, and is left on for three days.

Spicy Assistance for Women

In many cases, the chile folk remedies for treating women are highly anecdotal and we don't know precisely how the chiles are used. For example, we read that the juice from pepper leaves "stimulates childbirth" in Indonesian villages, yet details of the usage are unavailable.

On the other hand, some remedies are quite specific. In his 1931 volume, *The Ethno-Botany of the Maya*, Ralph Roys noted that delayed childbirth is treated by preparing a drink that contains crushed chile peppers, juice from a *jicara* gourd, water from the house, and water from the well. Less specific is the cure to hasten childbirth from the Andokes of the northwest Amazon, which calls for crushed chile pods mixed with the flowers of a species of the genus *Urtica*; apparently, the medicine is applied directly to the vagina, which would cause intense burning. Perhaps the simplest chile aid to induce childbirth comes from Sonora, Mexico, where powdered chiltepins are inhaled by overdue pregnant women to induce sneezing, which then induces childbirth. After giving birth, Guatemalan Indian women use a drink of chile powder and water as purge, and in African folk medicine, a poultice is made from the ground chile pods, kaolin, and bark of *Newbouldia laevis* as a postpartum medication.

Hispanic nursing mothers in California and other Western states avoid eating chiles while they are nursing for fear that their milk will become too hot and their babies will suffer from eating less of it. However, when it comes time to wean babies, many cultures depend on chiles. The Shushufinidi Indian mothers of the northwest Amazon smear pepper juice on their nipples to wean their babies, while the Navajo and Ramah Navajo mothers of New Mexico rub red chile powder on their nipples for the same purpose, as do Indians of various tribes in Arizona and Sonora, Mexico.

Chiles as Stomachics and Beyond

Here is another instance where chiles are seen as a cure for the very conditions they are rumored to cause: stomach problems. "Taken moderately, chile helps and comforts the stomach for digestion," wrote José de Acosta, the Jesuit priest and historian, in 1590, which is probably the first written indication of the use of chile as a stomachic, or digestive tonic.

In our research of worldwide chile folk cures, it was soon evident that chile pods were of great value in appetite enhancement. They are consumed for that purpose by the East Indian community of Trinidad, and the same usage is reported in Russia, Jamaica, and The Bahamas. In herbal medicine, cayenne has long been reputed to stimulate gastric juices.

Cayenne also is used as a cure in England for seasickness, which is a severe form of indigestion. In Southeast Asia, a decoction of the leaves is drunk to combat upset stomach, but in most parts of the world it is the pods that are used for this purpose. "Bird peppers," also known as chiltepins, are swallowed whole in Trinidad and Sonora, Mexico, to combat indigestion, while in Russia, the pods are steeped in —what else?—vodka before being swallowed.

Teas and pills for stomach disorders also contain chiles. A tea made from dried chile pods is used in Ecuador to treat stomach pains and colic, while in Ayurvedic medicine, a pill made from chile powder, ginger, and rhubarb is used to combat severe indigestion. The Bribri Indians of Costa Rica drink a root decoction of chile plants as a bitter tonic to overcome colic or stomach discomfort due to overeating. Some sources state that the root of chile plants is toxic, and that the current Maya Indians in the Yucatán Peninsula use it for deliberate poisoning.

Remember chiles being used as a vermifuge? Well, they are used internally for that purpose as well. In Mexican villages, jalapeño leaves and flowers are consumed in an infusion to eliminate worms, and in the French Antilles, dried pepper leaves mixed with milk are drunk in the morning on an empty stomach as a cure for internal parasites.

Chiles have long been reputed to cause ulcers but once again are used as a treatment for them. "Cayenne rebuilds the tissue in the stomach and heals stomach and intestinal ulcers," wrote Diane Robertson in *Jamaican Herbs* (1982). Her view is upheld by Bolivian Indians who suffer from stomach ulcers. In what is probably an extremely painful treatment, the ulcerous patients are fed fresh *locoto* chiles (*Capsicum pubescens*), one of the hottest varieties in the world. For fourteen to eighteen days, patients are fed the chiles, beginning with one the first day, two the second day, and so on until they are cured. It is difficult to imagine consuming eighteen of these chiles raw in a single day.

What goes in must come out, so we would be remiss if we didn't quote Diane Robertson again, who wrote: "Cayenne produces natural warmth and stimulates the peristalic motion of the intestines, aiding in assimilation and elimination." She adds ominously, "It can be hot, going in and coming out for the first three days." This condition, well known to lovers of red chile who live in New Mexico, has been dubbed "jaloproctitis." No wonder chiles are considered to be a purge by the Guatemalan Indians!

Chiles may sometimes burn upon elimination, but they are reputed to cure a number of bowel disorders. The raw pods are consumed to fight flatulence among Amazonian Indians along the Rio Apaporis in Brazil; the same cure is used in many parts of Africa. In India, pills made of chile powder, rhubarb, aloe, and ginger, in equal parts, are taken as a carminative, to expel gases from the stomach and intestines.

Natives of the state of Sonora in Mexico not only treat indigestion with wild chiltepins, they eat them whole to treat diarrhea, which of course, chile is reputed to cause. But perhaps they don't use chiltepins for chiltepin-induced diarrhea. In Gold Coast, Africa, the fruits of the *nsatea* chile are crushed and mixed with lime juice to make an enema to cure constipation. In Senegal, the long, hot *foronto* chile is a remedy for piles.

The ancient Maya treated a condition known as "yellow stools" (dysentery) by combining nine chile pods with the seed of the yellow fruit *Mammea americana* (a mamey), together with the bark of *Spondeas lutea*. These are all mashed together and then soaked in—get ready—urine, overnight. The afflicted person drinks the concoction with chocolate or wine and the yellow stools will cease.

Heating Up Your Hemorrhoids

One of the most pervasive uses of chiles we found at this end of the body was as a treatment for hemorrhoids. We know it sounds excruciating, but here's the story. In 1956, L. Stevenel, a French Army officer, noted an interesting medicinal usage of chiles in Africa. Writing in *The Bulletin of the Society of Exotic Pathology*, Stevenel attributed the absence of varicose veins and hemorrhoids in the natives to the constant use of red chiles in their diets.

"Native workers on the railroad always carry a supply with them and consider them as a panacea necessary for good health," he wrote. Stevenel claimed that he had cured his own hemorrhoid problem and that of his fellow officers by adding red chile pulp to their food. The cure worked quickly—in a matter of days—but only with red chiles; green chiles were ineffective. Although Stevenel did not state why red chiles worked and green did not, we suspect the reason could be connected with the high concentration of vitamin A in red chiles.

Chile as an internal cure for hemorrhoids is used all over the world. In Cuba and Guadeloupe, for example, the pods are eaten in salads to combat hemorrhoids. In Argentina and Cuba, powdered chiles are mixed with honey and made into pills to treat hemorrhoids, and tinctures of chiles are taken internally for hemorrhoids and flatulence in Venezuela. However, we were surprised to find so many external cures. Crushed chiles are used as a rub for hemorrhoids in Colombia. In Peru, the leaves and the pods are macerated together and applied to the hemorrhoids.

These days, Dr. Richard A. Wright, chief of the gastroenterology/hepatology division of the department of medicine at the University of Louisville, is designing a trial study to examine the association of chile peppers and hemorrhoidal symptoms. He is just one of hundreds of researchers who are investigating the healing powers of peppers as used by folk practitioners.

➤ *Foronto.* Term for chile pepper in Senegal.

FRUTESCENS *SPECIES*

The Tabasco chile is the best-known variety of this species, being the primary ingredient in the famous sauce by the same name that is now more than 125 years old. Another famous variety is the *malagueta*, which grows wild in the Amazon Basin in Brazil, where the species probably originated. Curiously, there are not as many names for the wild varieties as there are for some other species, the most common name being "bird peppers." No domesticated *frutescens* has ever been found in an archaeological site in Central or South America, but ethnobotanists speculate the domestication site was probably Panama and from there it spread to Mexico and the Caribbean.

At any rate, we know the Tabasco variety of *frutescens* was being cultivated near Tabasco, Mexico, in the early 1840s because it was transferred to Louisiana in 1848,

where it was eventually grown to produce Tabasco sauce. Demand outstripped supply, and today Tabascos are commercially grown in Central America and Colombia and shipped in mash form to Louisiana.

In Louisiana, Tabasco peppers fell victim to the tobacco etch virus, but were rescued in 1970 with the introduction of 'Greenleaf Tabasco,' a TEV-resistant variety. Today at Avery Island, the site of the original Tabasco-growing and -manufacturing operation, there are still fields of Tabasco under cultivation—but mostly for crop improvement and seed production.

Some varieties of *frutescens* found their way to India and the Far East, where they are still called "bird peppers." There they are cultivated to make hot sauces and curries. *Capsicum frutescens* plants have a compact habit, an intermediate number of stems, and grow between one and four feet high, depending on climate and growing conditions. The leaves are ovate, smooth, and measure two and a half inches long and two inches wide.

Tabasco chiles. DAVE DEWITT

The flowers have greenish-white corollas with no spots and purple anthers. The pods are borne erect and measure up to one and a half inches long and three-eighths inch wide. Immature pods are yellow or green, maturing to bright red. The *frutescens* species is quite hot, measuring between 30,000 and 50,000 Scoville Units.

The height of the plants depends on climate, with the plants growing the largest in warmer parts of the country. The plant is particularly good for container gardening, and one of our specimens lived as a perennial for four years in a pot, but gradually lost vigor and produced fewer pods each year. A single plant can produce 100 or more pods.

The species *C. frutescens* and *C. pubescens* have fewer pod shapes, sizes, and colors than *C. annuum*, *C. chinense*, and *C. baccatum*. No one knows the real reason for this. One must remember that the diversity of pod morphology is human-guided. In other words, the differences one sees in pod size and shape and because humans conscientiously made choices on which pods to save for the next growing season. In nature, wild chile plants usually have small red, erect fruits that drop off easily. The small fruit and easy fruit drop traits are beneficial for bird dispersal. However, humans prefer large fruit and fruit that stays attached to the plant until harvested. Thus, under domestication these traits are modified.

The *C. frutescens* plant has small fruits that drop off easily. Therefore, an explanation for the lack of fruit shapes in *C. frutescens* is that it is still mostly a wild form. It is found growing in the same areas as *C. annuum* and *C. chinense*, so selection may have been on *C. annuum* and *C. chinense*, while *C. frutescens* had little or no selection.

The most common use for the pods is making hot sauces; they are crushed, salted, fermented, and combined with vinegar. However, the pods can be used fresh in salsas and can be dried for adding to stir-fry dishes.

Fukien rice. Extremely pungent chile pepper grown in China.

Funtua. Principal chile grown in Nigeria.

Furtu. Name for peppers in French Guiana.

HOMEMADE "TABASCO" SAUCE

Because the Tabasco chiles are not aged in oak barrels for three years, this will be only a rough approximation of the famous McIlhenny product. This recipe calls for fresh Tabasco, so you will have to grow your own or substitute dried ones that have been rehydrated. Other small, hot, fresh red chiles, such as piquins, can also be substituted for the Tabascos. Note that this recipe requires advance preparation.

MAKES 2 CUPS
HEAT SCALE: **Hot**

1 pound fresh red Tabasco chiles, chopped
2 cups distilled white vinegar

2 teaspoons salt

Combine the chiles and the vinegar in a saucepan over medium-low heat. Stir in the salt and simmer for 5 minutes. Remove from the heat, cool, and place in a blender. Puree until smooth, strain, and place in a glass jar. Allow to steep for 2 weeks in the refrigerator.

Strain the sauce again, and adjust the consistency by adding more vinegar if necessary. The sauce keeps indefinitely in the refrigerator.

Gachupín. Name for piquin chile in Veracruz, Mexico.

GARDENING

Hundreds of articles and at least one book — *The Pepper Garden* — have been written on the home and commercial cultivation of the Capsicums, so there's far too much information available for us to go into great detail in this section. This is designed as a basic gardening guide for beginners using organic techniques.

The Strategy

The combination of the long growing times of the increasingly popular exotic chile varieties and the medium to short growing seasons in many parts of North America forces many gardeners to examine their strategy. In order to get the maximum number of peppers from these potentially prolific varieties, the plants need enough time to produce and ripen up the pods. That often means extending the natural growing season at the front end, the back end, or both.

Starting Seeds

To stretch the beginning of the pepper growing season, start the plants indoors around January or February (January if the garden is in the North; February in the South). Plant the pepper seeds in "recycled" plastic six-packs (from plants bought at nurseries) filled with a loose seed-starting mix. Plant far more seeds than the actual number of plants needed for the garden,

Labeled seedlings in the greenhouse. DAVE DEWITT

Chile plants mulched with newspaper. DAVE DEWITT

thinning out the weakest plants later, and perhaps even planting a few of the extra seedlings in pots that can be moved back indoors come fall.

After sowing the seeds in the premoistened seed-starting mix, set the six-packs (or seed-starting flat or pots or whatever) on a source of bottom heat (such as a heating cable, a seed-starting mat, or the top of the refrigerator) to boost germination. Cover the setup loosely with plastic to retain moisture, spritz the surface lightly with tepid water every day if it seems dry, and then, after the seeds have sprouted, remove the plastic and move the containers someplace where the seedlings will receive plenty of bright light — either the sill of a super-bright, clean window; very close to a four-tube fluores-

cent fixture; or under some high-intensity grow lights.

The pepper plants will grow more foliage and flowers (and therefore more fruit) if the seedlings are prevented from becoming rootbound, when the roots are cramped. So either start them in large containers or transplant them into increasingly larger pots, starting when the seedlings hit the four-leaf stage. Then, when the seedlings are finally transplanted outside, their roots will be vigorous and spread out and the plants will get off to a running start.

Pests

A couple of pests do go after pepper seedlings — aphids especially like to attack young plants indoors. Fight these little pests with fire by knocking the aphids off the seedlings with a spray mixture of soapy water and chile powder. To make it, add about one half to one teaspoon of the hottest, most finely ground chile powder to a quart of ready-made insecticidal soap solution (mixed according to the label) or to a quart of water containing two drops of dishwashing soap, well mixed.

The other "pest" most known for its tendency to damage pepper seedlings (and thus reducing potential yields) is a cat, who will graze on your pepper seedlings if

Rows of habanero plants, Texas Hill Country. DAVE DEWITT

he/she has the chance, so keep the six-packs and seedling tray out of reach.

Transplanting

Soon the pampered peppers will be moved from the protected sanctuary of the home or greenhouse into the brutal spring environment of high winds, low temperatures, and bright light. To toughen the seedlings' stems so that they can withstand those outdoor winds, place them in front of a fan for three to seven days before they are scheduled to go outside. Keep the fan on day and night at a setting that's just high enough for a moderate breeze. Don't blow the seedlings over—just create some good air circulation.

Then sometime around the last frost date, begin to further prepare the seedlings for their move outdoors by "hardening them off": Place the seedlings outside for increasing periods of time each day—even overnight if a nice warm spell hits—over a one- to two-week period.

Preparing the Plot

While hardening off those seedlings, prepare their future garden site. They'll grow best in raised beds in most regions, and in sunken beds in dry climates. The pepper garden should ideally be located somewhere that peppers haven't grown for several years to help prevent disease problems. Admittedly, a strict crop rotation is hard to do in a small garden, but a pepper planting can at least follow a spring crop of peas. Try not to grow peppers in the same spot two years in a row.

Dig some compost or aged manure into the pepper bed before planting. This will be all the nutrition the peppers will need for the growing season to come. Use aged (not fresh) manure to ensure against nitrogen overdose, which can cause low yields. There have been cases of six-foot-tall jalapeño plants with plenty of foliage but no pods on them because the grower fed them too much nitrogen too fast.

If growing peppers in the North (or anyplace where the ground is chilly), warm up the soil by covering it with black plastic for a few days before the planting. Don't pull up this "mulch" later on; leave it right where it is and plant the peppers in holes cut into the plastic—this will keep the soil warm, decrease the water needs, and prevent weeds.

When planting, use only the healthiest and most vigorous seedlings. Leggy, stunted, or aphid-damaged plants will not recover sufficiently to fulfill their yield potential. Space the seedlings about six to twelve inches apart. Many garden guidelines suggest a 12-inch spacing between pepper plants, but smaller-podded varieties can easily be squeezed into a six-inch space.

But don't plant all of the seedlings in the ground. Save some of the plants for growing in containers outside, so the pots can be moved indoors to a brightly lit area when the weather turns cool in the fall.

The newly transplanted peppers will need as much warmth as they can get. Protect the peppers from low temperatures by covering the plants with a floating row cover, such as Reemay. Some gardeners surround their seedlings with water-filled inner tubes or Wallo'Waters (flexible plastic tubes arranged in a circle that are filled with water; they're sold at garden centers, nurseries, and by mail order). The water absorbs heat from the sun during the day, and then holds onto that heat after temperatures start to cool. Overnight, the water releases that heat, keeping the soil and air around the seedlings nice and warm. Another warm-water technique is to fill several gallon-sized plastic milk jugs with water and bury them halfway in the ground next to each seedling (be careful not to disturb the plant's roots when digging).

The Growing Season

When summer arrives, weeds may try to seize control of the pepper patch. Prevent them at all costs. Weeds not only look ugly, they can harbor pests like leafhoppers, which spread curly top virus to pepper plants (which happened with devastating effect throughout New Mexico in 1995). So keep those hoppers homeless by making the garden weed-free.

For gardeners who live in warm zones, the summer sun can be more of a hindrance than a help to getting high yields. Intense sunlight can actually cook peppers (a problem called sunscald) and decrease the yield of usable fruits. If gardening in a high-altitude region with intense sunlight, shade the peppers by covering the plants with shade netting (available at garden centers or by mail order). Rig up a makeshift frame over the peppers and drape the shade cloth over this frame so it remains easy to tend the peppers under their "tent." Varieties such as habaneros and *rocotos* are especially prone to sunscald—and both perform and yield better under the netting than they do in open, unshaded plots.

During the hottest days of July and August, pepper plants can lose a lot of water through their leaves. When this occurs, the leaves wilt and the flowers (and sometimes fruit) drop right off the plants. Reduce this water loss by boosting the humidity around the plants with a thick layer of mulch such as dried grass clippings (placed over top of the plastic mulch, if using it).

Once the plants start producing their peppers, there's another little trick to use to maximize the yields—at least with the pepper varieties that are eaten green, such as jalapeños, serranos, and the New Mexican varieties. Increase the total yield of these varieties by continually picking the peppers when they reach their largest "mature green" size, and not waiting for them to fully ripen on the plant. When a pepper plant reaches its "fruit load" (the maximum weight of peppers the plant can support), it will stop flowering and fruiting even though there may be a month or more left in the growing season. Removing the mature green fruits signals the plant to continue flowering and setting fruit throughout the remainder of the season—and the result is more pods per plant.

Harvesttime

Often, the first frost of the year does not signal the end of the growing season. The early frost is followed by an "Indian Summer" that brings enough warm weather to keep peppers growing for another three or four weeks. But to make use of this extended season, it is necessary to cover the plants. There are many good crop protectors—cotton bedsheets, clear or black plastic, nylon netting, plastic row covers, even large cardboard boxes placed over individual plants. The material should be thick and dense enough to retain ground heat, but not so thick that it will break off branches if it gets weighted down by rain or snow.

Place the covers in position as early in the day as possible, say between 4 and 6 P.M. on the evening of the frost—so that there's still some heat to retain (it gets cool fast at night in the fall). And be sure to remove such covers as soon as it's warm enough the following day.

If the temperature is going to drop below 28°F, though, the covering efforts will probably not be enough to protect the plants from the cold. But there are other plants, those peppers that have been growing in pots. Move them indoors before the first frost, and the plants will overwinter (survive the winter) nicely. If there are not any peppers in pots, dig up a few of the healthiest favorites in the garden (don't dig up a struggler hoping it'll recover inside—it won't), pot them in soil that drains well, and move them inside. These plants may drop most of their leaves over the winter, but most will survive and come back strong—especially if you prune them in the spring, cutting off any branches that look dead and brown, rather than green. The plants will sprout new growth vigorously after such a pruning, even if you cut them back severely.

Gardeners can even make this indoor overwintering and spring pruning a perennial event, because peppers are perennials when grown in frost-free conditions. Wintered-over pepper plants need regular watering, but unless you are actively growing them by providing artificial light, there is no need to fertilize them until they resume growing in the spring. (See Harvesting and Processing.)

◢ *Goan.* A variety of *annuum* grown in Goa, India, that resembles a pointed *cascabel*.

◢ **Goat pepper.** Local name for the *chinense* species in The Bahamas and some parts of Africa.

◢ *Gril koreni.* In the Czech Republic, a dry rub composed of mild paprika, salt, and spices.

◢ *Guaguao.* Term for piquin chiles in Cuba.

◢ *Guajillo.* A common chile in northern and central Mexico, it resembles a small dried red New Mexican chile. It is used primarily in sauces. Grown primarily in Zacatecas, Durango, and Aguascalientes.

◢ *Güero.* "Blonde"; a generic term for yellow chiles in Mexico. (See *Xcatic*.) Other terms are *carrocillo*, *cristal*, and *cristalino*.

◢ **Guinea pepper.** Thought to be of the *chinense* species, it is grown in Nigeria, Liberia, and the Ivory Coast. Introduced into England in 1548.

◢ *Gulasove koreni.* In the Czech Republic, a spice mixture for goulashes composed of hot paprika, salt, caraway seeds, and other spices.

◢ **'Guntur Red.'** A variety of *annuum* that is named for Guntur, reputedly the chile capital of India. It resembles a dried red jalapeño.

HABANEROS

This section concerns the culinary aspects of habaneros. History and varieties are covered in the entry *Chinense* Species.

Flavor Elements

American chefs and cookbook authors love to wax poetic about the unique flavor of the fresh habanero relatives. Chef Mark Miller described fresh habaneros as having "tropical fruit tones that mix well with food containing tropical fruits or tomatoes," and Scotch bonnets as possessing a "fruity and smoky flavor." Cookbook author Steven Raichlen agreed, describing the Scotch bonnets as "floral, aromatic, and almost smoky." As far as the dried habaneros were concerned, Miller detected "tropical fruit flavors of coconut and papaya, a hint of berry, and an intense, fiery acidic heat."

The Heat Level

Although the species is renowned for the high heat level of its pods, we should remember that all heat levels are found in the *chinense* species, from zero to the hottest ever measured. The typical commercial habanero averages between 80,000 and 150,000 Scoville Units but has great variability depending upon climate and stress. In a series of experiments at New Mexico State University, Dr. Paul Bosland and Peggy Collins tested the same variety of *chinense*, an orange habanero from Yucatán, grown under different conditions. In 1992, grown outside in a field, the pods measured 357,992 Scoville Units. The same variety, grown in the greenhouse, measured 260,825 Scoville Units. The variability of pungency approached 30 percent, which illustrates the role played by the environment in the heat levels of chile peppers. Regarding the heat levels, because habaneros and their relatives are being used, cooks can assume that the recipes are hot. Of course, the heat level can be adjusted by varying the number of habaneros used, or by increasing the amounts of the other ingredients in the recipes.

Cooks can also remove the seeds and placental tissue, to decrease the heat of the habaneros. Cooks should also remember that the habaneros themselves vary in heat, so it's a good idea to taste-test the habaneros first by placing a tiny sliver on the tongue and then chewing it up.

Handling

Since habaneros have the highest concentration of capsaicin, they are the most dangerous in terms of burns. For people sensitive to capsaicin, it can cause contact dermatitis just like poison ivy. It is particularly dangerous when it comes into contact with sensitive body parts like the eyes.

It is not merely enough to wear gloves when handling habaneros. The gloves and the cutting board used to chop them should be cleaned with bleach and a strong dish detergent to avoid moving the capsaicin to other surfaces where it might be transferred accidentally to the eyes. Cooks talented with knives have learned how to clean and chop a habanero without touching it with the fingers.

If you should get capsaicin in your eyes, immediately flush them with water or an eyewash. The pain will be intense, but it will soon go away. Should your fingers or hands burn from capsaicin contact, the best treatment is to submerge them in vegetable oil.

Preserving the Pods

The simplest preserving method is simply to wash and dry the pods and place them in a plastic bag in the freezer. They will lose some of their firmness when defrosted, but the flavor, heat, and aroma are all preserved. Habaneros can also be pureed with a little vinegar and the mixture will keep in the refrigerator for weeks.

Another common preservation method is drying the pods. They should be cut in half vertically, seeds removed, and placed in a food dehydrator. After they are thoroughly dried, they can be stored in jars, in plastic bags in the freezer, or ground into powders (be sure to wear a dust mask!). Drying does not affect the heat level of the pods, but pods that are rehydrated will lose some flavor and aroma.

Remember, sauces and salsas are a great way to utilize excess habaneros from the garden!

Habanero Substitutions and Products

Any of the habanero relatives can be substituted for any other—Scotch bonnets for datil peppers, for example. Other varieties of chiles can be used in place of habaneros, but why bother? There are many habanero products available in the marketplace, but the cook has to be resourceful. In addition to scouring gourmet shops and natural foods stores, cooks should explore Latin and Caribbean markets, and in some cases, Asian markets that carry Latin and Caribbean products.

Dried pods—These should be rehydrated for about a half hour in hot water and then drained before using. Smoked pods are also available, and they should also be rehydrated.

Powders—Generally speaking, use about one teaspoon powder for a single fresh pod.

Pickles—Usually West Indian in origin, these imports are used in two ways. The vinegar can be sprinkled over foods like a hot sauce, and the pods can be washed and used as a substitute for fresh pods.

Crushed or pureed habaneros—A highly concentrated form that sometimes has lime juice or vinegar added. One teaspoon substitutes for a single fresh pod.

Hot sauces—Generally speaking, about two teaspoons of a commercial habanero sauce will substitute for a single fresh pod.

BELIZEAN SPICY SALBUTES

These fried, puffed-up tortillas are common throughout the Yucatán Peninsula. Although usually served as an appetizer, we enjoyed ours in Belize as a lunch entree sprinkled with liberal doses of habanero hot sauce. These are probably the most common fast food found in the region.

MAKES 12 SERVINGS
HEAT SCALE: **Varies**

Tortillas
2 cups masa harina
¼ cup all-purpose flour
1 teaspoon salt
½ teaspoon baking powder
¾ cup water
3 cups vegetable oil for frying

Topping
2 chicken breasts, poached, skin removed, and
  shredded
1 small onion, thinly sliced
Shredded cabbage
Commercial habanero hot sauce

To make the tortillas, in a bowl, mix together the *masa*, flour, salt, and baking powder. Add the water, mixing well, using just enough to make a stiff dough. Let the dough sit for 5 minutes.

Pinch off pieces of dough to make 1-inch balls. Flatten them into tortillas about 4 inches in diameter. Coat a griddle with 1 tablespoon of the oil and heat over medium-high heat. Cook the tortillas on the griddle for 30 seconds a side, turning once. Add the remaining oil to a large sauce pan and heat to high. Fry each tortilla until it puffs, about 1 minute. Drain on paper towels.

Top the *salbutes* with the chicken, onion, and cabbage, and sprinkle with hot sauce.

HABANERO CRISPY FISH WITH CARAMELIZED ONION RELISH

In the Caribbean islands this dish might be made with the popular flying fish; substitute snapper or other whitefish such as bass, perch, or flounder. For a tamer version, omit the ground habanero. Note that this recipe requires advance preparation.

MAKES 4 TO 6 SERVINGS
HEAT SCALE: **Medium**

Crispy Fish

2 pounds red snapper fillets

2 limes, cut in half

1 tablespoon commercial habanero hot sauce or
   Habanero Hot Sauce—Belize-Style (page 159)

2 cloves garlic, minced

2 scallions, minced (white and green parts)

1 cup all-purpose flour

2 tablespoons cornstarch

1 teaspoon powdered ginger

1 teaspoon salt

½ teaspoon ground dried habanero chile

¼ teaspoon freshly ground white pepper

Vegetable oil for frying

1 large egg, beaten

Caramelized Onion Relish

1 tablespoon oil from frying fish

1 medium red onion, sliced

1 medium yellow onion, sliced

1 tablespoon honey

2 tablespoons red wine vinegar

2 tablespoons dry red wine (Cabernet or Merlot)

Rub the fish with the limes. In a small bowl, combine the hot sauce, garlic, and scallions and rub the mixture into the fish. Place the fish in a glass dish, cover, and let sit in the refrigerator for at least 2 hours. The fish can either be left whole or cut into "fingers" (strips).

In another bowl, combine the flour, cornstarch, ginger, salt, ground habanero, and white pepper in a bowl and blend well.

Pour the oil into a frying pan to a depth of 2 inches. Heat to 370°F. Dip the fish in the egg and then the flour mixture, shaking off any excess. Fry the fish in the hot oil until golden brown and crispy, about 10 minutes; remove from the heat and keep warm.

To make the relish, pour off all but 1 tablespoon of the oil. Cook the onions in the oil, stirring, until soft, about 5 minutes. Stir in the honey and continue to cook, stirring, until the onions have caramelized, about 5 minutes. Add the vinegar and wine and cook until the liquid is reduced by about one half, 7 to 8 minutes.

To serve, if the fish is whole, place it on a platter and top with the onions; if it is in fingers, place the fish on a bed of the onions.

SHRIMP FROM HELL
Camarones de Infierno

The key to this rather intense recipe is to always use fresh shrimp, never canned or frozen. It is usually served over rice or pasta, but can also be wrapped up in soft corn tacos with some chopped tomatoes and shredded lettuce or cabbage.

MAKES 2 TO 4 SERVINGS
HEAT SCALE: **Hot**

12 large fresh shrimp, peeled and deveined
2 tablespoons vegetable oil
4 cloves garlic, minced
1 teaspoon minced fresh habanero chile

1 teaspoon fresh lime juice
¼ cup white wine, such as Chardonnay
2 tablespoons butter
Chopped fresh cilantro for garnish

In a skillet over medium heat, cook the shrimp in the oil, tossing constantly, until they just turn pink, about 1 minute. Remove the shrimp and keep warm. Add the garlic, chile, lime juice, and wine to the skillet and cook, stirring constantly, for 2 minutes. Return the shrimp to the pan and cook, stirring, for 30 seconds.

Remove from the heat and add the butter a little at a time, stirring until an emulsion is formed, 2 to 3 minutes.

Serve over white rice with the cilantro as a garnish.

BRAZILIAN CHINENSE CHICKEN
Xin-Xin

This Brazilian dish reflects the African influence on the cuisine in Bahia. It is usually cooked with the *chinense* variety of chiles known as *pimenta do cheiro*.

Traditionally, this version of chicken in shrimp and nut sauce would use *dende* (palm) oil to add color, but since it is difficult to find and is loaded with saturated fat, we have substituted paprika. Note that this recipe requires advance preparation.

MAKES 4 TO 6 SERVINGS
HEAT SCALE: Medium

¼ cup fresh lemon juice

One 3- to 4-pound chicken, cut into serving pieces

1 onion, minced

3 cloves garlic, minced

¼ cup dried shrimp (available in Latin and Asian markets)

1 habanero chile, seeds and stem removed, minced

2 teaspoons grated fresh ginger

2 to 3 tablespoons olive oil

½ teaspoon paprika

1 large tomato, seeds removed, coarsely chopped

1 cup chicken broth

½ pound shrimp, shelled and deveined

2 tablespoons ground cashew nuts

2 tablespoons ground peanuts

Chopped fresh parsley for garnish

In a glass dish, sprinkle the lemon juice over the chicken and marinate, covered, for ½ hour.

In a skillet over medium heat, cook the onion, garlic, dried shrimp, habanero, and ginger in the oil, stirring, until the onions are soft, 3 to 5 minutes. Add the drained chicken pieces and cook, stirring, until browned, adding more oil if necessary, about 5 minutes.

Stir in the paprika, tomato, and broth. Reduce the heat to low, cover, and simmer until the chicken is done, 30 to 45 minutes. Add the shrimp and ground nuts, raise the heat slightly, and cook until the shrimp is done and the sauce is thickened, about 10 minutes. Garnish with the parsley and serve.

⌦ **Harissa.** A North African chile paste.

HARVESTING AND PROCESSING

Pepper gardening experts recommend the technique of staggered harvesting, which means that the chiles in the garden can be used for most of the growing season. Usually the first chiles available are those which are small and used green in fresh salsas—the serranos, jalapeños, and other varieties such as the habanero.

Some chiles, especially the New Mexican varieties, can be eaten or processed as soon as they are about four inches long, or they can be allowed to turn red before picking and drying. However, there are a few varieties that are generally used only in their dried state, such as cayenne and *santaka* chiles.

It is important to continue harvesting the ripe pods as they mature. If the pods are allowed to remain on the plant, few new ones will form, whereas if the pods are continuously harvested, the plants will produce greater numbers of chiles. The best time to pick chiles for drying is when they first start to turn red. This timing will stimulate the plant into further production and the harvested chiles can be strung to dry and will turn bright red.

Haphazard harvesting can result in waste, so careful planning is essential to ensure the maximum efficiency of the practical chile pepper patch. Choose pods that have smooth, shiny skins and are firm to the touch. A good rule to follow is that if the

Sorting habaneros, California. SUNBELT ARCHIVES

pod comes off the stem easily, the chile is ready. If you have to tug on the pod, it is too early to pick it. The small chiles do not have to be peeled or processed in any way before being used. They can be picked, washed, and used in any recipe.

Drying is the oldest and most common way to preserve chile pods and works well for most chiles—except the very meaty ones such as jalapeños, which are smoke-dried and called chipotle. For hundreds of years, New Mexicans have been stringing chiles onto *ristras* (strings) and hanging them in the sun to dry.

To dry chiles, select those that have turned red or another mature color. If the chile is picked before starting to turn, it is very unlikely that it will ever turn red. Avoid any pods that have black spots, since these will mold and rot. In warm, arid climates, string the chiles through the stem using a large needle and fishing monofilament, and hang until dry. In cool, moist climates, the best bet for drying chiles is to use a food dehydrator.

Dried chiles can be reconstituted in a variety of ways. They can be roasted very lightly on a griddle, fried in a little oil until they puff and reconstitute slightly, or soaked in hot water for 15 to 20 minutes.

All dried chiles can be ground into powder—and most are, including the habanero. Crushed chiles, or those coarsely ground with some of the seeds, are called *quebrado*. Coarse powders are referred to as *caribe*, while the finer powders are termed *molido*. The milder powders, such as New Mexican, can also be used as the base for sauces, but the hotter powders such as cayenne and piquin are used when heat is needed more than flavor. In some kitchens there are more

Ristras *are the traditional method of drying red chiles.*
DAVE DEWITT

powders available than whole pods because the powders are concentrated and take up less storage space. Store the powders in small, airtight bottles. The fresher the powders, the better they taste, so don't grind up too many pods. Use an electric spice mill and be sure to wear a painter's mask to protect the nose and throat from the pungent powder. The colors of the powders vary from a bright, electric red-orange (chiltepins), to light green (dried green jalapeños), to a dark brown that verges on black (ancho). Many cooks experiment by changing the powders called for in recipes.

Poblanos and the New Mexican varieties that are harvested green must be roasted and peeled before using them in a recipe. Blistering or roasting the chile is the process of heating the chile to the point that the tough transparent skin is separated from the meat of the chile so it can be removed. The method is quite simple.

While processing the chiles be sure to wear rubber gloves to protect yourself from the capsaicin that can burn your hands and any other part of your body that you touch. Before roasting, cut a small slit in the chiles close to the top so that the steam can escape. The chiles can then be placed on a baking sheet and put directly under the broiler or on a screen on the top of the stove.

One favorite method is to place the pods on a charcoal grill about five to six inches from the coals. Blisters will soon indicate that the skin is separating, but be sure that the chiles are blistered all over or they will not peel properly. Sometimes the chile pods will blacken slightly, but this does not affect the taste. Immediately wrap the chiles in damp towels or place in a plastic bag with damp paper towels for ten to fifteen minutes—this "steams" them and loosens the skins. For crisper, less cooked chiles, plunge them into ice water to stop the cooking process.

Green chile is a low-acid fruit and for that reason dietitians do not recommend it for home canning. It can be done, however, but only by using a pressure canner and by carefully following all the manufacturer's specific instructions. We find freezing to be a much easier and more flavorful method of preservation.

If they are to be frozen whole (rather than chopped), the pods do not have to be peeled first. In fact, they are easier to peel after they have been frozen. After roasting the chiles, freeze them in the form in which you plan to use them—whole, in strips, or chopped. If you are storing in strips or chopped, peel the pods first. A handy way to preserve chopped or diced chiles is to freeze them in ice cube trays with sections. When frozen, they can be "popped" out of the trays and stored in a bag in the freezer. When making a soup or a stew, just drop in a cube. This eliminates the problems inherent in hacking apart a large slab of frozen chiles when you just need a couple of ounces.

Roasted and peeled green chiles can also be dried. String the chiles together, cover with cheesecloth, and dry in a well-ventilated location. One ounce of this chile *pasado* (dried green chile) is equivalent to ten to twelve fresh chile pods. Excess chile peppers can also be pickled or used to make vinegars, oils, pastes, salsas, and sauces. (See Hot Sauce History; Salsa.)

HOT SAUCE DEFINITIONS

Picante sauces are thin, cooked combinations of tomatoes, onions, chiles, garlic, salt, and vinegar. They have no cilantro, and they are not thickened.

Salsas are thicker and chunkier than picante sauce and generally have a wider range of ingredients and spices. They have two forms, uncooked (also called fresh-cut or fresh-pack), which is sold in the chilled deli case, or cooked, which is shelf-stable and is usually packed in bottles but sometimes in cans. There are literally dozens of types of salsa. (See Salsa.)

Taco sauces are cooked and contain finely pureed chiles and onions in a sweetened tomato base; they are, obviously, poured over tacos.

Enchilada sauces usually are designated red or green (usually so colored by tomatoes or tomatillos). They are cooked sauces with chiles, spices, a high oil content, and a smooth, creamy texture. They are used in the preparation of enchiladas, burritos, and other Mexican-based specialties. In New Mexico, red and green sauces are so colored by the green or red chiles used to make the sauce.

Barbecue sauces generally have a tomato sauce base and are then flavored with vinegar, spices, and sweeteners. Generally speaking, they are used to finish a barbecue after smoking the meat; however,

A Swedish habanero hot sauce. DAVE DEWITT

contain chiles or not. There is a subcategory of hot pepper sauces termed Asian. (See below.)

Hot pepper sauces are thin, pourable sauces (usually vinegar-based) that are intensely flavored with concentrations of pureed chiles. They are primarily used as a table condiment and are secondarily used as a cooking ingredient. Salsas, picante sauces, barbecue sauces, marinades, and chile pastes are excluded from this category.

All types of hot pepper sauces are manufactured in North America these days, no matter what their first origin, so the attribution of a type of sauce only to a particular location no longer applies.

Louisiana-Style — Usually a strained sauce made of crushed or ground cayenne, jalapeño, or Tabasco chiles that are sometimes fermented and then combined with salt and vinegar.

Caribbean — Usually containing habanero-related chiles, these tend to be thicker than Louisiana sauces and often contain additional ingredients such as mustard or fruits.

Asian — The most popular of the thinner Asian sauces is *sriracha*, made from red serrano chiles. It often is marketed in squeeze bottles.

Mexican/Southwestern — These range widely in taste and heat. There are chipotle (smoked jalapeño) sauces, New Mexican–based hot sauces, which tend to be milder, and piquin-based sauces, which are quite hot.

many people use them as marinades and grilling sauces. An increasing percentage of the barbecue sauce category is now hot and spicy.

Cooking sauces are used for grilling, roasting, and stewing meats and include *adobos*, *pipiáns*, *moles*, and jerk sauces, among others. There are only a few commercial brands but there are a great number of home recipes for these sauces.

Oriental sauces include soy sauces, fish sauces, stir-fry sauces, and condiments such as *sambals*, which are chile pastes. Depending on the type of oriental sauce and the country of origin, these sauces can

HOT SAUCE HISTORY

There is little doubt that the United States leads the world in at least the number of brands of hot sauce produced—probably well over 1,000. And although we think of the hot sauce boom as a relatively new phenomenon, hot sauces have been popular here for about two centuries.

Much of what we know about now-extinct brands of hot sauces comes from bottle collectors. There is not a great body of material on the subject of collectible hot sauce bottles, but we are indebted to Betty Zumwalt, author of *Ketchup, Pickles, Sauces: 19th Century Food in Glass*, who dutifully cataloged obscure hot sauce bottles found by collectors. Many bottles in the hands of collectors were uncovered by archaeological digs and from shipwrecks.

Other sources of information about early hot sauces are city directories, which often contained advertisements for sauces, and newspapers. We know from these sources that the first bottled cayenne sauces appeared in Massachusetts around 1807. These were probably homemade and similar to English sauces that were decorated with silver labels. Sometime between 1840 and 1860, J. McCollick & Company of New York City produced a Bird Pepper Sauce in a large cathedral bottle that was nearly eleven inches tall. This sauce is significant because it was probably made with the wild chiles called chiltepins or "bird peppers." We also know that in 1849, England's Lea and Perrins Worcestershire

Sauce was first imported into the United States via the port of New York.

That year was important in the history of hot sauces because it marked the first recorded crop of Tabasco chiles, the vital ingredient of McIlhenny Company's Tabasco Pepper Sauce. That crop was grown by a prominent Louisiana banker and legislator, Colonel Maunsell White on his Deer Range Plantation. The *New Orleans Daily Delta* printed a letter from a visitor to White's plantation, who reported, "I must not omit to notice the Colonel's pepper patch, which is two acres in extent,

An early bottle of Tabasco sauce with metal cap. SUNBELT ARCHIVES

all planted with a new species of red pepper, which Colonel White has introduced into this country, called Tobasco red pepper. The Colonel attributes the admirable health of his hands to the free use of this pepper." Tobasco was an early misspelling of Tabasco, the Mexican state.

Colonel White manufactured the first hot sauce from the "Tobasco" chiles and advertised bottles of it for sale in 1859. About this time, he gave some chiles and his sauce recipe to a friend, Edmund McIlhenny, who promptly planted the seeds on his plantation on Avery Island. McIlhenny's horticultural enterprise was interrupted by the Civil War and invading Union troops from captured New Orleans. In 1863, McIlhenny and his family abandoned their Avery Island plantation to take refuge in San Antonio, Texas.

When the McIlhenny family returned to Avery Island in 1865, they found their plantation destroyed and their sugarcane fields in ruin. However, a few volunteer chile plants still survived, providing enough seeds for McIlhenny to rebuild his pepper patch. Gradually, his yield of pods increased to the point where he could experiment with his sauce recipe, in which mashed chiles were strained, and the resulting juice was mixed with vinegar and salt and aged in fifty-gallon white oak barrels. In 1868, McIlhenny packaged his aged sauce in 350 used cologne bottles and sent them as samples to likely wholesalers. The sauce was so popular that orders poured in for thousands of bottles priced at one dollar each, wholesale, which was quite a bit of money in those days.

In 1870, McIlhenny obtained a patent on his Tabasco brand (as it was now called) hot pepper sauce and by 1872 had opened an office in London to handle the European market. The increasing demand for Tabasco sauce caused changes in the packaging of the product as the corked bottles sealed with green wax were replaced by bottles with metal tops.

Around this same time, a cookbook entitled *Mrs. Hill's New Cookbook*, by Annabella Hill of Georgia, contained an interesting recipe for barbecue sauce that contained butter, mustard, vinegar, black pepper, and red pepper—almost certainly cayenne. So it is evident that there was a general tradition of the home cooking of hot sauces in the South. Mrs. Hill also included a recipe for a curry sauce using prepared curry powder.

From an excavated wreck of the good ship *Bertrand*, dated 1874, we know that Western Spice Mills of St. Louis was making hot sauce around that time because 173 of their bottles were uncovered. That same year (some say 1875), Eugene R. Durkee of Brooklyn, New York, applied for a patent on a hexagonally shaped "Chilli Sauce" bottle, but although the patent application survives, no actual bottle has ever been found. E. R. Durkee & Company became a rather large spice and condiment company; the brand name exists to this day. Around this same time, W. K. Lewis & Co. in Boston was producing a pepper sauce in a square cathedral-shaped bottle.

In 1877, Willam H. Railton, a Chicago businessman who owned the Chicago Preserving Works, began using a Maltese cross–shaped label for table sauces "prepared from a Mexican formula." He applied for a trademark in 1883, and by 1884 he was buying large ads for his Chili Colorow Sauce. Interestingly enough, although it was a "chili" sauce, the advertising copy claimed: "It is expressly suitable for family dining, possessing a fine, rich body of exquisite flavor and has neither the fiery nor nauseous taste which characterizes most sauces." With a typical nineteenth-century patent medicine pitch, the copy went on to claim: "It relieves indigestion and cures dyspepsia. Physicians recommend it highly."

During the 1880s and 1890s, several hot sauces sprang up, including C&D Peppersauce, manufactured by Chace and Duncan in New York City in 1883, but we have nothing left but the bottle. Sometime around 1900, the Bergman and Company Pioneer Pickle Factory in Sacramento, California, began selling Bergman's Diablo Pepper Sauce in five-inch-tall bottles with narrow necks that resembled the typical hot sauce bottle of today.

In 1893, it is said that Popie Devillier developed his legendary hot sauce Hotter 'n Hell. Born in southern Louisiana in the "Bayou Country," Arthur "Popie" Devillier left home at the ripe-old age of thirteen, settling into work as a lumberjack in one of the area logging camps. According to his late great-grandson, Kent Cashio, Popie Devillier ("Popie" was a name usually given to a Cajun grandfather by his grandson) became a cook for a lumber camp, taught the ropes by a French cook and a Choctaw Indian assistant.

Relying on his Choctaw/Cajun influence, he created the sauce blending eight spices, including cloves, which many of the workers placed in their mouth after a meal to ease the burn and soothe the tongue. He then slow-cooked the sauce to yield a spicy hot, yet full-flavored hot sauce. The sauce is not only a hot sauce, but a marinade and an injector for meat and wild game.

Hotter 'n Hell was passed down the family tree for more than ninety years, until 1992, when Mr. Cashio, seeing the potential in the market for a recipe that had endeared itself to the lumberjacks and families of the former French-owned Louisiana Territory, introduced the product to the public as Popie's Hotter 'n Hell Sauce. Tragically, Kent Cashio became terminally ill, and in May 1994, sold Popie's to Café Companies, Inc. An instant hit, Café Louisane Hotter 'n Hell Sauce, now made in Baton Rouge, carries the legend of Popie to the future generations of customers at the Café Louisiana Cajun Seafood and Oyster Bar, as well as throughout the Bayou Country and beyond. The Café Companies has set up a royalty for Mr. Cashio's children—another true legacy of Popie Devillier.

From hot sauce bottle collectors, we

know that Koonyik Chilies Sauce appeared along the West Coast of the United States around 1900. About the same time, a Detroit company, Horton-Cato, manufactured Royal Pepper Sauce in a bottle with a bulbous bottom. And sometime shortly after 1889, Heinz produced Heinz's Tabasco Pepper Sauce in an elegant bottle; but alas, even Heinz couldn't compete with the "real" Tabasco sauce.

After the death of Edmund McIlhenny in 1890, the family business was turned over to his son John, who immediately inherited trouble in the form of a crop failure. John attempted to locate Tabasco chiles in Mexico but could not find any to meet his specifications. Fortunately, his father had stored sufficent reserves of pepper mash, so the family business weathered the crisis. However, that experience taught the family not to depend solely upon Tabasco chiles grown in Louisiana. Today, Tabascos are grown under contract in Honduras, Colombia, and other Central and South American countries, and the mash is imported into the United States in barrels.

John McIlhenny was quite a promoter and traveled all over the country publicizing his family's sauce. "I had bill posters prepared," he once said, "and had large wooden signs in the fields near the cities. I had an opera troupe playing a light opera. At different times I had certain cities canvassed by drummers, in a house-to-house canvass. I had exhibits in food expositions, with demonstrators attached. I gave away many thousands of circulars and folders,

and miniature bottles of Tabasco pepper sauce."

In 1898, another Louisiana entrepreneur (and former McIlhenny employee) named B. F. Trappey began growing Tabasco chiles from Avery Island seed. He founded the company B. F. Trappey and Sons and began producing his own sauce, which was also called "Tabasco." The McIlhenny family eventually responded to this challenge and a several decades-long feud by receiving a trademark for their Tabasco brand in 1906.

The trademark did not deter other companies from using the name Tabasco in their products. In 1911, the Joseph Campbell Company began selling Campbell's Tabasco Ketchup and described it as "the appetizing piquancy of Tabasco Sauce in milder form."

Obviously noticing the success of McIlhenny's Tabasco pepper sauce, other companies sprang up all over the country. Charles E. Erath of New Orleans began manufacturing Extract of Louisiana Pepper, Red Hot Creole Peppersauce in bottles nearly eight inches tall in 1916. A year later, La Victoria Foods began manufacturing Salsa Brava in Los Angeles, California. In Louisiana in 1923, Baumer Foods began manufacturing Crystal Hot Sauce and in 1928 Bruce Foods started making Original Louisiana Hot Sauce— two brands that are still in existence today.

The Louisiana hot sauce boom continued when, in 1929, Trappey's expanded to two plants, one in Lafayette and one in New Iberia. That same year, the McIlhenny family won a trademark infringement suit against the Trappeys. From that time on, only the McIlhenny sauce could be called "Tabasco," and competitors were reduced to merely including Tabasco chiles in their list of ingredients. The two companies had competed with identically named sauces for thirty-one years.

Undoubtedly because of the Wall Street collapse and the Great Depression, no further hot sauce start-ups were uncovered during our research for this book until the beginning of World War II. In 1941, Henry Tanklage formed La Victoria Sales Company to market a new La Victoria salsa line. He introduced red taco sauce, green taco sauce, and enchilada sauce—the first of their kind in the United States. He took over the entire La Victoria operation in 1946, which today has ten different hot sauces covering the entire salsa spectrum, including Green Chili Salsa and Red Salsa Jalapeña.

During the 1940s and 1950s, hot sauces were sold exclusively in small grocery stores, and manufacturers were always searching for new products. In 1952 Henry Tanklage of La Victoria Foods invented and introduced the first commercial taco sauce in the United States. And in 1955, La Preferida began manufacting a line of salsas.

The 1960s saw the rise of ready-to-eat products such as TV dinners, supermarkets gaining ground over the small, neighborhood grocery stores, and the increasing fascination with all things "gourmet." *Gourmet* magazine, which had been launched in 1941, and *Bon Appétit*, launched in 1955, became the arbiters of American food tastes. But where could one find the exotic ingredients for many of the recipes that appeared in those magazines? Cheese shops were the only incarnation of what would later become gourmet shops, and they were rare. "In California," wrote food historian Evan Jones, "cooks who bought esoteric ingredients did so mostly through mail orders. Stores making and selling fresh pasta were unheard of."

A wave of food change swept the country in the 1970s. Sometimes called the "whole foods movement," the trend emphasized cooking with fresh, unadulterated ingredients. Vegetarianism increased in popularity, health food stores sprang up all over, and a new concept in selling food was launched—the gourmet retail shop, which specialized in selling exotic, imported foods and products from smaller manufacturers that were not available in the large supermarkets. The stage was set for yet another boom in hot sauces, and this one was led by the smaller manufacturers.

In 1975, Patti Swidler of Tucson, Arizona, launched Desert Rose Salsa, a line that was specifically designed to be sold in the specialty food shops. When her business took off, the reporters came calling and Patti told them bluntly, "People are making salsa that is no longer salsa. I still find people gravitate toward authentic flavors."

Four years later, in Austin, Texas, Dan Jardine began production of Jardine's commercial salsa, perhaps starting Austin's reputation (disputed by San Antonio) as the hot sauce capital of America. "Austin is a unique place in the United States," he said. "There seems to be a lot more salsa companies trying to start here." A count by *Austin American-Statesman* food editor Kitty Crider in 1993 totaled forty-eight Austin-made salsas.

Another Texas company, the El Paso Chile Company, was started in 1980 by W. Park Kerr and Norma Kerr. "When my mother and I started the El Paso Chile Company," Park said, "adding cilantro to a basic salsa was considered innovative. Three years later, we came out with cactus salsa—which has two kinds of green chiles and diced prickly pear cactus—and everyone thought that was weird. Now everyone has knocked it off."

New salsas and hot sauces began springing up all over the country and some manufacturers went for both the gourmet and supermarket customers. Datil peppers and homemade sauces with them have existed for centuries in St. Augustine, Florida. In 1981, Chris Way opened Barnacle Bill's in St. Augustine, a fresh seafood restaurant, and he soon made a hot sauce with the datil peppers to serve with his fish and other seafood specialties. Each table had its own jar of Dat'l Do It sauce, but they began disappearing at an alarming rate.

Way soon realized that his best customers were stealing the bottles of hot sauce. But then he reasoned that they had to steal it—because he had never offered it

for sale! About this same time, Chris was approached by one of his customers, who happened to be a vice president of Winn-Dixie, a huge supermarket chain. He liked the Dat'l Do It sauce, he said, and if Chris was willing to upgrade his packaging, the Winn-Dixies would carry it. So was born the Dat'l Do It operation, which now has nine products, including Dat'l Do It Hot Sauce and Hellish Relish. To complete his field to manufacturing to retail cycle, Way has also opened several retail Dat'l Do It shops.

Between the years of 1982 and 1987, Mexican sauce sales jumped 16 percent, and Mexican sauces suddenly were at the top of the sauce and gravy category. In 1983, Panola Pepper Company in Lake Providence, Louisiana, began with 2,000 gallons of sauce made by Bubber Brown from his mother's recipe. That same year, Frank's Red Hot Cayenne Pepper Sauce was introduced by Durkee-French in an advertising blitz; Red Hot would eventually challenge Tabasco for U.S. market share. And to prove just how far afield salsa manufacturing had gone, in 1986 Miguel's Stowe Away in Vermont launched a salsa line.

In April 1986, Sauces & Salsas, Ltd., began manufacturing the Montezuma brand of hot pepper sauces and salsas in Columbus, Ohio. The company was founded by Chuck Evans and over the years established the most diverse line of chile pepper sauces in the world, including the nation's number one brown sauce, Smokey Chipotle.

In 1987, Pace was peeved at Pet over picante packaging. The largest salsa producer, Pace Foods of San Antonio, sued its biggest competitor, Pet Food's Old El Paso. Pace claimed Pet had imitated its label, the shape of the bottle, and even its slogan. Pace's slogan was "Pick Up the Pace," while Pet's Old El Paso slogan was "Pick of the Picantes."

Pace should have been even more upset at Rosarita's Salsa—their slogan was: "Enjoy a change of pace." Pace and Pet settled out of court in January 1988, after Old El Paso agreed to change the bottle and label. Pace also launched its famous national television campaign against its rival, where the cowboys mock the "made in New York City" attributes of an imaginary rival sauce. The campaign caused Pace to gain major market shares in the Midwest.

In 1987, Pace saw a major rival enter the fray as Geo. A. Hormel & Co. licensed the restaurant's name and introduced Chi-Chi's brand; it would eventually capture a large share of the market. The same year, Robert Spiegel, Dave DeWitt, and Nancy Gerlach founded *Chile Pepper* magazine, which would become the major national publication to feature hot sauces, their recipes, and advertisements for manufacturers, large and small.

The following year, Lisa Lammé opened Le Saucier in Boston; it is believed to be the first retail shop devoted to sauces and specializing in hot sauces. However, about the same time, the Chile Shop opened in Santa Fe and the Chili Pepper Emporium

ESTIMATED HOT PEPPER SAUCE BRAND SHARE, YEAR ENDING MARCH 1992	
Tabasco	26.6%
Durkee-French Red Hot	21.5
Crystal	9.5
Louisiana	6.7
Texas Pete	5.2
Red Devil	3.6
Albert's	2.0
Gebhardt	2.0
Pico Pica	1.8
Try Me	1.0
Melinda's	0.3
Private Label	4.4
All Other	15.0

Source: Packaged Facts

opened in Albuquerque; both are still in business. Macayo Foods of Phoenix introduced a line of taco sauces in *plastic pourable* bottles that same year, and the first National Fiery Foods Show was held in El Paso. That show, which started with a mere 37 exhibitors, would expand to 260 exhibitors by 1998, showcasing hundreds and hundreds of brands of sauces and salsas along the way.

Thirty-five sauce manufacturers in Louisiana were producing about a hundred different brands of hot sauce in 1989, and that same year the first two U.S. chipotle sauces were launched by U.S. manufacturers. Chuck Evans began selling Montezuma Smokey Chipotle, and San Angel Autentica Salsa Chipotle was produced by San Angel Mexican Foods in Stowe, Vermont; Don Peet and Manelick de la Parra were the founders. Over in Cambridge, Massachusetts, Chris

Schlesinger of the East Coast Grill began manufacturing his Inner Beauty hot sauce, which resembled a Barbadian or Trinidadian sauce. He made it specifically for chileheads, he said. "That's the kind of person who likes roller coasters, fast cars, and stays up late looking for excitement in his life. It's benign masochism . . . they experience danger without actually having it."

Nelson Thall, president of the Marshall McLuhan Center for Global Communications in Toronto, has a unique explanation for the ever-increasing popularity of hot sauces and other fiery foods: electronic technology, which has spread the word about salsas, for example. "Americans are becoming more 'tribal' in their tastes," said Thall. "And tribal Third World cultures embrace spicier foods, as opposed to the traditional ketchup-like blandness preferred by Western cultures."

➣ *Huachinango.* Another term for a large jalapeño; term for chipotle in Oaxaca, Mexico.

➣ *Huayca.* Amara (Peruvian) term for chile pepper.

TEXAS GREEN SAUCE

When you order green sauce on your enchiladas in Texas, this is what you will be served. It differs from New Mexico's green sauce in that the color is derived from tomatillos rather than from green chiles. This sauce can be used as a dipping sauce, with enchiladas, or as a topping for grilled poultry or fish.

MAKES 4 CUPS
HEAT SCALE: Medium

3 pounds tomatillos
1 bunch scallions
1 small bunch cilantro
1 tablespoon minced garlic
2 teaspoons sugar

2 teaspoons fresh lime juice
1 chicken bouillon cube dissolved in 2 tablespoons
 water
6 serrano chiles, stems removed

Roast the tomatillos in a roasting pan under the preheated broiler until they are brown and squishy, 5 to 7 minutes. Turn them over with a pair of tongs and repeat the process. Take the roasted tomatillos, including all the liquid from the roasting process, combine with the remaining ingredients in a food processor, and puree.

Simmer this mixture for 10 minutes before serving or incorporating into another recipe.

CLASSIC GREEN CHILE SAUCE, NEW MEXICO-STYLE

This all-purpose sauce recipe is from the southern part of New Mexico, where green chile is the number one food crop and is used more commonly than the red form. It is generally served over enchiladas.

MAKES 2 TO 2½ CUPS
HEAT SCALE: **Medium**

1 small onion, chopped
2 cloves garlic, minced
2 tablespoons vegetable oil
6 green New Mexican chiles, roasted (page 146),
   peeled, seeds and stems removed, chopped

1 teaspoon ground cumin
2 cups chicken broth or water

In a skillet over medium-high heat, cook the onion and garlic in the oil until softened, 3 to 5 minutes.

Add the chiles, cumin, and chicken broth or water and bring to a simmer. Reduce the heat to low and simmer for ½ hour. The sauce can be pureed in a blender to the desired consistency.

VARIATIONS: To thicken the sauce, make a roux by cooking 1 tablespoon flour in 1 tablespoon vegetable oil over medium-high heat, stirring constantly and taking care not to let it burn. Slowly stir the roux into the sauce and cook to the desired thickness. Coriander and Mexican oregano may be added to taste. For added heat, add more New Mexican chiles or a serrano or two.

HABANERO HOT SAUCE, BELIZE-STYLE

This is a classic Caribbean hot sauce from Belize. In order to preserve the distinctive flavor of the habanero chiles, don't cook them with the sauce but add them afterward. To cut the heat of this very hot sauce, increase the amount of carrots or decrease the number of habaneros. This sauce will keep for months in the refrigerator. Serve it over breakfast dishes, soups and stews, tacos, and anything else needing instant heat with full flavor.

MAKES 1 CUP
HEAT SCALE: **Extremely hot**

1 small onion, chopped
2 cloves garlic, chopped
1 tablespoon vegetable oil
1 cup chopped carrots
2 cups water

6 habanero chiles, seeds and stems removed,
   minced
3 tablespoons fresh lime juice
2 tablespoons white vinegar
1 teaspoon salt

In a skillet over medium-high heat, cook the onion and garlic in the oil, stirring, until softened, 3 to 5 minutes. Add the carrots and water. Bring to a boil, then reduce the heat to low and simmer until the carrots are soft, about 10 minutes. Remove from the heat.

Add the chiles, lime juice, vinegar, and salt to the carrot mixture. Place in a blender or food processor and puree until smooth.

INDIA

India is by far the largest producer of chile peppers in the world. *The Times of India Directory and Yearbook* for 1983 listed total acreage at 825,000 hectares (about 2 million acres), and this figure compares favorably to a 1986 total of 2.2 million acres.

The largest chile-production states are Andhra Pradesh, Madhya Pradesh, and Rajasthan. Together they produce nearly half of all the chiles grown in India. Other chile-producing states are Maharashtra, Karnataka, Orissa, and Tamil Nadu. Because of agricultural vagaries, production figures vary radically from state to state over the years.

As is true all over the world, chile nomenclature is in a state of confusion in India. The names of the agricultural cultivars bear no relation to the common names of the chiles. The most important chiles in India are *annuum* varieties that resemble cayennes or New Mexican types. The most common of these is called *Kashmiri* despite the fact that they are not exported from Kashmir. Other varieties include 'Guntur Red,' named after the most prolific pepper-producing region in India, Guntur; *Goan; Nellore; Reyadgi;* and *Reshampatti.* The cultivars listed by the Punjab Agricultural Institute include 'Andhra Jyoti,' 'Pusa Jwala,' 'Sindhur,' and designations such as 'NP46' and 'X-235.' On a trip to India, your author collected the most commonly available varieties in Rajasthan and they were Kashmiri and *lal mirch* (the equivalent of saying "red chile").

Some chiles are harvested in their green stage and are taken directly to produce markets, but most are allowed to dry to their red stage, harvested, and then spread out over sand to dry. Near Madurai in southern India, red chiles in the process of drying can be seen covering a vast area of dozens of acres. After they are sun-dried, the chiles are tossed into the air to allow the wind to blow away sand and straw. Then they are bagged and taken to spice markets where they are sold as whole pods or as various grinds of chile powder.

But how did chiles become such an important crop in India? The initial responsibility goes to the Portuguese. Under the leadership of Afonso de Albuquerque, the Portuguese conquered the city of Goa on the Malabar Coast in 1510 and gained control of the spice trade. Goa was rich in spices—cloves, cinnamon, cardamom, ginger, and black pepper—which were shipped to Lisbon in return for silver and copper. These spices were essential to Indian kari cooking. Kari is a Tamil, or South Indian, word for sauce—or, more correctly, the combination of spices that are added to meat, fish, or vegetables to produce a stew. It was the word kari that was Anglicized to become the famous "curry." Before chiles, Indian cooks used white pepper and mustard seeds to "heat up" their kari mixtures.

Shortly after the fall of Goa to the Portuguese, it is suspected chile peppers were introduced there by way of trade routes with Lisbon. Because of their familiarity with all kinds of pungent spices, the Indians of the Malabar Coast were undoubtedly quite taken with the fiery pods, and planted seeds that had been imported from monks' gardens on the Iberian Peninsula.

By 1542, three varieties of chiles were recognized in India, according to Dutch botanist Charles Clusius, and by the middle of that century chiles were extensively cultivated and exported. One variety of Indian chile was called 'Pernambuco,' after a town in Portuguese Brazil, giving rise to speculation that the chiles had passed from Brazil to Lisbon and then

Indian lal mirch *chile.* DAVE DEWITT

around the Cape to Goa. The difficulty with such a theory is the fact that the principal chile of Brazil was *Capsicum chinense,* yet that species is rare today in India—the *chinense* growing in India may actually be an extreme form of *frutescens,* the Tabasco chile. A more likely scenario is that the chiles introduced into India were *annuums* from the West Indies, the first chiles grown in Spain and Portugal. This theory is supported by the fact that *Capsicum annuum* became the most extensively cultivated chile in India and its main source of commerce.

Unlike Africa, where chiles were dispersed primarily by birds, in India they were spread by more deliberate cultivation. The Capsicums became known as *achar*, a term probably derived from the Native American name *ají*, and as *mirch* in northern India, and *mulagay* in the southern regions of the country and in Sri Lanka. Incidentally, *achar* is also the name of spicy pickles.

K. T. Achaya, in *Indian Food: A Historical Companion*, quotes "the great south Indian composer" Purandaradasa (1480–1564) about chiles: "I saw you green, then turning redder as you ripened, nice to look at and tasty in a dish, but too hot if an excess is used. Saviour of the poor, enhancer of good food, fiery when bitten."

The production of chiles was quite important during the British rule in India. By 1924, the British began to isolate varieties and work on breeding to improve yield and quality. The breeding was done by the Imperial Council of Agricultural Research and that agency classified fifty-two varieties of chiles.

S. N. Mahindru, author of *Spices in Indian Life*, commented that "poor sections of the Indian urbanites as well as the rural population were main consumers of green chiles. Middle and upper classes used chiles to a lesser extent."

No matter what the varieties were called, chiles eventually appeared in such a variety of ways in Indian cookery that the diversity and intensity of their use rivals

Indian chile vendors, c. 1890. SUNBELT ARCHIVES

that of Mexico, the Southwestern United States, and some parts of Asia. Four hundred years after chiles first entered India, the degree of their penetration into the various Indian cuisines was vividly illustrated by the cooking experiences of Robert H. Christie.

Christie, a British Army officer, collected recipes from India and used them to prepare elaborate banquets for his fellow members of the Edinburgh Cap and Gown Club in Scotland. In 1911, Christie published his landmark book on Indian cookery, *Twenty-Two Authentic Banquets from India*, which contained recipes for dishes from all parts of India, and from neighboring regions that are today separate countries. An examination of the ingredients of these recipes reveals that fully two thirds of the non-dessert and non-bread recipes contained some form of hot chiles!

In some regions, chiles totally dominated the food. In Christie's Bengal chapter, for example, twenty-two of twenty-three entrees contained chile peppers. In the Madras chapter, the count was eleven of thirteen, and in the Kashmir chapter, seven of eight recipes called for hot chiles in various forms, including fresh green and red plus dried red pods and powders.

Christie's recipes from some regions, such as Punjab, were not nearly so hot, but still it is evident that in 400 years chiles had completely conquered the cuisines of India, a land already rich in spices. They became an essential ingredient in both vegetarian and nonvegetarian cooking—imparting color, flavor, heat, and nutrients.

Spices in general and chiles in particular are so important to the Indian kitchen that they are purchased in monds, a unit of ninety pounds. Once in the kitchen, they are stored until the cook is ready to use them in freshly ground spice mixtures called *masalas*, which vary greatly from region to region and are designed for specific applications. The *masalas* generally combine red chile with cardamom, cinnamon, cloves, cumin, coriander, and black pepper. However, ginger, mustard seeds, fennel, mace, poppy seeds, nutmeg, and saffron also make an appearance in various incarnations of *masala*.

Whichever spices are chosen to blend with the chiles, they are first roasted separately and then are ground together in a *chakki*, a stone mill, or in a *kootani*, an iron mortar and pestle. The dry *masala* can then be stored in airtight containers or used immediately in cooking. When the dry *masala* is mixed with water, garlic, and fresh ginger, it becomes a "wet" *masala*. This paste is generally cooked by itself before the vegetables, meat, or fish are added to the pan.

Chile peppers not only transformed the *masalas* of India but also the chutneys, the primary condiments of the country. Chutney is an Anglicized version of the Hindi *chatni*, a word that refers to licking the fingertips, which were the utensils originally used to eat this mixture of chiles, fruits, various vegetables, and spices. Originally, the making of *chatni* was a method of preserving ripe fruits in the tropical climate. Today, Indian cooks prepare fresh chutney just hours before each meal by mixing fresh ingredients and then chilling them before serving.

Indian cooks are not impressed with Major Grey, the famed brand of bottled relish. They say that this commercial mango preserve bears no resemblance to homemade chutneys because it is too sweet and is not hot enough. Also, the prepared chutneys contain too much vinegar and ginger, but not enough of the other ingredients that make homemade chutneys superior: mixtures of different chiles and "exotic" ingredients (for bottled chutneys) such as tamarind, bananas, chopped green tomatoes, fresh coriander, coconut, and freshly ground spices.

Despite these complaints, the British and now the Americans are quite fond of the commercial chutneys and serve them with dishes prepared with commercial curry powders. Such a practice is mystifying, especially considering how easy it is to prepare much better-tasting chutneys from scratch.

In addition to their use in *masalas* and chutneys, chiles also appear as part of various styles of cooking such as vindaloo and tandoori. In vindaloo cooking, meats such as pork, goat, lamb, shrimp, or chicken are marinated for hours or even days in a mixture of vinegar, fiery chiles, fruit pulp, and spices. Then the meat is simmered in the same marinade, a process that melds the marinade with the meat juices and the chiles and reduces the entire mixture to an extremely powerful sauce.

The other style of cooking, tandoori, is very popular in Punjab and also uses chiles as a marinade ingredient; however, the method of cooking the meat is quite different. Instead of being stewed, it is baked in the intense heat generated in a tandoor, a clay oven that is sunk vertically into the ground. The chicken is first scored and then slathered with a yogurt-chile-lime paste. Then the bird is marinated for at least twelve hours in the mixture before it is skewered and inserted into the tandoor.

The fact that chiles occur in the majority of Indian entrees, side dishes, snacks, and festival specialties is not really surprising. In India it is said, "The climate is hot, the dishes are hotter, and the condiments are the hottest." This saying supports the legendary Indian tolerance for hot chiles. In southern India, a typical meal for four persons can include the following amounts and types of chiles: a handful of soaked and drained whole red chiles, two tablespoons of cayenne powder, two tablespoons of freshly chopped green chiles, and a bowl of whole green chiles on the table for snacking. These chiles are, of course, in addition to the *masalas* and chutneys that are also used.

In fiery south India, there is another saying, "Heat plus heat equals cool," an allusion to the gustatory sweating caused by hot chiles. The southern state of Andhra Pradesh is the chile capital of the entire country, and, according to *The Wall Street Journal*, the city of Guntur is the hottest city of that state and is another location competing for the title of the hottest city in the world. In 1988, that financial newspaper sent reporter Anthony Spaeth to India to investigate rumors that chile peppers had completely conquered the local cuisine. His report was shocking, to say the least.

"In Guntur," he wrote, "salted chiles are eaten for breakfast. Snacks are batter-fried chiles with chile sauce. The town's culinary pride are fruits and vegetables preserved in oil and chile, particularly its karapo pickles: red chiles pickled in chile." Another popular snack is deep-fried chiles dipped in chile powder.

Hot and spicy food is so predominant in Guntur that the agricultural market in town sells a single commodity: chile in its myriad forms. Legend and lore about chiles figure prominently in the culture of Guntur. The people often dream about them, and they believe that hot tempers arise from heavy chile eating and that chiles increase sexual desire. Children begin to eat chile at age five and quickly build up an incredible tolerance. In addition to culinary usage, the burning of red chile pods is said to ward off evil spells.

In Guntur, as in other worldwide hotbeds of chile consumption, those who do not eat chile are viewed with concern, if not suspicion. The people of Guntur attribute the abnormal avoidance of chile to several causes: the offenders have lived abroad, are from out of town, or have married someone from a less-fiery state.

In addition to their culinary usage, chile peppers have worked their way into the customs and traditions of the region to an unusual degree. Many people on the Indian subcontinent believe that the smoke of roasting or even burning chile peppers protects the house and gives a feeling of warmth and security. On the other hand, chiles can be an instrument of terrorism. In 1988, a gang of hoodlums boarded a train in India and began robbing the passengers. Anyone who dared to resist got a handful of chile powder thrown in the face and eyes.

On a lighter note, as an example of how ingrained chiles are in the cuisines of India, we present the kitchen of the Taj Majal Hotel in Bombay, which now serves Mexican food! Because this famous hostelry must cater to tastes of international guests, it now experiments with a cross-cultural cuisine known as Indian-Mexican food.

In this amalgamated cuisine, corn *masa* is replaced with yellow corn flour for making tortillas and tacos. In the tacos, lamb meat is spiced with ginger and turmeric, laced with a *panir* (cheese) salsa made with serrano-like chiles, and sprinkled with distinctive Indian cheeses. Nachos, the familiar snack of the American Southwest, are transformed with the addition of spiced garbanzo beans covered with a red chile sauce made with a combination of New Mexican–type chiles and the far hotter Japanese *santaka* variety. (See Curry.)

⬊ *'INIA.'* A cultivated variety of habanero in Mexico.

MANGO AND COCONUT CHILE CHUTNEY

This chutney from the southwest coast of India can be served with any curry and can be used as a dip for any kind of chip, including fried plantains.

MAKES 4 TO 6 CUPS
HEAT SCALE: **Medium**

One 1-inch ball of tamarind pulp (or substitute 2 teaspoons lime juice)
½ cup warm water
2 cups shredded unsweetened coconut
One 1-inch piece of ginger, peeled
4 green chiles, such as serranos, stems removed and halved
4 cloves garlic
1 cup fresh cilantro leaves
6 large green mangoes
1 teaspoon cumin seeds

1 teaspoon fenugreek seeds
¼ cup olive or vegetable oil
½ teaspoon yellow mustard seeds
1 teaspoon asafoetida (optional)
1 teaspoon greengram dal (optional)
1 teaspoon red chile powder
1 teaspoon turmeric powder
¼ cup curry leaves (optional) (available in Asian markets)
Salt to taste

Soak the tamarind in the warm water for 10 minutes, then strain the pulp and save the liquid.

In a food processor or blender, grind the pulp into a fine paste with the coconut, ginger, chiles, garlic, and ½ cup of the cilantro. Combine the paste with the tamarind water. Set aside.

Peel the mangoes, discard the seeds, and grind the pulp in a blender or food processor along with the cumin and fenugreek into a smooth paste.

Heat the oil in a large skillet over medium heat for 2 minutes. Reduce the heat, add the mustard seeds, asafoetida, and dal. When the seeds begin to pop, add the mango paste, chile powder, turmeric, and coconut-tamarind paste. Add a little water, mix well, and cook over low heat for 10 minutes, stirring occasionally.

Remove from the heat and add the curry leaves, remaining ½ cup cilantro, and salt. Place in a jar in the refrigerator; it keeps for at least 3 months.

MADRAS FRIED CHILE FRITTERS
Molagai Bajii

Bajiis, the unstuffed Madras version of chiles *rellenos*, are popular teatime snacks in Madras and other cities of Tamil Nadu. They are often accompanied by a mango chutney like the one in this section, and the taste combination is delicious. Serve with fruit drinks or beer.

MAKES 5 SERVINGS
HEAT SCALE: Medium

2 cups vegetable oil
½ cup corn flour
½ cup rice flour
1 teaspoon salt

½ cup water
2 teaspoons ground cumin
10 green New Mexican chiles, roasted and peeled (page 146), stems on, slit lengthwise on one side

Heat the oil in a skillet or wok over low heat.

In a bowl, combine the flours and the salt and add 1 teaspoon of the warm oil. Blend in the water and whisk to make a thick batter.

Turn the heat under the skillet or wok to high. Rub the ground cumin inside the chiles and dip them in the batter. Reduce the heat to medium and fry the chiles in the oil for 2 minutes, turning once, or until they are golden brown all over.

MOGHUL CHICKEN DILRUBA

This rich, spicy-sweet chicken dish from northwestern India has distinct Moghul influences. *"Dilruba"* means "sweetheart." The Moghuls controlled most of India for centuries, leaving behind some of India's most famous architecture, including the Taj Mahal. The Moghul emperors loved to eat, and twenty-course meals were common in the royal courts. Not surprisingly, Moghul rule had a greater influence on Punjabi cuisine than that of any other conqueror.

MAKES 4 SERVINGS
HEAT SCALE: **Medium**

2 medium onions

2 tablespoons chopped fresh ginger

6 tablespoons butter or vegetable oil

One 3- to 4-pound chicken, skin removed, cut into small serving pieces

1 cup plain yogurt

¼ cup almonds

¼ cup walnuts

¼ cup melon, pumpkin, or squash seeds (optional)

1 cup milk

2 tablespoons garam masala

1 teaspooon ground turmeric

2 to 3 fresh green cayenne peppers, minced (or substitute any small, hot chiles such as serranos or jalapeños)

Salt and ground cayenne to taste

A few strands whole saffron, soaked in 2 tablespoons warm milk

Minced fresh cilantro, whole almonds, and cashews for garnish

Put the onions and ginger into a blender or food processor and process to a smooth paste (about the consistency of applesauce). Heat the butter in a heavy, deep skillet over medium heat and cook the onion mixture, stirring often, until browned, about 5 minutes.

Add the chicken and yogurt. Combine well and cook until the mixture becomes rather dry and the chicken begins to brown, about 10 minutes.

Meanwhile, in a spice mill or a food processor, grind the almonds, walnuts, and melon seeds until quite fine. Stir them into the milk. Add this mixture to the chicken along with the *garam masala*, turmeric, chile peppers, salt, and ground cayenne pepper.

Cook, stirring often, until the chicken is very tender and the sauce is very thick, 10 to 15 minutes. Stir in the saffron and milk mixture and cook for 1 to 2 minutes longer.

Garnish with cilantro and nuts and serve hot.

 JUNGLI MANS

In the Mewari language of Rajasthan, *jungli mans* refers to a dish that would be prepared by a stranded hunter who only had the basics with him. It is amazingly tasty considering the limited ingredients. It is also quite hot, so serve it with some plain white rice.

MAKES 4 TO 6 SERVINGS
HEAT SCALE: Hot

2 cups ghee *(clarified butter) (or substitute vegetable oil)*

2 pounds lamb, cut into 1-inch cubes

10 lal mirch *chiles, stems removed and left whole (or substitute dried cayennes or* mirasol)

2 teaspoons salt

In a pot over medium heat, heat the *ghee* or oil and add the meat. Cook, stirring constantly, for 10 minutes. Add the whole chiles and salt and continue cooking. Add water as necessary to make sure that the meat neither fries nor boils, but is essentially braised. Continue cooking until the meat is tender, about 1 hour more, stirring occasionally. Remove the chiles before serving.

JALAPEÑOS

The Plant

The jalapeño chile, named after the city of Jalapa in Veracruz, Mexico, where it is no longer commercially grown, is a pod type of *Capsicum annuum*. Jalapeño plants usually grow from two and a half to three feet tall. They have a compact single stem or upright, multibranched, spreading habit. The leaves are light to dark green and measure about three inches long and two inches wide. The flower corollas are white with no spots. The pods, which are conical and cylindrical, are pendant and measure about two to three inches long and one inch wide. They are green (occasionally sunlight will cause purpling), maturing to red, and measure between 2,500 and 10,000 Scoville Units. The brown streaks, or "corking," on the pods are desirable in Mexico but not so in the United States.

Agriculture

In Mexico, commercial cultivation measures approximately 40,000 acres in three main agricultural zones: the Lower Palaloapan River Valley in the states of Veracruz and Oaxaca, northern Veracruz, and the area around Delicias, Chihuahua. The later region grows the American jalapeños, which are processed and exported into the United States. Approximately 60 percent of the Mexican jalapeño crop is used for processing, 20 percent for fresh consumption, and 20 percent in production of chipotle chiles, smoked jalapeños.

Jalapeño chiles. PAUL BOSLAND

In the United States, approximately 5,500 acres are under cultivation, with New Mexico the leading state for jalapeño production, followed by Texas. Home gardeners should remember that the U.S. varieties of jalapeños flourish better in semiarid climates—ones with dry air combined with irrigation. If planted in hot and humid zones in the United States during the summer, the yield of such jalapeños decreases and so Mexican varieties should be grown. The growing period is seventy to eighty days, and the yield is about twenty-five to thirty-five pods per plant.

Recommended Mexican varieties are 'Típico' and 'Peludo'; recommended U.S. varieties are 'Early Jalapeño' (hot) and 'TAM Jalapeño' (mild).

Culinary Usage

Jalapeños are one of the most famous chile peppers. They are instantly recognizable and a considerable mythology has sprung up about them, particularly in Texas. The impetus for the popularity of jalapeños starts from a combination of their unique taste, their heat, and their continued use as a snack food.

In 1956, *Newsweek* magazine published a story on a pepper-eating contest held in the Bayou Teche country of Louisiana, near the home of the famous Tabasco sauce. The article rated the jalapeño as "the hottest pepper known," more fiery than the "green Tabasco" or "red cayenne." (This, of course, is not true; the habanero is the hottest.) Thus the Tex-Mex chile was launched as the perfectly pungent pepper for jalapeño-eating contests, which have proliferated all over the country.

Many jalapeños are used straight out of the garden in salsas. Others are pickled in *escabeche* and sold to restaurants and food services for sale in their salad bars. Jalapeños are processed as "nacho slices," and "nacho rings" that are served over nachos, one of the most popular snack foods in arenas and ball parks. Jalapeños are commonly used in commercial salsas and picante sauces, which process a large percentage of the imports from Mexico. (See Chipotles; Smoking Chiles.)

JALAPEÑO FIRECRACKERS

These little explosions make perfect appetizers for chilehead guests.

MAKES 24 SERVINGS
HEAT SCALE: Medium to hot

24 jalapeño chiles
8 ounces Monterey Jack or Cheddar cheese, sliced
Vegetable oil for deep-fat frying

All-purpose flour for dredging
2 large eggs, beaten

Slit each pepper, remove the seeds with a small spoon or knife, and stuff the peppers with pieces of cheese. If necessary, insert a toothpick to hold the chiles together.

In a large pot, heat enough oil to deep-fry the chiles at 350°F. Dip each stuffed chile in the flour, then the eggs, then the flour again. Fry the chiles in the hot oil, in small batches, until the chiles are golden brown, 5 to 7 minutes. Drain on paper towels and serve.

⤸ *Japónes.* "Japan"; a small, pointed chile grown in Veracruz and San Luis Potosí, Mexico.

JERK FOODS

The word "jerk," as used in the Caribbean and particularly Jamaica, is thought to have originated from the word *"ch?arki"* (the question mark is part of the word), a Quecha Indian word from Peru. The Spanish converted the term to *"charqui,"* which meant smoked or dried meat. In English, this word became "jerk" and "jerky." Jamaica was controlled by both the Spanish and the English, so the derivation of the word seems clear.

The Caribbean technique of jerking meat was originated by the Maroons, Jamaican slaves who escaped from the British during the invasion of 1655 and hid in the maze of jungles and limestone sinkholes known as the Cockpit Country. The meat of preference at that time was wild boar, which could explain why jerk pork is particularly popular today. The Maroons seasoned the boar with a variety of spices and hot peppers and cooked it in a pit until it was dry. The meat would preserve well in the humidity of the tropics. During the twentieth century, the technique gained enormous popularity in Jamaica and jerk pork "shacks" are commonly found all over the island. The method has evolved, however, and the pork is no longer overcooked.

Although it began as a way to preserve meats, the technique of jerk is now used more to tenderize and add flavor. Basically, jerk seasonings are pungent combinations of island ingredients such as ginger, tamarind, nutmeg, thyme, scallions, native pimento berries (allspice), and, of course, Scotch bonnet chiles. These mixtures can be either dry rubs or wet mixtures in the form of marinades or pastes. Meat, fish, and poultry are coated with the jerk seasoning and marinated from four hours to overnight before cooking. The cooking technique is technically called "smoke grilling" and the Jamaicans used both dry and green pimento (allspice) wood to fuel the fire. They cover the marinated pork with sheets of corrugated aluminum to keep in the smoke. The smoke is an important part of the process, but it is not essential. If you lack a pit, then a barbecue grill, offset firebox smoker, or even an oven can be substituted; just be sure to cook the food very slowly.

◢ *Joto.* The term for ancho chile in Aguascalientes, Mexico.

Cooking jerk pork, Ocho Rios, Jamaica. MARY JANE WILAN

JAMAICAN JERK MARINADE

The number of versions of jerk marinades is nothing less than astonishing. Of course, every one of is "authentic, secret, and the most flavorful." Traditionally, the marinade should be very thick. It can be used with pork, chicken, or fish.

MAKES 2½ TO 3 CUPS
HEAT SCALE: **Extremely hot**

¼ cup whole Jamaican pimento berries (allspice)
3 Scotch bonnet or habanero chiles, stems and
    seeds removed, chopped
10 scallions, chopped
½ onion, chopped
4 cloves garlic, chopped
4 bay leaves, crushed
3 tablespoons chopped fresh ginger

⅓ cup chopped fresh thyme
1 tablespoon freshly ground black pepper
1 teaspoon ground nutmeg
1 teaspoon ground cinnamon
1 teaspoon salt (or more to taste)
¼ cup fresh lime juice
¼ cup vegetable oil

Roast the pimento berries in a dry skillet over medium heat until aromatic, about 2 minutes. Remove and crush them to a powder in a mortar or spice mill.

Add the pimento powder and the remaining ingredients to a food processor and blend to make a paste or sauce.

Store in the refrigerator; it will keep for a month or more.

JERK PORK, OCHO RIOS-STYLE

The Jamaican jerk cooks use a technique best described as "smoke grilling." It combines the direct heat of grilling with smoke produced by fresh pimento leaves and branches. It can best be duplicated by using a Weber-type barbecue with a round drip pan on the bottom to catch drippings and prevent flare-ups. Although the pork can be smoked in an indirect-heat smoker, the texture will not be the same. It is better to smoke-grill over wood rather than charcoal, as the flavor is far superior. Note that this recipe requires advance preparation.

MAKES 4 TO 6 SERVINGS
HEAT SCALE: **Hot**

4 pounds pork meat (roasts or chops, more needed if ribs), fat removed and coarsely cut into pieces 2 to 3 inches wide and 4 to 5 inches long

*2 cups Jamaican Jerk Marinade (page 174)
Hardwood chips such as apple, hickory, pecan, or oak (or substitute fresh branches and leaves)*

In a large bowl, toss the pork in the marinade, cover, and marinate overnight in the refrigerator.

Cover the wood chips with water and soak for 45 minutes to an hour before using.

Build a fire in the barbecue with charcoal and place the wet hardwood chips on top. It's preferable to only use hardwood to make the fire, but the use of charcoal is permissible. When the wood has burned to coals, spread them apart and place a metal drip pan, half-filled with water, in the center of the fire. Place the pork on the grill directly over the pan, and as far from the fire as possible. Cover the meat with either the barbecue cover, leaving a small vent for fresh air, or with a tent of aluminum foil which will keep in the smoke.

The trick for the next few hours is to add sufficient wood to keep the fire going while avoiding making it too hot. Every half-hour or so, add some soaked chips to the coals to produce smoke.

Cook the pork for 2 to 3 hours, depending upon the heat of the fire, turning the meat occasionally. Boil the marinade for 5 minutes and baste the meat with the marinade or the drippings from the pan. The pork should be crispy on the outside and tender on the inside, almost to the point of falling apart.

⮞ *Kashmiri.* Originally a variety of *annuum* grown in Kashmir, India, it is now the generic term for any medium-long dried red chile. An appropriate substitute would be *guajillo*.

⮞ *Kayensky* pepper. In Hungary, cayenne pepper.

⮞ *Kochikai.* Tamil (Southern India) word for chile pepper.

⮞ *Kochu.* In Korea, cayenne-like chiles. Also *gochu*.

KOREA

It is said that Koreans have the highest per capita chile consumption in the world. Of course, we are discussing the Republic of Korea, known in the West as South Korea. Total chile production there is about 200,000 tons on 326,000 acres, making South Korea the fifth-largest producer of chile peppers in the world. Chile peppers utilize 35 percent of the agricultural area for vegetables, far ahead of two other crops, Chinese cabbage and garlic. The main production areas are Chungcheongbuk-do and Kyungsangbok-do provinces, which are located in the central part of the country. The production technique calls for transplanting seedlings rather than direct seeding.

Before the mid-1970s, virtually all of the chile varieties grown in Korea were open-pollinated land races. But following extensive research by their Horticultural Experiment Station, now F1 hybrids constitute 80 percent of Korean production. There are ten major Korean varieties of these hybrids: 'Hongilpoom,' 'Bulamput,' 'Hanpyul,' 'Cheongyang,' 'Cheonghong,' 'Jinpoom,' 'Sinhong,' 'Hongsil,' 'Koreagon gochu,' and 'Ilwolgon gochu.' They were all introduced between 1979 and 1985. These varieties resemble the cayenne pod type in North America.

It is not a coincidence that chiles, cabbage, and garlic are South Korea's primary crops because they are all ingredients in what might be called the Korean national dish, *kimchi*. It is a fermented cabbage salad. Another important culinary use of chiles in Korea is in the manufacture of *kochujang* chile paste, the country's most popular condiment. Tall jars of homemade *kochujang*, condiments fermenting and mellowing in the sun, line terraces all across Korea. It is a salty hot pepper paste with a touch of sweetness. This is one of the most important ingredients in Korean cooking, and is as common in South Korea as ketchup is in the United States. Homemade *kochujang* requires months of work by Korean housewives, who must grow and dry the ingredients, grind them by hand, cook them, and cure the resulting mixture in the sun. Although some traditional households still prepare their seasonings in this way, the making of *kochujang* is now a dying art. Traditionally, *kochujang* contains glutinous rice, fermented soybean cake, hot red chile, salt, and malt syrup from barley and water. This mixture was placed in jars on March 3 of each year and allowed to ferment for a minimum of three months. Today, Korean grocery stores carry small jars of *kochujang* made from furnace-dried peppers and filled with preservatives and MSG. However, these mass-produced pastes are fairly good, especially when cooks add other spices to

them. Commercial *kochujang* is available in Asian markets.

◢ *Kulai.* A cayenne-like chile grown in Malaysia.

Korean hot chile. PAUL BOSLAND

KOREAN HOT PICKLED CABBAGE
Kimchi

Here is a classic Korean condiment that usually takes months to make because it is fermented in clay pots. This recipe takes only 3 or 4 days. Serve *kimchi* as an accompaniment to any stir-fried Asian dishes and to grilled or broiled meats. Note that this recipe requires advance preparation.

MAKES ABOUT 4 CUPS
HEAT SCALE: **Medium**

1 head Chinese cabbage, coarsely chopped

1 tablespoon salt

5 fresh green or red New Mexican chiles, roasted and peeled (page 146), seeds and stems removed, minced

2 tablespoons grated fresh ginger

6 scallions, green and white parts, chopped

2 cloves garlic, minced

In a large mixing bowl, sprinkle the cabbage with salt, cover, and let stand for 1 hour. Rinse well with cold water and drain. Return the cabbage to the bowl.

Add the remaining ingredients, stir well, and cover with water. Allow the mixture to pickle in the refrigerator for 3 or 4 days.

To serve, drain off the water and warm to room temperature.

KOREAN CHILE PASTE BARBECUE
Bulgogi

Many Americans first encounter *kochujang* at Korean restaurants when they order *bulgogi*, the Korean barbecue. Waiters grill thin strips of marinated beef over red-hot coals in a built-in grill in the table. Diners roll the beef up in lettuce leaves with a scoop of rice and a spoonful of *kochujang*. Feel free to grill the beef strips here instead of using a skillet. Note that this recipe requires advance preparation.

MAKES 4 TO 6 SERVINGS
HEAT SCALE: **Mild**

For the marinade
4 scallions, sliced
2 tablespoons toasted sesame seeds (see Note)
2 cloves garlic, sliced
2 tablespoons chopped fresh ginger
1/3 cup low-sodium soy sauce
1 tablespoon sesame oil
1 tablespoon rice vinegar
2 teaspoons sugar

To continue
1 1/4 pounds sirloin steak, very thinly sliced across the grain (this is easier if the steak is slightly frozen)
1 1/2 cups short- or medium-grain rice
3 cups water
1 head red leaf lettuce, leaves separated
1/4 cup kochujang (or substitute Chinese chile paste with garlic)

In a large, nonreactive bowl, combine all the marinade ingredients. Add the steak and toss to coat. Cover and marinate for at least 1 hour in the refrigerator.

In a pot, combine the rice and water and bring to a boil. Reduce the heat to low, cover and simmer until the water is absorbed, about 20 minutes.

Heat a heavy skillet, preferably cast-iron, until hot. If you own a tabletop burner, this is the time to use it. Remove the meat from the marinade and quickly cook, a few pieces at a time, turning the pieces to evenly brown, about 1 minute per batch.

To serve, line the edge of a serving platter with the lettuce leaves, mound the rice in the center, and place the beef around the rice. Serve the *kochujang* on the side.

To eat, add a scoop of rice and a few pieces of beef to a lettuce leaf, and top with a dollop of *kochujang*. Roll up the leaf and enjoy.

NOTE: Toast the sesame seeds in a dry skillet over medium heat for about 2 minutes, stirring constantly.

◥ *La-jiao.* Chile peppers in China. Also *hung fan jiao.*

◥ *'Largo.'* "Long or large"; a cultivated variety of serrano in Mexico.

LATIN AMERICA

Latin America, ancestral home of chile peppers, is an enigma when it comes to hot and spicy food. Since the fiery fruits originated there and proliferated for thousands of years before the Europeans arrived, it might be assumed that the prevalence of chiles had caused hot and spicy dishes to permeate throughout all of the cuisines of this vast region. But in Central and South America, countries such as Brazil and Peru are especially hot while Costa Rica, Venezuela, and Argentina are not.

In the countries where European influences had a great impact upon the cuisines, the food tends to be blander. The pockets of heat are the spicier countries where the indigenous Native American population had a greater effect on the cuisine than did the European settlers. And with the exception of Brazil, which had African influences, these pockets are the regions where the great civilizations of the Maya, Aztec, and Inca arose: the Yucatán Peninsula in Central America, the Valley of Mexico, and Peru and nearby Andean countries. (See Amazonia; Andes Region; Central America; Mexico.)

◥ *Loco.* "Crazy"; in Mexico, a term for mutants, especially those chiles hotter than normal.

◥ *Locoto. Capsicum pubescens.* (See *Rocoto.*)

◥ *Lombok.* Alternate Indonesian term for chile peppers.

◥ *'Loreto 74.'* A cultivated variety of *mirasol* in Mexico.

◣ *Macho.* "Manly"; another name for piquin in Mexico.

◣ *Mak phet.* Chile peppers in Laotian. *Mak phet dip* are fresh green chiles; *mak phet deng*, fresh red chiles; *mak phet nyai*, large chiles; *mak phet kuntsi*, small chiles; *mak phet kinou*, tiny, "rat-dropping" chiles; *mak phet haeng*, dried red chiles; *mak phet pung*, ground red chiles.

◣ *Malagueta.* *Capsicum frutescens*; a Brazilian chile related to Tabascos. It grows both wild and cultivated.

◣ **Mango.** Local term for bell peppers in Indiana and Illinois.

◣ *Mano.* Term for chile in Liberia.

◣ *Manzano* or *Manzana.* "Apple"; of the genus and species *Capsicum pubescens*. Grown in the Mexican states of Michoacán, Chiapas, Guerrero, and México, these chiles resemble small apples and are usually used in the red form. One variety is yellow and is termed *canario*. They have thick flesh and black seeds. The variety is also called *cirhuelo* in the Mexican state of Querétaro. The *manzano* is also called *cera*, *malinalco*, and *rocoto*.

◣ *'Marekofana.'* A cultivated variety of chile in Ethiopia.

◣ *Mata-frade.* In Brazil, friar-killer chile.

◣ *Max.* Another name for piquin in Yucatán, Mexico.

◣ *Meco.* A blackish-red smoked jalapeño in Mexico.

MEDICINAL USES

Chile peppers have been used medicinally in various parts of the world for hundreds of years. The earliest documented uses date back to the 1500s. They have been used in all

PARCHE POROSO
GUADALUPANO DE BELLADONA Y CÁPSICO

Al Comprador :- Certificamos que nuestro Parche Poroso Guadalupano de Belladona y Cápsico contiene el más alto grado de Extracto de Belladona. Un parche de calidad superior conteniendo .125% (.124 Granos) alcaloides de Belladona combinada con Cápsico.

Guadalupana Medicine Co.

Nuestra		Our
Señora de		Lady of
Guadalupe		Guadalupe

Marcas de Fábrica igualmente registradas en Mexico. M.I. Rgtrda. No.8469, 1 Octubre 1903. M.I. Rgtrda. No. 15022 y 15023, 24 Marzo 1917. M.I. Rgtrda. No.16702, 17 Junio 1919. M.I. Rgtrda. No.16758, No. 16759, y No. 16760, 24 Junio 1919. M.I. Rgtrda. No. 17239, 2 Octubre 1919. M.I. Rgtrda. No. 20113, 28 Octubre 1921.   Trade-Marks Registered in U.S.A. Patent Office Feb. 7, 1905, No. 44139. Aug. 6, 1907, No. 64451. Jan. 13, 1920, No.128775 and No. 128776. Also Registered in Foreign Countries.

GUADALUPANO BELLADONNA AND CAPSICUM POROUS PLASTER

Active Ingredients :- Belladonna extract (1/8 grain Alkaloids of Belladonna) and Capsicum.

PREPARED FOR
Dr. J. H. McLean Medicine Co., St. Louis, Mo. 63101, U.S.A.

Belladonna and Capsicum plaster.

forms, from fresh and powdered, to juiced and tinctured. While the ailments they treat are varied, including skin and eye infections, colds and asthma, heart conditions, circulatory problems, stomach ailments, and arthritis, there are basically two principles on which these treatments are based: increased circulation and nerve depletion.

Capsaicin, the chemical that makes chile hot, is the active ingredient to which the body initially reacts as though it were a poison. Upon ingestion, blood circulation to organs such as the heart, lungs, and stomach is at first decreased in a matter of minutes (a physical reaction to slow the dispersion of a poison); but when the body realizes it has not been poisoned, circulation throughout the entire body increases to above normal levels, starting with the internal organs, then radiating out toward the skin. This is why, even when taken internally, chile can help to heal skin lesions.

The increase in blood flow enhances the production of protective juices in the stomach, intestines, and lungs, making these organs more resistant to injury and infection; increased blood volume through the blood vessels helps to keep them clear and also nourishes the heart. This is why cayenne, when taken regularly, has been helpful in the treatment of heart disease and atherosclerosis.

When applied externally, capsaicin increases circulation to the site where it has been applied, and also depletes the nerves of substance P, a neurotransmitter that conveys pain signals to the brain. With regular use, the substance P can be depleted to such

Chiles exaggerated in the tabloid press. SUNBELT ARCHIVES

a degree that certain kinds of chronic pain, such as that associated with arthritis, are no longer perceived. In fact, capsaicin is one of the most powerful local pain relievers available and is the active ingredient in many over-the-counter arthritis medications. It is so effective that many doctors warn their patients not to overexert themselves when they find that their pain has lessened significantly. The capsaicin in chile has also been used to treat the pain of shingles, toothache, surgery scars, diabetic neuropathy, and mouth sores caused by chemotherapy.

The amount of the substance P depletion and the duration of desensitization depend upon how much capsaicin is applied. It often takes three or four days of regular use for full pain relief, with sensitivity returning anywhere from a few hours to a few weeks after capsaicin treatment has been discontinued. (See Folk Medicine.)

MEXICO

Chile is so ingrained in the culture of Mexico that chile expert Arturo Lomelí wrote: "Chile, they say, is the king, the soul of the Mexicans—a nutrient, a medicine, a drug, a comfort. For many Mexicans, if it were not for the existence of chile, their national identity would begin to disappear."

Early Origins

In southern Mexico and the Yucatán Peninsula, chile peppers have been part of the human diet since about 7500 B.C. and thus their usage predates the two great Central American civilizations, the Maya and the Aztecs. From their original usage as a spice collected in the wild, chiles gained importance after their domestication and they were a significant food when the Olmec culture was developing, around 1000 B.C.

About 500 B.C., the Monte Albán culture, in the Valley of Oaxaca, began exporting a new type of pottery vessel to nearby regions. These vessels resembled the handheld *molcajete* mortars of today and were called *Suchilquitongo* bowls. Because the *molcajetes* are still used to crush chile pods and make salsas, the *Suchilquitongo* bowls are probably the first evidence we have for the creation of crushed chile and chile powders. Scientists speculate that chile powder was developed soon after the *Suchilquitongo* bowls were invented, and both the tool and the product were then exported.

A carved glyph found in the ceremonial center of Monte Albán is further evidence of the early importance of chile peppers. It features a chile plant with three pendant pods on one end and the head of a man on the other. Some experts believe that the glyph is one of a number of "tablets of conquest," which marked the sites conquered by the Monte Albán culture.

The Spicy Legacy of the Maya

When the Europeans arrived in the Western Hemisphere, people of Mayan ancestry lived in southern Mexico, the Yucatán Peninsula, Belize, Guatemala, and parts of Honduras and El Salvador. The

A woman in Oaxaca grinds her mole *sauce* on a metate.
DAVE DEWITT

A chiltepinero measures out chiltepins in Sonora. DAVE DEWITT

Mayan civilization had long passed its height by that time, so there are no European observations about their classic culture. All that exists today are writings about their descendants; Mayan hieroglyphics, which are slowly being transliterated; and ethnological observations of the present Maya Indians, whose food habits have changed little in twenty centuries.

By the time the Maya reached the peak of their civilization in southern Mexico and the Yucatán Peninsula, around A.D. 500, they had a highly developed system of agriculture. Maize was their most important crop, followed closely by beans, squash, chiles, and cacao. Perhaps as

many as thirty different varieties of chiles were cultivated, and they were sometimes planted in plots by themselves but more often in fields already containing tomatoes and sweet potatoes. There were three species of chiles grown by the Maya and their descendants in Central America: *Capsicum annuum*, *Capsicum chinense*, and *Capsicum frutescens*—and they were all imports from other regions. The *annuums* probably originated in Mexico, while the *frutescens* came from Panama, and the *chinense* from the Amazon Basin via the Caribbean. The Maya also cultivated cotton, papayas, vanilla beans, cacao, manioc, and agave.

The importance of chiles is immediately

seen in the most basic Mayan foods. According to food historian Sophie Coe, "The beans . . . could be cooked in plain water or water in which toasted or untoasted chiles had been steeped. Such a chile 'stock' might be called the basis of the cuisine, so frequently does it turn up. It is in everything from the tortilla accompaniment of the very poorest peasant to the liquid for cooking the turkey for the greatest celebrations. There is even a reference to it in the *Popul Vuh* [Mayan sacred text], where the grandmother grinds chiles and mixes them with broth, and the broth acts as a mirror in which the rat on the rafters is reflected for the hero twins to see."

Coe speculates that the first sauces were used for tortilla-dipping. "The simplest sauce was ground dried chiles and water," she wrote in *America's First Cuisines*. "From this humble ancestor comes the line which terminates with trendy salsas beloved of a certain school of today's chefs." The ground or crushed chiles—sometimes in a thick sauce—were used to preserve and prolong the life of a piece of meat, fish, or other game. Since there was no refrigeration, fresh meat spoiled quickly, and by trial and error, the earliest cooks realized that chiles were an antioxidant, preserving the meats to some degree.

"But even the original inventors of tortilla-dipping sauces varied them when they could," Coe added. "The ground, toasted seeds of large and small squashes, always carefully differentiated by the Maya, could be added to the basic chile water, or you could mix *epazote* with the water and then add ground, toasted squash seeds to the flavored liquid." As more and more ingredients were added, a unique family of sauces was developed that led to the *pipiáns* and *moles* of today.

For breakfast the Maya ate a gruel of ground maize spiced with chile peppers, which is usually called *atole* but is sometimes known as *pozól*. A modern equivalent would be cornmeal or *masa* mixed with water and ground red chiles to the consistency of a milk shake. A favorite drink was chocolate mixed with water, honey, and chile powder.

For the main meal, stews of vegetables and meats heavily spiced with chiles were served. One of these was *chacmole*, which combined venison with chile, achiote, allspice, and tomato—it was an offering to the gods as well as a nourishing entree. Various reports describe sauces made with chiles and black beans being wrapped in corn tortillas and covered with chile sauce, which may be the earliest references to enchiladas. As Sophie Coe noted, "The accepted wisdom was that tortillas and beans were boring; it took chile to make the saliva flow."

The Maya seem to have invented tamales too, as the Spanish chronicler Gonzalo Fernández de Oviedo reported in 1526: "They brought certain well made baskets, one with the *pasticci* [filled pies] of maize dough stuffed with chopped meat . . . They ate it all, and praised that dish *pasticci*, which tasted as if it were spiced. It was reddish inside, with a good quantity of that pepper of the Indies which is called *asci* [the Antillean word for chile, modernized to *ají*]." Mayan tamales were quite sophisticated, with many different fillings, including toasted squash seeds, deer hearts, quail, egg yolks, dove breasts, squash blossoms, and black beans. The Maya kept domesticated turkeys, ducks, bees, and dogs, and their main game animals were deer, birds, iguana, and wild boar. Armadillos and manatees were considered delicacies. As with the Incas, meat dishes were reserved for Mayan royalty.

Chiles are highly visible today in areas with a Mayan heritage. In the Yucatán Peninsula, descendants of the Maya still grow habaneros, tomatoes, and onions in boxes or hollowed-out tree trunks that are raised up on four posts for protection against pigs and hens. These container gardens are usually in the yard of the house, near the kitchen.

Aztec Chiles

In 1529, Bernardino de Sahagún, a Spanish Franciscan friar living in Nueva España (Mexico), noted that the Aztecs ate hot red or yellow chile peppers in their hot chocolate and in nearly every dish they prepared! Fascinated by the Aztec's constant use of a previously unknown spice, Sahagún documented this fiery cuisine in his classic study, *Historia General de las Cosas de la Nueva España*, now known as the *Florentine Codex*. His work indicates that of all the pre-Columbian New World civilizations, it was the Aztecs who loved chile peppers the most.

The marketplaces of ancient Mexico overflowed with chile peppers of all sizes and shapes, and Sahagún wrote they included "hot green chiles, smoked chiles, water chiles, tree chiles, beetle chiles, and sharp-pointed red chiles." In addition to some twenty varieties of *chillis*, as the pungent pods were called in the Nahuatl language, vendors sold strings of red chiles (modern *ristras*), precooked chiles, and "fish chiles," which were the earliest known forms of *ceviche*, a method of preserving fish without cooking. This technique places the fish in a marinade of an acidic fruit juice and chile peppers.

Other seafood dishes were common as well in ancient Mexico. "They would eat another kind of stew, with frogs and green chile," Sahagún recorded, "and a stew of those fish called *axolotl* with yellow chile. They also used to eat a lobster stew which is very delicious." Apparently the Aztecs utilized every possible source of protein. The friar noted such exotic variations as maguey worms with a sauce of small chiles, newt with yellow chiles, and tadpoles with *chiltecpintl*.

Father Sahagún, one of the first behavioral scientists, also noted that chiles were revered as much as sex by the ancient Aztecs. While fasting to appease their rather bloodthirsty gods, the priests required two abstentions by the faithful: sexual relations and chile peppers.

Chocolate and chiles were commonly combined in a drink called *chicahuatl*, which was usually reserved for the priests and the wealthy. The Aztec versions of tamales often used banana leaves as a wrapper to steam combinations of *masa* dough, chicken, and the chiles of choice. Sahagún wrote that there were two types of sauces called "*chilemollis*": one with red chile and tomatoes, and the other with yellow chile and tomatoes. These *chilemollis* eventually became the savory *mole* sauces for which Mexican cuisine is justly famous.

Aztec cookery was the basis for the Mexican food of today, and, in fact, many Aztec dishes have lasted through the centuries virtually unchanged. Since oil and fat were not generally used in cooking, the foods were usually roasted, boiled, or cooked in sauces. Like the Maya, the Aztecs usually began the day with a cup of *atole* spiced with chile peppers.

The main meal was served at midday and usually consisted of tortillas with beans and a salsa made with chiles and tomatoes. The salsas were usually made by grinding the ingredients between two handheld stones, the *mocaljetes*. Even today, the same technique is used in Indian villages throughout Mexico and Central America. A remarkable variety of tamales were also served for the midday meal. They were stuffed with fruits such as plums, pineapple, or guava; with game meat such as deer or turkey; or with seafood such as snails or frogs. Whole chile pods were included with the stuffing, and after steaming, the tamales were often served with a cooked chile sauce.

It was this highly sophisticated chile cuisine that the Spanish encountered during their conquest of Mexico. Christopher Columbus "discovered" chile peppers in the West Indies on his first voyage to the New World. In his journal for 1493, he wrote,

"Also there is much *ají*, which is their pepper, and the people won't eat without it, for they find it very wholesome. One could load fifty caravels a year with it in Hispaniola."

Dr. Diego Chanca, the fleet physician for Columbus on his second voyage, wrote in his journal that the Indians seasoned manioc and sweet potatoes with *ají*, and that it was one of their principal foods. Of course, both Columbus and his doctor believed that they had reached the Spice Islands, the East Indies. Not only did Columbus misname the Indians, he also mistook chiles for black pepper, thus giving them the inaccurate name "pepper." But he did one thing right—he transported chile seeds back to Europe after his first voyage, which began the chile conquest of the rest of the world.

Explorers who followed Columbus to the New World soon learned that chiles were an integral part of the Indians' culinary, medical, and religious lives. In 1526, just thirty-four years after Columbus's first excursion, El Capitán Gonzalo Fernández de Oviedo noted that on the Spanish Main, "Indians everywhere grow it in gardens and farms with much diligence and attention because they eat it continuously with almost all their food."

Bernabe Cobo, a naturalist and historian who traveled throughout Central and South America in the early seventeenth century, estimated that there were at least forty different varieties. He wrote that there were "some as large as limes or large plums; others, as small as pine nuts or even grains of wheat, and between the two extremes are many different sizes. No less variety is found in color . . . and the same difference is found in form and shape."

The Aztec market in the capital, Tenochtitlàn, contained a large number of chiles, and most of those had been collected as tribute, a form of taxation used by the Toltecs and Aztecs and later adopted by the Spanish. The payers of the tribute were the *macehuales*, the serfs or commoners; the collectors were Aztec officials, or later on, officials who worked for the Spanish. The tribute consisted of locally produced goods or crops that were commonly grown, and the tribute of each village was recorded in boxes on codices of drawn or painted pictographs.

According to many sources, chiles were one of the most common tribute items. The chiles were offered to the government in several different forms: as fresh or dried pods, as seed, in two-hundred-pound bundles, in willow baskets, and in Spanish bushels. After the chile and the rest of the produce was moved to the capital, it was stored in warehouses and closely guarded, and then sold. Chile peppers were considered to be the most valuable of the tributes.

One of the most famous tribute codices is the *Matricula de Tributos*, which is part of the *Mendocino Codex*. This codex was compiled for the first viceroy of New Spain, Antonio de Mendoza, who ordered it painted in order to inform the Emperor Charles V of the wealth of what is now Mexico. Glyphs on the codex indicate the tribute paid to the Aztecs by conquered towns just before the Spanish conquest; the towns on one tribute list (in what is now San Luis Potosí) gave 1,600 loads of dry chiles to the imperial throne each year!

The *Mendocino Codex* also reveals an early use of chile peppers as a form of punishment. One pictograph shows a father punishing his young son by forcing him to inhale smoke from roasting chiles. The same drawing shows a mother threatening her daughter with the same punishment. Today, the Popolocán Indians, who live near Oaxaca, punish their children in a similar manner.

Wherever they traveled in the New World, Spanish explorers, particularly nonsoldiers, collected and transported chile seeds and thus further spread the different varieties. And not only did they adopt the chile as their own, the Spanish also imported foods that they combined with chiles and other native ingredients to create even more complex chile cuisines.

Creating a Chile Cuisine

The arrival of the Spanish in Mexico had a profound effect on the cuisine of the country as the ingredients the explorers brought with them soon transformed the eating habits of the Indians. However, the Aztecs and their descendants did not give up their beloved staples such as chiles, corn, and chocolate; they combined them with the new imports and thus created the basis for the Mexican cuisines of today.

Throughout the centuries, an astonishing variety in Mexican cooking developed as a result of geography. From the Yucatán Peninsula, Mexico stretches more than two thousand miles to the deserts of the north, so the length and size of Mexico, combined with the fact that mountain ranges separate the various regions, led to the development of isolated regional cuisines. This geographical variety is the reason that the cooking of tropical Yucatán differs significantly from that of the deserts of Chihuahua and Sonora.

One common factor, though, in Mexican cookery is the prevalence of chile peppers. Unlike South America, where chiles are still mostly consumed by the Indian population, in Mexico everyone fell in love with the pungent pods. Chile peppers are Mexico's most important vegetable crop; they are grown all over the country from the Pacific and Gulf coasts to mountainous regions with an altitude above 8,000 feet. Approximately 200,000 acres of cultivated land produce between 500,000 and 650,000 tons of fresh pods and 30,000 tons of dry pods, making Mexico number six of the chile-producing countries of the world. Although more than thirty different varieties are grown or collected in Mexico, the anchos/poblanos, serranos, *mirasols*, and jalapeños account for 75 percent of the crop. In 1988, Mexico exported 2,529 metric tons of fresh or dried chiles worth $4.6 million to the United States.

In 1985, each Mexican consumed about fourteen pounds of green chile and nearly two pounds of dried chile. In fact, the Mexicans eat more chile per capita than onions or tomatoes. The favorite chiles are about evenly divided between those harvested fresh and those utilized in the dry form.

The serranos and jalapeños are grown for processing and the fresh market, where they are the chiles of choice for salsas.

Over 90 percent of the serrano crop is used fresh in homemade *salsas* such as *pico de gallo*. About 60 percent of the jalapeño crop is processed, either by canning or pickling or as commercial salsas. Of the remainder, 20 percent is used fresh and 20 percent is used in the production of chipotles, the smoked and dried form of the jalapeño.

How Many Moles?

Perhaps the most famous Mexican chile dishes are the *moles*. The word *mole*, from the Nahuatl *molli*, means "mixture," as in *guacamole*, a mixture of vegetables (*guaca*). Some sources say that the word is taken from the Spanish verb *moler*, meaning to grind. Whatever its precise origin, the word used by itself embraces a vast number of sauces utilizing every imaginable combination of meats, vegetables, spices, and flavorings—sometimes up to three dozen different ingredients. Not only are there many ingredients, there are dozens of variations on *mole*—red *moles*, green *moles*, brown *moles*, fiery *moles*, and even mild *moles*.

The earliest *moles* were simple compared with what was to come after the Spanish invasion. Ana M. de Benítez, who reconstructed pre-Columbian dishes based on Sahagún's descriptions, used four different chiles (ancho, *mulato*, pasilla, and chipotle), plus tomatoes, garlic, pumpkins, tomatillos, and chayote as the basis of her *moles*. The addition of Eastern Hemisphere ingredients such as almonds, raisins, garlic, cinnamon, and cloves would eventually transform the basic *mole* of the Aztecs into a true delicacy.

Mole poblano, originally called *mole de olores* ("fragrant *mole*"), is the sauce traditionally served on special occasions such as Christmas that combines chiles and chocolate, a popular and revered food of the Aztecs. Montezuma's court consumed fifty jugs of chile-laced hot chocolate a day, and warriors drank it to soothe their nerves before going into battle. However, the story of how chocolate was combined with chile sauces does not involve warriors, but rather nuns.

Legend holds that *mole poblano* was invented in the sixteenth century by the nuns of the convent of Santa Rosa in the city of Puebla. It seems that the archbishop was coming to visit, and the nuns were worried because they had no food elegant enough to serve someone of his eminence. So, they prayed for guidance and one of the nuns had a vision. She directed that everyone in the convent should begin chopping and grinding everything edible they could find in the kitchen. Into a pot went chiles, tomatoes, nuts, sugar, tortillas, bananas, raisins, garlic, avocados, and dozens of herbs and spices. The final ingredient was the magic one: chocolate. The chocolate, they reasoned, would smooth the flavor of the sauce by slightly cutting its heat. Then the nuns slaughtered their only turkey and served it with the *mole* sauce to the archbishop, who declared it the finest dish he had ever tasted.

This is a great legend, but a more likely scenario holds that the basic *mole* of the Aztecs was gradually transformed by a collision of cuisines. Regarding the use of chocolate, since that delicacy was reserved for Aztec royalty, the military nobility, and religious officials, perhaps Aztec serving girls at the convent gave a royal recipe to the nuns so they could honor their royalty, the archbishop. At any rate, the recipe for *mole poblano* was rescued from oblivion and became a holiday favorite. De Benítez noted: "In the book on Puebla cooking, published in Puebla in 1877, we find recipes for making forty-four kinds of *mole*; there are also sixteen kinds of *manchamanteles* [tablecloth stainers] which are dishes with different kinds of chiles."

In Mexico today, cooks who specialize in *moles* are termed *moleros*. In 1963 a group of *moleros* formed a *mole* cooperative of sixty partners who banded together for the good of their craft. They shared equipment such as pulverizers and mills, and eventually organized a fair exclusively dedicated to *moles*, so they formed the *Feria Nacional del Mole*, the National *Mole* Fair, held in conjunction with the fairs of the local pueblos.

At the fair, thousands of people sample hundreds of different *moles* created by restaurateurs and *mole* wholesalers. By 1982, the fair had grown so large that the committee moved the location and the date to accommodate all the visitors. The *mole* fair became a national event and was eventually placed on the Secretary of Tourism's calendar of fairs and fiestas. Each year bigger and better events were presented. As a result, restaurants began featuring more *mole* specials and tourists had more opportunities to experience the various *moles*.

The National *Mole* Fair has certainly become one of the premier chile pepper events in the world. This fair is the Mexican equivalent of chili con carne cook-offs in the United States; the *moleros* take great pride in their fiery creations and consider each *mole* a work of art in the same way that chili cook-off chefs regard their chili con carne. Often the preparation of a family *mole* recipe takes as long as three days. Their recipes are family secrets not to be revealed to others under any circumstances; indeed, they are passed down from generation to generation.

"If one of my children wants to carry on my business as a *molero* and is serious about it," *molero* Villa Suarez told reporter William Stockton, I will tell them all the secrets when the time comes." But he went on to indicate that if his children were not interested in becoming *moleros*, his secrets would die with him.

The color of a particular *mole* depends mostly upon the varieties of chiles utilized. A green *mole* consists of poblano chiles while a red *mole* could contain three or four different varieties of dried red chiles, such as chiles *de árbol*, or *cascabels*. The brown and black *moles* owe their color to pasillas and anchos, both of which are sometimes called "chile *negro*" because of their dark hues when dried. The dark color of *mole negro* can also be the result of roasting the chiles until they are almost black, as is the custom in Oaxaca.

Other than chiles, there are literally dozens of other ingredients added to the various *moles,* including almonds, anise, bananas, chocolate, cinnamon, cilantro, cloves, coconut, garlic, onions, peanuts, peppercorns, pine nuts, pumpkin seeds, raisins, sesame seeds, toasted bread, tomatillos, tomatoes, tortillas, and walnuts.

Undoubtedly, some *moleros* add coriander, cumin, epazote, oregano, thyme, and other spices to their *moles.*

But Puebla is not the only state in Mexico with a reputation for *moles.* Oaxaca, in the south, lays claim to seven unique *moles*—and dozens and dozens of variations. In *Tradiciones Gastronómicas Oaxaqueñas*, the author, Ana Maria Guzmán de Vasquez Colmenares, noted: "There must be something magical in the number seven, for the number of Oaxacan moles coincides with the wonders of the world, the theological virtues, the wise men of Athens—and for their wisdom which elected the number seven to represent justice."

"There may be seven *moles,*" say the locals, "but of thousands and thousands of cooks, each has their own private version of all of the *moles,* so how many does that make?" One magazine writer suggested: "Oaxaca should be the land of 200 moles!"

For the record, the seven *moles* are: *mole negro, mole coloradito, mole verde, mole amarillo, mole rojo, manchas manteles* ("tablecloth stainer"), and *mole chichilo.* They are all descendants of *clemole,* believed to be the original *mole* of Oaxaca. It was quite simple, being composed of ancho and pasilla chiles, garlic, cloves, cinnamon, and coriander.

The Oaxacan *moles* are characterized by unusual chiles that are unique to the region. There are sixty chiles grown only in the state of Oaxaca and nowhere else in Mexico. Of those sixty, about ten commonly appear in the Oaxaca city market. Some of these unusual chiles include chiles *de agua,* which grow erect and are pointed at the end.

The chiles *chilhuacle*, which are short and fat, come in two varieties, black and red. The red variety is called "the saffron of the poor" because a small amount of ground *chilhuacle rojo* gives a similar coloring to foods. Other unique chiles are the red-orange chiles *onzas*, the yellow *costeño*, and the pasilla *Oaxaqueña* (sometimes called pasilla *Mexicana*), a smoked chile *de agua* pasilla that adds a chipotle-like flavor to *moles*.

Instead of tediously grinding all the ingredients on a *metate* these days, many cooks go to the Benito Juárez market, buy all their chiles, nuts, and seeds, and have them custom-ground in the special *molinos*, or mills in another section of the market. The result is a dark paste that is later converted into a *mole* sauce. The chiles are toasted black, soaked and ground, and blended with fried tomatoes, tomatillos, and roasted garlic and onions. Then come nuts and seeds—some toasted, some fried. Almonds, peanuts, pecans, chile seeds, and sesame seeds. There are almost always more sesame seeds than any other seed or nut. They have to be fried slowly and carefully, with lots of love and attention. Hence the affectionate Mexican *dicho* (saying): "You are the sesame seed of my *mole*."

Many different meats are added to *moles*, from chicken to beef to fish, but by far the most common meat served is turkey. In fact, turkey is so important in *mole negro*, that Mexican writer Manuel Toussaint noted that the turkey in the *mole* was as important as the eagle in the Mexican flag, and another writer suggested that to refuse to eat *mole negro* was a crime of treason against the homeland!

TORTILLA SOUP WITH PASILLA CHILES
Sopa de Tortilla con Chiles Pasillas

The broth in this recipe is about the only thing that stays the same from cook to cook. Basic to Mexican cuisine, this soup from Chihuahua is served with a multitude of ingredients, and even they vary widely from place to place. The garnishes vary too; it's all part of the fun of making or eating this soup!

MAKES 8 SERVINGS
HEAT SCALE: **Medium**

4 pasilla chiles, seeds and stems removed
4 quarts rich chicken broth
3 large tomatoes, peeled
2 onions, quartered
2 cloves garlic
1 teaspoon salt
¼ cup chopped fresh cilantro
2 tablespoons vegetable oil
3 dozen small corn tortillas, cut into ¼-inch strips, fried and drained (or substitute 4 cups broken tortilla chips)

Garnishes
2 pasilla chiles, seeds and stems removed, lightly fried and coarsely ground in blender
1 cup chopped avocados
1 cup crumbled cheese, such as panela, feta, or mozzarella

Tear the 4 pasilla chiles into strips, cover with hot water in a bowl, and rehydrate for 15 minutes.

Heat the chicken broth in a large saucepan almost to the boiling point, reduce the heat to low, and simmer while you prepare the rest of the ingredients.

Put the drained rehydrated chiles in a blender, add the tomatoes, onions, garlic, salt, and cilantro, and puree for 10 seconds.

Heat the oil in a small skillet over medium-high heat, add the blended chile mixture, and cook, stirring, for 5 minutes. Stir this mixture into the simmering chicken broth, cover, and simmer for 30 minutes.

Divide the fried tortilla strips into 8 bowls, ladle the simmering chicken-chile stock over the strips. Garnish with the ground pasilla chiles, avocado, and cheese.

SPICY NORTEÑO BEEF SALAD
Salpicón

This recipe is extremely popular in northern Mexico, particularly Ciudad Juárez. It crossed the border into the United States because of Julio Ramirez. Ramirez opened his first Julio's restaurant in 1944 in Juárez on Avenida 16 de Septiembre and a second location in El Paso in 1985, and this recipe immediately became the restaurant's best-selling dish. Note that this recipe requires advance preparation.

MAKES 12 SERVINGS
HEAT SCALE: **Medium**

One 3-pound beef brisket
2 cloves garlic, minced
Salt to taste
1 cup diced white Cheddar cheese
½ cup chopped fresh cilantro
½ cup diced, seeded tomatoes

½ cup vegetable oil
½ cup white wine vinegar
4 chipotle chiles in adobo, minced
Diced avocado for garnish
1 head iceberg lettuce

Put the brisket in a large pot with enough water to cover. Add the garlic and salt and bring to a boil. Reduce the heat to medium-low and simmer for about 1½ hours, uncovered, until the meat is tender and can be shredded. Cool the meat in the broth and then shred finely by hand. Reserve the broth to make a stew or soup.

In a large bowl, toss the shredded brisket with the remaining ingredients (except the avocado and lettuce). Chill the mixture and allow it to marinate for a couple of hours or preferably overnight.

Line a platter with lettuce leaves, place the *salpicón* on the leaves, and garnish with the avocado. Serve with hot, buttered flour tortillas.

MEXICAN BREAKFAST SAUSAGE
Chorizo

This traditional Mexican sausage is often served with *huevos rancheros* for breakfast. Unlike other sausages, it is usually not placed in a casing but rather served loose or formed into patties. Note that this recipe requires advance preparation.

MAKES 8 SERVINGS
HEAT SCALE: **Medium**

1 clove garlic
½ cup hot red New Mexican chile powder
½ teaspoon freshly ground black pepper
¼ teaspoon each: ground cloves, ground cinnamon, ground cumin

1¼ teaspoons dried Mexican oregano
½ teaspoon salt
½ cup white vinegar
2 pounds ground pork

In a blender, combine all the ingredients except the pork and puree. Knead this mixture into the pork until it is thoroughly mixed together. Cover and let sit in the refrigerator for at least a day. At this point the chorizo may be frozen.

To cook, crumble it in a skillet over medium-high heat and cook thoroughly for about 15 minutes, stirring occasionally. Drain on paper towels before serving.

OAXACAN LITTLE RED MOLE
Mole Coloradito Oaxaqueño

Here is one of the seven classic Oaxacan *moles*. Although the spices for such *moles* are often ground in *molinos* in the markets, there are still many *señoras* in the small pueblos who insist on using their *mocaljetes* for the tedious grinding of the ingredients for this famous dish. Serve with black beans, rice, and tortillas.

MAKES 4 TO 6 SERVINGS
HEAT SCALE: **Medium**

1 whole chicken, cut into 8 serving pieces

6 cups chicken stock

5 ancho chiles, stems and seeds removed

2 guajillo chiles, stems and seeds removed (or substitute dried red New Mexican chiles)

5 whole black peppercorns

5 whole cloves

Two 2-inch cinnamon sticks, Mexican preferred

6 tablespoons lard or vegetable oil

1 white onion, peeled and quartered

10 cloves garlic

1 small French roll, sliced

1 small plantain (or substitute 1 banana)

2 tablespoons raisins

¼ cup sesame seeds

10 whole almonds

2 medium tomatoes, quartered

3 sprigs fresh marjoram or oregano

1 bar (2 ounces), or to taste, Mexican chocolate, such as Ibarra

1 or 2 avocado leaves (or substitute bay leaves)

Salt to taste

In a large pot over high heat, bring the chicken and stock to a simmer. Reduce the heat to medium-low and simmer until the chicken is tender, about 30 minutes. Remove the chicken and keep warm and reserve the stock.

In a large skillet or *comal* over medium heat, toast the chiles, turning once, until darkened but not burned. Toast the *guajillos* a little longer because of their tougher skins. Place the chiles in a bowl and cover with hot water to soak for 30 minutes to soften. Remove the chiles, place in a blender or food processor, and puree, adding a little chile water if necessary. Strain.

In the skillet or *comal* over medium heat, toast the peppercorns, cloves, and cinnamon sticks until aromatic, 1 to 2 minutes, stirring often. Cool and grind in a *mocaljete* or spice grinder.

In the same skillet, heat 1 tablespoon of the lard and sauté the onion and garlic over medium heat until slightly browned. Cool and place in a blender or food processor and puree with a little water.

Heat 3 tablespoons of the lard in the skillet until smoking hot, and fry the bread slices until lightly brown. Remove and drain on paper towels. In the same hot skillet, fry the peeled plantain on both sides until browned (about 3 minutes), remove, and drain. Quickly fry the raisins for about 1 minute and remove. Reduce the heat to low and add the sesame seeds. Cook, stirring constantly, for 2 minutes, then add the almonds and continue to cook, stirring, until both are well browned. Remove, drain, and combine in a food processor or blender with the bread, plantain, and raisins, reserving a bit of the sesame seeds for garnish. Puree, adding a little water if necessary.

Wipe out the skillet with a cloth and add 1 tablespoon of the lard. When hot, add the tomatoes and cook well, stirring, for about 3 minutes. Place in a blender or food processor and puree until smooth. Remove.

Heat the remaining tablespoon of lard in a *cazuela* or heavy pot over medium-high heat until smoking. Add the chile puree and cook, stirring constantly, so it does not burn, for

2 minutes. It tends to splatter about, so be careful! Add the tomato puree, the ground spices, onion-garlic mixture, and the marjoram and heat through. Stir in the bread mixture and continue to heat, stirring constantly. Add the chocolate and avocado leaves and thin with the reserved chicken stock. Reduce the heat to low and simmer for 30 minutes.

Add the chicken and adjust the salt. Heat through and serve.

Querétaro-Style Enchiladas
Enchiladas Estilo Querétaro

This recipe from the state of Querétaro calls for chile-infused vinegar, which is easy to find in gourmet shops and hot shops. These enchiladas are unusual because they are fried instead of baked.

MAKES 24 ENCHILADAS, 8 SERVINGS
HEAT SCALE: Medium

6 cups water
3 medium potatoes, peeled and diced
4 carrots, peeled and diced
2 cups vegetable oil
10 ancho chiles, seeds and stems removed, chopped
2 cloves garlic, chopped
½ teaspoon dried Mexican oregano
2 cloves
½ teaspoon ground cinnamon

Salt to taste
24 small corn tortillas
5½ ounces packaged chorizo, fried for about 15 minutes over medium heat, or use Mexican Breakfast Sausage (page 196)
¼ cup chile-infused vinegar
1½ cups grated asadero cheese (a mild Cheddar cheese) (or substitute Monterey Jack)
1 onion, chopped
½ head lettuce, shredded

In a large pot, heat 4 cups of the water to boiling. Add the potatoes and carrots and boil until they are half cooked, about 7 minutes. Remove from the pot and drain. In a skillet, heat ⅔ cup of the vegetable oil over medium heat and cook the potatoes and carrots, stirring occasionally, until lightly browned, about 10 minutes.

Place the remaining 2 cups water in a large saucepan. Add the chiles, garlic, oregano, cloves, cinnamon, and salt and bring to a boil. Boil for 5 minutes. Remove the pan from the heat, place the mixture in a blender, and process until smooth. Place the tortillas on a flat surface. Carefully put 1 tablespoon of the chile mixture onto the center of each tortilla and spread it around. Reserve the remaining chile mixture.

In a bowl, combine the chorizo and potatoes and carrots. Spoon about 3 tablespoons of the mixture on top of the chile mixture on each tortilla. Starting at one end, roll each tortilla into a cylinder and set aside.

Pour the remaining 1⅓ cups oil and the chile-infused vinegar into a large skillet over medium-high heat and heat until the oil is hot. Place the enchiladas in the oil and fry quickly until almost crisp, turning once, for about 2 minutes on each side. Drain the enchiladas on paper towels. Place the fried enchiladas on a plate and cover with the remaining chile mixture, cheese, onion, and shredded lettuce, and serve.

SONORAN SHREDDED BEEF WITH CHILES
Machaca Estilo Norteño

The word *"machaca"* derives from the verb *machacar*, to pound or crush, and that description of this meat dish is apt. The shredded meat is often used as a filling for burritos or chimichangas and is sometimes dried. Serve the meat wrapped in a flour tortilla along with shredded lettuce, chopped tomatoes, grated cheese, and sour cream to reduce the heat.

MAKES 6 TO 8 SERVINGS
HEAT SCALE: Hot

One 3-pound pot roast
10 to 15 chiltepins, crushed
1½ cups chopped green New Mexican chiles,
    roasted and peeled (page 146), stems and
    seeds removed

1 cup chopped tomatoes
½ cup chopped onion
2 cloves garlic, minced

Place the roast in a large pot and add enough water to cover. Bring to a boil, then reduce the heat to medium-low, cover, and simmer until tender and the meat starts to fall apart, 3 to 4 hours. Check it periodically to make sure it doesn't burn, adding more water if necessary.

Remove the roast from the pan and remove the fat. Remove the broth from the pan, chill, and remove the fat. Shred the roast with a fork.

Return the shredded meat and then the defatted broth to the pan. Add the remaining ingredients and bring to a simmer over medium-high heat. Reduce the heat to medium-low and simmer until the meat has absorbed all the broth.

🌿 *Miahuateco.* Grown only in the states of Puebla and Oaxaca, Mexico, this large variety of poblano is used in its green form.

🌿 *Mirasol.* "Looking at the sun"; the erect (sometimes pendant) pods are two to four inches long, are quite hot, and are used both fresh and dry. *Mirasol* is primarily grown in Zacatecas, Mexico. Also called *miracielo*, "looking at the sky." In the United States, a pod type of the *annuum* species. Varieties include: 'De Comida,' 'Guajillo,' and 'Costeño.'

🌿 *Mirch.* Hindi term for hot Capsicums in northern India. *Lal mirch* is red chile; *hari mirch* is green chile. Cayenne is *pisi hui lal mirch.* Dried red chiles are *sabut lal mirch. Kashmiri* chiles are *degi mirch.*

🌿 *Miri.* Sinhalese word for chile.

🌿 *'Mississippi Hot.'* A variety of *Capsicum annuum* grown in the American South for pickling. Also 'Mississippi Red Hot.'

🌿 **Mombasa.** Principal chile variety cultivated in Uganda.

🌿 *Mora.* "Mulberry" or "blackberry"; a smoked red serrano or jalapeño that is pliable. Also called *morita* in many parts of Mexico and *chilaile* in Quintana Roo, Mexico.

🌿 *Morelia.* A variety of poblano that is grown only in Queréndaro, Michoacán, Mexico. The pods dry to a black color, so it is also known as chile *negro.* Named for the capital of Michoacán.

🌿 *'Morita.'* A cultivated variety of jalapeño. This variety is also smoked. (See *Mora.*)

🌿 *Morrón.* Generally, in Mexico, a bell pepper but also another name for pimiento.

🌿 *Mosquito.* "Mosquito chile"; in Mexico, another name for the piquin.

🌿 *Mukuru.* Local name for the wild *Capsicum tovarii* of Peru.

🌿 *Mulagay.* Sri Lankan (Tamil) term for peppers.

🌿 *Mulato.* A variety of dried poblano chile in Mexico that has very dark brown—almost black—pods. Grown primarily in Jalisco, Guanajuato, and Puebla.

🌿 *Murici.* A name for the *chinense* species in Brazil.

🌿 **Mutton pepper.** Local name for *Capsicum chinense* in Belize.

Negro. "Black." (See *Morelia*.) Also sometimes refers to a dark pasilla chile in Mexico.

Nellore. A variety of *annuum* grown in India that resembles the Mexican *de árbol* variety.

New Mexican. Formerly called Anaheim, this pod type is grown in Chihuahua and other northern states of Mexico and then imported into the United States. It is also grown extensively in New Mexico, Arizona, and California. It is a long (to eight inches), fairly mild pod that is used both in green and red forms.

NEW MEXICAN VARIETIES

According to many accounts, cultivated chile peppers were introduced into what is now the United States by Capitán General Juan de Oñate, the founder of Santa Fe, in 1609. However, they may have been introduced to the Pueblo Indians of New Mexico by the Antonio Espejo expedition of 1582–83. According to one of the members of the expedition, Baltasar Obregón, "They have no chile, but the natives were given some seed to plant." By 1601, chiles were not on the list of Indian crops, according to colonist Francisco de Valverde, who also complained that mice were a pest that ate chile pods off the plants in the field.

After the Spanish began settlement, the cultivation of chile peppers exploded, and soon they were grown all over New Mexico. It is likely that many different varieties were cultivated, including early forms of jalapeños, serranos, anchos, and pasillas. But one variety that adapted particularly well to New Mexico was a long green chile that turned red in the fall. Formerly called "Anaheim" because of its transfer to the more settled California around 1900, the New Mexican chiles were cultivated for hundreds of years in the region with such dedication that several distinct varieties developed. These varieties, or "land races," called 'Chimayó' and 'Española,' had

Freshly harvested 'New Mexico No. 6–4' chiles. SUNBELT ARCHIVES

adapted to particular environments and are still planted today in the same fields they were grown in centuries ago; they constitute a small but distinct part of the tons of pods produced each year in New Mexico.

In 1846, William Emory, Chief Engineer of the Army's Topographic Unit, was surveying the New Mexico landscape and its customs. He described a meal eaten by people in Bernalillo, just north of Albuquerque: "Roast chicken, stuffed with onions; then mutton, boiled with onions; then followed various other dishes, all dressed with the everlasting onion; and the whole terminated by chile, the glory of New Mexico."

Emory went on to relate his experience with chiles: "Chile the Mexicans consider ʰef-d'oeuvre of the cuisine, and seem

really to revel in it; but the first mouthful brought the tears trickling down my cheeks, very much to the amusement of the spectators with their leather-lined throats. It was red pepper, stuffed with minced meat."

The Plant

New Mexican chiles are pod types of the *annuum* species. The plant has mostly a compact habit with an intermediate number of stems, and grows between twenty and thirty inches high. The leaves are ovate, medium green, fairly smooth, and about three inches long and two inches wide. The flower corollas are white with no spots. The pods are pendant, elongate, bluntly pointed, and measure between two and twelve inches. They are dark green, maturing to various shades of red. Some ornamentals are yellow or brown. Their heat ranges from quite mild to medium, between 500 and 2,500 Scoville Units. More than 40,000 acres of New Mexican chiles are under cultivation in New Mexico, California, Arizona, and Texas. The growing period is about eighty days, and each plant produces between ten and twenty pods, depending on variety and cultural techniques.

Varieties of the New Mexican pod type are: 'Anaheim M' (eight-inch pods, mild); 'Anaheim TMR 23' (eight-inch pods that are etch-resistant, mild); 'Chimayó' (a land race from northern New Mexico with thin-walled, six-inch pods, medium-hot); 'Española Improved' (pods five to six inches, medium heat); 'Fresno' (erect, two-inch pods, medium-hot); 'New Mexico No. 6-4' (the most commonly grown New Mexican variety, pods are seven inches long, medium heat); 'NuMex Big Jim' (long pods, up to twelve inches, medium heat); 'NuMex Eclipse' (chocolate-brown, five-inch pods, mild); 'NuMex Joe E. Parker' (improved 6-4 variety); 'NuMex Sunrise' (bright yellow, five-inch pods, mild); 'NuMex Sunset' (orange, five-inch pods, mild); 'NuMex R Naky' (pods are five to seven inches long, mild); and 'Sandia' (six-inch pods with thin walls, medium-hot).

'Española Improved' chile. DAVE DEWITT

Agriculture

The earliest cultivated chiles in New Mexico were smaller than those of today; indeed, they were (and still are, in some cases) considered a spice. But as the land races developed and the size of the pods increased, the food value of chiles became evident. There was just one problem—the bewildering sizes and shapes of the chile peppers made it very difficult for farmers to determine which variety of chile they were growing from year to year. And there was no way to tell how large the pods might be, or how hot. The demand for chiles was increasing as the population of the state did, so it was time for modern horticulture to take over.

In 1907, Fabian Garcia, a horticulturist at the Agricultural Experiment Station at the College of Agriculture and Mechanical Arts (now New Mexico State University), began his first experiments in breeding more standardized chile varieties, and, in 1908, published *Chile Culture*, the first chile bulletin from the Agricultural Experiment Station. In 1913, Garcia became director of the experiment station and expanded his breeding program.

Finally, in 1917, after ten years of experiments with various strains of pasilla chiles, Garcia released 'New Mexico No. 9,' the first attempt to grow chiles with a dependable pod size and heat level. The 'No. 9' variety became the chile standard in New Mexico until 1950, when Roy Harper, another horticulturist, released 'New Mexico No. 6,' a variety that matured earlier, produced higher yields, was wilt-resistant, and was less pungent than 'No. 9.'

Corn and chile harvest, Santa Cruz, New Mexico, c. 1913. MUSEUM OF NEW MEXICO, NEG. 8088

The 'New Mexico No. 6' variety was by far the biggest breakthrough in the chile breeding program. According to Dr. Roy Nakayama, who succeeded Harper as director of the New Mexico Agricultural Experiment Station, "The 'No. 6' variety changed the image of chile from a ball of fire that sent consumers rushing to the water jug to that of a multipurpose vegetable with a pleasing flavor. Commercial production and marketing, especially of green chiles and sauces, have been growing steadily since people around the world have discovered the delicious taste of chile without the overpowering pungency."

Recognized in the 1970s as "Mr. Chile," Roy Nakayama helped expand New Mexico chile growing, which totaled 1,200 acres between 1949 and 1959, into a thriving industry that reached 15,000 acres in 1979, and 28,700 acres in 1996. As a researcher at the Agricultural Experiment Station in Las Cruces, New Mexico (now New Mexico State University), he improved the pod type called the 'New Mexico No. 6-4' in the late 1950s. Nakayama's improvements helped the 'New Mexico No. 6-4' become one of the most popular chiles grown in the state because of its moderate size (six to seven inches long), thick flesh, and uniform skin texture, which made it easy to work with and dehydrate.

In 1975, Nakayama introduced the 'NuMex Big Jim,' a cross between a small Peruvian chile and various types from New Mexico. This medium-heat chile is easy to grow, harvest, and stuff for chiles *rellenos*, and quickly became popular because of its size (the average pod is twelve inches).

Before he retired in 1985, Nakayama developed one of his most important contributions, 'NuMex R Naky.' Before the introduction of this low heat chile in 1985, the United States had imported paprika, a spice and a coloring agent, from Hungary and Spain. However, this new variety turned out to be a great source for paprika, which enabled New Mexico farmers to turn the tables and export about one third of their harvest to worldwide markets, including Africa, Hungary, and Spain.

Today, Dr. Paul Bosland, who took over the chile breeding program from Dr. Nakayama, is developing new varieties that are resistant to chile wilt, a fungal disease that can devastate fields. He has also created varieties to produce brown, orange, and yellow *ristras*, strings of chiles, for the home decoration market. The breeding and development of new chile varieties—in addition to research into wild species, post-harvest packaging, and genetics—is an ongoing, major project at New Mexico State. But modern horticultural techniques finally produced fairly standardized chiles. New Mexico is by far the largest commercial producer of chile peppers in the United States, with about 30,000 acres under cultivation.

Culinary Usage

All of the primary dishes in New Mexico cuisine contain chile peppers: sauces, stews, *carne adovada*, enchiladas, *posole*, tamales, *huevos rancheros*, and many combination vegetable dishes. The intense use of chiles as a food rather than just as a spice or condiment is what differentiates New Mexican cuisine from that of Texas or Arizona. In neighboring states, chile powders are used as a seasoning for beef or chicken broth–based "chile gravies," which are thickened with flour or cornstarch before they are added to, say, enchiladas. In New Mexico, the sauces are made from pure chiles and are thickened by reducing the crushed or pureed pods.

New Mexico chile sauces are cooked and pureed, while salsas utilize fresh ingredients and are uncooked. Debates rage over whether tomatoes are used in cooked sauces such as red chile sauce for enchiladas. Despite the recipes in numerous cookbooks, traditional cooked red sauces do not contain tomatoes, though uncooked salsas do.

New Mexicans love chile peppers so much that they have become the de facto state symbol. Houses are adorned with *ristras*. Images of the pods are emblazoned on signs, T-shirts, coffee mugs, posters, wind socks, and even underwear. In the late summer and early fall, the aroma of roasting chiles fills the air all over the state and produces a state of bliss for chileheads.

"A la primera cocinera se le va un chile entero," goes one old Spanish *dicho,* or saying: "To the best lady cook goes the whole chile." And the chile pepper is the single most important food brought from Mexico that defines New Mexican cuisine.

CLASSIC NEW MEXICAN RED CHILE SAUCE

This basic sauce can be used in any recipe calling for a red sauce, either traditional Mexican or New Southwestern versions of beans, tacos, tamales, and enchiladas.

MAKES 2 TO 2½ CUPS
HEAT SCALE: Medium

10 to 12 dried whole red New Mexican chiles	3 cloves garlic, chopped
1 large onion, chopped	3 cups water

Preheat the oven to 250°F. Place the chiles on a baking pan and put in the preheated oven for 10 to 15 minutes or until the chiles smell like they are toasted, taking care not to let them burn. Remove the stems and seeds and crumble the chiles into a saucepan.

Add the remaining ingredients and bring to a boil. Reduce the heat to low and simmer for 30 minutes until it's thickened.

Puree the mixture in a blender until smooth and strain if necessary. If the sauce is too thin after straining, place it back on the stove and simmer until it is reduced to the desired consistency.

VARIATIONS: Spices such as cumin, coriander, and Mexican oregano may be added to taste. Some versions of this sauce call for the onion and garlic to be sautéed in lard—or vegetable oil these days—before the chiles and water are added.

GREEN CHILE STEW

This is the beef stew or macaroni and cheese of New Mexico—a basic dish with as many variations as there are cooks. Add a warmed flour tortilla and you have a complete meal.

MAKES 6 SERVINGS
HEAT SCALE: Hot

2 pounds lean pork, cubed
2 tablespoons vegetable oil
1 large onion, chopped
2 cloves garlic, minced
1 large potato, peeled and diced (optional)

6 to 8 green New Mexican chiles, roasted and
*   peeled (page 146), seeds and stems removed,*
*   chopped*
2 tomatoes, chopped
3 cups water

In a skillet over medium-high heat, cook the pork in the oil until browned, about 5 minutes. Add the onion and garlic and cook, stirring, for 2 to 3 minutes more.

Combine all the ingredients in a kettle or crockpot and bring to a simmer over medium-high heat. Reduce the heat to low and simmer until the meat is very tender, 1½ to 2 hours.

NEW MEXICAN CARNE ADOVADA

This simple but tasty dish evolved from the need to preserve meat without refrigeration, since chile acts as an antioxidant and prevents the meat from spoiling. It is a very common restaurant entree in New Mexico. Serving suggestions: Place the *carne adovada* in a flour tortilla to make a burrito, or use it as filling for enchiladas. If quartered potatoes are added during the last hour of baking, the dish becomes a sort of stew. Note that this recipe requires advance preparation.

MAKES 6 SERVINGS
HEAT SCALE: Hot

1 1/2 cups crushed dried red New Mexican chiles, seeds included
4 cloves garlic, minced

3 teaspoons dried Mexican oregano
3 cups water
2 pounds pork, cut into strips or cubed

In a bowl, combine the chiles, garlic, oregano, and water and mix well to make a *caribe* sauce.

Place the pork in an oven-proof glass pan and cover with the chile *caribe* sauce. Marinate the pork overnight in the refrigerator.

Preheat the oven to 300°F. Bake the pork until it is very tender and starts to fall apart, about 2 hours.

POSOLE WITH CHILE CARIBE

Here is the classic version of *posole* as prepared in northern New Mexico. Serving the chile *caribe* as a side dish instead of mixing it with the *posole* allows guests to adjust the heat to their own taste. Note that this recipe requires advance preparation.

MAKES 4 SERVINGS

HEAT SCALE: **Medium, but varies according to the amount of chile *caribe* added**

For the *posole*

2 dried red New Mexican chiles, stems and seeds removed

8 ounces frozen posole *corn or dry* posole *corn that has been soaked in water overnight then drained (available in Latin-American markets)*

1 teaspoon garlic powder

1 medium onion, chopped

6 cups water

1 pound pork loin, cut into ½-inch cubes

For the chile *caribe*

6 dried red hot New Mexican chiles, stems and seeds removed (see Note)

2 quarts water

1 teaspoon garlic powder

To serve

Warm flour tortillas

Minced fresh cilantro

Chopped onion

Combine all the *posole* ingredients except the pork in a pot and boil over medium heat until the *posole* is tender, about 3 hours, adding more water if necessary.

Add the pork and continue cooking for ½ hour, or until the pork is tender but not falling apart. The result should resemble a soup more than a stew.

To make the chile *caribe*, in a large pot, boil the chile pods in the water for 15 minutes. Remove the pods to a blender, add the garlic powder, and puree. Transfer to a serving bowl and allow to cool.

The *posole* should be served in soup bowls accompanied by the tortillas. Serve the chile *caribe*, freshly minced cilantro, and freshly chopped onion in 3 separate bowls for guests to add according to individual taste.

NOTE: For really hot chile *caribe*, add dried red chile piquins, cayenne chiles, or chiles *de árbol* to the New Mexican chiles.

SOUTHWESTERN SPICED SQUASH
Calabacitas

This recipe combines two other Native American crops, squash and corn, with chile. One of the most popular dishes in New Mexico, it is so colorful that it goes well with a variety of foods.

MAKES 4 TO 6 SERVINGS
HEAT SCALE: **Medium**

3 zucchini squash, cubed

½ cup chopped onion

¼ cup (½ stick) butter or margarine

½ cup chopped green New Mexican chiles,
    roasted and peeled (page 146), stems removed

2 cups whole kernel corn

1 cup milk

½ cup grated Monterey Jack cheese

In a skillet over medium-high heat, cook the squash and onion in the butter until the squash is tender, 6 to 7 minutes.

Add the chiles, corn, and milk. Bring the mixture to a simmer. Reduce the heat to low and simmer for 15 to 20 minutes to blend the flavors. Add the cheese and heat until the cheese is melted.

⤳ *Nga yut thee.* Burmese term for chiles.

NOMENCLATURE

A great deal of discussion and controversy has erupted over the terminology of the *Capsicum* genus in English. As a quick glance at the chile definitions this book will indicate, there are hundreds of terms for the pods in languages from all over the world, so it is curious that the following terms have been debated with such passion.

Ají. This word, from the Arawaks of the West Indies, was transferred to South America by the Spanish and became the general term there for *Capsicums* of all varieties, but usually the species *baccatum.* It is used in South America the way the word chile is used in Central America and Mexico.

Capsicum. From the Greek *kapto*, "to bite," this is the botanical name for the genus and the one preferred by the scientific community. We would assume that there would be little controversy here, except for two drawbacks. First, the term is unfamiliar to most people; and second, the term *Capsicum* specifically means bell pepper in the United Kingdom, Singapore, and other English-speaking parts of Southeast Asia.

Pepper. Of course, we know that Christopher Columbus used the Spanish term *pimiento*, which means black pepper, to describe the *Capsicums.* According to some writers, this means that the word pepper should never be used for the *Capsicums* because of the confusion with black pepper. However, in English, the word pepper is either plural ("give me some peppers"), or modified by either chile or chili, so the possibility of confusing green pods with black peppercorns is reduced.

Chile. This is the Mexican-Spanish term for *Capsicums*, supposedly derived from chilli (see below). It is also used in New Mexico as both a noun and an adjective before the word pepper. It is spelled with an "e" to avoid confusion with chili, meaning chili con carne. Surprisingly, many newspapers in the United States have changed the spelling from chili pepper to chile pepper over the past decade. This is probably because of the popularity of *Chile Pepper* magazine and the many cookbooks using the spelling that have been published.

Chili. This is the Anglicized version of chile that is probably the most popular spelling in the United States and Canada. It is also both a noun and an adjective when followed by pepper. It is also the shortened version of chili con carne, the dish with *Capsicums*, meat, spices, and occasionally beans, so there can be confusion in a headline such as FRED JONES WINS CHILI CONTEST. Did he win for his pods from his garden or his bowl of red?

Chilli. Pepper expert Jean Andrews believes that the proper English term is chilli. This is also the British spelling for hot peppers, but her argument goes back to the Aztecs. She writes that the Nahuatl language spelling, as transliterated by Dr. Francisco Hernández (1514–78), was chilli. She observes: "That Spanish spelling was later changed to chile by the Spanish-speaking Mexicans, and 'chili' in the United States. Chilli is the name most used by English speaking people throughout the world." This may be so, but the question arises as to the original transliteration. When translating a nonwritten word into a written language, all kinds of linguistic problems can occur, which is why we now call the city Beijing instead of Peking. If Hernández was correct, the proper pronunciation of the word would be "chee-yee" because the double L in Spanish is pronounced like an English Y. Since no one pronounces either chile, chili, or chilli this way, why is the spelling so important?

Chile (or Chili) Peppers. This is either a redundant or an extremely precise term, depending on your point of view. It is used to distinguish the plants and the pods from dishes made with them, but purists object to both using chile or chili as an adjective and to using the word pepper.

In conclusion, the many spellings and the syntax of the words used to describe the *Capsicum* genus will never be standardized. This is because—and we're not being flip—no one really cares outside of academia, and even the experts there disagree. Languages evolve, and because of the increasing popularity of *Capsicums*, the terms to describe them are better known and there is less chance of confusion.

NUTRITION

Chile peppers don't have to be healthy to be fun to eat but, fortunately, they are. In fact, they have quite a long history as a folk remedy for all kinds of ailments, from anorexia to vertigo. Some of the more scientifically recognized medical applications of chile peppers include treatments for asthma, arthritis, blood clots, cluster headaches, postherpetic neuralgia (shingles), and severe burns (see Folklore and Mythology; Folk Medicine).

Chile peppers contain only a few calories (thirty-seven per 100 grams of green chile, about three and a half ounces), and possibly have the ability to burn off those calories and others as well. This intriguing possibility comes from researchers at Oxford Polytechnic Institute in England, who conducted an experiment in TEF, an acronym meaning "thermic effects of food." Twelve volunteers ate identical 766-calorie meals. On one day, three grams each of chile powder and mustard were added to the meals; on the next day, nothing was added. On the days chile and mustard were added, the volunteers burned between four to seventy-six additional calories, with an average of forty-five.

The researchers concluded that the test was "a possible lead to a different approach to weight reduction," but also warned that the effect had been demonstrated in only one instance. They also cautioned that six grams (one-fifth ounce) of the chile-mustard mixture "may be a large amount for the average American. If you are used to Mexican, Spanish, or Indian food, though, it's reasonable."

A possible explanation for the result is the fact that certain hot spices—especially chiles—temporarily speed up the body's metabolic rate. After eating, the metabolic rate increases anyway—a phenomenon known as "diet-induced thermic effect." But chiles boost that effect by a factor of twenty-five, which seems to indicate that increasing the amount of chile in a recipe could reduce the effective caloric content—provided, of course, that one does not drink more beer to counter the added heat.

Most of the research on the nutritional properties of hot peppers has concerned the New Mexican pod types because they are consumed more as a food than as a condiment. The long green pods are harvested, roasted and peeled, and are stuffed or made into sauces. Some of the green pods are allowed to turn red on the bush; after harvesting, the red chiles are used as the primary ingredient in red chile sauces. The green chiles are quite high in vitamin C, with about twice the amount by weight found in citrus, while dried red chiles contain more vitamin A than carrots. Vitamin C is one of the least stable of all the vitamins; it will break down chemically by heating it, by exposing it to air, by dehydrating it, and by dissolving it in water. Vitamin A, however, is one of the most stable vitamins and is not affected by canning, cooking, or time.

A high percentage of vitamin C in fresh green chiles is retained in the canned and frozen products, but the vitamin C content drops dramatically in the dried red pods and powder. Each 100 grams of fresh ripe chile pods contains 369 milligrams of vitamin C, which diminishes by more than half to 154 milligrams in the dried red pods. Red chile powder contains less than 3 percent of the vitamin C of ripe pods, a low 10 milligrams.

The amount of vitamin A dramatically increases as the pod turns red and dries, from 770 units per 100 grams of green pods to 77,000 in freshly processed dried red pods. This hundred-fold rise in vitamin A content is the result of increasing carotene, the chemical that produces the orange and red colors of ripe peppers. The recommended daily allowances for these vitamins are 5,000 International Units for A and 60 milligrams for C. These allowances can be satisfied daily by eating about a teaspoonful of red chile sauce for A and about one ounce of fresh green chile for C.

Each 100 grams of green chile contains less than two tenths of a gram of fat—a very low amount. Since no cholesterol is found in vegetable products, peppers are free of it. The fiber content of fresh hot peppers is fairly high (between 1.3 and 2.3 grams per 100 grams of chile), and many of the dishes prepared with them utilize starchy ingredients such as beans, pasta, and tortillas. And the sugar in chiles is in the form of healthy complex carbohydrates.

Fresh green chile contains only 3.5 to 5.7 milligrams of sodium per 100 grams—a very low amount. Chile peppers can be very useful for the low-sodium dieter. The substitution of hot peppers for salt makes gustatory sense because the pungency of the peppers counteracts the blandness of the meal resulting from salt restrictions. In other words, the heat masks the absence of salt.

However, canned green chile peppers should be avoided because of the salt used in the canning process, which can be over a hundred times the amount in fresh or frozen chiles. For people on a potassium-restricted diet, the opposite is true: canned chiles have one half the potassium content of fresh ones. Some experts blame this anomaly on the hot lye bath method of removing the tough pepper skins, a technique that provides additional sodium by absorption and reduces the potassium through leaching. It should be noted that some processors have switched to a high-pressure steam treatment to remove skins—a far more healthy and tasty method.

CHILE AND HERB SALT SUBSTITUTE

Use this recipe to eliminate excess salt from your diet or salt from any recipe in this cookbook. It tastes the best, of course, when you grow and dry your own herbs, but commercially purchased dried herbs will work as well. Try this mixture on baked potatoes, pasta, and vegetables—and especially on corn on the cob.

MAKES ½ CUP
HEAT SCALE: **Mild to medium**

¼ cup dried parsley
¼ cup dried basil
2 teaspoons dried rosemary
1 tablespoon dried tarragon
2 tablespoons dried thyme
1 tablespoon dried dill weed

2 tablespoons paprika
1 teaspoon celery seeds
1 teaspoon crushed, dried red chiles such as
    piquins or 2 teaspoons New Mexican red chile
    powder

Place all of the ingredients in a food processor and blend for 10 seconds or so. Put the mixture into a shaker jar and cover tightly until ready to use. You can keep this for several months.

OLEORESINS FROM CAPSICUMS

Oleoresins are highly concentrated extracts, or oils, made from the dried pods of both hot and nonpungent Capsicums, used from culinary, medicinal, coloring, and many other purposes. There are three types from most to least pungent: oleoresin capsicum, oleoresin red pepper, and oleoresin paprika.

Oleoresin capsicum is made from the hottest chiles available, usually from African, Indian, or Asian chiles, although any hot chile can be used. The heat rating is generally between 500,000 and 1,800,000 Scoville Units, or about 4 to 14 percent capsaicin. A single pound of 500,000 S.U. oleoresin will replace twenty pounds of cayenne pods. This extremely hot oleoresin is used in personal defense pepper sprays, in super-hot sauces such as Dave's Insanity Sauce, in pharmaceuticals such as topical analgesic creams, and in some manufactured foods. Since its heat can be precisely measured, manufacturers can make foods consistently of the same heat level.

A milder extract is oleoresin red pepper, produced from larger, milder red chile pods grown in Mexico, the United States, India, and Turkey. It ranges from 80,000 to 500,000 Scoville Units and a pound of 200,000 S.U. oleoresin red pepper will replace ten pounds of good-quality red chiles. It is mainly used in food processing.

Oleoresin paprika is extracted from a large number of paprika varieties and is nonpungent. However, the milder the chiles, the higher their color content, so oleoresin paprika is used primarily as a red dye in food manufacturing.

Oleoresin manufacture is a process that takes a large, expensive plant with a lot of machinery. The chiles are ground to a coarse powder and then treated with a solvent. To produce a fat-soluble oleoresin, dichloroethane, hexane, or benzene are used. For a water-soluble oleoresin, acetone or ethanol is the usual solvent.

The solvent, sometimes heated, is percolated through a bed of the powdered chiles. Then the solvent must be removed from the crude oleoresin by distillation, a tricky process because if the mixture is overheated, there is a loss of flavor and solubility. After distillation, the oleoresin is sometimes purged of fats with ethanol, which keeps it from turning rancid and further concentrates the capsaicin. The result is a very thick, dark reddish-brown liquid concentrate. The percentage of capsaicin varies according to the chiles used and the methods used to extract the oleoresin.

The Rezolex plant in Radium Springs, New Mexico, is one of four oleoresin extraction plants in the United States; there are additional plants in Spain, India, South Africa, and Japan. Rezolex has great access to the raw product because operator Lou Biad owns extensive farming operations and three pepper-dehydrating plants. They process mostly nonpungent American paprika types.

The Rezolex process begins with dehydrating the pods to 3 percent moisture. The pods are then ground into a powder and pelletized. The pellets are washed with hexane continuously until they release their natural oils. The spent pellets that are left over are turned into feed for sheep and goats, and they are so tasty that longhorn cattle used to break down the fences around Rezolex to feed on spilled spent pellets.

The oil and hexane mixture is called miscella, and this must be carefully heated to remove the hexane, which constitutes 90 percent of the miscella. The heating reduces

Rezolex oleoresin extraction plant, Radium Springs, New Mexico.
DAVE DEWITT

the hexane to 2 percent, and then to get it below the federal regulations of twenty-five parts per million, the miscella is treated in a thin-film evaporator under a heavy vacuum. It takes fifteen pounds of pods to make one pound of oleoresin paprika.

When processing highly pungent pods for oleoresin capsicum, the oleoresin would be recovered by further treating with methanol, which binds with the capsaicin. The mixture settles and can be drained off, and then the methanol is distilled off and the result is concentrated oleoresin capsicum.

The oleoresin paprika produced by Rezolex is used primarily by food processors to add color to their products. It is an ingredient in chicken feed because it enriches the color of egg yolks and gives gray chicken meat a pinkish hue. It is sprayed on potato chips to give them a golden color when baked. One of the oleoresin's principal uses is by the meat industry, particularly by the manufacturers of pepperoni, bologna, and wieners. It gives meat the appearance of being leaner than it really is, and is used in spice blends such as black pepper and garlic oil that are used to treat processed meats. It also shows up in ketchup, margarine, and in frozen-food batters for fish and chicken.

Oleoresin capsicum is used in food processing to provide a precise heat level for various foods. For example, it could be added to tortilla chips to give color and a measured level of pungency. Besides its use in food processing and pharmacology, other uses of oleoresin capsicum include mixing it with paint to make an antifouling coating for the hulls of boats. The coating prevents the accumulation of barnacles. In 1995, a U.S. patent was issued for the coating, which is also used to prevent zebra mussels from fouling water intake valves along the Great Lakes. Other uses include spraying it on lambs to repel coyotes in Wyoming and Colorado, and on fence posts to prevent "cribbing"—excessive chewing by cattle and horses.

Oleoresin capsicum is also sold in a con-centrated "hot sauce" form as a repellent for deer, rabbits, and mice and is applied to fruit and nut trees, vegetables, and shrubs. Hot pepper wax, a concentrate which is also mixed with water and sprayed on foliage, is a repellent for aphids, spider mites, thrips, and white fly.

ORNAMENTAL CHILES

Although edible, ornamentals are grown primarily for their unusual pod shapes or for their dense foliage and colorful, erect fruits. Other pod types can be used as ornamentals, such as the piquins.

Many ornamentals have multiple stems and a compact habit. They seldom grow over twelve inches high. In low-light situations, some ornamentals adopt a vine-like habit. The leaves are one to two inches long and one half to one inch wide. The flower corollas are white with no spots. The pods vary greatly in shape, from small, piquin-like pods to extremely long and thin cayenne-like pods. In between, they can assume nearly any shape imaginable. The pods also vary greatly in heat, ranging between zero and 50,000 Scoville Units. One distinguishing factor of ornamentals is their ability to live in pots as perennials. In the garden, they often grow larger than they do in pots. Ornamentals are used mostly for decoration, but they can be pickled or dried.

Recommended varieties include: 'Black Plum,' with small, erect, dark purple hot pods; 'Bolivian Rainbow,' with purple foliage, stems, and flowers, and very hot

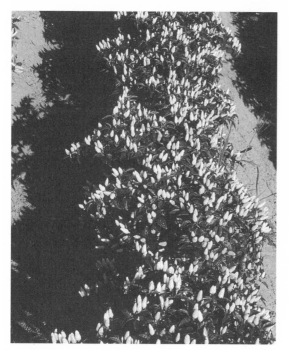

'Sweet Pickle' variety of ornamental. DAVE DEWITT

pods that turn orange and red; 'Fiesta Hot,' a compact plant with slender, red, two-inch pods; 'Fips,' very small plants with conical, erect, red pods; 'Jigsaw,' small, hot, red pods on small plants with attractive, variegated foliage; 'NuMex Centennial,' with small, erect pods ranging in color from purple to cream to red; 'Peter Pepper,' with mild pods that resemble a human penis; and 'Super Chili,' a hybrid with two-and-a-half-inch, erect, cone-shaped, hot pods.

⌟ *Ot.* General Vietnamese term for chile peppers. Dried chiles are *ot kho* and chile sauces are *tuong ot.*

⟩ *'Pabellón 1.'* A cultivated variety of pasilla in Mexico.

⟩ *Panameño.* A name for the *chinense* species in Costa Rica.

⟩ *Panco.* A name for the *chinense* species in Peru.

⟩ *'Pánuco.'* A cultivated variety of serrano in Mexico. Named for a river in northern Veracruz.

⟩ *'Papaloápan.'* A cultivated variety of jalapeño in Mexico.

PAPRIKA

The word *paprika* derives from the Hungarian *paparka*, which is a variation on the Bulgarian *piperka*, which in turn was derived from the Latin *piper*, for "pepper." In the United States, the term paprika simply means any nonpungent red chile, mostly New Mexican pod types that have

had their pungency genetically removed. In Europe, however, paprika has much greater depth, having not only distinct pod types but also specific grades of the powders made from these pod types.

There is a minor debate about how Capsicums arrived in Hungary from the Western Hemisphere. Some historians credit their spread to the invasion of the Ottoman Turks into Central Europe. The armies of Turkey conquered Syria in 1516 and Egypt in 1517, Yugoslavia in 1521, and Hungary in 1526. The year 1526 is the date usually given for the introduction of paprika into Hungary by the Turks, but this date is plausible only if the Turks had somehow acquired chiles from either Spanish, Italian, or Greek traders in the Mediterranean.

Zoltan Halasz, author of *Hungarian Paprika Through the Ages*, believes: "Most probably the Turks got into the possession of Paprika through Italian intermediaries, and since a great many nations fond of gardening lived on the Balkan Peninsula, which was under Turkish occupation, the cultivation of the spice, winning favor among all these peoples, soon became widespread."

A more likely scenario holds that the Turks first became aware of chile peppers when they besieged the Portuguese colony of Diu, near Calicut, in 1538. This theory suggests that the Turks learned of chile peppers during that battle and then transported them along the trade routes of their vast empire, which stretched from India to Central Europe. According to Leonhard Fuchs, an early German professor of medicine, chiles were cultivated in Germany by 1542, in England by 1548, and in the Balkans by 1569. Fuchs knew that the European chiles had been imported from India, so he called them "Calicut peppers." However, he wrongly assumed that chiles were native to India.

So, sometime between 1538 and 1548, chiles were introduced into Hungary, and the first citizens to accept the fiery pods were the servants and shepherds who had more contact with the Turkish invaders. Zoltan Halasz tells the tale: "Hungarian herdsmen started to sprinkle tasty slices of bacon with Paprika and season the savoury stews they cooked in cauldrons over an open fire with the red spice. They were followed by the fishermen of the Danube . . . who would render their fish-dishes more palatable with the red spice, and at last the Hungarian peasantry, consuming with great gusto the meat of fattened oxen and pigs or tender poultry which were prepared in Paprika-gravy, professed their irrevocable addiction to

Woman stringing paprika in Hungary. PAUL BOSLAND

Paprika, which by then had become a characteristically Hungarian condiment."

From that point on, the landed gentry, the aristocracy, and the royal courts readily adopted the hot spice, and the Danube region developed Europe's only genuine chile cuisine. In the sunny south of Hungary, the brilliant red pods decorated gardens everywhere, and even today, that part of the country is the heart of paprika growing. In 1569, an aristocrat named Margit Szechy listed the foreign seeds she was planting in her garden in Hungary. On the list was *"Turkisch rot Pfeffer"* (Turkish red pepper) seeds, the first recorded instance of chiles in Hungary. Upon Mrs. Szechy's death and the subsequent division of her estate, her paprika plots were so valuable they were fought over bitterly by her daughters.

The famous "Hungarian flavor," which is unique to the cuisine of that country, is created by the combination of lard, paprika, and spices. Chopped onions are always cooked to translucency in the lard; paprika and sour cream are added to pan drippings after meats have been browned to make a rich sauce, which is then served over meat and peppers. There are many versions of hot and spicy recipes with the generic terms of *gulyas* ("goulash") and *paprikas* ("paprikash").

In the Hungarian countryside, paprika peppers are threaded onto strings and hung from the walls, porches, and eaves of farmhouses, much like the chile *ristras* in the American Southwest. Today Hungary produces both pungent and sweet paprikas, but originally all Hungarian paprika was aromatic and quite hot. It was evidently too hot for some tastes, for by the turn of this century other countries were requesting that Hungary develop a nonpungent variety. By accident, farmers produced a sweet variety in their fields when they planted milder "eating" paprika with hotter "seasoning" paprika in proximity, and insects cross-pollinated the two. The resulting hybrid reduced the pungency of the paprika pods and probably led to the nonpungent varieties now grown in Spain.

Food authority Craig Claiborne has noted, "The innocuous powder which most merchants pass on to their customers as Paprika has slightly more character than crayon or chalk. Any Paprika worthy of its name has an exquisite taste and varies in strength from decidedly hot to pleasantly mild but with a pronounced flavor." We recommend that cooks use imported Hungarian

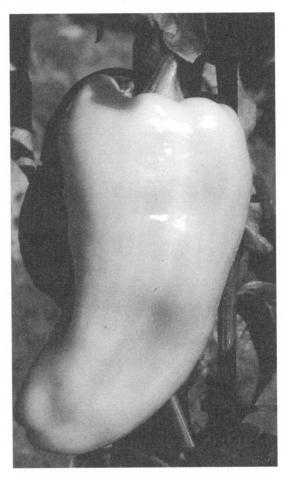

Szentesi *variety of Hungarian paprika.* PAUL BOSLAND

paprika such as Szeged, and if it is too mild, they should heat it up with ground cayenne.

Types of Hungarian Paprikas

NOTE: The hottest paprikas are not the bright red ones, but rather the palest red and light brown ones.

Special Quality (*Különleges*): The mildest and brightest red of all Hungarian paprikas, with excellent aroma.

Delicate (*Csípmentes Csemege*): Ranging from light to dark red, a mild paprika with a rich flavor.

Exquisite Delicate (*Csemegepaprika*): Similar to Delicate, but more pungent.

Pungent Exquisite Delicate (*Csípös Csemege, Pikant*): A yet more pungent Delicate.

Rose (*Rózsa*): Pale red in color with strong aroma and mild pungency.

Noble Sweet (*Édesnemes*): The most commonly exported paprika; bright red and slightly pungent.

Half-Sweet (*Félédes*): A blend of mild and pungent paprikas; medium pungency.

Hot (*Erös*): Light brown in color, this is the hottest of all the paprikas.

CHICKEN PAPRIKASH
Csírkepaprikás

This is one of the classic paprika recipes from Hungary. Be sure to use only imported paprika in this dish, or the flavor will not be the same. It is traditionally cooked with lard or goose fat and served with dumplings. Serve over egg noodles, plain rice, or boiled potatoes.

MAKES 6 SERVINGS
HEAT SCALE: **Medium**

3 tablespoons corn oil

2 tablespoons butter

One 2½- to 3-pound chicken, cut into serving
  pieces

2 medium onions, chopped

3 large cloves garlic, minced

1 rounded tablespoon medium-hot paprika

1 tablespoon hot paprika

2 rounded tablespoons mild paprika

2 tablespoons brandy

¾ cup chicken stock

1 whole, fresh, long, red chile, such as New
  Mexican

⅓ to ½ cup sour cream

Salt to taste

In a large, heavy skillet over medium-high heat, heat the oil and butter. Add the chicken pieces and cook until browned, 8 to 10 minutes. Using a slotted spoon, remove the chicken and set aside. Add the chopped onions to the skillet and cook, stirring, until the onions are translucent, about 5 minutes. Add the garlic and cook for 1 to 2 minutes more. Reduce the heat to very low, stir in all the paprika, and cook for an additional minute, stirring constantly. Add the brandy and stir to deglaze the pan. Add the browned chicken pieces and mix well. Add the chicken stock and whole hot red pepper.

Bring the mixture to a boil over high heat, reduce heat to low, cover, and simmer for 45 to 60 minutes. Using a slotted spoon, remove the chicken to a serving platter and keep warm. Bring the liquid in the casserole to a boil over high heat, and cook until the liquid is reduced by about one third. Turn the heat to low, and slowly stir in the sour cream, until the sauce is smooth. Add salt to taste. Pour the sauce over the chicken and serve immediately.

CREAM OF PAPRIKA SOUP

This recipe combines the Hungarians' love of paprika and things creamy. You may use any of your favorite vegetables for this dish, but make sure that they have a similar cooking time or adjust the size of the pieces accordingly.

MAKES 4 TO 6 SERVINGS
HEAT SCALE: **Mild**

1 onion, chopped
2 stalks celery, chopped
1 quart chicken broth
1 pound vegetables, coarsely chopped (such as asparagus or carrots)

2 tablespoons all-purpose flour
2 tablespoons hot Hungarian paprika
¼ cup water
½ cup heavy cream
Salt and freshly ground black pepper to taste

In a large skillet, combine the onion, celery, and broth. Bring to a boil over high heat, then reduce the heat to low and simmer until tender, 8 to 10 minutes. Remove and puree in a blender until smooth. Return to the heat, add the vegetables, and simmer until the vegetables are tender, about 20 minutes.

In a small bowl, mix the flour and paprika with the water to make a paste and stir into the soup mixture. Heat until the soup thickens, about 5 minutes. Remove from the heat and slowly stir in the cream. Return to the heat and simmer for 10 minutes or until hot, taking care not to let the soup boil. Season with salt and pepper and serve.

Pasilla chiles. CHILE PEPPER INSTITUTE

⟟ **Paprika** *Paliva.* In Slovakia, a very pungent mix of hot paprika and salt.

⟟ **Paprika** *Sladka.* A mild, bright red paprika from Slovakia.

⟟ *Parado.* A name for piquin in Oaxaca, Mexico.

⟟ *Pasado.* In Mexico, another name for *chilaca*; in New Mexico, roasted and peeled New Mexican chiles that are sundried.

PASILLA

In Spanish, pasilla means "little raisin," an allusion to the dark brown pods of this type. In California, the ancho is sometimes called pasilla, causing much confusion. In western Mexico it is sometimes called chile *negro*, a term that also refers to the darker anchos. In the fresh form, the pod is known as *chilaca*.

The Plant

Pasillas are pod types of the *annuum* species. The plant has an intermediate number of stems, an erect habit, and grows two to three feet high or more. The primary branches begin over five inches from the lowest stem portion so the pods will not touch the ground. The leaves are ovate, smooth, medium green in color, and measure three inches long and one and a half inches wide. The flowers have white corollas with no spots. The pods are extremely elongate, cylindrical, furrowed, and measure six inches long (or more) by one inch wide. Immature fruits are dark green, maturing to dark brown. The growing period is 90 to 100 days, and the yield is twenty pods or more to the plant. This type is not particularly pungent, measuring between 1,000 and 1,500 Scoville Units.

Agriculture

It is likely that the pasilla is the immediate predecessor of the New Mexican type. It has adapted particularly well to the temperate regions of Mexico. About 7,500 acres of pasillas are cultivated in Mexico, primarily in Aguascalientes, Jalisco, Zacatecas, and Guanajuato. The annual yield is approximately 3,500 tons of dried pods. The most popular Mexican varieties are 'Pabellon One' and 'Apaseo.' There is no commercial U.S. production. The pasilla does well in the home garden, and the pods should be allowed to dry on the plant.

Culinary Usage

The pasilla is part of the legend of the origin of *mole* sauces, which also contain anchos. (See Mexico.) Because it is very flavorful, the pasilla is a favorite of Mexican *moleros*, cooks who specialize in preparing unique *mole* sauces. The pasilla is mainly used in the dried pod or in powder form in sauces such as *moles* and *adobos*. It adds an interesting taste and color to standard red chile enchilada sauce as well.

ROAST PORK WITH PASILLA ADOBO SAUCE

Adobo is a thick sauce of chiles, vinegar, and spices that is popular in both Mexico and the Philippines. This roast makes a wonderful entree, sliced and served with a sauce made from the pan drippings, and any leftover meat can be made into tasty shredded pork enchiladas. Accompany this roast with Mexican rice and a salad of avocados, tomatoes, onions, and sweet and hot peppers dressed with olive oil, wine vinegar, crushed garlic, and a mix-and-match collection of minced fresh herbs such as cilantro, Mexican oregano, mint, basil, tarragon, parsley, sage, rosemary, or thyme. Note that this recipe requires advance preparation.

MAKES 6 SERVINGS
HEAT SCALE: **Mild**

6 pasilla chiles, stems and seeds removed
2 cups chicken broth
1 medium onion, chopped
3 cloves garlic, chopped
3 tablespoons vegetable oil
½ teaspoon ground cumin

½ teaspoon dried oregano, crushed
2 tablespoons white vinegar
1 cup beer, preferably a Mexican lager (such as Bohemia)
3 cloves garlic, chopped
One 3-pound pork roast

In a saucepan, combine the chiles and chicken broth and bring to a simmer. Reduce the heat to low and simmer until soft, about 5 minutes.

In a skillet over medium-high heat, cook the onion and garlic into the oil until softened, about 5 minutes. Add the rehydrated chiles with their broth and the remaining ingredients, except the pork, and simmer for 10 minutes to blend the flavors. Place the sauce in a blender and puree until smooth.

Make deep gashes in the roast and push the sauce into the gashes. In a roasting pan, pour the remaining sauce over the meat and marinate in the refrigerator overnight.

Preheat the oven to 425°F. Place the pork on a rack in a roasting pan. Put it on the middle shelf of the oven, and immediately reduce the heat to 350°F. Cook the meat for 30 to 45 minutes per pound or until the internal temperature reaches 185°F. Baste frequently with the sauce. Place foil over the top of the roast if the roast starts getting too brown.

⩗ *Pasilla oaxaqueño.* A smoke-dried chile *de agua* in Oaxaca, Mexico.

⩗ *Pátzcuaro.* A dark variety of pasilla grown in Michoacán, Mexico. Named for the famous lake.

⩗ *'Peludo.'* "Hairy"; a cultivated variety of jalapeño in Mexico.

⩗ *Peperone.* Italian term for peppers.

⩗ *Pepperoncini.* "Small pepper"; a mild, Italian variety of *annuum* that is often pickled. In the United States, it is considered to be a variety of the Cuban pod type.

PEPPER SPRAYS

The power of oleoresin capsicum is so great that it has become a popular ingredient in personal defense sprays, virtually replacing tear gas products such as Mace. The tear gas products had proven to be virtually ineffective against many violent attackers, especially those under the influence of narcotics and alcohol. Additionally, the tear gas products have a fairly long reaction time of three to thirty seconds.

Pepper sprays have a reaction time of one to three seconds, and have been touted as a safe, effective response to attackers. One article in a security magazine stated: "One blast of pepper spray will cause respiratory spasms, choking, and temporary closure of the eyes, preventing any further aggressive behavior. It will work against persons under the influence of narcotics and alcohol."

But some of these claims are apparently exaggerated. Pepper sprays vary considerably in the amount of oleoresin they contain. Manufacturers tout the percentage of oleoresin in their products and make claims that theirs is best because it contains 10 percent oleoresin. But what is the strength of the oleoresin? One manufacturer, BodyGuard, states: "Remember, a spray containing ten percent of 500,000 Scoville Heat Unit oleoresin capsicum is not as effective as a spray containing five percent of 2,000,000 Scoville Heat Unit oleoresin. The more capsaicinoid content the oleoresin has, the hotter and more effective the spray will be."

Pepper sprays quickly became popular with law enforcement agencies after first being introduced in 1977. By 1990, *Time* magazine reported that the FBI and more than 1,000 agencies were using one spray called Cap-Stun. Generally speaking, the sprays used by law enforcement personnel are five times more powerful than those sold to the general public.

The sprays are quite popular with the public, as evidenced by steadily growing sales. But there has been some backlash. The sprays are now forbidden to be carried on aircraft, and they were banned for personal defense use in California until a law permitting their use was passed in 1994. Before then, the only pepper spray permitted in that state was a diluted antianimal spray called Dog Shield; however, many different sprays were sold illegally in California and are commonly available.

In 1994, the American Civil Liberties Union in Los Angeles claimed to have documented fourteen fatalities involving people who had been sprayed. Alan Parachini, director of public affairs, stated that even if the spray itself was not the cause of death, autopsy results showed that it was a factor. He urged the Los Angeles Police Department to curtail its use of pepper spray until more research is done.

But more research had already been done. The International Association of Chiefs of Police examined twenty-two deaths linked to pepper spray and concluded that the spray was not a factor in any of them. They based their estimation on the report of Dr. Charles Petty, a former Dallas County medical examiner, who examined autopsy reports. Most of the deaths resulted from "positional asphyxia," which means that police had restricted the breathing of suspects while restraining them. Suspects are often hog-tied, forced to lie on their stomachs while their handcuffs and leg shackles are linked behind their backs. Their bellies can be pushed into their chest cavities, causing suffocation.

The study also brought up questions of the effectiveness of the pepper spray in subduing violent and irrational people. The FBI report "Chemical Agent Research, Oleoresin Capsicum" concluded that pepper sprays were effective against intoxicated people, and told the story of a large, intoxicated biker who was successfully disabled. "Two agencies reported oleoresin capsicum is frequently used to subdue inmates who were violent and uncontrollable."

However, the report "Pepper Spray and In-Custody Deaths" referred to by the International Association of Chiefs of Police stated: "In the majority of cases, oleoresin capsicum spray was either ineffective or less than totally effective." Since drugs or alcohol were involved in most of these cases, the conclusion to be reached is that the pepper spray was unable to subdue the suspects effectively, so the police resorted to forceful procedures that caused the deaths. In addition to "positional asphyxia," other factors in the deaths were cocaine intoxication and excited delirium from the cocaine.

Denver police indicated some doubts about pepper spray in 1990. Officer Marc Frias sprayed a suspect at point-blank range and found the man still standing. "Unless it hits you right in the open eyes, it takes too long to incapacitate you," said Sergeant Dave Abrams, supervisor of the Denver Police Department's SWAT team. "I've seen it take more than a minute."

The inventor of the Cap-Stun spray used, Gardner Whitcomb, countered that the police were spraying at too close a range to allow formation of a mist that can be inhaled.

⤳ *Pequín.* See Piquin.

⤳ *Peri-peri.* See *Pili-pili.*

⤳ *Perón.* "Pear-shaped"; a regional name for the *rocoto* or *manzano* chile in Mexico.

⤳ *Petit Malice.* In Haiti, little prank chile.

PHYSIOLOGY AND ADDICTION

The power of chiles is enough to inspire mythology and folk tales, so it is not surprising that some people believe in its ability to control our minds—or at least our bodies. In 1980, Dr. Andrew Weil noted the mind-altering properties of chiles in his book *The Marriage of the Sun and Moon.* "The chile lover knows that pain can be transformed into a friendly sensation whose strength can go into making him high," he wrote. "The secret of this trick lies in perceiving that the sensation follows the form of a wave: It builds to a terrifying peak, then subsides, leaving the body completely unharmed. Familiarity with the sensation makes it possible to eat chile at a rate that keeps the intensity constant. One is then able to glide along on the strong stimulation, experiencing it as something between pleasure and pain that enforces concentration and brings about a high state of consciousness." Weil even gave this drug-like sensation a catchy name: mouth surfing.

Then Weil related a story from Santha Rama Rau's book, *The Cooking of India,* where an Indian woman visiting London became ill from the bland food and craved chiles so much that she poured three quarters of a bottle of Tabasco sauce plus sixteen red-hot South American chiles over her omelet before she was satisfied. His own experiences of turning previously inexperienced people on to chiles has been "uplifting." "It is especially meaningful to see that by a change of mental attitude, perseverance, and openness to new experience something that previously appeared painful and injurious can become pleasureful and beneficial."

As if Weil's theory that chiles are a drug wasn't shocking enough, the front-page headline in the *Albuquerque Journal* on February 9, 1990, sparked quite a controversy: "THAT CRAVING FOR CHILE JUST MIGHT BE AN ADDICTION." The story involved a theory by Dr. Frank Etscorn, then an experimental psychologist at the New Mexico Institute of Mining and Technology in Socorro, that the warm afterglow and the constant craving for chile are due to capsaicin triggering the release of endorphins, the body's natural painkillers.

"We need a fix of red or green chile with a side order of endorphins," said Etscorn. "We get slightly strung out on endorphins, but it's no big deal." Etscorn has experience with treating addiction—he was the one who invented the nicotine patch.

To prove that eating chile releases endorphins, Etscorn used a drug called naloxone, which can reverse the effects of a heroin overdose by blocking brain receptors that respond to the heroin. In an experiment, he had one of his students consume the hottest jalapeños he could find until his mouth was burning up and perspiration was pouring off his face. The student was asked to tell them when the pain began to diminish. When that happened, the subject was given a naloxone injection, and the pain increased as the endorphins were blocked from the brain.

These endorphins, of course, are the

same ones that cause the so-called runner's high, and they have been called "the body's natural opiates." But just how addictive are they? Dr. John Prescott, an Australian scientist, made a similar splash in Australia in 1994 as Etscorn did in the United States with his claims of the addictive qualities of chiles. Although the chiles do not promote physical dependence like alcohol, nicotine, or heroin, he said, five weekly doses could get an adult "hooked." Warned Prescott: "The more you have, the more you crave."

Many chile lovers exhibit distinctly druggie habits. We've seen people who always travel with their stash of hot sauce, Texans who carry their tiny *chilipiquin* pods in silver snuffboxes, and Californians who mix chile powder with their cocaine before snorting it. "The pink fix," it's called.

While people do become habituated to chiles because of their flavor, their stimulating properties, and their healthfulness, they don't necessarily crave additional chiles or hotter chiles. People tend to reach a plateau between stimulation and pain that they are comfortable with, and tend to stay at that heat level. This tendency is similar to a social drinker who doesn't get drunk, or a smoker limiting himself to four cigarettes a day.

A study at Duke University Medical Center found that in smaller doses capsaicin and nicotine induce some of the same physiological responses, including irritation, secretion, sneezing, vasodilation, coughing, and peptide release; however in larger, injected doses, capsaicin destroys many of the neurons containing its receptors, while nicotine actually increases the number of nicotine acetylcholine receptors. What this means is that large doses of capsaicin result in the body becoming less responsive to capsaicin, but that large doses of nicotine cause the body to become more responsive to nicotine. While people may develop a mental preference for chile, they definitely do not develop a physical addiction.

According to Paul Rozin, Ph.D., a psychologist at the University of Pennsylvania, who has done extensive research on the acquisition of chile preference, chile does not meet the criteria for true physical addiction, which involves these symptoms:

Craving: for chile, this exists to a degree, but it never becomes a physical necessity.
Loss of control: only by choice.
Withdrawal: we miss it, but we don't get sick without it.
Tolerance: we adjust to higher heat levels, but we don't need increasing amounts just to feel normal.

However, we can speak from experience that there is an intense longing for the heat because certain foods associated with chile—breakfast eggs, for example—now seem incredibly bland. And remember, with chile abstention, desensitization wears off and when you attempt to return to your heat plateau, the chiles on the way there will seem to be hotter. Marijuana users report a more intense high from the same batch if they abstain from smoking for a few days, so perhaps chile is psychologically addictive in this way.

Interestingly enough, chile is a substance that most mammals (birds and reptiles seem to be unaffected by its heat properties) will avoid as they would a poison. A study at the University of Pennsylvania found that it is practically impossible to induce a preference for chile peppers in rats, and subsequent studies with dogs and chimpanzees have had limited success. The 1979 study states that humans are the only mammals that "reverse their natural rejection" to bitter "innately unpalatable substances" such as nicotine, coffee, alcohol, tobacco . . . and chile peppers. They can learn to prefer the flavor and physiological effects of these ingredients to the point of choosing to eat them regularly.

One reason might be practical in nature. Dr. Rozin found that the most common reason Mexican people gave for eating chile is that it "adds flavor to food." He also observed that chile might be a digestive aid. "With a mealy and bland starch-base diet, typical of the areas where chili pepper is commonly eaten, chili aids in the ingestion and swallowing of food and may enhance the palatability of food."

But why do we choose to eat chile in the first place? It does not create physical need like the aforementioned substances. Babies and young children reject it, as do "uninitiated adults" who have never tried it before. The only animals Dr. Rozin found during the course of his studies who exhibited true, laboratory-proven preference for chile were two chimpanzees and a dog, all of which had strong relationships with humans.

And therein lies the key—socialization. Just as young people develop a taste for cigarettes, coffee, and alcohol from repeated use through a desire to be included and identified with a certain group, be it family or peers, so do they become accustomed to chile. "No explicit rewards are given for eating chili in the home," said Rozin. There is, however, the possibly more subtle reward for being adult and doing what members of one's society do, as well as the less subtle encouragement of parents and peers."

Among American college students asked about their chile-eating histories, the most common responses to "How did you get to start eating chile?" was that it was used at home, or that their parents put it on food. In Mexico, where chile-eating is a part of everyday life, very young children are protected from exposure to it, then allowed to develop their own preference, which usually starts between the ages of four and eleven.

The socialization theory explains possibly why people start eating chile in the first place, but in a non-chile-centered society, the reasons they keep eating it are less clear.

The "opponent-endorphin responses" theory has to do with endorphins turning a painful experience into pleasurable one so that a person seeks out this experience again and again. This does not provide a complete explanation because it implies attaining a certain level of physical addiction, which, as we have explained, does not happen with chile peppers. Dr. Rozin also cites contradictions such as: People who do not like chile do not reverse their preference as the negative taste of chile wears off (which is what happens with addictive substances), and there is no evidence that preference for chile wears off, even after long periods (weeks to years) of not eating it. Former smokers, for instance, can become ill if they try a cigarette after having not smoked for a certain amount of time.

The "Benign Masochism" or "Constrained Risk" theory seems a bit more likely. This holds that people like chile peppers for the same reasons they like roller coasters, scary movies, and stepping into hot baths. All of these activities provide methods of exciting the body by making it respond to a dangerous situation, while the mind is certain that circumstances are safe. This body/mind disparity may be a source of feelings of mastery and pleasure, a case of body over mind. The study cited additional supporting arguments for this theory, which include:

It is not uncommon for people to like the body's defensive responses, for instance, the nose and eye tearing that result from eating hot peppers.

People often eat chile at a heat level close to the highest they can tolerate, which means that liking chile is related to pushing the limits of pain and tolerance.

Many of the people who like hot and spicy foods tend to be a little more outgoing than those who do not. They like traveling, wearing colorful clothing, meeting new people, and trying new things. Perhaps eating chile peppers is the culinary expression of an adventurous spirit and a fun-seeking nature.

⤳ *Pichichi.* A name for piquin in Puebla, Mexico.

⤳ *Pico de pájaro.* "Bird's beak"; in Mexico, another name for chile *de árbol*; also, *pico de paloma*, "dove's beak."

⤳ *Pili-pili.* Swahili term for the chiltepin, or "bird's eye" pepper in tropical Africa. Generically, all hot chile peppers in Africa.

⤳ *Pilipili hoho.* In East Africa, a chile that makes you say "ho-ho" after you eat it.

⤳ *Piment.* French term for peppers.

⤳ *Pimenta-de-bode.* A name for the *chinense* species in Brazil.

⤳ *Pimenta do chiero.* "Chile of aroma"; small-podded *Capsicum chinense* variety in Brazil.

⤳ *Piment bouc.* A name for the *chinense* species in Haiti.

⤳ *Pimento.* Portuguese term for peppers. Also, West Indian term for allspice.

⤳ **Pimiento.** The familiar, mild, olive-stuffing pepper. They are also used fresh in salads and are pickled. Some varieties are grown and dried for their powder, which is marketed in the United States as paprika.

A pod type of the *annuum* species. Varieties include 'Pimento Select,' 'Pimiento Sweet,' and 'Red Heart Pimiento.' Sometimes spelled pimento.

✎ *Piperies.* Greek term for peppers.

PIQUIN

The piquin is a pod type of the *annuum* species. The word "piquin," also spelled "pequin," is probably derived from the Spanish word *"pequeño,"* meaning small, an obvious allusion to the size of the fruits. Variations on this form place the words "chile" or "chili" before or in combination with both "pequin" and *"tepin"* forms. The wild form of the piquin type is variously called chiltepin or chilipiquin (see Chiltepin) and it is possible that the word *"chilipequin"* is derived from the Nahuatl (Aztec) word *"chiltecpin"* rather than from *"pequeño."*

The piquins are also known by common names such as "bird pepper" and "chile *mosquito.*" Most are unnamed varieties, both wild and domesticated, varying in pod size and shape from BBs to *de árbol*–like fruits. Generally speaking, the wild varieties (spherical *"tepins"*) are called chiltepins and the domesticated varieties (oblong *"piquins"*) are called piquins or pequins, but in Texas the wild varieties are called chilipiquins.

The Plant

Piquins vary greatly, usually having an ~~diate number of stems and an erect

habit. In the wild, piquins can grow six feet high or more, and in the greenhouse they have grown fifteen feet high in one season. However, some varieties have a prostrate habit, spreading across the ground like a ground cover. The leaves are medium green and are lanceolate or ovate, measuring about three and a half inches long by one and a half inches wide. The flower corollas are white with no spots. The pods are borne erect, are round or oblong, and measure between one quarter and one half inch long and wide. Domesticated varieties have elongate, pointed pods, usually borne erect but occasionally pendant, sometimes measuring up to two inches long. Piquins are extremely hot, measuring between 50,000 and 100,000 Scoville Units. In Mexico, the heat of the chiltepin is called *arrebatado* ("rapid" or "violent"), which implies that although the heat is great, it diminishes quickly.

Agriculture

Piquins were part of the prehistoric migration of *Capsicum annuum* from a

'NuMex Bailey Piquin.' PAUL BOSLAND

nuclear area in southern Brazil or Boliva north to Central America and Mexico. Ethnobotanists believe that birds were responsible for the spread of most wild chiles—and indeed, the chiltepin is called the "bird pepper." (See "Bird Peppers.") Attempts at domestication of the wild plants have led to the development of the commercial chile piquin, which grows under cultivation in Mexico and Texas (some wild forms have escaped). A cultivated form of the chiltepin has been grown successfully in Sonora and in the Mesilla Valley of New Mexico, where they are planted as annuals. In all cases of domestication, the cultivated forms tend to develop fruits larger than the wild varieties; botanists are not certain whether this trait is the result of better cultural techniques or the natural tendency for humans to pick the largest fruits, which contain next year's seed.

In Mexico, a number of different varieties of piquins grow wild in the mountains along both coasts: from Sonora to Chiapas on the Pacific and Tamaulipas to Yucatán on the Gulf. They are collected and sold as fresh green, dried red, and in salsas, but the amount of total production is unknown. Some Mexican food companies bottled the chiltepins *en escabeche* and sell them in supermarkets. In the United States, retail prices for wild chiltepins have been as high as forty-eight dollars per pound.

In the United States, about a thousand acres of what is termed "small chili" are cultivated, mostly in Texas and New Mexico. Many of these chiles are packaged and labeled as piquin regardless of the shape of their pods—from those resembling red peppercorns to those which look like small New Mexican varieties—and there is no way to tell which are cultivated and which are collected in the wild.

Piquins do well in the home garden and are particularly suited to being grown in containers as perennials. Garden writer Paul Bessey of the *Arizona Daily Star* reports that rosy-headed house finches regularly decimate his ripening chiltepins, so some netting protection from birds may be necessary when growing this variety. The growing period is at least ninety days, and the plant can produce between 50 and 100 pods, depending on its size and growing period.

Legend and Lore

The Tarahumara Indians of the Sonoran Desert in Mexico believe that chiltepins are the greatest protection against the evils of sorcery. One of their proverbs holds that "The man who does not eat chile is immediately suspected of being a sorcerer." The Papago Indians of Arizona maintain that the chiltepin "has been here since the creation of the earth."

Medical applications of chiltepins are numerous. In Mexico they are habitually used for the relief of acid indigestion; they are crushed and mixed with garlic, oregano, and warm water. Other maladies reputedly treated by chiltepins include sore throats, dysentery, rheumatism, and tumors.

Popular folklore holds that Texans love chile piquins so much they eat them right off the bush. In fact, their infatuation is so great that piquin-heads rarely travel far from home without an emergency ration of the tiny pods, either whole or crushed, in a silver snuffbox or pillbox. Texans also reputedly use the chile piquin in place of soap to punish children for using "cuss words."

Culinary Usage

In 1794, Padre Ignatz Pfefferkorn, an early observer of Sonoran culinary customs, described how chiltepins were primarily used, and of course piquins can be substituted: "It is placed unpulverized on the table in a salt cellar, and each fancier takes as much of it as he believes he can eat. He pulverizes it with his fingers and mixes it with his food. The *chiltepin* is still the best spice for soup, boiled peas, lentils, beans, and the like . . ." Today the red dried chiltepin is used precisely the same way—crushed into soups, stews, and bean dishes. The green fruit is chopped and used in salsas and bottled *en escabeche*.

For recipes, see Chiltepin.

◄ *Piri-piri.* See *Pili-pili.* Also describes dishes made with this hot pepper in Mozambique and Kenya. In the Caribbean, a spicy hot Portuguese pepper oil.

◄ **Poblano.** "From Puebla"; one of the most common Mexican chiles, it is heart-shaped and dark green, about three inches wide and four inches long. Called *miahuateco* in southern Mexico and the Yucatán Peninsula. The dried form is ancho.

◄ *Pochilli.* In Mexico, the Nahuatl name for smoked chiles.

POD TYPES

Pod types are divisions between the species level and the cultivar (cultivated variety) level in *Capsicum* species that have great diversity in pod shapes. The wild species and the two domesticated species with the least diversity in pod shapes, *frutescens* and *pubescens*, have no pod types. The remaining three domesticated species have varying numbers of pod types. The naming of types is left up to botanists and horticulturists, mostly from the United States, so the South American pod types have not been organized yet.

The *annuum* species has the largest number of pod types because the species is the most commonly cultivated. The pod type system listed here was developed by Paul W. Bosland and Jaime Iglesias with the assistance of Alton Bailey. It primarily refers to *Capsicums* grown in the Western Hemisphere. The pod types of *annuum* are:

Ancho/Poblano
Bell
Cayenne
Cherry
Cuban
De árbol
Jalapeño
Mirasol
New Mexican
Ornamentals

Caribbean seasoning pepper, pod type of Capsicum chinense.

DAVE DEWITT

Paprika
Pasilla
Pimiento
Piquin
Serrano
Squash
Wax

The most important of these pod types have separate articles in this encyclopedia; the remainder are briefly described in the text.

The pod type designations are in their infancy for the *chinense* species because only a few pod shapes are grown commercially, and because most of the South American varieties have not been studied enough. Cur-

rently, four pod types of *chinense* are cultivated in the Caribbean and North America:

Orange Habanero
Caribbean Red
Scotch Bonnet
Caribbean Seasoning Pepper

The *baccatum* species has an enormous diversity in pod shapes, and commercial cultivation of distinctly different varieties occurs mostly in the Andes region. However, these shapes have not yet been categorized into specific pod types.

PREHISTORY AND DOMESTICATION

According to botanist Barbara Pickersgill, the genus *Capsicum* originated in the remote geologic past in an area bordered by the mountains of southern Brazil to the east, by Bolivia to the west, and by Paraguay and northern Argentina to the south. Not only does this location have the greatest concentration of wild species of chiles in the world, but here, and only here, grow representatives of all the major domesticated species within the genus. Another chile botanist, W. Hardy Eshbaugh, believes that the location for the origin of chile peppers was further east, in central Bolivia along the Rio Grande.

Scientists are not certain about the exact time frame or the method for the spread of both wild and domesticated species from the southern Brazil-Bolivia area, but they suspect that birds were primarily responsible. The wild chiles (like their undomesticated cousin of today, the chiltepin) had erect, red fruits that were quite pungent and were very attractive to various species of birds, which ate the whole pods. The seeds of those pods passed through their digestive tracts intact and were deposited on the ground encased in a perfect fertilizer. In this manner, chiles spread all over South and Central America long before the first Asian tribes crossed the Bering land bridge and settled the Western Hemisphere.

When mankind arrived in the Americas more than 10,000 years ago, about twenty-five species of the genus *Capsicum* existed

Selection of larger pods by early farmers led to the varieties of today. SUNBELT ARCHIVES

in South America. Five of these species were later domesticated; however, some of the other wild species were and still are occasionally utilized by man. Two of the five domesticated species of chiles, *Capsicum baccatum* and *C. pubescens*, never migrated beyond South America. *Baccatum*, known as *"ají,"* merely extended its range from southern Brazil west to the Pacific Ocean and became a domesticated chile of choice in Bolivia, Ecuador, Peru, and Chile. Likewise, *C. pubescens* left Brazil to be domesticated in the Andes, where it is known as *"rocoto."* Its range today is primarily in the higher elevations of Bolivia, Peru, and Ecuador, although it was introduced during historical times into mountainous areas of Costa Rica, Honduras, Guatemala, and Mexico.

Three other *Capsicum* species that were later domesticated are *annuum*, *chinense*, and *frutescens*. These closely related species shared a mutual, ancestral gene pool and are known to botanists as the *annuum-chinense-frutescens* complex. They seem to have sprung up in the wilds of Colombia and later migrated individually to Central America and Amazonia. These three species were all in place when mankind arrived on the scene, and, apparently, each type was domesticated independently—*annuum* in Mexico, *chinense* in Amazonia (or possibly Peru), and *frutescens* in southern Central America. These three species have become the most commercially important chiles, and the story of their domestication and further spread is revealed in the archaeological record.

The earliest evidence of chile peppers in the human diet is from Mexico, where archaeologist R. S. MacNeish discovered chile seeds dating from about 7500 B.C. during his excavations at Tamaulipas and Tehuacán. This find and an intact pod from Peru's Guitarrero Cave (dated 6500 B.C.) seem to indicate that chiles were under cultivation approximately 10,000 years ago. However, that date is extremely early for crop domestication and some experts suggest that these specimens are chiles that were harvested in the wild rather than cultivated by man. The common bean (*Phaseolus vulgaris*) was also found in the same excavation levels, and scientists cannot be sure if they were wild or domesticated varieties. Experts are certain, however, that chile peppers were domesticated by at least 3300 B.C.

Ethnobotanists, scientists who study the relationship of plants to man, have theorized that during the domestication process, chiles were first accepted as "tolerated weeds." They were not cultivated but rather collected in the wild when the fruits were ripe. The wild forms had erect fruits that were deciduous, meaning that they separated easily from the calyx, and fell to the ground. During the domestication process, whether consciously or unconsciously, early Indian farmers selected seeds from plants with larger, nondeciduous, and pendant fruits.

The reasons for these selection criteria are a greater yield from each plant and protection of the pods from the chile-hungry birds. The larger the pod, the greater will be its tendency to become pendant rather

Chile merchant from the Codex Florentino. SUNBELT ARCHIVES

than to remain erect. Thus the pods became hidden amid the leaves and did not protrude above them as beacons for birds. The selection of varieties with the tendency to be nondeciduous ensured that the pods remained on the plant until fully ripe and thus were resistant to dropping off as a result of wind or physical contact. The domesticated chiles gradually lost their natural means of seed dispersal by birds and became dependent upon human intervention for their continued existence.

Because chiles readily cross-pollinate, hundreds of varieties of the five domesticated chiles developed over thousands of years. The color, size, and shape of the pods of these domesticated forms varied enormously. Ripe fruits could be red, orange, brown, yellow, or white. Their shapes could be round, conic, elongate, oblate, or bell-like, and their size could vary from the tiny fruits of chiltepins or Tabascos to the large pods of the anchos and New Mexican varieties. However, no matter what the size or shape of the pods, they were readily adopted into the customs and cuisines of all the major civilizations of the Western Hemisphere. (See *Annuum* Species; *Baccatum* Species; "Bird Peppers;" *Chinense* Species; *Frutescens* Species; *Pubescens* Species.)

⤳ *Prik.* The Thai word for chile peppers. *Prik khee noo* (translated: rat turd chiles) are the tiny, slender chiles that are often labeled as "Thai chiles" or "bird pepper." (Sometimes spelled *prik khee noo suan.*) *Prik khee nu kaset* is the term for serrano-type chiles. *Prik leuang* is a yellow, medium-length, slender chile used in southern Thailand. *Prik khee fah* (sometimes *prik chee far*) is a term used to refer to cayenne chiles, while *prik yuak* is similar to the 'Hungarian Yellow Wax Hot' variety. The long, green, New Mexican types are *prik num.* Dried red chiles are *prik haeng,* while *prik pon* is red chile powder. *Prik bod* is chile paste; *nam prik* is chile sauce, while *nam prik pao* is chile tamarind paste.

PUBESCENS *SPECIES*

Pubescens is the only domesticated *Capsicum* species with no wild form; however, two wild species, *C. cardenasii* and *C. eximium,* are closely related. The center of origin for this species was Bolivia, and the species was probably domesticated about 6000 B.C., making it one of the oldest domesticated plants in the Americas. Botanist Charles Heiser, citing Garcilaso de la Vega (1609), notes that *pubescens* was "the most common pepper among the Incas, just as it is today in Cuzco, the former capital of the Incan empire."

It is grown today in the Andes from Chile to Colombia, mostly in small family plots. It is also cultivated in highland areas of Central America and Mexico. The common name for this species in South America is *rocoto* or *locoto.* In Mexico, it is also called chile *manzano* (apple pepper), and chile *perón* (pear pepper), allusions to its fruit-like shapes. In some parts of Mexico and Guatemala, *pubescens* are called chile *caballo,* "horse pepper." Yellow *pubescens* in Mexico are called *canarios,* or canaries, in parts of Mexico, particularly Oaxaca.

Pubescens has a compact to erect habit (sometimes sprawling and vine-like) and grows up to eight feet tall, but two feet is more usual in U.S. gardens. In Bolivia, they grow to fifteen feet. The leaves are ovate, light to dark green, very pubescent (hairy), and measure up to three and a half inches long and two inches wide.

The flowers have purple corollas, purple and white anthers, and stand erect above the leaves. The pods are round, sometimes pear-shaped, measuring about two to three inches long and two to two and a half inches wide, but some pods as large as bell peppers have been reported. The pods are green in their immature state, maturing to yellow, orange, or red.

Rocoto *chile, Peru. Note the apple shape.* PAUL BOSLAND

Their heat level is 30,000 to 50,000 Scoville Units and higher. The *pubescens* varieties contain a unique set of capsaicinoids (pungency compounds), causing some people to believe they are hotter than habaneros. In parts of the Americas they are referred to as *el mas picante de los picantes*, "the hottest of the hot."

As with *C. frutescens*, there is a lack of pod diversity with *C. pubescens*. The fruits are large and stay attached to the plant. There are wild forms of *C. annuum*, *C. chinense*, and *C. baccatum*; however, with *C. pubescens*, no plant with small fruits that easily separate from the plant has ever been found. It has been suggested that *C. pubescens* was domesticated so long ago that its wild form is extinct. So, even if it had been domesticated for so long, why is the variability less? One explanation is that when *C. pubescens* was domesticated it went through a "founders effect." Founders effect is when the establishment of a new population is founded by a few original individuals that carry only a small fraction of the total genetic variation of the parental population. If this was the case, there is not enough genetic diversity to allow for genetic recombination to produce the assortment of pod forms seen in the other species.

Furthermore, *C. pubescens* is isolated from other domesticated species and cannot cross-pollinate with them. This reduces the genes available. Another factor may be the climate it grows best in. Because it thrives only in a narrow temperature range, it may not have been grown in as many places,

thus reducing the opportunity for selection by humans.

Scientists are presently addressing this question with sophisticated molecular techniques. Their work may make it possible for us to have an answer to the lack of pod diversity in a few years. Of course, their work depends on having the genetic resources available—the seeds of the future.

The *pubescens* are traditionally grown in high mountain areas of tropical countries. They can survive very light frosts but not hard freezes. Some sources state that because of their long growing season and need for long day length, the *pubescens* varieties are unsuitable for cultivation in the United States. However, our experiments have shown that plants started early can achieve fruiting in one season. Some plants may not fruit because there is mostly self-incompatibility in the species. To set fruit, pollen must be transferred by bees or humans from a neighboring plant of the same variety. The species also responds well to shading because the foliage has a tendency to burn in full sun. The growing season is long, 120 days or more, and the plants produce up to thirty pods, depending on the length of the growing season.

Because it is adapted to the cooler highland temperatures, *pubescens* grows best under cooler conditions. This can be in a cool coastal climate, a mountain garden, or an artificial climate, such as a greenhouse. In southern New Mexico, the summer heat is too strong to get good growth on the plants, as the leaves tend to burn. All *C. pubescens* plants are grown in a greenhouse that has evaporative coolers to keep the temperature within an adequate range. The seeds are sterilized with sodium hypochlorite, then planted in plastic trays. After planting, the trays are watered as needed to maintain optimum plant growth, usually a once-a-day watering. The trays are placed on a greenhouse bench where the air temperature is maintained at 80°F during the day and 55°F at night. The seedlings are thinned to the most vigorous plant per cell.

Once the seedlings have six to eight true leaves, they are transplanted to pots. Either two plants are planted in an eight-inch pot or a single plant to a six-inch pot. Fertilizer is keep to a minimum because *C. pubescens* plants if given more than adequate nitrogen will grow profusely without flowering and consequently without setting fruit. Plants can live for several years in a pot.

Pubescens varieties are usually consumed in their fresh form because the pods are so thick they are difficult to dry. They are commonly used in fresh salsas, and the larger pods can be stuffed with meat or cheese and baked.

STUFFED ROCOTO CHILES
Rocotos Rellenos

The heat factor in this dish can be very high, but the other ingredients will temper it somewhat. Serve it with hot slices of fresh corn and rounds of sweet potatoes. Note that you'll need a meat grinder to prepare this recipe.

MAKES 20 STUFFED CHILES, 4 OR 5 SERVINGS
HEAT SCALE: **Hot**

20 red rocoto chiles (or substitute the largest jalapeños available)
1 pound pork, cubed
3 cups water
2 tablespoons vegetable oil, plus 2 cups for frying
2 onions, chopped
2 cloves garlic, minced

1 cup peanuts, toasted (see Note) and ground
1 pound green peas (see Note)
½ teaspoon salt
¼ teaspoon freshly ground black pepper
2 large hard-boiled eggs, chopped
4 large eggs, separated

Wash the chiles, leave the stems intact, open halfway, and carefully remove the seeds. Place the chiles in a large pot, cover with water, and bring to a boil. Reduce the heat to medium-high and boil the chiles for 3 minutes. Drain the chiles carefully, keeping them intact, and set aside.

Place the pork in a medium saucepan, add the 3 cups of water, and bring to a boil. Reduce the heat to low and simmer until the pork is tender, about 1 hour. Drain the mixture and reserve the cooking liquid. Grind the pork using a coarse setting on a meat grinder and set aside.

Heat the 2 tablespoons of oil in a medium skillet and cook the onions and garlic, stirring, until softened, about 5 minutes. Add the ground pork, peanuts, peas, salt, and black pepper and enough of the reserved pork stock to keep the mixture moist. Mix in the chopped eggs, remove from the heat, and let the mixture cool for a few minutes.

Cut a slit in each chile and stuff the chiles with this mixture. Push the edges of the slit in each chile together tightly.

In a bowl, beat the egg whites until they are quite stiff. In a separate bowl, beat the egg yolks and fold them into the whites.

Heat 2 cups of oil to 400°F, and when it is ready, dip each pepper into the egg mixture and deep fry about 3 peppers at a time for 30 to 60 seconds, until their outsides are golden brown. Drain on paper towels and keep warm until all the peppers have been cooked.

NOTE: Toast peanuts in a dry skillet over medium heat for about 3 minutes, stirring constantly.
NOTE: Before using, simmer peas in water for 15 minutes.

➤ *Pujei.* Term for chile in Sierra Leone.

➤ *Pulga.* "Flea chile"; another name for piquin chiles in Mexico.

➤ *Pulla.* See *Puya*.

PUNGENCY

Determining the precise pungency of the varieties of chiles and the foods prepared with them has long been a goal of cooks and researchers alike. In 1912, Wilbur L. Scoville, a pharmacologist with a Detroit company, Parke Davis, the drug company using capsaicin in its muscle salve, Heet, developed the Scoville Organoleptic Test. This test used a panel of five human heat samplers who tasted and analyzed a solution made from exact weights of chile peppers dissolved in alcohol and then diluted with sugar water. The hotter the sample, the greater the amount of water required to dilute it until the pungency was no longer detectable to the palate. Thus, if the dilution required was 1,000 units of water to 1 unit of the alcohol sample, the sample was said to have a pungency of 1,000 "Scoville Units." A majority of three of the tasters had to agree before a value was assigned to a given chile or food. Total analysis took sixteen to twenty-four hours and the number of daily tests were limited due to panel fatigue.

Says Louis Sanna, technical director of the Santa Maria Chili Company: "Any test relying on human judgment is bound to be subjective. Not only were there differences of opinion within each company producing chile pepper products, there were also alarming differences among the different companies. Test results of the same material could vary as much as fifty percent from company to company, which made life difficult for food processors who needed to know how hot a final product was going to be. In short, the Scoville test was not reproducible." And that is why the Scoville test was replaced by high technology.

The technique for determining Capsicum pungency by high performance liquid chromatography (HPLC) was developed by James Woodbury of Cal-Compack Foods in 1980. Woodbury wrote: "Previously published methods include organoleptic, spectrophotometric, gas chromatographic, and thin layer chromatographic. Most were time consuming, inaccurate, or imprecise at lower pungency levels."

The HPLC process dissolves the powdered chile sample in ethanol saturated with sodium acetate and separates out the capsaicinoids. The capsaicinoids are then analyzed with a spectrofluorimeter that measures the capsaicin levels in parts per million (ppm), which is then converted to Scoville Units, the standard industry measurement.

The test is sensitive to two parts per million, about thirty Scoville Units, which means that testing individual chiles is now much more accurate. Home cooks wishing to test their chiles will need to buy an Altex Model 322 Liquid Chromatograph equipped with a solvent programmer and dual pumps or perhaps a Varian Model 5060 LC with a data integrator.

Despite the accuracy of HPLC testing, we should remember, as Dr. Ben Villalon, former director of the Texas Agricultural Experiment Station points out, "Capsaicin can and is quantitatively measured by high performance liquid chromatography, to exactness for that particular pod only, that particular plant, that particular location, and that particular season only." Thus, chiles will often deviate from published heat levels because of local conditions.

One chromatograph rates a jalapeño at 2,000 Scoville Units, while another machine in another laboratory measures a different jalapeño at 12,000 Scovilles. What is going on here? How could there be a factor of six difference in these measurements? Isn't, after all, a jalapeño a jalapeño?

Scientifically speaking, not necessarily so. Dr. Ben Villalon's statement above indicates that there is great variance in heat levels of the same variety. This is due to a number of factors. Different varieties are bred to different pungencies, for example, so that's why we have a 'TAM Mild Jalapeño' that is used for nacho slices and is much milder than most other varieties. Thus genetics plays a major role in determining pungency.

The environment plays an equally important role in pungency. The chemical makeup of the soil and the fertilizers used can be factors. It has been proven that stress can increase the capsaicin levels in the pods and such stress could be overwatering or underwatering; excessive summer heat, winds, and solar radiation; excess or lack of humidity; as well as ambient insecticides and air pollution.

So, are we no better off than we were with the old Scoville Organoleptic Test? That too depends on several factors. We wondered if perhaps some of the problem in measuring the heat came from the instrumentation or operator error, and we suspected that perhaps there was no national standard by which all the heat levels were judged. But when we interviewed capsaicin expert Marlin Bensinger, he said that there was a national standard, and that was 98 percent pure crystalline capsaicin manufactured by the Sigma company. All laboratory equipment is calibrated to this standard before the testing begins, so the Sigma capsaicin is the benchmark for all of the HPLC testing in the country—on a voluntary basis, of course.

What this country lacks is a national protocol for HPLC testing, a methodology of sampling and testing that every lab follows. Because the most important part of the entire testing process is the sampling procedure, not the actual test. The principle working here is the same as the computer principle GIGO: garbage in, garbage out.

There is no standard method for sampling the chile peppers to measure for the heat level. Do you take all the pods on one plant in a field, or take one pod from each of 100 plants? Everyone removes the stems prior to measurement, but do you remove the seeds? Some do, some don't, and the seeds provide a lot of weight but a small amount of pungency. At what degree of ripeness do you pick the chiles? Immature, they have greater weight (more water) but less capsaicin, making them a lot milder but more profitable to sell by the pound.

Bensinger suggests using a scientific method that calculates the square root of number of bushels of chiles you have from a harvested field. If, for example, you had 100 bushels, you would take a sample from 10 bushels, analyze each of the ten samples, and see what the variance in heat level is from bushel to bushel. If the variance is low, the sample will be accurate, in general, for that field. If there is a wide variance, the seed used probably was not true to type (cross-pollinated) or there were microclimates in the field causing stress in some parts. In that case, the measurements from all ten samples would be averaged to provide some estimation of the heat of a field, which in all likelihood would be processed together.

Part of the protocol agreement should be procedures for the two major testing results, wet weight basis and dry weight basis. In the standard technique, fresh chiles are sliced, dried in a tray dryer with forced air at 140°F, and ground to pass through a thirty-mesh screen. This sample is then dissolved in solvents and tested with HPLC. The final values are compared to the original wet weight. If the values are compared to the dry weight, the Scoville ratings will be much higher, and will skew the result. It is a sim-ple fact that drier chiles are hotter: their capsaicin is diluted by less water.

But what about testing wet products? That can be done, but the results are usually not as accurate as the preceding procedure. With salsa or hot sauce, scientists wash the sample three times with petroleum ether, which dissolves out the capsaicinoids. The ether is then evaporated off and the dry residue contains the capsaicinoids, which are measured by HPLC and compared to the original wet weight.

But can the labs be fooled? Easily, says Bensinger, because there is no national protocol. It all depends on the sample delivered to the laboratory, and if the laboratory is not particular in demanding a large sampling of whole fresh pods, then a sample could be adulterated by adding a large amount of placental tissue, which has a much higher percentage of capsaicin than the pod wall.

It's not a major scandal, but certain claims of growers and manufacturers need more substantiation, and a national HPLC testing protocol would be one way to achieve accuracy in all Scoville measurements. (See Scoville Scale.)

◣ *'Pusa Jwala.'* Cultivated chile in Liberia.

◣ *Puya.* See *De árbol.* Also, a form of *mirasol* or *guajillo.*

⤷ **'Ramos.'** A cultivated variety of poblano in Coahuila, Mexico.

⤷ **'Real Mirasol.'** A cultivated variety of *mirasol* in Mexico.

RELLENOS: *STUFFED CHILES*

One of the best ways to enjoy the unique flavors of chiles is to eat them whole with a filling. The larger chiles are easier to stuff, but even serranos can be stuffed if the cook has patience and a small spoon. The most commonly stuffed chiles are the green poblanos and New Mexican chiles. They are roasted and peeled first (page 146) and the seeds are removed. Even dried chiles, such as anchos and pasillas can be stuffed, but they must be rehydrated first in warm water and the seeds should be removed.

"The Healing Pods"—old botanical print. SUNBELT ARCHIVES

NEW MEXICAN CHILES RELLENOS

No collection of chile recipes could be complete without including one for stuffed green New Mexican chiles. In late summer when the fresh crop comes in, no chile dish tastes better. They can be stuffed with cheese, meat mixtures, or a combination of meats, dried fruits, and nuts. Serve them covered with green chile sauce.

MAKES 4 SERVINGS
HEAT SCALE: Medium

4 large green New Mexican chiles, roasted and
peeled (page 146), stems left on, seeds removed
1 pound Cheddar cheese or Monterey Jack, cut
into 4 sticks, 5 inches long and 1 inch wide
All-purpose flour for dredging, plus 3 tablepoons

3 large eggs, separated
1 tablespoon water
¼ teaspoon salt
Vegetable oil for frying

Make a slit in the side of each chile and stuff the chiles with the cheese sticks. Dredge the chiles in the flour.

In a bowl, beat the egg whites until they form stiff peaks.

In another bowl, beat the yolks with the water, 3 tablespoons flour, and salt until thick and creamy. Fold the yolks into the whites. Dip the chiles in the mixture.

In a large skillet, heat 2 to 3 inches of the oil over high heat to 375°F to 400°F. Fry the chiles until they are a golden brown, turning once. Cook for about 3 minutes on each side.

STUFFED ANCHO CHILES
Chiles Anchos Rellenos

Ancho chiles, with their raisiny flavor, make excellent *rellenos*. However, be careful to choose anchos that are fairly fresh. Look for chiles that are still bendable and that have a prevalent aroma through their packaging.

MAKES 4 TO 6 SERVINGS
HEAT SCALE: Medium

For the salsa
1/4 cup vegetable oil
2 onions, minced
2 green tomatoes, minced
1/2 cup water
1/4 teaspoon dried Mexican oregano
2 tablespoons chopped fresh cilantro

For the stuffed chiles
4 cups water
6 large ancho chiles, stems and seeds removed

13 ounces aged cheese, such as Romano, sliced
* into 6 equal pieces*
5 tablespoons butter
1/3 cup vegetable oil
6 small corn tortillas
6 large eggs, scrambled
1 head lettuce, shredded or chopped
1 avocado, sliced
7 ounces Cheddar cheese, grated

To prepare the salsa, heat the oil in a saucepan over medium-high heat. Add the onions and cook, stirring, until softened, about 5 minutes. Add the tomatoes, water, oregano, and cilantro and cook over high heat, stirring, until the tomatoes are fully cooked, about 5 minutes. Set aside.

To prepare the chiles, pour the water into a large saucepan. Bring to a boil over high heat. Place the chiles in the boiling water and cook for 2 minutes to rehydrate. Drain the chiles and carefully pat dry on paper towels. Fill each chile with a slice of aged cheese and set aside.

In a large skillet, melt the butter over medium heat, then add the oil and turn the heat to high. Add the chiles and cook until browned, turning once. Cook for about 3 minutes on each side. Remove from the oil, drain on a paper towel, and place on a platter.

Briefly dip the tortillas in the hot oil and place them on a separate plate. Place 1 chile on top of each tortilla, then top them with a spoonful of salsa and some of the scrambled egg.

Decorate the plates with the lettuce, avocado slices, and shredded cheese.

CRAB-STUFFED CHILES
Chiles Rellenos de Jaiba

The use of chipotle chiles in this recipe from Sinaloa, Mexico, adds a smoky depth of taste to the crab. We recommend the meat from freshly cooked crab legs, but if unavailable, good-quality canned crabmeat can be substituted.

MAKES 4 SERVINGS
HEAT SCALE: **Medium**

4 tomatoes, chopped, plus 2 tomatoes, deseeded, chopped

1 cup chopped onion, plus ½ cup minced onion

½ cup chicken broth, vegetable broth, or clam juice, plus 2 to 3 tablespoons more, if needed

½ cup water

3 chipotle chiles in adobo sauce, minced

½ teaspoon salt

¼ teaspoon freshly ground black pepper

2 cups shredded cooked crab

1 teaspoon dried Mexican oregano or 2 teaspoons minced fresh

8 green poblano chiles, roasted and peeled (page 146), seeds removed

1½ cups corn oil

½ cup all-purpose flour

3 large egg whites, stiffly beaten

In a small saucepan, combine the 4 chopped tomatoes, 1 cup chopped onion, ½ cup chicken broth, water, chipotle chiles, salt, and black pepper. Bring the mixture to a boil, then reduce the heat to low. Allow the mixture to simmer while you stuff the chiles.

In a small bowl, mix together the crab, ½ cup minced onion, oregano, and 2 remaining tomatoes. If the mixture seems dry, add 1 tablespoon of the chicken stock at a time. Stuff the poblano chiles with this mixture.

In a large skillet over high heat, heat the corn oil. Dredge the stuffed chiles in the flour and dip them into the egg whites. Deep fry the stuffed chiles in the oil for 2 minutes per side, or until golden brown. Drain on paper towels.

Arrange the *rellenos* on a warm dinner plate and top with the hot salsa.

REMEDIES WITH CHILES

Herbal remedies with chiles predate recorded history, so it is not possible to know when mankind first discovered the healing powers of peppers. But it is likely that the tiny wild pods encountered by early man at least 12,000 years ago were used as a medicine before they spiced up food. (See Folk Medicine).

There are some improbable remedies from various sources that utilize chiles to "cure" typhoid, cholera, tetanus, and tuberculosis, among other diseases, but they are not included here. Instead, there are remedies that treat conditions and symptoms rather than specific diseases.

Commercial cayenne is, in reality, the powder from any hot red chile pepper pod. So in these remedies, when cayenne is called for, any pungent chile powder, such as habanero, piquin, Asian, and hot New Mexican may be substituted. However, do not use the chili powder mixtures made for use in chili con carne—they are blends that contain other spices, such as cumin.

We have grouped the remedies according to their methods of application:

Powders and Capsules. These are the most basic of Capsicum applications. Externally, chile powder is applied directly to open wounds and wrapped with gauze to stop bleeding. Warning: Some people are so sensitive to capsaicin that direct application of chile powder, oils, salves, and ointments can occasionally cause contact dermatitis with mild blistering of the skin. It's always advisable to test a small area of skin first before more widespread application. The powder is also applied with a swab to a painful tooth cavity. For internal use, the powder is placed in gelatin capsules, often in conjunction with other herbs, and they are taken as part of a regular regimen or to relieve certain symptoms. However, be forewarned that people who are sensitive to chile peppers should start with low doses and gradually build up to the suggested dosage. People who suddenly begin taking large doses of cayenne capsules can sometimes experience stomach and bowel discomfort.

Tinctures. Tinctures combine chiles and ethyl alcohol. They are used in their basic form or as an ingredient in other remedies. Fluid extracts are concentrated tinctures.

Syrups. Chiles, herbs, and sugar are combined to make syrups that are generally used to treat throat ailments. Syrups that are thickened and dried become lozenges.

Infusions. These are basically water-based teas or gargles containing chile and often additional ingredients.

Oils and Salves. Chiles are often steeped in vegetable oils, sometimes in combination with other herbs, and the oil is used externally. A salve is an oil to which beeswax has been added to give it a much thicker consistency.

Liniments. These are fluid extracts specifically applied to the skin to treat strained muscles, sore joints, and inflamations.

Poultices and Plasters. A poultice is a powdered mass of herbs that are moistened with water, or a tincture, infusion, oil, or salve, placed on the skin, and wrapped with a cloth. A plaster is similar to a poultice except that the herbs are moistened with water and spread on a linen or cotton cloth, then applied to the skin and covered with plastic to keep the moisture in.

No specialized laboratory equipment is needed to prepare the remedies; needed are a kitchen scale and a mortar and pestle or a spice mill.

HERBAL CAYENNE CAPSULES #1

Use as you would in any instructions for cayenne capsules. This combination is said to reduce fevers and blood pressure and to aid in circulation. The dosage is 1 to 4 capsules per day. Use yogurt in the diet the same day. Empty capsules are available at herb and drug stores.

MAKES 100 CAPSULES

¼ cup cayenne
⅛ cup powdered dried ginger

2 tablespoons powdered goldenseal

Place the herbs in a mortar or spice mill and grind to a fine powder. Place in #00 gelatin capsules until full. Store in a jar with a lid and they will last indefinitely.

VARIATION: Add 1 ounce of chaparral to the above herbs and grind to a powder.

HERBAL CAYENNE CAPSULES #2

This old remedy is also said to treat fever, headache, and liver complaints. The dosage is 2 capsules at bedtime, or as needed.

MAKES 75 CAPSULES

2 teaspoons powdered lobelia seed
2 teaspoons cayenne
2 teaspoons powdered valerian

2 teaspoons powdered slippery elm
4 teaspoons powdered dandelion leaf

Place the herbs in a mortar or spice mill and grind to a fine powder. Place in #00 gelatin capsules. Store in a jar with a lid and they will last indefinitely.

TINCTURE OF CAPSICUM

This is a classic formula for a tincture, using vodka. However, vodka is alcohol diluted with water, which is not very miscible with capsaicin. So people wishing a more concentrated tincture can substitute grain, or ethyl alcohol. Any hot red chile powder may be substituted for the chile pods. The alcohol tincture will last for years if tightly sealed. For a nonalcoholic tincture, substitute white vinegar for the vodka; but the result will not be nearly as powerful.

MAKES 4 CUPS

1/2 cup dried hot red chiles, such as piquin,
    habanero, santaka or other Asian hots, seeds
    and stems removed

4 cups inexpensive vodka or grain alcohol

In a blender or food processor, grind the chile pods as finely as possible. Place the resulting powder in a glass jar and pour the vodka over it. Cover the jar. Allow to steep for 1 week, shaking the jar daily.

Strain the tincture by pouring it through several layers of cheesecloth. Pour into a clean glass jar for use as a liniment. It will keep indefinitely in the medicine cabinet.

CHILE-GARLIC COUGH SYRUP

This is a remedy for persistent coughs. Take it in 1 tablespoon doses every hour as long as the coughing persists. A doctor should be consulted if the cough persists for more than a few days.

MAKES 1½ CUPS

½ teaspoon hot chile powder such as habanero, piquin, or cayenne

1 cup freshly squeezed lemon juice

6 cloves garlic, minced

1 tablespoon grated fresh ginger

¼ cup sugar or honey

Place all ingredients in a blender and puree. Store in a sealed clean glass jar in the refrigerator. It will last for 2 weeks.

"BIRD PEPPER" VINEGAR FOR FLU

This is a remedy from the West Indies; it is also used to treat sore throat. Combine this vinegar with honey and barley water to make a mouthwash and gargle. Interestingly enough, this remedy can be applied to a cloth and used as a poultice for gout.

MAKES 2¼ CUPS

2 tablespoons "bird peppers" or chiltepins

2 tablespoons salt

1 cup boiling water

1 cup cider vinegar

In a mortar, combine the chiles and salt and crush. Add to the boiling water and let steep 10 minutes. Strain, allow to cool, and add the vinegar. Drink as a tea.

THAI TEA FOR FEVER

The combination of ginger and hot chiles is reputed to induce sweating to reduce fever in Southeast Asia. The dosage is ¼ cup 4 times a day or until the fever breaks.

MAKES 2 CUPS

Two 3-inch pieces gingerroot, grated
2 fresh Thai chiles, seeds and stems removed,
    minced (or substitute serranos)

2 cups water
Juice of 1 lemon
2 teaspoons honey

Combine all the ingredients in a pot and bring to a boil, stirring often. Turn off the heat and let steep for ½ hour. Strain and drink hot.

HABANERO OIL

This oil is used to treat arthritis pain and sore muscles. A couple of drops help to soothe toothaches. It should be stored in the refrigerator, where it will last for a couple of weeks.

MAKES 2 CUPS

2 tablespoons habanero powder
2 cups sunflower oil

In a saucepan, combine the powder and the oil. Cook over low heat for about 2 hours. Strain through a cheesecloth into a clean glass jar. Cover and it will keep in the refrigerator for 2 to 3 weeks.

NOTE: To make a salve, add 1½ ounces of beeswax.

HOT HERBAL OINTMENT

Clean the wound, sore, or insect bite with strong soap and water and then apply this ointment. Cover with a bandage or gauze.

MAKES 3 CUPS

2 ounces dandelion leaves
2 ounces plantain leaves
2 ounces yellow dock leaves
1 quart boiling water

1/4 cup lard
2 ounces beeswax
1 teaspoon cayenne

In a pot, combine the dandelion, plantain, and yellow dock. Add the boiling water and continue boiling until the liquid is reduced by one half. Strain the mixture into a bowl and add the remaining ingredients, stirring well. Transfer to a clean jar for storage and cover. It will last 2 to 3 weeks in the refrigerator.

CAPSICUM LINIMENT WITH HERB OILS

This is used for sprains, bruises, and the symptoms of rheumatism and neuralgia.

MAKES 1/2 CUP

1/4 cup Tincture of Capsicum (page 253)
1/4 cup fluid extract of lobelia
1 teaspoon oil of wormwood

1 teaspoon oil of rosemary
1 teaspoon oil of spearmint

Combine all the ingredients and mix well. Spread over the afflicted area and massage well. Transfer the excess liniment to a clean glass jar and cover. It will last 2 to 3 weeks in the refrigerator.

COSTA RICAN PAIN COMPRESS

This remedy is for external use only and should not be eaten because it is so extremely hot. Any hot chiles can be used, but why not use the habaneros that are cultivated in Costa Rica for export?

MAKES 4 CUPS

1 cup chopped garlic
1 cup chopped fresh ginger
1 cup chopped habanero chiles

3 cups coconut oil (or substitute peanut or
   sesame oil)

In a bowl, combine the garlic, ginger, and chiles and mix well. Heat the oil in a large pan over medium-high heat. Add the garlic mixture, reduce the heat to low, and simmer, stirring occasionally, for 10 minutes. Remove from the heat and let cool before using.

Spread the mixture over a clean cloth and apply to the afflicted area. Transfer the excess mixture to a clean jar and cover. It will last 2 to 3 weeks in the refrigerator.

❧ **Reshampatti.** A variety of *annuum* grown in India. The single *reshampatti* resembles a straight dried cayenne, while the double *reshampatti* resembles the ancho.

❧ **Ristra.** In Mexico and the American Southwest, a string of red chile pods.

❧ **Rocotillo.** A mild *chinense* grown on various Caribbean islands including Cuba and the Cayman Islands.

❧ **Rocoto.** The Peruvian name for *Capsicum pubescens* that are grown in mountainous regions of Mexico, where they are called *manzana* and *canario* (when yellow). The pods are thick-walled, quite hot, and have black seeds. Also spelled *rocote*.

❧ **'Roque.'** A cultivated variety of *mulato* in Mexico.

Sakaipilo. Term for chile in Madagascar.

SALSA

Salsa is the Spanish word meaning "sauce," but salsa in a commercial in the United States and Canada means a chunky sauce with a tomato base and onions, usually spiced with jalapeños or serranos. The manufactured sauce must be cooked in order to bottle it. In home and restaurant cooking, salsa is an uncooked sauce with an enormous number of variations. There are fruit salsas, bean salsas, vegetable salsas, and even dessert salsas—all with a common theme: hot peppers.

In Texas, salsa manufacturing began in 1947. Dave and Margaret Pace operated a small food-packing operation in the back of their liquor store in San Antonio. They were manufacturing syrups, salad dressings, and jellies and sold their products door-to-door. Dave, by trial and error, began to make picante sauce and test it on his friends. When it was introduced commercially, it was so popular that the Paces were forced to drop all the other products and concentrate on the picante sauce. But the salsa business was not easy.

"In forty-seven my sauce bottles exploded all over the grocery shelves because I couldn't get the darned formula right," said Dave Pace in 1992. "In the seventies, the business exploded when the hippies came along. No question but this health stuff made the whole category explode, and it just tickles me to see these people take the ball and run with it."

Between 1985 and 1990, Mexican sauce sales grew 79 percent; between 1988 and 1992, the percentage of American households buying salsa increased from 16 percent to 36 percent. And despite the claims of Austin, the real Mexican sauce capital of the United States was Los Angeles, which gobbled up 3.3 million gallons of it in 1990. This appetite was due to numerous barrio immigrants living in the east and central parts of the city.

A fruit salsa. SUNBELT ARCHIVES

By 1992, the top eight salsa manufacturers were Pace, Old El Paso, Frito-Lay, Chi-Chi's, La Victoria, Ortega, Herdez, and Newman's Own. Pace owned 32.3 percent of the market, according to a study by Information Resources, Inc., published in *The New York Times.* The market share figures change when different sources are consulted, but Pace is always in the lead. Pace spent $10 million in advertising in 1992 to maintain that lead, outspending Pet Foods' $5 million for the Old El Paso sauce lines.

That same year fifty new salsa products were introduced in Texas alone, including new brands or additional products by established brands. By 1993, competition from the smaller salsa companies was so fierce that Pace, Old El Paso, and a total of six of the top-ten brands saw Texas sales decline 3 percent from the year before. During the first seven months of 1993, according to *New Product News,* 147 new salsa products were introduced, including Heinz's Salsa Style Ketchup.

Salsa became America's number one condiment in dollar sales around the middle of 1992, which reflects a growing love of all forms of this condiment. Salsa experts describe a profusion of different styles of both homemade and commercial salsas. Reed Hearon, in his book *Salsa,* divides salsas into fiery, mild, modern, and dessert. Mark Miller, in *The Great Salsa Book,* divides his salsas into chile, tropical, fruit, corn, bean, garden, nut-seed-herb, ocean, and exotic. And Chris Schlesinger and John Willoughby, in their book *Salsas, Sambals, Chutneys & Chowchows,* categorize these similar condiments as: salsas, chutneys, *blatjangs, atjars,* sambals, chowchows, piccalillies, relishes, and catsups.

There are many more uses for salsa than just as a premeal dip with corn tortilla chips, a vegetable dip, or a condiment served with fish and over eggs. The newer uses of salsa include: a sauce over grilled chicken, baked chicken, pan-fried steak, veal, or fish; a barbecue sauce; over pizza; a base for cooked sauces; a marinade; a salad dressing; over pasta; over enchiladas, burritos, huevos rancheros, fajitas, and chicken wings; spoon-eaten like gazpacho; and on baked potatoes and French fries.

Total sales of Mexican sauces in the United States are expected to top $2 billion in 2000. "The future for salsa looks strong indeed," wrote Robert Spiegel, former publisher of *Chile Pepper* magazine. "We believe there's plenty of growth left in this upward trend. We expect salsa to remain America's favorite condiment for years, or even decades, to come simply because salsa lends itself to adaptation to changing tastes. Plus salsa satisfies the broader trends in food. It is healthy, low calorie, spicy, and diverse in its ethnic applications and its versatility. Salsa, in one form or another, has been gaining in popularity for decades and decades. In our lifetime we don't expect to see it stop gaining."

TOP U.S. SALSAS AND PICANTE SAUCES, 1992

Brand	Sales (Millions)	Share
Pace	$160.4	32.3
Old El Paso	91.9	18.5
Frito-Lay	54.6	11.0
Chi-Chi's	47.4	9.5
La Victoria	30.2	6.1
Ortega	28.2	5.7
Herdez	9.1	1.8
Newman's Own	7.5	1.5

Source: Information Resources, Inc.

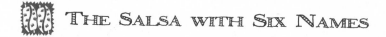 # THE SALSA WITH SIX NAMES

This blend of hot chiles and fresh garden vegetables is known both north and south of the border as salsa *fria*, *pico de gallo*, salsa *cruda*, salsa *fresca*, salsa *Méxicana*, and salsa *picante*. No matter what it's called, or what part of Mexico it's from, the Salsa with Six Names will always triumph over bottled salsas for the dipping of tostadas, as a taco sauce, or as a relish for roasted or grilled meats. The key to proper preparation is to never use a food processor or blender. A marvelous consistency will be achieved by taking the time to chop every ingredient finely by hand. Note that this recipe requires advance preparation.

MAKES 2 CUPS
HEAT SCALE: **Medium**

4 serrano or jalapeño chiles, seeds and stems removed, minced

1 large onion, minced

2 medium tomatoes, minced

2 cloves garlic, minced

¼ cup minced fresh cilantro

2 tablespoons vegetable oil

2 tablespoons, or less to taste, red wine vinegar or lime juice

Mix all the ingredients together in a glass or other nonreactive bowl. Let stand at room temperature for at least 1 hour before serving.

Serve with tortilla chips as a dip. This salsa is also good with tacos, burritos, and fajitas.

NORTHERN MEXICAN SALSA CRUDA

This salsa is popular in the state of Chihuahua. Note the use of fresh poblanos in a salsa, which is uncommon. Grilling the tomatoes over an open flame enhances the tastes of the salsa. Note that this recipe requires advance preparation.

MAKES ABOUT 2 CUPS
HEAT SCALE: **Hot**

¼ cup seeded and chopped serrano chiles
¼ cup seeded and chopped jalapeño chiles
¼ cup seeded and chopped poblano chiles
¼ cup chopped onion
¼ cup chopped scallions, white and green parts
¼ to ½ teaspoon salt to taste
½ cup fresh lime juice

2 medium tomatoes, chopped, plus 1 medium tomato, broiled, peeled, and blended until smooth
¼ cup minced fresh cilantro
1 medium avocado, peeled, seeded, and chopped (optional)

Place the chiles, onion, scallions, and salt in a glass or other nonreactive bowl with the lime juice. Mix well and refrigerate for 1 to 2 hours. Drain off the liquid and discard. Then add the chopped tomatoes and just enough of the broiled, blended tomato to bind the mixture into a sauce. Add more salt, if desired. Stir in the cilantro and avocado, if you are using it. Although the avocado is optional, it adds a great deal to the sauce.

YELLOW, RED, AND GREEN SALSA WITH HABANEROS

One great thing about chile peppers is that they come in quite a variety of bright colors. Here we match red habaneros with yellow tomatoes, although orange habaneros work fine and may be substituted for the red ones. Serve this salsa over grilled seafood or chicken. Note that this recipe requires advance preparation.

MAKES ABOUT 4 CUPS
HEAT SCALE: Hot

2 pounds small yellow tomatoes, cut into ½-inch cubes

2 red habaneros, seeds and stems removed, minced

½ cup thinly sliced scallions, white and green parts

½ cup minced celery with leaves

1 small red bell pepper, roasted (page 146) and cut into ¼-inch dice

1 small red tomato, cut into ½-inch cubes

2 tablespoons olive oil

1 tablespoon fresh lime juice

1 tablespoon chopped fresh cilantro

1 teaspoon minced fresh mint

½ teaspoon minced garlic

Salt and freshly ground black pepper

Combine all ingredients in a large glass or other nonreactive bowl and mix well. Let stand 30 minutes before serving to let the flavors mix.

⊌ *Sambal.* A Malaysian and Indonesian chile paste.

⊌ **Scotch bonnet.** A pod type of *chinense* grown in Jamaica. Also, the generic name for the species in other Caribbean islands.

SCOVILLE SCALE

The food industry unit of measurement for the pungency of hot peppers is the Scoville Unit. It is named for the pharmacologist Wilbur L. Scoville (for the story, see Pungency). Although the Scoville Organoleptic Test is still occasionally used, it has mostly been replaced by high performance liquid chromatography. This process measures the amount of capsaicin present in parts per million, which are then converted into Scoville Units. Pure capsaicin is 16 million Scoville Units. The pungency of peppers measures from trace amounts in some bell peppers to 577,000 Scoville Units in a 'Red Savina' variety of habanero, believed to be the hottest ever tested. It should be pointed out that not all 'Red Savinas' have tested this hot. Most are in the 200,000 to 400,000 Scoville Unit range. As there are many factors affecting the pungency of any variety, and there are many varieties within the various species, the measurements below are necessarily approximate.

⊌ **Seasoning pepper.** In the Caribbean, mild, elongated *Capsicum chinense* varieties.

SERRANOS

In Spanish, *serrano* is an adjective that means "from the mountains." The chile described by this adjective was first grown in the mountains of northern Puebla and Hidalgo, Mexico.

The Plant

Serranos vary in habit from compact to erect, have an intermediate number of stems, and grow from one and a half to five

SCOVILLE UNITS	CHILE VARIETIES AND COMMERCIAL PRODUCTS
100,000–500,000	habanero, Scotch bonnet, South American *chinenses*, African "bird's eye"
50,000–100,000	*santaka*, chiltepin, *rocoto*, Chinese *kwangsi*
30,000–50,000	piquin, 'Cayenne Long,' Tabasco, Thai *prik khee nu*, Pakistan *dundicut*
15,000–30,000	*de árbol*, crushed red pepper, habanero hot sauce
5,000–15,000	early jalapeño, *aji* amarillo, serrano, Tabasco sauce
2,500–5,000	'TAM Mild Jalapeño,' *mirasol*, 'Cayenne Large Red Thick,' Louisiana hot sauce
1,500–2,500	*sandia, cascabel*, 'Yellow Wax Hot'
1,000–1,500	ancho, pasilla, 'Española,' Old Bay Seasoning
500–1000	'NuMex Big Jim,' 'NuMex No. 6-4,' chili powder
100–500	'NuMex R-Naky,' 'Mexi-Bell,' 'Cherry,' canned green chiles, Hungarian hot paprika
10–100	pickled *pepperoncini*
0	mild bells, pimiento, 'Sweet Banana,' U.S. paprika

Serrano chiles. DAVE DEWITT

Agriculture

Mexico has about 37,500 acres of serranos under cultivation, compared to only 150 acres in the United States, mostly in the Southwest. The states of Veracruz, Sinaloa, Nayarit, and Tamaulipas are the biggest producers of Mexican serrano chiles, growing about 180,000 tons of pods a year. Despite the proliferation of canned serranos, only 10 percent of the crop is processed. The vast majority is used fresh. A very small amount of red serranos is dried out for sale in markets. Recommended varieties are the Mexican cultivars 'Altamira,' 'Panuco,' and 'Tampiqueño.' In 1985, the Texas Agricultural Experiment Station released 'Hidalgo,' a mild, multiple-virus-resistant strain which is now popular in the United States.

Culinary Usage

Relatively unknown in the United States until a couple of decades ago, serranos have become popular because of their pickling. Many different brands of serranos *en escabeche,* or serranos pickled with carrots and onions, have gained favor in the Southwest, where they are consumed as a snack or hors d'oeuvre. By far, the most common use of serranos is in fresh salsas. The chiles are picked fresh from the garden or purchased in produce departments, minced, and then combined with a variety of vegetables. The resulting salsas can be used as dips or as condiments for meats, poultry, seafood, and egg dishes.

feet tall. The leaves vary from light to dark green, are pubescent (hairy), and measure three and a half to five inches long and one and a half to two inches wide. The flower corollas are white with no spots. The pods grow erect or pendant, are bluntly pointed, and measure between one and four inches long and a half inch wide. Serranos measure between 10,000 and 15,000 Scoville Units.

Fresh Tomatillo Salsa with Serranos

In Mexico, all sauces are salsas, regardless of whether or not they are cooked. But in the United States, a salsa usually refers to an uncooked sauce. This is one of the simplest—yet tastiest—uses of serrano chiles. Serve this as a dip for chips or as a marinade and basting sauce for grilled poultry and meat.

MAKES ABOUT 2 CUPS
HEAT SCALE: Medium

1 pound fresh green tomatillos
3 tablespoons minced red onion
2 serrano chiles, seeds and stems removed, minced
1 small bunch cilantro, coarsely chopped

Juice of 1 lime
1 to 2 tablespoons olive oil (optional)
Sugar to taste (optional)

Husk the tomatillos and wash them thoroughly under very hot water. Cool under running cold water, and coarsely puree in a food processor or blender. Add the onion, serrano chiles, cilantro, and lime juice and pulse until coarsely chopped.

Remove the bowl from the machine and add olive oil if you wish to adjust the consistency. Add some sugar if the tomatillos are too sour.

➣ *Shatta.* Arabic term for hot chile pepper.

➣ *Siling.* The Filipino (Tagalog) word for Capsicums in general. *Siling bilog* is bell pepper; *siling haba* is the long green or red chile; *siling labuyo* is the "bird pepper," very small and very hot (*Capsicum frutescens* or *C. chinense*).

➣ *Sinteh.* Name for the *chinense* species in Cameroon.

SMOKING CHILES

Why did Native Americans smoke chiles in the first place? Perhaps some thick-fleshed chiles such as early jalapeños were dropped near the communal fire and later, a leathery, preserved chile was the result. Since smoking is believed (along with salting) to be one of the earliest preservation methods, it would make sense that the "meaty" chiles could be smoked right along with the meat.

In the town of Delicias in northern Mexico, the red jalapeños are smoked in a large pit on a rack that can be made out of wood, bamboo, or metal. Another nearby pit contains the fire and is connected to the smoking pit by an underground tunnel. The pods are placed on top of the rack where drafts of air pull the smoke up and over the pods. A farm may have a smoker of a different design at the edge of the fields, and it may be a fireplace of bricks with grates at the top and a firebox below. This smoker is for small batches.

Chipotles smoked in the Mexican manner are not always available north of Mexico. And with prices of chipotles topping $15 per pound when they are available, an attractive alternative for cooks is to smoke their own chiles. As chile expert Paul Bosland of New Mexico State University commented in an article in *Chile Pepper* magazine, "It is possible to make *chipotle* in the backyard with a meat smoker or Weber-type barbecue with a lid. The grill should be washed to remove any meat particles because any odor in the barbecue will give the chile an undesirable flavor. Ideally, the smoker or barbecue should be new and dedicated only to smoking chiles." The result of this type of smoking is a chipotle that more resembles the red *morita* than the classic tan-brown *típico*.

There are five keys to the quality of the homemade *chipotles*: the maturity and quality of the pods, the moisture in the pods, the type of wood used to create the smoke, the temperature of the smoke drying the pods, and the amount of time the fruits are exposed to the smoke and heat. But remember that smoking is an art, so variations are to be expected and even desired.

Recommended woods are fruit trees or other hardwoods such as hickory, oak, and pecan. Pecan is used extensively in parts of Mexico and in southern New Mexico to flavor *chipotle*. Although mesquite is a smoke source in Mexico, we prefer the less greasy hardwoods. Mesquite charcoal (not briquettes) is acceptable, however, especially when soaked hardwood chips are placed on top to create even more smoke. It is possible, however, that the resinous mesquite smoke (from the wood, not charcoal) contributes to the tan-brown coloration of the *típico* variety of chipotle.

Wash all the pods and discard any that have insect damage, bruises, or are soft, and remove the stems from the pods. Start two small fires on each side of the barbecue bowl, preferably using one of the recommended hardwoods. If you are using a meat smoker with a separate firebox, simply build the fire in the firebox.

Place the pods in a single layer on the grill rack so they fit between the two fires. For quicker smoking, cut the pods in half lengthwise and remove the seeds. Keep the fires small and never directly expose the pods to the fire so they won't dry unevenly or burn. The intention is to dry the pods slowly while flavoring them with smoke. If you are using charcoal briquettes, soak hardwood chips in water before placing them on the coals so the wood will burn more slowly and create more smoke. The barbecue vents should be opened only partially to allow a small amount of air to enter the barbecue, thus preventing the fires from burning too fast and creating too much heat.

Check the pods, the fires, and the chips hourly and move the pods around, always keeping them away from the fires. It may take up to forty-eight hours to dry the pods completely, which means that your fire will probably burn down during the night and will need to be restoked in the morning. When dried properly, the pods will be hard, light in weight, and brown in color. After the pods have dried, remove them from the grill and let them cool. To preserve their flavor, place them in a Ziploc bag.

Ten pounds of fresh jalapeños yield just one pound of chipotles after the smoking process is complete. A pound of chipotle goes a long way, as a single pod is usually enough to flavor a dish.

A quick smoking technique involves drying red jalapeños (sliced lengthwise, seeds removed) in a dehydrator or in a gas oven with just the pilot light on. They should be desiccated but not stiff. This takes days, depending on heat and humidity in the oven. Then smoke them for three hours over fruitwood in a traditional smoker with a separate firebox, or in the Weber-style barbecue as described above. This technique separates the drying from the smoking so you spend less time fueling the smoker.

Hot sauce manufacturer Chuck Evans has experimented with smoke-drying pods on a large scale with jalapeños grown near Toledo, Ohio. The large red pods had a lot of white "corking," which is a desirable trait for jalapeños in Mexico. Thus they resembled the variety called 'Huachinango.' He took the pods to a local catering firm that specialized in barbecue and used one of their revolving rack smokers. With hickory wood as his smoke source, he smoked the pods at 110°F for three days. He was attempting to duplicate the *típico* ("cigar-butt") variety but the result was much more like the *mora* or *morita*, with their bright red-brown leathery appearance.

The second attempt at duplicating the *típico* variety was in another meat-packing plant in a modern room with climate-controlled, injected smoke. The result was identical to the first try.

Then Chuck repeated the experiment a third time with a primitive smoker in a sausage-making facility. It was a small room with racks set on the ground and smoke that circulated continuously. He left the pods in the room for a week, and the chipotles were closer to the desired tan-brown color, but the pods still had too much moisture in them. He concluded that the raw red jalapeños contained extra moisture to begin with.

Obviously, the Mexicans have perfected the *típico* technique, while we Americans are struggling to duplicate it with more modern equipment. It is a delicate balance of the pit temperature, the amount of smoke, the type of smoke, and the length of time that produces the perfect *chipotle*. Perhaps we shall be forced to dig smoking pits in our backyards and begin growing mesquite trees.

Rob Polishook is one of the owners of Chile Today-Hot Tamale, a company that introduced the Smoked Habanero chiles to American chileheads. When we asked him about his technique for smoking the hottest chiles in the world, he wouldn't reveal his exact trade secrets, but he did give us some general techniques.

"Producing the smoked habanero chile is an intricate and time-consuming process,"

he wrote. "The habaneros are smoked over a medley of exotic woods, herbs, and spices. The habaneros are smoked for sixteen to thirty hours and must be turned and sorted depending on their density and size at least once an hour. This process ensures that the habaneros do not burn and will have a rich, smoky, citrus, incendiary flavor. Chile Today-Hot Tamale's homemade habanero smoker has smoked thousands of pounds of habaneros. Similar to a chef's favorite pan, it has seasoned perfectly." Rob's final comment is good evidence for devoting a smoker strictly to chipotles.

Storage

Many cooks have success storing chipotles in a Ziploc bag in a cool and dry location. If humidity is kept out of the bags, the chipotle will last for twelve to twenty-four months. A more secure method to store them at room temperature is to keep them in glass jars with a tight-fitting, rubber-sealed top.

Of course, the best storage of all is to freeze them. Use heavy-duty freezer bags and double-bag the chipotles. They will keep for years with no noticeable loss of flavor or smoke.

Making Chipotle Powder

A "dried" chipotle usually has about 80 to 90 percent of its moisture removed, which is enough, with the smoke, to preserve it and retard bacterial growth, but not enough to create a powder. Therefore, regardless of whether you are using the *típico* chipotle or the *morita*, they must be further dried in a food dehydrator or in the oven on the lowest possible heat, until they are so dry that you can snap them in half.

Put on a painter's mask to protect you from breathing the dried chipotle fumes and sneezing, and break the chipotles into manageable pieces. Use an electric spice mill or a coffee grinder to reduce the pod pieces to a powder.

Because the chiles are so desiccated, the chipotle powder stores well in air-tight containers such as small jars. But remember, powders will oxidize and absorb odors from the air or the freezer, so if you intend to freeze the powders or store them in bags at room temperature, triple-bag them first.

➷ *Spanischcher oderkercher pheffer.* German term for peppers.

➷ *Spansk peppar.* Swedish term for peppers.

SPICE ISLANDS — INDONESIA, MALAYSIA, AND SINGAPORE

In Indonesia, Malaysia, and Singapore, the words for rice (*nasi*), chicken (*ayam*), hot sauce (*sambal*), and many other food terms are often identical from region to region, so it is difficult to separate the Malaysian and Indonesian elements of the food of the spiciest islands. After the Portuguese won control of the Malacca Strait in 1511, it is probable that chile peppers were imported soon afterward by traders sailing to and from the Portuguese colony of Goa, India. The spice trade was one of the primary motivating factors in European exploration of the rest of the world, so it is not surprising that many countries sought to control the output of the "Spice Islands." These islands, which now comprise parts of the countries of Indonesia, Malaysia, and Singapore, produced cinnamon, cloves, nutmeg, black pepper, and many other spices. What is surprising about the Spice Islands is that they were infiltrated and "conquered" by a New World spice — chile peppers.

Asian food authority Copeland Marks has observed that the cuisine of the region would be "unthinkable without them . . . When the chile arrived in Indonesia it was welcomed enthusiastically and now may be considered an addiction." An addiction they may be, but their nomenclature is as confusing as ever. They have a common term in the region, *cabe* (also spelled *cabai*). *Cabe hijau* refers to green chiles while *cabe merah* means red chiles and *cabe rawit* are the notoriously hot bird chiles (*Capsicum*

Malaysian chiles and garlic in a Singapore market. DAVE DEWITT

frutescens). But another word for chiles in Java and other parts of Indonesia is *lombok*, while *cili* is the operative alternate in Malaysia. *Cili padi* are apparently the same as *cabe rawit*, the small bird chiles, while dried red chiles are *cili kering*.

The nomenclature gets even more muddled when the chilehead travels to Bali, a Hindu outpost in predominately Muslim Indonesia. There, chiles are *tabia*. *Tabia lombok* (sometimes called *tabia jawa*) is finger-length and resembles cayenne, while *tabia bali* is about an inch long and is the most popular chile on the island. *Tabia kerinyi* are the "bird's eye" chiles, or piquins, and *tabia gede* is the bell pepper.

Chiles are the number one vegetable crop in Indonesia, occupying 18 percent of the total acreage with an astonishing 500,000 acres under cultivation. That figure placed Indonesia third in world chile production in 1986, after India and Mexico. In agricultural terminology, there are two varieties under cultivation: *cabe rawit* ("chile pepper" or "bird pepper"), a variety of *C. frutescens*, and *cabe merah*, or "cayenne." The Indonesian chiles are planted in alternating rows with shallots and sometimes with rice.

In Indonesia, chiles are used in a wide variety of dishes and are often combined with coconut cream or milk. On the island of Java, sugar is added, making that cuisine a mixture of sweet, sour, and fiery hot. Some cooks there believe that the addition of sugar keeps the power of the chiles and other spices under control.

A hot and spicy stir-fry at the Newton Hawker Centre, Singapore. DAVE DEWITT

Perhaps the principal use of chiles in this part of Asia is in sauces called *sambals* that are spread over rice or are used as a dip for satay, barbecued small chunks of meat. Chiles are often combined with peanuts for the satay dips. One word in particular frequently comes up in discussions of Indonesian food, and that is *rijsttafel*, which means "rice table" in Dutch. It is not a dish, but rather a feast of many dishes, including curries. The term derives from the Dutch settlers, who staged elaborate dinner parties in an attempt to upstage one another. It was up to the creative chef never to duplicate flavors, types of meat, or cooking styles, and for every dish that was spicy hot, there had to be a bland dish to offset it. Likewise, sweet dishes were offset by sour dishes, warm dishes by cold dishes, wet by dry, and firm-textured by soft-textured.

Often, as many as fifty or sixty dishes were served, but despite such attention to detail, the food was not as important as the spectacle in a *rijsttafel*, and the quality of the party was judged by the number of servants it took to produce the affair. If fifty servants were required, the party was known as a "fifty-boy *rijsttafel*," which the Indonesians naturally found offensive. Today the term is considered to be a degrading holdover from colonial times; however, scaled-down *rijsttafels* are still staged for tourists—but without all the servants. Some of the curry dishes included in early *rijsttafels* were the *gulais*,

"curried stews," and the *rendangs* (sometimes spelled *randang*), which are meat dishes cooked in coconut milk and spices.

By comparison with the Indonesian figures, chiles are grown on a scant 2,500 acres in Malaysia—but still are the most important vegetables grown in the country in terms of total acreage, value, and per-capita consumption. There are two main varieties of *C. annuum* under cultivation, 'Kulai' and 'Langkap.' They are grown by themselves or are intercropped with coconut, rubber, or pineapple. Malaysia provides more than 90 percent of Singapore's needs for fresh chile, with the remaining coming from Thailand.

In Malaysia too, chiles play an important role in the curries. For example, *lemak kuning* is a coconut-based sauce made with most of the regional curry ingredients; *kerabu kerisik* is made with fried, pounded coconut, lime juice, dried shrimp, shallots, and chiles; and *kacang* blends together the flavors of peanuts, lemongrass, *galangal*, chiles, and coconut milk.

Similarly, the famous *sambals* range from simple chile sauces to curry-like pastes and are primarily used to spice up other dishes, such as mild curries. The basis for most *sambals* is chiles, onions (or shallots or garlic), and citrus, but many other ingredients are used, including lemongrass, *blacan*, ginger, *galangal*, candlenuts, kaffir lime leaves, and coconut milk. Thus the *sambals* resemble a curry paste, but with a much greater amount of chiles.

✺ Spice Islands Chile Paste
Sambalan

This Malaysian paste is the culinary equivalent of harissa in North Africa and *berbere* in Ethiopia. Its most common use is in making quick main dishes. About 1 tablespoon of the *sambalan* is stir-fried with every 8 ounces of the already-cooked meat, such as chicken or beef. Coconut milk is added to make a gravy, the mixture is reduced, and the dish is served over rice.

MAKES ABOUT 2 CUPS
HEAT SCALE: **Medium to hot**

20 dried red New Mexican chiles, seeds and stems removed, soaked in hot water for 20 minutes

8 dried chiltepins, piquins, or Thai chiles, seeds and stems removed, soaked in hot water for 20 minutes (optional, for a hotter paste)

3 onions, chopped

7 cloves garlic

2 teaspoons fish or shrimp paste (optional)

¾ cup peanut oil, or more if needed

1 teaspoon tamarind paste dissolved in 1 cup warm water

2 teaspoons salt

2 tablespoons light brown sugar

Combine the chiles, chiltepins (if you are using them), onions, garlic, fish paste, and ½ cup of the peanut oil in a food processor and puree to a smooth paste. Heat the remaining ¼ cup peanut oil in a wok or skillet over high heat, add the chile paste, and fry until it is dark in color and the oil starts to separate, about 1 minute. Add the tamarind-water mixture, salt, and brown sugar, reduce the heat to low, and simmer for 5 minutes, stirring occasionally. Store in bottles, tightly covered, in the refrigerator for up to a week.

BALINESE GADO GADO SALAD

This popular salad from Bali is a meal in itself. Traditionally, the salad is composed of a wide array of raw and parboiled ingredients, arranged in layers, and is served with the spicy peanut dressing.

MAKES 8 SERVINGS
HEAT SCALE: **Medium**

Peanut Dressing

1 cup peanut butter, smooth or crunchy

$1/2$ cup water

1 to 2 'bird's eye' chiles (chiltepins), stems removed, finely minced (or substitute piquin or cayenne chiles)

$3/4$ teaspoon garlic powder

2 teaspoons light brown sugar

2 tablespoons dark soy sauce

1 tablespoon fresh lemon or lime juice

$1/2$ to 1 cup canned coconut milk

Salad

$1/2$ pound mung bean sprouts, brown ends pinched off

$1/2$ pound green beans, cut into 2-inch-long pieces

2 large carrots, cut into matchstick-size pieces

1 small head cauliflower, separated into small florets

3 hard-boiled eggs, peeled and quartered

3 large potatoes, boiled until tender (about 30 minutes) and sliced into rounds about $3/8$ inch thick

1 large cucumber, skin scored, sliced very thinly

To make the dressing, place the peanut butter and water into a saucepan over low heat and stir until mixed. Remove from the heat and add all the other dressing ingredients. Combine well to make a thick dressing with a pouring consistency. Set aside.

To make the salad, drop the bean sprouts into a pot of boiling water and immediately remove, drain, and rinse under cold tap water. If you use a strainer to remove the beans, you can use the same water to cook the rest of the vegetables.

In the same pot of boiling water, cook the green beans, carrots, and cauliflower until only just tender, about 10 minutes. Alternatively, you can place the vegetables in a steamer basket in a pot with just ½ inch of water and steam the vegetables until cooked. Rinse the vegetables in cold water to cool.

Arrange the cooked green beans, carrots, and cauliflower in separate sections on a large platter, with wedges of egg and potato rounds in the center and the cucumber surrounding the platter. Serve cold, accompanied by the peanut sauce, which is spooned over the individual servings by each guest.

PENANG CHICKEN SATAY

This recipe is from Penang, Malaysia. It is a classic Spice Islands dish that combines the heat of chiles with the exotic fragrances of the Spice Islands. It is usually served with a peanut-chile sauce such as *katjang saos*. Note that this recipe requires advance preparation. Satay sticks can be found in Asian markets or gourmet shops.

MAKES 4 SERVINGS
HEAT SCALE: **Medium**

Four 3-inch pieces ginger, peeled
4 piquin chiles, chopped
5 cloves garlic
3 shallots
1 teaspoon cumin seeds
1 teaspoon anise seeds

1 tablespoon ground turmeric
3 stalks lemongrass
2 teaspoons sugar
1 pound boneless chicken, cut into strips
Asian Peanut Dressing (page 275) for serving
Diced cucumbers and onions for garnish

Combine the ginger, chiles, garlic, shallots, cumin, anise, turmeric, lemongrass, and sugar in a food processor and puree, adding water if necessary. Marinate the chicken strips in this mixture for 12 hours, covered, in the refrigerator.

Light a charcoal fire in your grill. Thread the chicken strips onto separate satay sticks that have been soaked in water. Grill the satay sticks over coals until the meat is done, about 12 minutes, turning often. Serve the satays with an Asian peanut sauce on the side and garnished with the diced cucumbers and onions.

SUMATRAN CHILE RENDANG
Rendang

Here is the traditional way the Sumatrans cook the often-tough meat of the water buffalo—by slowly simmering it in coconut milk. This recipe takes some time to make, but it's worth it. It keeps for months in the freezer. Serve the *rendang* with any rice dish.

MAKES 6 SERVINGS
HEAT SCALE: Medium

8 cups coconut milk

½ cup Spice Islands Chile Paste (page 274)

3½ pounds chuck roast, cut into 1-inch cubes

Heat the coconut milk in a large pot over low heat for about 3 minutes. Add the paste and the meat. Cook, uncovered, for 1½ to 2 hours, or until the meat is quite tender. Stir the mixture every 15 minutes or so. The sauce will become very thick.

Raise the heat to medium-high and, stirring continuously, continue to cook the mixture until all the sauce has been incorporated into the meat and the meat becomes golden brown, about 30 minutes.

MALAYSIAN SEAFOOD WITH GREEN CHILES AND NOODLES
Laksa Lemak Melaka

The Malaysian people love chile peppers, select them carefully at the market, and use them liberally as a source of heat in most recipes. This dish features serranos or jalapeños, but piquins may be added if more heat is desired.

MAKES 6 TO 8 SERVINGS
HEAT SCALE: **Medium**

1 pound shrimp, peeled and deveined
1 pound halibut or other whitefish, cut into
    ¾-inch chunks
3 cups water
8 candlenuts (or substitute Brazil nuts)
3 serrano chiles or jalapeños, seeds and stems
    removed, chopped
1½ teaspoons ground turmeric
¾ teaspoon ground ginger
Pinch ground cinnamon
2 large cloves garlic

1 teaspoon grated lemon peel
¼ cup vegetable oil
2 cups minced onion
2 cups coconut milk
2 tablespoons fresh lime juice
1 pound bean sprouts
1 pound vermicelli or spaghetti
1 cucumber, peeled, seeded, and cut into strips for
    garnish
Fresh or dried mint for garnish (optional)

Place the shrimp and fish in a large skillet; add 1 cup of the water and simmer over low heat for about 5 minutes. Remove from the heat and let cool. Be sure to reserve the cooking liquid.

In a food processor, combine the nuts, chiles, turmeric, ginger, cinnamon, garlic, and lemon peel and process to a paste. Heat the vegetable oil in another skillet over medium-high heat. Add the onion and chile paste and cook, stirring, until the onions are soft, about 5 minutes. Add the coconut milk, remaining 2 cups water, and lime juice to the onion mixture. Bring to a simmer, then reduce the heat to low and simmer, stirring occasionally, for 8 minutes.

Add the cooked shrimp, fish, and the fish cooking liquid. Simmer for 10 minutes. Meanwhile, bring a small pot of water to a boil. Add the bean sprouts to the boiling water and cook for 1 minute. Cool the bean sprouts under cold water. In another pot of boiling water, cook the noodles as noted on the package and drain. In individual bowls, divide the noodles and bean sprouts equally. Pour the shrimp, fish, and sauce over each serving and garnish with cucumber and mint.

❧ **Squash pepper.** In the United States, a pod type of the *annuum* species. Also called cheese or tomato peppers, the squash type is best known for the flattened shape of the pods. Varieties include 'Red Squash Hot' and 'Yellow Squash Hot.'

❧ *Struchkovy pyerets.* Russian term for peppers.

⩗ *Taa' tɕ'itɕin itɕ.* "Chile excreted by birds"; term for chiltepin in Huastec Mayan language of Mexico.

⩗ *Tabia.* Balinese word for chile peppers. *Tabia lombok* (sometimes called *tabia jawa*) is finger-length and resembles cayenne; *tabia bali* is about an inch long and is the most popular chile in Bali; *tabia kerinyi* are the "bird's eye" chiles, or piquins. *Tabia gede* is bell pepper.

⩗ *Tabiche.* A chile in Oaxaca, Mexico, similar to a jalapeño, consumed both fresh and dry.

⩗ *'Tampiqueño-74.'* A cultivated variety of serrano in Mexico.

TASTE AND FLAVOR

The sensation of heat created by capsaicin in chiles is caused by the irritation of the trigeminal cells, which are pain receptors located in the mouth, nose, and stomach.

These sensory neurons release substance P, a neuropeptide chemical messenger that tells the brain about pain or skin inflammation. Repeated consumption of chile peppers confuses the substance P receptors, which is the reason people eventually build up a tolerance to capsaicin and can eat hotter and hotter foods.

When applied topically to treat skin pain, capsaicin "triggers a burst of the neuropeptide substance P from the C fibers," according to the *Journal of the American Medical Association*, and this is the initial burning sensation. Capsaicin also prevents the nerve endings from making more substance P, and thus further pain signals from the skin are greatly diminished or completely eliminated. Capsaicin is the only compound known to block the transmission of substance P to the brain. When the capsaicin treatment is concluded, the substance P stores revert to normal.

There is a great deal of confusion about the effects of capsaicin on the tongue and taste buds, starting with the notion that

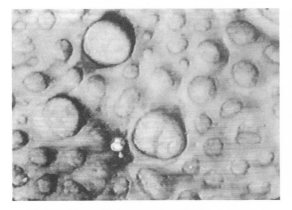

Taste papillae on the tongue of a nontaster. SUNBELT ARCHIVES   *Taste papillae on the tongue of a supertaster.* SUNBELT ARCHIVES

men who can eat the hottest peppers are somehow more masculine or "macho." The real truth is that these men are not macho, they're nontasters. About 50 percent of the population are regular tasters, meaning that they have an average number of taste buds per square centimeter on their tongue. The remaining population is evenly divided between super-tasters, who have many more taste buds, and the nontasters, who have less to practically none. The super-tasters are almost twice as sensitive to sweet, bitter, and burning tastes, while the nontasters enter jalapeño-eating contests.

Sometimes, of course, normal tasters and supertasters eat food that is simply too hot and the tongue and mouth can suffer blistering from contact dermatitis. This certainly harms the taste buds, but they are usually replaced in about two weeks, according to John Kinnamon, a University of Colorado neurobiologist. But let's take a closer look at those taste buds.

Capsaicin mostly affects the apex (tip), not the radix (base) of the tongue, and those little bumps on the front of the tongue are really taste papillae, in which the taste buds are housed. These papillae are all over the mouth, and you can actually taste with the roof of your mouth. Along with the taste buds in the mouth are the trigeminal cells mentioned earlier, which are sensitive to touch, temperature, and pain.

Generally speaking, people who love chiles claim that they enhance the tastes of other foods, while people who avoid fiery foods contend that chiles reduce or mask food flavors. In fact, it has long been rumored that the capsaicin in chile peppers damages or destroys the taste buds; in interviews noted chef Julia Child has made such a claim. There have been numerous studies on the subject of capsaicin desensitization, which generally have people judge the intensity of the taste of salt or citric acid after the mouth is treated with varying strengths of a capsaicin solution. Desensitization does occur, causing a decrease in both the taste and tactile sensations on the tongue, but this effect seems to be temporary and does not destroy the taste buds.

In fact, in one study done by Tracey Karrer and Linda Bartoshuk of the Yale University School of Medicine, it was reported that in the sour and bitter taste tests: "As subjects recovered from capsaicin desensitization, their responses were enhanced in some cases to values higher than the pre-condition." This would seem to indicate that although capsaicin desensitizes the taste buds, after recovery tastes seem to be enhanced. They also noted: "Anecdotally, several subjects gave ratings that seemed to indicate that, after desensitization, they developed sensitivity to tactile components or taste components that they had previously not sensed." An earlier study by Karrer and Bartoshuk indicated that people who eat chiles every day are in a constant state of desensitization, and consequently have less of an ability to perceive tastes. But desensitization also means more of a tolerance for capsaicin, so the same level of heat would not seem so hot to them.

Interestingly enough, there may be a methodology factor at work as well. In an experiment by Beverly Cowart of the Monell Chemical Senses Center, where the capsaicin was actually mixed with what was being tasted, "no reduction in perceived taste intensity, relative to the control condition, was observed." Cowart noted that periodic rinses always cause desensitization where mixtures do not, leading her to conclude: "Much of the apparent masking of taste intensity in the presence of oral irri-

tation is not directly related to the irritation level but is sensitive to procedural variation." So typically, we are left with conflicting scientific studies.

Dr. Barry Green of the Monell Chemical Senses Center theorizes that the conflict may have something to do with cognitive psychology. In his experiments, some people were able to taste many flavors after eating chiles, but others were not. As there are holistic people and analytical people, he sees the same dichotomy in the world of food. Some people see fiery foods and think, "This is ridiculously hot — I can't taste a thing," while others use their analytical abilities and think, "This is great — I can taste all these incredibly strong flavors." After all, no matter how scientific the experiment, taste is still subjective. Dr. Green noted: "The easiest explanation for why people like pain from their food is simply that it adds a whole new dimension to flavor."

Cooling the Burn

Many substances have been proposed as an antidote in the mouth to the heat of chiles, including water, milk, sugar, bread, citrus fruits, beer, and other carbonated beverages. The theory is that such substances can either wash away or dilute the capsaicin, or, like the bread, can absorb it. The problem is that the capsaicin is bound to the nerve receptor sites in the mouth and is not easily dislodged or diluted. Remember that capsaicin is very miscible with alcohol, fats, and oils, but not very miscible with water.

In 1989, the late John Riley, editor-publisher of the quarterly journal *Solanaceae,* tested various remedies reputed to remove the heat of the capsaicin in chile peppers. In each test, a slice of serrano chile was chewed for one minute, and then one of the remedies was applied. The amount of time until the burning sensation eased was measured and the results were recorded.

Remedy	Total Minutes
Rinse the mouth with water only	11
Rinse the mouth with 1 tablespoon olive oil	10
Drink ½ cup heavy fruit syrup	10
Rinse mouth with 1 tablespoon glycerine	8
Drink ½ cup milk, rinsing well	7

Milk was the winner, and indeed, dairy products have long been reputed to be the best cool-downs for the burning effects of capsaicin in chiles. But why?

Scientists now believe that casein in the milk is responsible for its cooling effects. According to Robert Henkin of the Taste and Smell Clinic in Washington, D.C., casein is a phosphoprotein that acts as a detergent and strips the capsaicin from the nerve receptor binding sites in the mouth that are contained in the taste papillae. The casein in milk is in the form of calcium caseinate, which constitutes about 3 percent of milk. Other possible cool-downs containing casein include milk chocolate and some beans and nuts.

In a 1990 study at the University of California, Davis, Christina Wu Nasrawi and Rose Marie Pangborn reported that a 10 percent sucrose solution at 20°C was just as effective as milk at 5°C. A 5 percent ethanol solution was no more effective than water at cutting the burn. The effectiveness of sugar in warm water revives folk tales of it being an Asian cure for a chile overdose in the mouth. Richard Sterling, travel editor of *Fiery Foods Magazine,* wrote to us that a waiter in Pattaya Beach, Thailand, once dropped a cube of sugar into Richard's too hot Dom Yom, or spicy prawn soup. The heat level dropped noticeably and then Richard observed that the condiment trays in Thai restaurants often include a small jar of sugar.

The Joseph Cerniglia Winery of Cavendish, Vermont, issued a press release in 1992 claiming that the malic acid contained in the apples used in their Woodchuck Draft Cider "washes away the heat" of fiery foods. It is interesting that malic acid would be used to "wash away" the heat when it is already present in the pods.

THAILAND AND ITS NEIGHBORS

Thai food is extensively spiced with chiles but, contrary to popular belief, there is not just one "Thai chile," but rather many different varieties that are used in cooking. When your author toured the wholesale market in Bangkok in 1991, he found literally tons of both fresh and dried chiles in baskets and in huge bales five feet tall. The chiles ranged in size from piquin-like, thin green pods barely an inch long to yellow and red pods about four inches long.

A total of seventy-nine different varieties of chiles have been collected in Thailand from three species: *Capsicum annuum,*

C. chinense, and *C. frutescens*. Given the volatile state of chile nomenclature all over the world, it is not surprising that some confusion exists over the terms for the Thai chiles. For example, one reference book states that *prik khee noo* is a New Mexican pod type, while the general consensus is that it is the tiny, elongated "bird pepper" so associated with Thai cooking. *Prik kee noo* translates, inelegantly, as "mouse-dropping chile." The chiles that resemble the New Mexican type are called *prik num*, "banana peppers," and *Kashmiri*, because they are grown extensively in Kashmir, India.

Confusion exists here too, because the *Kashmiri* chiles are also called *Sriracha*, or *Siracha* chiles. They are so named because a sauce made from these chiles originated in the Thai seaside town of Sriracha as an accompaniment to fish, and it became so popular that it has been bottled and sold around the world. However, the chiles used in *Sriracha* sauce now are red serranos. *Prik khee fah* is a term used to refer to cayenne chiles, while *prik yuak* is the 'Hungarian Yellow Wax Hot' variety.

In agricultural terminology, the two types of chiles grown commercially in Thailand are "bird pepper" (*prik khee nu*) and "chili" (*prik khee fah*). Chiles accounted for about 12 percent of the total agricultural land in Thailand in 1985 (the most recent year we have statistics for), and about 100,000 acres were planted in "bird pepper" and 45,000 acres in "chili." For comparison, the approximate number of acres devoted to chiles in New Mexico, the number one chile producing state in the United States, varies between 35,000 and

Thai women enjoy a curry feast, c. 1880. SUNBELT ARCHIVES

Chiles and vegetables are sold at Thailand's floating markets.
DAVE DEWITT

40,000 acres. The Thai chiles are grown on terraces, on hillsides, and in irrigated paddy fields after the rice season is over.

The same trade routes that introduced the chile pepper into Thailand also spread the concept of curries from India to all parts of the globe. Consequently, Thailand is a perfect example of a culinary collision of cultures: Indian curry spices were combined with the latest exotic import—chile peppers—to create some of the hottest curries on earth.

Most commonly in Thailand, fresh chiles are ground up with other ingredients to make the famous Thai curry pastes that are staples in Thai cooking and take several forms. *Kaeng* (often spelled *gaeng*) is the term for a bewildering variety of Thai curries. Some *kaengs* resemble liquid Indian curry sauces and are abundant with traditional curry spices such as turmeric, coriander, and cardamom. Another type of *kaeng* curry omits these curry spices and substitutes herbs like cilantro, but the chiles are still there. This second group of *kaeng* curries is said to be the original Thai curries, invented long before they were influenced by Indian spices. As with the curries of Sri Lanka, these *kaeng* curries are multicolored; depending upon the color of the chiles and other spices and the amount of coconut milk added, they range from light yellow to green to pale red. *Kaeng kari* is yellow-colored because it contains most of the curry spices, including turmeric, and is fairly mild. One of the more pungent of these *kaeng* curries, *kaeng ped*, is made with tiny red chiles, coconut milk, and basil leaves, and is served with seafood.

Chiles are also important to another aspect of Thai cuisine: the presentation of the meal. "The Thais are as interested in beautiful presentation as the Japanese are," writes Asian food expert Jennifer Brennan. "The contrasts of color and texture, of hot and cold, of spicy and mild are as important here as in any cuisine in the world." Considering the emphasis on both heat and presentation in their cuisine, it is not surprising that the Thais love to garnish their hot meals with—what else?—hot chiles. Their adoration for the chile pepper extends to elaborately carved chile pod flowers. They use multicolored, small chiles for the best flower effect, with colors ranging from green to yellow to red to purple. The procedure for creating chile pod flowers is quite simple. Hold the chile by the stem on a cutting board and use a sharp knife to slice the chile in half, lengthwise, starting one-eighth inch from the stem down to the point (or apex, for the botanically minded). Rotate the chile 180 degrees and repeat the procedure until the chile is divided into sixteenths or more. The thinner the "petals," the more convincing the chiles when finished. Immerse the chiles in ice water until the slices curl—a few hours—and remove the seeds with the tip of a knife. The chile flowers can then be arranged artistically on the platter and later devoured as a spicy salad condiment, which accompanies the traditional Thai curries.

Hot and spicy curries also appear commonly in the cuisine of Myanmar (formerly Burma), Thailand's neighbor to the west and northwest. There, chiles are known as *nga yut thee*, and they are used to make *balachuang*, a spicy relish that not only accompanies curries, but is served at every meal. To make a Burmese curry, the cooks make a curry paste out of their five basic ingredients: onions, garlic, chiles, ginger, and turmeric. Burmese cooks add other spices as well, including an occasional prepared curry powder. But the hallmark of the Burmese curry is its oiliness. The cooks use a combination of peanut oil and sesame oil, about a cup of each, heated in a wok until it smokes—this is called "cooking the oil." The curry paste is added, the heat is reduced, and the paste is cooked for fifteen minutes. Then meat is added, cooked, and eventually the oil rises to the top. This state is called *see byan*, "the return of the oil." When the oil floats on top, the dish is done. The oil is not skimmed off the top, but rather is absorbed by the side dish of rice when it is served. Surprisingly, the curries do not taste greasy.

'Angkor Sunrise' chile from Cambodia. DAVE DEWITT

In Laos, which borders Thailand to the east and northeast, chiles are known collectively as *mak phet*. There are many characterizations of *mak phet* chiles in the Laotian language, such as by color and size. *Mak phet ∂ip* are fresh green chiles while *mak phet ∂eng* are fresh red chiles. *Mak phet nyai* are large chiles, *mak phet kuntsi* are small chiles, and *mak phet kinou* are the tiny, "rat-dropping" chiles — undoubtedly a variety similar to the Thai *prik khee noo*, as they share the same terminal word. Other characterizations of Laotian chiles are *mak phet haeng*, dried red chiles, and *mak phet pung*, ground red chiles.

Fresh small red and green chiles are used extensively in a number of chile pastes in Laos. Jalapeño- and serrano-like chiles are beaten with pestles in huge mortars, and locally available spices are added. Larger chiles are stuffed, as with a favorite Laotian creation called *mawk mak phet*. It features poblano or New Mexican chiles that are stuffed with vegetables, spices, and whitefish, and then steamed.

According to Richard Sterling, who has traveled extensively in the region, chiles are also ubiquitous in Cambodia, Thailand's neighbor to the southeast. "Every grand market and merchant's corner of Phnom Penh offers them in baskets, piles, and bags," he wrote, "We don't know precisely when or by whom the chile was introduced to this part of the world, but it was certainly by the Spanish or Portuguese in the late sixteenth century." Sterling referred to the first documented official contact between what is now Cambodia and Europeans, which occurred in 1596 when the Portuguese governor of Manila sent an official expedition to the king of Angkor in 1596. "We don't know what the expeditions' supplies, provisions and gifts for the king included," added Sterling, "but one hundred years after Columbus, the Portuguese were well supplied with Capsicums from the New World. It is delicious to speculate that though the military missions came to naught, a chile culinary mission enjoyed great success."

In Vietnam, the heart of the chile cuisine coincides with the center of the country, principally the city of Hue. There, a fish and chile sauce called *nuac cham* reigns supreme. It consists of fish sauce, lime, sugar, garlic, and fresh, small, red serrano-like chiles called *ot*, which is the generic Vietnamese term for chile peppers. Dried chiles are *ot kho*, chile sauces are *tuong ot*, and chile pastes are *tuong tuoi*.

THAI RED CURRY PASTE
Nam Prik Kaeng Ped

A popular condiment and cooking ingredient in Thailand, this curry paste can be added to any dish to enhance its flavor. It is, of course, a primary ingredient in many of the famous Thai curries. Traditionally, it is patiently pounded by hand with a heavy mortar and pestle, but a food processor does the job quickly and efficiently.

MAKES ABOUT 1 CUP
HEAT SCALE: Hot

5 New Mexican dried red chiles, seeds and stems removed

10 small dried red chiles, such as piquins, seeds and stems removed

2 teaspoons coriander seeds

2 teaspoons cumin seeds

2 small onions

1 teaspoon black peppercorns

½ cup chopped fresh cilantro

¼ cup chopped fresh basil or mint leaves

1 teaspoon salt

Three 2-inch stalks lemongrass, including the bulb

One 1-inch piece of galangal, peeled

1 tablespoon chopped garlic

1 tablespoon shrimp paste

1 tablespoon corn or peanut oil

1 tablespoon grated lime zest

¼ cup water

Soak all the chiles in water for 20 minutes to soften, then remove and drain. Roast the coriander and cumin seeds for about 2 minutes in a dry skillet, and when they are cooled, grind to a fine powder in a spice mill.

Combine the chiles and all remaining ingredients in a food processor or blender and puree into a fine paste. Store it in a tightly sealed jar in the refrigerator. It will keep for several weeks.

BEEF IN THAI RED CURRY SAUCE
Kaeng Nuea

This is a classic hot and spicy Thai curry dish that is often prepared at home. Traditionally, one of the many kinds of Thai eggplants are used, *makeua poh* or *makeua peuang*, but they are sometimes difficult to find. The flavor won't be the same, but feel free to add cubes of Japanese eggplant, or, for the look of a traditional Thai curry, add some green peas.

MAKES 6 SERVINGS
HEAT SCALE: **Hot**

3 cups coconut milk

5 tablespoons Thai Red Curry Paste (page 288)

1½ pounds chuck steak, thinly sliced

1 teaspoon grated lemon zest or 2 crushed kaffir lime leaves

½ teaspoon salt

¾ cup bamboo shoots

3 tablespoons fish sauce (nam pla)

2 teaspoons palm sugar (available at Asian markets) or brown sugar

1 cup eggplant, zucchini, or yellow squash cut into ¾-inch cubes

2 green serrano or jalapeño chiles, seeds and stems removed, sliced into rings

½ cup coarsely chopped fresh basil leaves

Heat 1 cup of the coconut milk in a large, heavy Dutch oven over medium heat. When it is hot, stir in the Thai Red Curry Paste and cook the mixture until some little drops of oil appear on the surface, about 1 minute. Continue to cook, stirring, for 1 minute more.

Add the meat and simmer the mixture for 5 minutes. Make sure there is some liquid in the pan at all times—add a little more of the coconut milk if necessary. At the end of the 5 minutes, add the remaining coconut milk, lemon zest or lime leaves, salt, bamboo shoots, fish sauce, palm sugar, and eggplant and simmer for 15 minutes.

Stir in the chiles and the basil and simmer for 2 minutes. Serve with steamed rice.

THAI BAKED FISH-STUFFED CHILES
Prik Khee Sy Moo

This low-calorie dish is from Thailand. This recipe reminds one of chiles *rellenos*, the stuffed green chile dish of the American Southwest.

MAKES 4 SERVINGS
HEAT SCALE: Mild

¾ pound fresh or frozen snapper fillets, minced
⅓ cup minced canned water chestnuts
1 large egg white, lightly beaten
2 whole scallions, minced, white and green parts

2 teaspoons peanut oil
2 teaspoons soy sauce
8 New Mexican green chiles, stems on, roasted and peeled (page 146), seeded

Preheat the oven to 350°F. Spray a baking dish with nonstick vegetable coating. In a bowl, combine the fish with the water chestnuts, egg white, scallions, 1 teaspoon of the oil, and soy sauce. Mix well.

Make a slit in the side of each chile. Carefully spoon the fish filling into the slit, to avoid splitting. Place in the prepared baking dish; brush the chiles lightly with the remaining oil.

Bake for 30 minutes, or until the chiles are tender and the filling is cooked.

BURMESE CHILE PORK WITH GREEN MANGO
Wettha Thayet Thi Chet

In Burma, the most popular meat is pork for a number of reasons. Upper Burma is heavily populated by Chinese, who are traditionally big pork consumers; pork is cheaper than lamb or beef; and pork combines well with a number of diverse ingredients, including the green mango.

MAKES 5 TO 6 SERVINGS
HEAT SCALE: **Medium**

One 2-inch piece of fresh ginger, sliced

3 cloves garlic

1 large onion, cut into eighths

3 tablespoons vegetable oil

½ teaspoon ground turmeric

1 tablespoon crushed chile piquin or other small, hot dried chile

½ teaspoon fish sauce (nam pla)

1 teaspoon shrimp paste

1 teaspoon shrimp sauce (optional)

2 pounds boneless, lean pork, cut into pieces 2 inches long and 1 inch wide

½ teaspoon salt

¾ cup grated unripened (green) mango

1 teaspoon paprika

3 cups water

In a blender or small food processor, puree the ginger, garlic, and onion. Heat the oil in a large, heavy skillet over low heat and lightly cook the ginger puree, turmeric, and chile, stirring, until the mixture becomes red-brown, 3 to 5 minutes. Stir in the fish sauce, shrimp paste, and shrimp sauce (if you are using it) and cook, stirring, for 1 minute.

Raise the heat to medium-high, add the pork, salt, green mango, and paprika and cook, stirring, until the pork is no longer pink and starts to brown, 8 to 10 minutes.

Stir the water into the simmering pork mixture, bring to a boil, reduce the heat to low, cover, and simmer until the liquid is reduced to 1 cup. It should take about 1¼ hours. Check the meat and stir occasionally to prevent sticking and burning. At the end of the cooking period, the sauce should be thick, about the consistency of a white sauce.

Serve with steamed rice and stir-fried vegetables.

VIETNAMESE DIPPING SAUCE
Nuoc Cham

This version of the famous Vietnamese chile sauce is from Hanoi. *Fiery Foods Magazine* correspondent Richard Sterling noted: "No Vietnamese table is complete without a dish of *nuoc cham* for dipping and drizzling over the dishes. It is as ubiquitous as rice." It is particularly good with Vietnamese spring rolls.

MAKES ½ CUP
HEAT SCALE: **Medium**

1 or 2 cloves garlic
1 fresh red chile, such as serrano or jalapeño, seeds
   and stem removed
2 teaspoons sugar

¼ lime
2½ tablespoons water
2 tablespoons fish sauce (nam pla)

Traditional method: With a mortar and pestle, pound the garlic, chile, and sugar into a paste. Squeeze the lime juice in. With a paring knife, remove the pulp from the lime and pound it into the paste. Add the water and fish sauce and mix well.

   Modern method: Combine all ingredients, including the lime juice and pulp, in a food processor and puree, adding more water if necessary.

VARIATION: To make the traditional Vietnamese sauce for roast beef, *nuac cham tuong gung*, omit the lime juice and pulp and add 2 tablespoons minced fresh ginger.

CURRIED FROG'S LEGS WITH NUOC CHAM
Ech Nau Ca-Ri

This Vietnamese recipe is a classic use of *nuoc cham*. Serve it over rice accompanied by a tropical fruit salad. Chicken or shrimp may be substituted for the frog's legs. Note that if you are using dried lemongrass this recipe requires advance preparation.

MAKES 4 SERVINGS
HEAT SCALE: **Mild**

4 pairs of large frog's legs, skinned and deboned

1 stalk fresh lemongrass or 1 tablespoon dried lemongrass

2 fresh piquin chiles, seeds and stems removed, chopped (or substitute any small, hot chiles)

3 shallots, sliced

3 cloves garlic, minced

1½ teaspoons sugar

1 teaspoon Thai Red Curry Paste (page 288) (or substitute commercial curry paste)

2 teaspoons imported curry powder

¼ teaspoon salt

2 tablespoons Vietnamese Dipping Sauce (page 292)

2 ounces cellophane noodles

2 tablespoons peanut oil

1 small onion, chopped

1 cup chicken broth

½ cup coconut milk or heavy cream

1 tablespoon cold water

1 teaspoon cornstarch

2 limes, quartered, for garnish

Cut the frog's legs into bite-sized pieces. Rinse with cold water, pat dry with paper towels, and refrigerate. If you are using fresh lemongrass, peel away the outer leaves and cut so that only the lower part of the stalk remains. Cut this part into thin slices and mince. If you are using the dried lemongrass, soak it for 1 hour in warm water, then drain and mince.

In a food processor, place the lemongrass, chiles, shallots, garlic, sugar, curry paste, curry powder, salt, and 1 tablespoon of the Vietnamese Dipping Sauce. Process the ingredients until they are a very fine paste. Remove the frog's legs from the refrigerator, and rub the paste over them. Cover the legs and return them to the refrigerator for 30 minutes. While the legs are marinating, soak the noodles in water for 30 minutes, then drain them and cut into 2-inch lengths.

Heat the oil in a large skillet over medium heat. Add the onion and cook, stirring, until the onion is translucent, about 5 minutes. Add the frog's legs, and brown well on all sides, for 3 to 4 minutes. Add the chicken broth and bring to a boil. Reduce the heat to low, cover, and simmer for 15 minutes.

Next, add the coconut milk or heavy cream, leaving the lid off. In a separate bowl, combine the 1 tablespoon of cold water, the remaining 1 tablespoon Vietnamese Dipping Sauce, and the cornstarch, and stir well. Add the cornstarch mixture to the skillet, and cook, stirring, until the mixture thickens. Add the cellophane noodles and bring the mixture to a boil. Remove from the heat, place on a platter, and garnish with lime wedges. This dish is also great when served over rice.

➤ **Tiger tooth.** A variety of *chinense* grown in Guyana.

➤ *'Tinnevelly.'* A variety of *annuum* grown in India that resembles a *cascabel*.

➤ *'Típico.'* A cultivated variety of jalapeño in Mexico and the United States.

➤ *Togarishi.* Chile peppers in Japanese.

TOXICITY OF CAPSAICINOIDS

In order to determine the lethal toxic level of capsaicinoids in animals, and to extrapolate that level for humans, researchers in 1980 performed a rather gruesome experiment with mice, rats, guinea pigs, and rabbits. Pure capsaicin was administered intravenously, subcutaneously, in the stomach, and applied topically until the animals died. The lethal toxic doses of capsaicin, measured in milligrams per kilogram of animal weight ranged from a mere .56 milligrams when administered intravenously to 190 milligrams when consumed to 512 milligrams when applied topically—which means that the poor animals were drowned in it. Indeed, the probable cause of death in all cases was presumed to be respiratory paralysis. Guinea pigs were the most sensitive to capsaicin, while rabbits were less susceptible. The author of the study, T. Glinsukon, concluded that the acute toxicity of capsaicinoids as a food additive in mankind was neglible. If humans are

about as sensitive as mice, the theoretical acute fatal toxicity dose for a 150-pound person would be about thirteen grams of pure, crystalline capsaicinoids (approximately half an ounce), which frankly, sounds high to us. We think that less than that would be lethal.

There have been investigations of dangerous doses in humans of the various substances that have capsaicin as an ingredient. For example, C. L. Winek conducted a study, published in *Drug and Chemical Toxicology*, that examined the overdose potential of Tabasco sauce. He concluded that a person of average weight would have to consume nearly a half gallon of the sauce to overdose and become unconscious.

In a related study, rats were fed large amounts of Tabasco sauce and there were "no gross or microscopic pathological changes or any significant biochemical changes in the animals." Their growth rate also remained normal. In a similar study, rats were fed crude extracts of chile pods and crystalline capsainoids by stomach tube while allowed access to normal food and water. None of the rats died and they all appeared normal throughout the study. Of course, the rats were killed and then autopsied, but no gross pathological changes were detected.

Humans have also acted as guinea pigs with oleoresin capsicum. It is an ingredient in super-hot sauces with names like Insanity, Death, and Suicide. These sauces are tasted at food shows by people who have no idea of how hot they are. Some people, with few taste buds in their mouths, are not bothered by the extreme heat. But most people react very negatively to the super-hot sauces, experiencing severe burning and sometimes blistering of the mouth and tongue. Other immediate responses have included shortness of breath, fainting, nausea, and spontaneous vomiting. People should be very careful of commercial hot sauces that list oleoresin capsicum as an ingredient.

Aside from the above adverse effects, the super-hot sauce will not hurt you. "Comprehensive nutritional studies have not shown any adverse effects of chile or capsaicinoids even at ten times the maximum use levels," wrote one of the world's experts on capsaicin, V. S. Govindarajan, author of the mammoth study *Capsicum— Production, Technology, Chemistry and Quality*. But even if you do overindulge in capsaicinoids, do not worry, for they are quickly metabolized in the liver and excreted in urine within a few hours.

◣ *Travieso.* "Naughty"; another Mexican term for *guajillo*.

◣ *Trompo.* "Child's top"; another Mexican term for a *cascabel*.

◣ *Tuong.* Chile paste in Vietnam. Also *tuoi*. *Tuong ot* is *Sriracha* hot sauce.

◣ *Tuxtla.* A piquin from southern Mexico.

◢ *Uchu.* Quecha word for chiles in Peru.

◢ *Ulupica.* Local name for the wild chiles *Capsicum eximium* and *Capsicum cardensaii* in Bolivia.

◢ *Umbigo-de-tainha.* In Brazil, mullet's navel chile.

◢ *'Uxmal.'* A cultivated variety of habanero in Mexico.

⌍ **Variegated.** Varieties of chiles with partially white leaves and usually purple flowers.

VEGETARIAN CHILE CUISINE

Hot and spicy food lends itself to the absence of meat because of the intense flavors and sensations produced by a number of varieties of chiles. This regimen also works perfectly with low-salt, low-cholesterol, and low-fat diets, and so vegetarian chile recipes reflect these health considerations as much as possible without sacrificing flavor. In India, for example, chiles are used heavily to spice up vegetarian dishes. (See Nutrition.)

⌍ *'Veracruz S-69.'* A cultivated variety of serrano in Mexico.

⌍ *Verde.* "Green or unripe"; in Mexico, any green chile, but typically serrano.

⌍ *'Verdeño.'* A pale green, cultivated Mexican variety of poblano.

 ## TWO-CHILE OIL

Use this oil in place of other vegetable oils for a double-whammy of peppers, both red and black. When mixed with Herbally Hot Vinegar (page 299), it makes a dynamite oil and vinegar salad dressing. Note that this recipe requires advance preparation.

MAKES 4 CUPS

HEAT SCALE: **Hot**

3½ cups corn oil
½ cup sesame oil (see Variation)
8 cloves garlic, crushed

2 dry red New Mexican chiles, seeds and stems
   removed, crushed
6 piquin chiles, seeds and stems removed, crushed
1 tablespoon black peppercorns

Combine all the ingredients in a saucepan and cook over medium heat, stirring occasionally, for 10 minutes. Remove from the heat and let cool.

Remove the garlic and pour the remaining oil mixture into a sterilized glass jar and cap it. Store in a cool, dark place for 2 weeks. Strain the oil through a cheesecloth-lined sieve into another sterilized bottle and store in the refrigerator until you're ready to use it. It will keep in the refrigerator for about a month.

VARIATION: Replace the sesame oil with others such as olive, peanut, or almond.

HERBALLY HOT VINEGAR

For those who enjoy intensely flavored vinegars, here's the one to use in place of those store-bought varieties. Try it over salads, in salad dressings, or in any recipe calling for vinegar.

MAKES 1 QUART
HEAT SCALE: **Medium**

1 quart white wine vinegar
5 chiltepins or other small, hot chiles, crushed

Six 3-inch-long sprigs fresh rosemary or oregano
3 tablespoons minced fresh ginger

In a large saucepan, heat the vinegar to boiling. Add the remaining ingredients, stir well, and turn off the heat. Allow to cool to room temperature.

Strain the vinegar through a cheesecloth-lined sieve, pour into a quart bottle, and cap. Store in a cool, dry place or in the refrigerator. The vinegar will keep indefinitely.

CHIPOTLE MAYONNAISE WITH ROASTED GARLIC

The smoky flavor of the chipotle adds a spicy dimension to ordinary mayonnaise. Serve this condiment over hard-boiled eggs, on vegetarian sandwiches, or use it as a salad dressing.

MAKES ABOUT 2 CUPS
HEAT SCALE: **Medium**

1 chipotle chile in adobo *sauce, stem removed*
2 tablespoons fresh lime juice
2 cups mayonnaise

2 teaspoons minced roasted garlic (see Note)
½ finely minced scallion, green and white parts

In a blender, combine the chipotle and lime juice and puree. In a bowl, combine the chile puree and the remaining ingredients and mix well. The mayonnaise will keep in the refrigerator for 1 week.

NOTE: To roast garlic, take 4 cloves of unpeeled garlic and sprinkle with olive oil. Bake the garlic in an uncovered ovenproof bowl at 350°F until it is soft, about 20 minutes. Let cool and squeeze the garlic out of the skins.

Roasted Fresh Red Chiles with Garlic

This recipe was originally of Italian origin, and called for roasted red bell peppers. By substituting New Mexican chiles, the element of pungency is added. It's best served over focaccia bread.

MAKES 8 SERVINGS AS AN APPETIZER
HEAT SCALE: Medium

4 large fresh red New Mexican chiles, cut in half, stems and seeds removed

2 large tomatoes

4 cloves garlic, thinly sliced

¼ cup olive oil

Salt and freshly ground black pepper

1 small bunch fresh cilantro for garnish

Move the oven rack to the highest shelf, and preheat the oven to 350°F. Lightly oil a baking sheet. Lay the chiles on the prepared sheet, cut side up. Bring a pot of water to a boil. Add the tomatoes to the boiling water and cook for just 1 minute. Remove the tomatoes and rinse under cool water. The peels will come off easily. When all of the tomatoes are peeled, cut them into quarters and place 1 quarter in each chile half.

Next, divide the garlic slices equally among the chile halves, then sprinkle some of the olive oil into each chile. Season to taste with salt and pepper. Place the peppers in the oven and roast for 1 hour. The chiles and tomatoes should be soft to the touch and lightly browned.

When done roasting, place the peppers on a platter in a circular design and pour the pan juices over the top. Garnish with the fresh cilantro.

GREEN CHILE VEGETABLE BISQUE

The complexity of vegetable flavors in this thick green soup is intensified by the addition of the ginger. Since the chiles are eventually pureed, there is no need to roast and peel them. For a hotter bisque, replace half of the New Mexican chiles with jalapeños.

MAKES 6 SERVINGS
HEAT SCALE: **Medium**

1 cup chopped fresh New Mexican chiles
1 cup chopped celery
1 cup diced potatoes
1 small zucchini, chopped
⅓ cup basmati rice
⅛ teaspoon white pepper
1 bay leaf
Pinch dried thyme

Pinch dried basil
7 cups vegetable stock
4 cups chopped fresh green beans
¼ cup chopped fresh parsley
One 3-inch piece of fresh ginger
Salt and freshly ground black pepper
Chopped fresh cilantro, chopped fresh chives, and
    chopped tomato for garnish

In a large pot, combine the chiles, celery, potatoes, zucchini, rice, pepper, bay leaf, thyme, basil, and stock. Bring to a boil, then reduce the heat to low and simmer, uncovered, until the potatoes are tender, about 15 minutes. Add the beans and simmer until tender, about 10 minutes. Remove the bay leaf and add the parsley.

Remove from the heat and puree in batches until smooth, adding more stock if necessary. Return to the pot. Peel the ginger, grate, and press out the juice into the soup. If the ginger is dry and there is not much juice, add the grated ginger to the soup. Stir and heat for 1 minute and add salt and pepper to taste.

Serve garnished with chopped cilantro, chives, and tomato.

DEVIL RICE
Arroz del Diablo

We recommend a hot habanero salsa for this recipe, such as Yellow, Red, and Green Salsa with Habaneros, page 264. You can also use any hot commercial salsa.

MAKES 4 SERVINGS
HEAT SCALE: **Hot**

2 cups long-grain white rice
3 tablespoons olive oil
1 medium onion, chopped
2 cloves garlic, chopped

1 cup habanero salsa (see above)
4 cups vegetable broth
Salt

In a large skillet over medium-high heat, cook the rice in the olive oil, stirring, until it begins to color, 1 to 2 minutes. Add the onion and garlic and cook, stirring, until the rice is a golden brown, being careful not to burn.

Add the habanero salsa and 1 cup of the vegetable broth, and bring to a simmer. Reduce the heat to low and simmer for about 5 minutes. Add the remaining stock, cover the pan with a tight-fitting lid, and simmer until the liquid is absorbed, about 20 minutes. Add salt to taste and serve.

HOT AND SOUR TEMPEH

Tempeh is available in health food and whole food stores. It has long been popular in Indonesia, but not long ago few people in this country knew about it. The intense flavors of this dish make for a very satisfying entree. Serve it over cooked rice, or with a crisp salad and some warm pita bread.

MAKES 4 SERVINGS
HEAT SCALE: Hot

1 small fresh pineapple, cleaned

3 tablespoons Two-Chile Oil (page 298) (or substitute any chile-infused oil)

1 tablespoon minced fresh ginger

3 cloves garlic, minced

2 tablespoons minced onion, plus ½ cup coarsely chopped onion

2 tablespoons white wine or rice vinegar

½ cup water

½ cup brown sugar

3 tablespoons miso

1 teaspoon dark soy sauce

8 ounces 5-grain tempeh, cubed

1 teaspoon sesame oil

2 dried Thai chiles

¼ cup cubed red bell pepper

1 cup sliced bok choy

½ cup chopped jícama

¾ cup bean sprouts

¼ cup sliced white mushrooms

Cut the fresh pineapple into ½-inch cubes and set aside; you'll need 1½ cups. Puree some of the remaining pineapple in a food processor, drain and measure out 2 tablespoons, and set aside.

Over high heat, heat 1 tablespoon of the oil in a small wok or a heavy skillet and cook the ginger, garlic, and minced onion for 30 seconds, stirring so the garlic doesn't burn.

Add 1 tablespoon of the remaining oil, vinegar, and water, stirring constantly. Add the reserved pineapple puree, brown sugar, miso, and dark soy sauce, and stir until the miso is dissolved. Stir in the cubed pineapple, remove the mixture from the heat, and reserve.

Heat the remaining 1 tablespoon chile oil in a wok or large skillet over medium-high heat and cook the cubed tempeh, stirring, until it is crisp, about 4 minutes. Remove it from the wok and drain on paper towels.

Wipe out the wok with a paper towel. Heat the sesame oil in the wok over medium-high heat and quickly cook the Thai chiles, bell pepper, coarsely chopped onion, bok choy, jícama, bean sprouts, and mushrooms, stirring, until everything is heated through but still crisp, 1 to 2 minutes. Remove the Thai chiles and stir in the reserved tempeh and the pineapple sweet and sour sauce; heat through and serve immediately.

SICHUAN FRIED EGGPLANT IN CHILE SAUCE

This recipe, from Sichuan Province in the People's Republic of China, has the mixed tastes of salty, sweet, sour, and spicy.

MAKES 4 SERVINGS
HEAT SCALE: **Medium**

4 cups peanut oil

1 eggplant, peeled and cut into pieces 2 inches long, 1 inch wide, and ¾ inch thick (3½ cups total)

¼ cup chopped pickled chiles, jalapeño suggested

1 tablespoon minced fresh ginger

1 tablespoon minced garlic

1 scallion, chopped, green and white parts

⅓ cup vegetable broth

1 tablespoon soy sauce

1 tablespoon white vinegar

1 tablespoon sugar

1 teaspoon dry white wine (optional)

1 teaspoon cornstarch dissolved in 2 tablespoons warm water

Heat the oil in a wok over medium heat. Add the eggplant and deep fry until soft, about 3 minutes. Remove, drain, and keep warm. Pour off all but 1 tablespoon of the oil.

Add the chiles and cook, stirring, until the oil becomes red. Add the ginger, garlic, and scallion and cook, stirring, until fragrant, about 1 minute. Add the vegetable broth, reserved eggplant, soy sauce, vinegar, sugar, and wine, and cook, stirring, for 2 minutes.

Stir in the cornstarch paste and simmer until the sauce is thickened. Serve with rice.

"DRUNKEN" PINTO BEANS

Frijoles Borrachos

Not only do these "drunken" beans contain fine Mexican beer, they are usually consumed with the same. Serve as an accompaniment to any barbecued meat or poultry dishes. Use as a filling for burritos or *sopaipillas*, or serve by itself with a flour tortilla. Note that this recipe requires advance preparation.

MAKES 6 TO 8 SERVINGS
HEAT SCALE: **Medium**

2 cups dried pinto beans, sorted and rinsed clean
¼ cup chopped jalapeño chiles
12 ounces dark Mexican beer, such as Negra
　　Modelo

1 small onion, chopped
1 large tomato, chopped
1 teaspoon Worcestershire sauce

In a large bowl, cover the beans with water and soak overnight. Drain.

In a large pot, cover the beans with fresh water, bring to a boil, reduce the heat to medium-low, and simmer until the beans are done, about 2 to 2½ hours. Add more water if the beans start to dry out. Remove and drain, reserving 1½ cups of the bean liquid, adding water to make 1½ cups if necessary.

Combine the remaining ingredients, the beans, and the reserved bean liquid. Simmer the beans for 30 minutes to blend the flavors.

GREEN CHILE FOCACCIA BREAD

Green chile is the perfect addition to this wonderful Italian bread. Perfect for an hors d'oeuvre or with a meal, this recipe is easily doubled or tripled.

MAKES 2 LOAVES
HEAT SCALE: **Medium**

2 cups warm tap water (about 110°F)
2 envelopes active dry yeast
¾ cup olive oil
10 cups unbleached all-purpose flour

4 teaspoons salt
½ cup chopped New Mexican green chiles
2 cups milk
2 teaspoons coarse salt

Place the water in a bowl, then whisk in the yeast, and half of the olive oil. In a large mixing bowl, combine the flour, salt, and green chiles. Stir the yeast mixture and milk into the flour mixture with a sturdy spatula, until the flour is well combined. Cover the bowl with a kitchen towel and allow the dough to rise until it has doubled in size, about 1 hour.

Spread 1½ teaspoons of the remaining oil in two 11 × 17-inch jelly-roll pans. (You can do this in batches if you only have 1 pan.) Turn the dough out of the bowl and divide between the 2 pans. Pat and press the dough to fill each pan completely.

Using your pinkie finger, poke cavities in the focaccia about every 2 inches. Drizzle each pan with equal amounts of the remaining oil, and sprinkle with the coarse salt.

Cover the pans with kitchen towels and allow the dough to rise again, until it doubles in size, about an hour.

Set a rack in the lower third of the oven, and preheat the oven to 450°F. Bake the bread for 25 minutes, or until it is a light golden-brown color. Remove from the oven and serve immediately or cool in the pan on a rack for later use. The bread can be reheated at 375°F for 6 or 7 minutes.

BLUE CORN BREAD WITH GREEN CHILES

Spiced corn bread is highly popular in New Mexico. Adjust the heat upward by substituting jalapeños in this recipe, and serve it with your favorite spicy soup. If blue cornmeal is not available, substitute the yellow variety.

MAKES 6 SERVINGS
HEAT SCALE: Medium

1 cup coarse blue cornmeal	¼ teaspoon garlic powder
1 cup all-purpose flour	1½ cups buttermilk
2 teaspoons sugar	¼ cup minced hot New Mexican green chiles
1 teaspoon baking soda	1 cup minced onion
1 teaspoon baking powder	2 large eggs, beaten
1 teaspoon salt	1 cup grated Cheddar cheese

Preheat the oven to 350°F. Grease a 9-inch square pan.

Combine all the dry ingredients in a large bowl.

In a saucepan over medium-low heat, heat the buttermilk with the chiles and onion for 3 minutes, then allow to cool.

In another bowl, combine the eggs and cheese. Add the milk mixture and the egg mixture to the dry ingredients and blend until smooth.

Pour this mixture into the prepared pan and bake 40 to 50 minutes or until the corn bread is browned and firm.

WAX CHILES

The shiny appearance of the pods of these varieties is the reason the type is called wax. They vary greatly in size, shape, and pungency.

The Plant

Wax peppers have multiple stems and a compact habit, growing up to thirty inches high. The leaves are ovate, medium green, and up to five inches long and three inches wide. The flower corollas are white with no spots. The pods vary greatly in size and shape, from the small, two-inch 'Caloro' to the giant 'Banana Supreme' with eight-inch pods. Generally speaking, the small pods are borne erect and the long ones pendant. The pods are conical but tapering, and bluntly pointed at the end. Yield is twenty-five or more pods per plant, and the heat scale varies from zero to 40,000 Scoville Units.

Agriculture

Most wax varieties are very prolific in the home garden, fruiting early and producing well. The growing season is seventy or more days. Recommended varieties are 'Banana Supreme,' 'Caloro,' 'Gold Spike,' 'Hungarian Yellow Wax Hot,' 'Santa Fe Grande,' and 'Sweet Banana.'

Culinary Usage

The milder wax varieties are used fresh in salads. All varieties can be pickled, which is the most common use of commercially grown wax peppers.

PICKLED 'HUNGARIAN YELLOW WAX HOT' CHILES

This recipe can be used to pickle virtually any fresh chile, but 'Hungarian Yellow Wax Hots' are one of the favorites. It will pickle approximately 2 pounds of ripe chiles. Remember, despite the name, these chiles are not particularly hot. Note that this recipe requires advance preparation.

MAKES 4 PINTS
HEAT SCALE: **Medium**

Brine
3 cups water
1 cup pickling salt
2 pounds ripe 'Hungarian Yellow Wax Hot' chiles

Pickling solution
3 cups 4 to 5 percent distilled white vinegar
3 cups water
3 teaspoons pickling salt

For the brine, in a bowl, combine the water and salt and add the chiles. Place a plate over the chiles to keep them submerged in the brine. Soak the chiles overnight to crisp them. Drain, rinse well, and dry.

For the pickling, poke a couple of holes in the top of each chile to keep them from floating in the liquid. Pack the chiles tightly in sterilized jars.

In a saucepan, combine the vinegar, water, and salt. Bring the solution to a boil and pour over the chiles in the sterilized jars, leaving ¼-inch headway. Gently tap the side of the jar to remove any trapped bubbles.

Seal the jars and store at room temperature for 4 to 6 weeks before serving. The chiles will keep for up to a year.

'Hungarian Yellow Wax Hot' chile. DAVE DEWITT

⊾ *Xcatic.* A fairly mild chile grown in the Yucatán Peninsula that is related to wax and banana chiles. Sometimes called *güero* ("blonde"), it usually is yellow in color.

Resources

There are hundreds of mail-order companies selling chile-related products. The following is not an exhaustive list, but rather those companies that have the widest selection of products to choose from.

ORGANIZATION

The Chile Pepper Institute
NMSU, Box 30003, MSC 3Q
Las Cruces, NM 88003
(505) 646-3028
www.nmsu.edu/~hotchile/index.html

This organization provides publications and bibliographies and publishes a quarterly newsletter.

CHILES AND FIERY FOODS BY MAIL-ORDER

Heat Seekers Catalog
Hot Spicy Foods Company
P.O. Box 1986
Morgan Hill, CA 95038
(800) 648-8439

Hot Sauce Harry's
3422 Flair Drive
Dallas, TX 75229
(800) 588-8979
(214) 902-8552

Mo Hotta Mo Betta
P.O. Box 4136
San Luis Obispo, CA 93403
(800) 462-3220

Pendery's
1221 Manufacturing Avenue
Dallas, TX 75207
(800) 533-1870

Salsa Express
100 North Tower Road
Alamo, TX 78516
(800) 43-SALSA

Santa Fe School of Cooking
116 West San Francisco Street
Santa Fe, NM 87501
(505) 983-4511

SEED SOURCES

The Largest Capsicum Germ Plasm Bank

The U.S. Department of Agriculture Plant Introduction Station in Georgia holds a vast collection of the seed of more than 2,000 Capsicum varieties. Gardeners interested in growing unusual peppers can petition the station for a few seeds of selected varieties. There is no guarantee that the station can or will supply seed for these varieties, but it's worth a try for dedicated gardeners. Send a self-addressed, stamped envelope for the return of seed. Contact:

Director, USDA-ARS Plant Introduction
    Station
1109 Experiment Street
Griffin, GA 30223-1797

Heirloom Seeds

Seed Savers Exchange is dedicated to the preservation of heirloom seed varieties, including hundreds and hundreds of Capsicums. They publish an annual yearbook listing available varieties, which can be ordered through individual collectors.

Seed Savers Exchange
3076 North Winn Road
Decorah, IA 52101

Native Seeds/SEARCH is another source for heirloom pepper varieties, mostly from the Southwest and Mexico.

Native Seeds/SEARCH
2509 North Campbell Avenue 325
Tucson, AZ 85719

Other Recommended Seed Sources

Enchanted Seeds
P.O. Box 6087
Las Cruces, NM 88006
(505) 233-3033

The Pepper Gal
P.O. Box 23006
Fort Lauderdale, FL 33307
(305) 565-4972

Plants of the Southwest
Agua Fria Route 6, Box 11A
Santa Fe, NM 87501
(505) 438-8888

Redwood City Seed Co.
P.O. Box 361
Redwood City, CA 94064
(415) 325-SEED

Seeds of Change
P.O. Box 15700
Santa Fe, NM 87506-5700
(505) 438-8080

Tomato Grower's Supply Co.
P.O. Box 2237
Fort Myers, FL 33902
(813) 768-1119

Commercial Seed Sources

The following suppliers offer seeds in bulk quantities.

Enchanted Seeds
P.O. Box 6087
Las Cruces, NM 88006
(505) 233-3033

Liberty Seed Co.
P.O. Box 806
New Philadelphia, OH 44663

Petoseed Co.
P.O. Box 4206
Saticoy, CA 93004
(805) 647-1188

Rogers NK
P.O. Box 4188
Boise, ID 83711

WEB SITES

Archival Information

Chile-Heads Home Page (www. netimages.com/~chile/). A compendium of chile pepper information and Internet discussion.

Fiery Foods Super Site (www.fiery-foods.com). A vast amount of information on chiles and the Fiery Foods Industry.

Firegirl (www.firegirl.com). An entertaining site about all things hot and spicy.

Graham Caselton Chile-Head (easyweb. easynet.co.uk/~gcaselton/chile/chile.html). The best British site for detailed information on chiles and fiery foods.

Chili con Carne

International Chili Society (www. chilicookoff.com). This site offers informa-

tion on the ICS, with history of the society, merchandise, sanctioned cook-offs, and recipes.

Chili Appreciation Society—International (www.bigbend.com/casi/chili/ssi). Information on CASI, plus recipes, events, and history.

Chili.Net (ourworld.compuserve.com/ homepages/mgrabois/chilinet.htm). Information on chili con carne around the world.

Curry

The Curry House (www.dwsmith.demon. co.uk/index.htm). This site from Oxfordshire in the U.K. is devoted to the love of worldwide curries. It features recipes from all over the world as well as curry spices for sale.

Hot Sauces—Recipes and Mail-Order Sources

Hot Hot Hot (www.hothothot.com). A retail catalog of hot sauces.

Hot Pursuits (www.hotpursuits.com). Canada's first on-line hot sauce catalog.

The Mole Page (www.slip.net/ ~bobnemo/whatmole.html). Information and recipes on *mole* sauces.

Pepperfest (www.tabasco.com). This official site of the world-famous Tabasco sauce has history, recipes, and merchandise.

Peppers (www.peppers.com). A huge catalog with more than 600 hot sauces.

Bibliography

There are hundreds of thousands of citations involving Capsicums in dozens of academic and popular disciplines, so a complete bibliography would be a masterwork of scholarship and a valuable CD-ROM or Internet database. Until that is completed, however, it is fortunate that several extensive bibliographies of Capsicums have already been compiled. Most exist only in printed format, but some, such as the ones supplied by the Chile Pepper Institute, are in word processing formats on disk. In this volume, after the list of specialized bibliographies, there is a general bibliography of sources. It is important to note that more extensive bibliographies are found in the volumes carrying Dave DeWitt's byline; they have not been duplicated in this encyclopedia, although some important citations in them have been repeated here.

SPECIALIZED BIBLIOGRAPHIES

Andrews, Jean. "Bibliography." In *Peppers: The Domesticated Capsicums.* Austin: University of Texas Press, 1984, 155–66.

Bosland, Paul W. *Capsicum: A Comprehensive Bibliography.* Las Cruces, N.M.: Chile Pepper Institute, 1997. Available on disk, 7,000+ citations, mostly scientific.

Casili, V. W. D. *Pigmentao e Pimenta (Capsicum sp.), Bibliograffia Brasileira Comentada.* Vicosa, Brazil: Universidade Federal de Vicosa, Ser. Técnica, Bol. 23, 1970.

Coe, Sophie. "Bibliography." *In America's First Cuisines.* Austin: University of Texas Press, 1994.

Commonwealth Bureau of Horticultural and Plantation Crops. *Annotated Bibliographies on Capsicum Growing and Cultivars in the Tropics and Other Countries.* East Malling, England: Query Files 4777, 5891, 6159, 1964–73.

Commonwealth Bureau of Soils. "Bibliography on Peppers: Soils, Fertilizers, and Nutrition." East Malling, England: Bibliography No. 1324, 1969.

DeWitt, Dave. *Chile Peppers: A Selected Bibliography*

of the Capsicums. Las Cruces, N.M.: Chile Pepper Institute, 1994. Available on disk.

DeWitt, Dave, and Nancy Gerlach. "Bibliography." In *The Whole Chile Pepper Book.* Boston: Little, Brown, 1990.

Ferrari, J. P., and G. Ailluad. "Bibliography of the Genus Capsicum." J. d'Agric. Trop. et Bot. Appl., Vol. 18, No. 11, 1971, 385–479.

Gallardo, Pablo Velásquez, and J. Alberto Arellano Rodríguez. *Bibliografía Mundial de Chile, Capsicum spp. (1965–1982).* Mexico: Instituto Nacional de Investigaciones Agrícolas México, 1984. 6,107 citations.

Lippert, L. F., and R. S. Scharffenberg, *Garden Pepper (Capsicum sp.).* Vol. 1 of *Vegetable Crops Bibliographies.* West Covina, Calif.: Bibliographic Associates, 1964.

Long-Solis, Janet. "Bibliografía Citada." In *Capsicum y Cultura: La Historia del Chilli.* Mexico: Fondo de Cultura Económica, 1986.

Marshall, Dale E. "A Bibliography on the Mechanical Harvesting of Capsicum Peppers and Related Subjects." St. Charles, Ill.: Pickle Packers International, 1992. (P.O. Box 606, 60174.)

Purseglove, J. W., et al. "References of Chillies: Capsicum spp." In Purseglove, *Spices.* London: Longman's, 1981.

BIBLIOGRAPHY OF *THE CHILE PEPPER ENCYCLOPEDIA*

A-As-Saqui. "Tomato and Pepper Production and Its Problems in Liberia." In *Tomato and Pepper Production in the Tropics*, ed. by T. D. Griggs and B. T. McLean. Taipei, Taiwan: Asian Vegetable Research and Development Center, 1989.

Achaya, K. T. *Indian Food: A Historical Companion.* Delhi, India: Oxford University Press, 1994.

Acosta, José D. *The Natural and Moral History of the Indies* (1590). New York: Lennox Hill Publishing, 1979.

Ainsley, Whitelaw. *Materia Indica: Or, Some Account of Those Articles Which Are Employed by the Hindoos and Other Eastern Nations in Their Medicine, Arts, and Agriculture.* London: Longman, Reese, Orme, Brown, and Green, 1826.

Anderson, E. N. *The Food of China.* New Haven: Yale University Press, 1988.

Andrews, Jean. *Peppers: The Domesticated Capsicums.* Austin: University of Texas Press, 1984.

Baudin, Louis. *Daily Life in Peru Under the Last Incas.* New York: Macmillan, 1968.

Bensinger, Marlin. Personal correspondence, February 1997.

Benson, Elizabeth P. *The Maya World.* New York: Crowell, 1967.

Brennan, Jennifer. *The Cuisines of Asia.* London: Macdonald, 1984.

Bridges, Bill. *The Great American Chili Book.* New York: Rawson, Wade Publications, 1981.

Brown, David. Personal correspondence, June 1994.

Chile Pepper, ed. by Dave DeWitt, Vol. 1, No. 1 (Summer 1987) to Vol. 10, No. 5 (October 1996).

Chopra, R. N., R. L. Badhwar, and S. Ghosh. *Poisonous Plants of India.* New Delhi, India: Indian Council of Agricultural Research, 1965.

Christie, Robert H. *Twenty-Two Authentic Banquets from India* (1911). New York: Dover Publications, 1975.

Cobo, Father Bernabe. *History of the Inca Empire.* Austin: University of Texas Press, 1979.

Coe, Sophie D. *America's First Cuisines.* Austin: University of Texas Press, 1994.

Coetzee, Renata. *The South African Culinary Tradition.* Cape Town, South Africa: C. Struik Publishers, 1977.

Cooper, Joe. *With or Without Beans.* Dallas: William S. Henson, 1962.

De Benítez, Ana M. *Pre-Hispanic Cooking.* Mexico: Ediciones Euroamericanas Klaus Thiele, 1974.

DeGaray, Rodolfo, and Thomas Brown. "Cuban Foods That Bite Back." *Chile Pepper*, January/February 1992, 29.

De la Vega, Garcilaso (*El Inca*). *Royal Commentaries of the Incas.* Trans. by Harold V. Livermore from the 1609 work. Austin: University of Texas Press, 1966.

De Schlippe, Pierre. *Shifting Cultivation in Africa.* London: Routledge & Kegan Paul, 1956.

DeWitt, Dave, and Paul Bosland. *The Pepper Garden.* Berkeley, Calif.: Ten Speed Press, 1993.

———. *Peppers of the World: An Identification Guide.* Berkeley, Calif.: Ten Speed Press, 1996.

DeWitt, Dave, and Chuck Evans. *The Hot Sauce Bible.* Freedom, Calif.: Crossing Press, 1996.

———. *The Pepper Pantry: Chipotles.* Berkeley, Calif.: Celestial Arts, 1997.

DeWitt, Dave, and Nancy Gerlach. *The Whole Chile Pepper Book.* Boston: Little, Brown, 1990.

———. *The Habanero Cookbook.* Berkeley, Calif.: Ten Speed Press, 1995.

———. *The Pepper Pantry: Habaneros.* Berkeley, Calif.: Celestial Arts, 1997.

DeWitt, Dave, and Arthur Pais. *A World of Curries.* Boston: Little, Brown, 1994.

DeWitt, Dave, Mary Jane Wilan, and Melissa T. Stock. *Hot & Spicy Chili.* Rocklin, Calif.: Prima Publishing, 1994.

———. *Hot & Spicy & Meatless.* Rocklin, Calif.: Prima Publishing, 1994.

———. *Hot & Spicy Latin Dishes.* Rocklin, Calif.: Prima Publishing, 1995.

———. *Hot & Spicy Southeast Asian Dishes.* Rocklin, Calif.: Prima Publishing, 1995.

———. *Hot & Spicy Caribbean.* Rocklin, Calif.: Prima Publishing, 1996.

———. *Hot & Spicy Mexican.* Rocklin, Calif.: Prima Publishing, 1996.

———. *Hot & Spicy & Meatless 2.* Rocklin, Calif.: Prima Publishing, 1997.

———. *Flavors of Africa.* Rocklin, Calif.: Prima Publishing, 1998.

DeWitt, Dave, Melissa T. Stock, and Kellye Hunter. *The Healing Powers of Peppers.* New York: Three Rivers Press, 1998.

Fernándo de Oviedo, Gonzalo. "*Della Naturale e Generale Istoria dell'Indie.*" In *Giovanni Batista Ramusio, Navigazione e Viaggi*, Vol. 5. Turin, Italy: Einaudi, 1985.

———. *Historia Natural y General de las Indias.* Madrid, Spain: Atlas, 1959.

Fritz, G. Lorenzo. "Searching for the Chile Peppers of Highland Bolivia." (Manuscript.) Tucson, Az.: October 1995.

Gerard, John. *The Herball or General Historie of Plantes.* London: John Norton, 1597.

Guzmán de Vásquez Colmenares, Ana María. *Tradiciones Gastronomicas Oaxaqueñas.* Oaxaca, Mexico: 1982.

Hachten, Harva. *Kitchen Safari.* New York: Atheneum, 1970.

Haile, Y., and Y. Zewdie. "Hot Pepper and Tomato Production and Research in Ethiopia." In *Tomato and Pepper Production in the Tropics*, ed. by T. D. Griggs and B. T. McLean. Taipei, Taiwan: Asian Vegetable Research and Development Center, 1989.

Halász, Zoltán. *Hungarian Paprika Through the Ages.* Budapest, Hungary: Corvina Press, 1963.

Heiser, Charles B., Jr. *The Fascinating World of the Nightshades.* New York: Dover, 1987.

Hillman, Howard. *The Book of World Cuisines*. New York: Penguin, 1979.

Hudgins, Sharon. "Types of Hungarian Paprikas." (Manuscript.) Munich, Germany: October 1990.

———. "Red Gold: The Paprikas of Hungary." *Chile Pepper*, July/August 1990, 22.

Jaffrey, Madhur. *Madhur Jaffrey's Indian Cooking*. Hauppauge, N.Y.: Barron's, 1995.

Jain, Girilal (ed.). *The Times of India Directory and Yearbook*. Bombay, India: The Times of India, 1983.

Jordan, Shirley. "Savoring the Isle of Spice." *Chile Pepper*, September/October 1994, 16.

Kang, K. Y. "Tomato and Pepper Production and Research in Korea." In *Tomato and Pepper Production in the Tropics*, ed. by T. D. Griggs and B. T. McLean. Taipei, Taiwan: Asian Vegetable Research and Development Center, 1989.

Kelly, Isabel. *Folk Practices in North Mexico*. Austin: University of Texas Press, 1965.

Kirtikar, K. R., and B. D. Basu. *Indian Medicinal Plants*. Panini, India: Sudhindra Asrama Bahadurganj, 1918.

Krajewska, Anna M., and John J. Powers. "Sensory Properties of Naturally Occurring Capsaicinoids." *Journal of Food Science*, Vol. 53 (May/June 1988), 902.

Libín, Tita. "The Voodoo Foods of Bahia." *Chile Pepper*, July/August 1994.

Lin, C. Y., and S. H. Lai. "Production and Utilization of Pepper and Tomato in Taiwan, China." In *Tomato and Pepper Production in the Tropics*, ed. by T. D. Griggs and B. T. McLean. Taipei, Taiwan: Asian Vegetable Research and Development Center, 1989.

Lomelí, Arturo. *El Chile y Otros Picantes*. Mexico: Editorial Premeteo Libre, 1986.

Lusk, Jim. "Pepper Acreage by Variety in the U.S." *Lusk's Processor Notebook*, Saticoy, Calif: PetoSeed, October 1996.

MacNeish, R. S. "Ancient Mesoamerican Civilization." *Science* 143: 531–37.

Mahindru, S. N. *Spices in Indian Life*. New Delhi, India: Sultan Chand & Sons, 1982.

Marks, Copeland. *The Exotic Kitchens of Indonesia*. New York: M. Evans, 1989.

Mesfin, D. J. *Exotic Ethiopian Cooking*. Falls Church, Va.: Ethiopian Cookbook Enterprises, 1990.

Miller, Mark. *The Great Chile Book*. Berkeley, Calif.: Ten Speed Press, 1991.

Morgan, Jinx, and Jennifer Morgan. "Guadeloupe: Island with a French Accent." *Bon Appétit*, July 1990, 30.

Nabhan, Gary. "The Red-Hot Mother of Chiles." In *Impact: The Albuquerque Journal Magazine*, Vol. 9, No. 3 (November 1985), 4.

Nagai, H. "Tomato and Pepper Production in Brazil." In *Tomato and Pepper Production in the Tropics*, ed. by T. D. Griggs and B. T. McLean. Taipei, Taiwan: Asian Vegetable Research and Development Center, 1989.

Naj, Amal. *Peppers: A Story of Hot Pursuits*. New York: Knopf, 1992.

Narikawa, T., et al. "Pepper and Tomato Cultivation, Production and Research in Japan." In *Tomato and Pepper Production in the Tropics*, ed. by T. D. Griggs and B. T. McLean. Taipei, Taiwan: Asian Vegetable Research and Development Center, 1989.

Nikornpun, Manee, and Pipob Lumyong. "Tomato and Pepper Production and Improvement in Thailand." In *Tomato and Pepper Production in the Tropics*, ed. by T. D. Griggs and B. T. McLean. Taipei, Taiwan: Asian Vegetable Research and Development Center, 1989.

Ortiz, Elizabeth Lambert. *The Complete Book of Mexican Cooking*. New York: Bantam, 1968.

Panjabi, Camellia. *The Great Curries of India*. New York: Simon & Schuster, 1995.

Payne, Bob. "Martinique: Romance, Rum and Red Peppers in the French Caribbean." *Bon Appétit*, February 1994.

Pfefferkorn, Ignatz. *Sonora: A Description of the Province*. Trans. by Theodore Treutlein. Albuquerque: University of New Mexico Press, 1949.

Pickersgill, Barbara. "The Archaeological Record of Chili Peppers (Capsicum spp.) and the Sequence of Plant Domestication in Peru." *American Antiquity*, Vol. 34, No. 1, 1969, 54–61.

Purseglove, J. W., et al. "Chillies: Capsicum spp." In Purseglove, *Spices*. London: Longman's, 1981.

Raichlen, Steven. "Hot, Hot, Hot! Caribbean Pepper Has Fire-Power." *Medina County Gazette*, June 30, 1990.

Rengade, Jules. *Las Plantas que Curan y Las Plantas que Matan*. Barcelona, Spain: Montanery Simon, 1887.

Robertson, Diane. *Jamaican Herbs*. Montego Bay, Jamaica: Island Herbs Limited, 1982.

Roeder, Beatrice A. *Chicano Folk Medicine from Los Angeles, California*. Berkeley, Calif.: University of California Press, 1988.

Roys, Ralph L. *The Ethno-Botany of the Maya*. New Orleans: Tulane University, 1931.

Sahagún, Bernardino de. *The General History of the Things of New Spain (1590)*. Trans. by A. J. O. Anderson and C. E. Dibble. Santa Fe, N.M.: School of American Research, Monograph No. 14, 1963.

Sahni, Julie. *Classic Indian Cooking*. New York: William Morrow, 1980.

Sax, Richard. "The Paprika of Hungary." *Bon Appétit*, October 1993, 40.

Seed Savers Staff. *Seed Savers 1994 Yearbook*. Decorah, Ia.: Seed Saver's Exchange, 1995.

———. *Seed Savers 1995 Yearbook*. Decorah, Ia.: Seed Saver's Exchange, 1996.

———. *Seed Savers 1996 Yearbook*. Decorah, Ia.: Seed Saver's Exchange, 1997.

Singh, J. H., and D. S. Cheema. "Present Status of Tomato and Pepper Production in India." In *Tomato and Pepper Production in the Tropics*, ed. by T. D. Griggs and B. T. McLean. Taipei, Taiwan: Asian Vegetable Research and Development Center, 1989.

Spaeth, Anthony. "In Guntur, India, Even at 107 Degrees, It's Always Chili, Chili and More Chili." *The Wall Street Journal*, June 30, 1988.

Sterling, Richard. "Return to the Land of the Ascending Dragon." *Chile Pepper*, November/December 1993, 30.

Stevenel, L. "Red Pepper, A Too Much Forgotten Therapeutic Agent Against Anorexia, Liver Congestion, and Vascular Troubles." *Bulletin of the Society of Exotic Pathology*, Vol. 49, No. 5, 1956, 841–43.

Stockton, William. "Hunt for Perfect Mole Leads to Rich Delights." *Albuquerque Tribune*, December 12, 1985, B-6.

Van der Post, Laurens. *African Cooking*. New York: Time-Life Books, 1970.

———. *First Catch Your Eland*. New York: William Morrow, 1978.

Whitlock, Ralph. *Everyday Life of the Maya*. New York: Dorset Press, 1976.

Wiegand, Ronn. "On Pairing Food and Beverages." In Marlena Spieler, *Hot & Spicy*. Los Angeles: Jeremy P. Tarcher, 1985.

Williams, Deborah. "The Land of Five Rivers." *Chile Pepper*, July/August 1992, 48.

Wilson, Ellen Gibson. *A West African Cookbook*. New York: M. Evans, 1971.

Yacovleff, E., and F. Herrera. *El Mundo Vegetal de los Antiguos Peruanos*. Lima, Peru: Imprenta del Museo Nacional, 1935.

Yang, C. Y., T. W. Zhu, and S. D. Lee. "Production of Tomato and Pepper in China." In *Tomato and Pepper Production in the Tropics*, ed. by T. D. Griggs and B. T. McLean. Taipei, Taiwan: Asian Vegetable Research and Development Center, 1989.

Zumwalt, Betty. *Ketchup, Pickles, Sauces: 19th Century Food in Glass*. Sand Point, Id.: Mark West Publishers, 1980.

Index